BOOK of NAMES

Especially Relating to
THE EARLY PALATINES

And the First Settlers in the
MOHAWK VALLEY

———

COMPILED AND ARRANGED BY
LOU D. MacWETHY

———

CLEARFIELD

Originally published
St. Johnsville, New York, 1933

Reprinted by
Genealogical Publishing Co., Inc.
Baltimore, Maryland
1969, 1981, 1985

Reprinted for
Clearfield Company by
Genealogical Publishing Co.
Baltimore, Maryland
1999, 2002, 2007

Library of Congress Catalogue Card Number 69-17132
ISBN-13: 978-0-8063-0231-7
ISBN-10: 0-8063-0231-3

Made in the United States of America

Dedicated to the Memory of
two faithful co-workers
who labored until
called

BOYD EHLE, C. E.

HUBERT W. HESS, A. B.

FOREWORD

The demand for information concerning early Mohawk Valley Families led to the within publication. War, the great destroyer, not only levels immediate opposition but destroys records which embarrass succeeding generations. The early French and Indian wars took their toll, which followed by the ravages of the Revolution, removed many documents which would have been of assistance to the present generation. It was to rescue such information as was available which led to the undertaking in 1925 of publishing in the Enterprise and News, all material bearing on early days which came to hand. The movement caught the fancy of descendants of the Mohawk Valley in many parts of the country. Thus it came about that we enlarged the scope of our work and began a systematic search for individuals antedating the Revolution and especially pioneers. The undertaking presented an ever widening field until we were staggered even by the prospect. But through the loyal support of several historically minded sons of the Mohawk we were kept to the task. The present work is the result of combined effort of many interested individuals. We are moved to acknowledge these services but hardly know where to begin. Two devoted and enthusiastic supporters have passed away during the building of the book. In a way this book is a corner stone in the monument erected to their memory by their co-workers in the project. They were Prof. Hubert W. Hess and Boyd Ehle. The former was an early supporter of the movement. The latter gave liberally of his time and substance, especially in the matter of the London List and the Hunters Food List. These he procured at his own expense and carefully classified in order that posterity might the more readily trace their lineage. Other able assistants to whom we wish to make acknowledgment are L. F. Bellinger, Lt. Commander, U. S. N., retired who is an authority on the German Flatts settlement. He also traced out the names of those taking the oath of allegiance. For the Kocherthal Records we are indebted to the Lutheran Quarterly, of Harrisburg and for valuable comment and the life of Kocherthal we thank the Rev. H. F. Vesper of Canajoharie. For data on Stone Arabia we are indebted to the Rev. A. L. Dillenbeck of Johnstown and for assistance in the Roster of Oriskany we owe much to Nelson Greene, author of the "Gateway to the West" and several other valuable histories.

For assistance in locating the casuals in the various regiments we are indebted to many individuals. It would be impossible to enumerate them all.

When we consider that the book has been a gradual accumulation of facts covering several years of research, one can appreciate the difficulty in making all the proper acknowledgments.

The arrangement of the book will be found practical. In most cases the names are arranged alphabetically. This is an innovation. In no instance previously have these names been so arranged. It is possible in a very few minutes to trace an individual through all the developments following the initial appearance. Thus valuable time is saved.

A departure never before attempted by valley historians will be found in the Tryon County Militia in which casual records of individuals are attempted. From this a considerable number of individuals who were killed, wounded or took part at Oriskany are identified. This has taken a great amount of research and of course is not complete. It constitutes a start, however, towards a desired end.

The book is far from perfect. There are undoubtedly duplications and in some cases entire omissions, But so far as possible the original records have been followed and the spellings faithfully copied. The book is presented for just what it claims to be, a book of names. No attempt is made to trace descent or to amplify on the individual. The object for which we set out was to learn, if possible, who was who in the days of the first settlers. This book is the result. Wherever we found a name we incorporated it. We even went across the water and located the London List, because part of that list became our pioneers and our ancestors. The name is now available, and thus far the task is completed. The effort of tracing down from the common ancestor to the present is another task, and this we leave to the genealogist. Our task was to prove the name and individual as actually having existed. Having given the start we leave it to others to carry on.

LOU D. MacWETHY.

St. Johnsville, N. Y., February 6, 1933.

AUTHORITIES CONSULTED

Documentary History of the State of New York.
Colonial Documents of the State of New York.
The Clinton Papers of the State of New York.
Greene's Gateway to the West, Nelson Greene.
Report of the State Historian, Colonial Series.
Ecclesiastical Records of the State of New York.
The British Museum, Manuscript Division, London England.
The Manuscript Division, State Education Dept., Albany, N. Y., Edna L. Jacobson in charge.
New York in the Revolution, State of New York.
Archives of the State of New York, Furnow.
The Colonial Laws of New York.
The Lutheran Quarterly Harrisburg.
Frontiersmen of New York, Simms.
Schoharie and the Border Wars, Simms.
The Minutes of Tryon County, Frye.
Minutes of the Albany Committee of Correspondence, State of New York, Vol. 1.

TABLE OF CONTENTS

Page

Our Early Citizens, Those taking the Oath of Allegiance............ 1
French and Indian War, Names of Militiamen 7
Kocherthal Records by Rev. Joshua Kocherthal 15
London Documents, First Consignment of Palatines 51
Joshua Kocherthal, Sketch by Rev. H. V. Vesper.............................. 53
Stone Arabia Graveyard by Rev. A. L. Dillenbeck.......................... 59
Congregational Register of Stone Arabia and Cani-schoharie........ 60
Palatine Heads of Families, the Hunter Ration Lists...... 65
Review of Food List by Boyd Ehle 73
Mohawk School at Fort Hunter 74
List of Palatines 1909 (First London List) 75
List of Palatines (Second List).. 81
List of Palatines (Third List)... 88
List of Palatines (Fourth List).. 102
Abstract of 3 Lists of Pal. who came from Germany ...._..... 111
Further Classification of London List by Occupation 111
Prisoners of War, Colonial.. 112
Sufferers at German Flatts 116
Colonial Census of Palatines in America.. 120
Volunteers to Canadian Expedition 1711... 125
Palatine Orphan List.. 128
Oriskany, Roster of Names on Monument... 131
Tryon County Militia First Regiment (Campbell)........................... 137
Tryon County Militia, Second Regiment, (Klock) 143
Tryon County Militia, Third Regiment, (Fisher).......... 155
Tryon County Militia, Fourth Regiment, (Bellinger)...................... 163
References from List, 4th. Reg. 169
Tryon County Rangers and Exempts 174
Johnson's Ledger ....--...... 178
Nicknames and Equivalents 179
Tryon Co., Committee of Correspondence 181
Albany Co., Committee of Correspondence 182
Oath of Secrecy of Albany Co. Committee of Correspondence 182
Index to Kocherthal Records 193

ILLUSTRATIONS

Page

Old Church at Schoharie 64
General Herkimer Home ...._....... 209
Fort Plain Block House 142
Fort Keyser 148
Grave of Hendrick Klock 148
Old Palatine Church 148
Col. Marinus Willett 154
Dedicating Memorial Gateway at Oriskany Battlefield 162

MAPS

Stone Arabia 180
Harmanus VanSlyck's tract of land 189
Burnetsfield Patent 190
Francis Harrison Patent 191
Sir John Johnson's Raid 1780 192

THE COMPILER AND COLLABORATORS

Top left to right—L. F. Bellinger, C. E., Lt. Com. Ret., U. S. N.; the late
H. W. Hess, A. B.; the late Boyd Ehle, C. E.
Center—L. D. MacWethy.
Bottom, left to right—Milo Nellis; Col. O. W. Bell, U. S. A.

OUR EARLY CITIZENS

Names of Those Taking the Oath of Allegiance From 1715 to 1773

Compiled from the Colonial Laws by
Lt. Com. L. F. Bellinger, U. S. N., Retired

How old is your family?
Who was the first pioneer in your family?
How far back can you trace your citizenship?
All of these are natural questions.

The following names have been gathered from the Colonial Laws, as they were set down at the time of the occurrence. The significance is that the parties taking such oath were present, and of lawful age, and did on that occasion by their act, furnish documentary evidence of their existence. Perhaps they sleep in unmarked graves. Perhaps no Bible record has come down to us. Perhaps no other proof is available or ever will be, but it is evident that on the day and date given below these men were alive and active and were taking the most important step in their careers. Just what that citizenship was to lead to is a story in itself. They could not foresee the great drama in process of unfolding. But they were there and it is our duty to preserve these names for the benefit of those who come after. The following columns constitute one of the most important contributions to history yet published. It is the first time these names have been made available in printed form outside the records. The work of Lt. Bellinger in preparing these names will be appreciated by the present generation and let us hope by many generations yet to come.

PALATINE NATURALIZATIONS
BY L. F. BELLINGER

As a boy I understood perfectly why foreigners desired to become citizens of this land of the free and home of, for, and by the brave, but never did understand there could be any question of property rights, and thought if a man bought property, it belonged to him regardless of his nationality, present or past. Later in life I learned that Hayti, foreigners cannot acquire real estate, and the same is true in Japan at present. It appears that about 1700 one who was naturalized in one of the American Colonies; was by no means naturalized in all of them Also, there were certain questions about owning property and buying property which seem queer to us. First, it was necessary to obtain a legal permit or licinse before any purchasing of lands from the Indians could be instituted. Undoubtedly there were "costs" connected with the issuance of these permits. Next, after the land was deeded by the Indians, aliens were always in trouble with the Colonial Government about quit rents, and transfers of the land to others, that did not cause trouble to citizens of the Colony, and a law was passed July 5, 1715 to remove some of these troubles. Fifty years or so later it was necessary to fix up the 1715 law so the property belonging to the first naturalized aliens could be received and held by their children born in the Colony of New York.

It is of interest to note how the scare of loss of land and the passage of new laws and privileges brought about surges in the desire for naturalizations.

It is noteworthy that some of our ancestors failed to save up the necessary 19 or 20 shillings in six months or a year as the requirement was, and their names had to go on later special acts for their benefit.

After all that trouble of theirs to acquire the land, how many in your "Descendants" column live now on the land that troubled their ancestors so much? Count 'em Mr. Editor!

Following this is given a list of names of the Palatines in the valley, so far as I can pick out names with which we are all more or less familiar.

I have tried to put in parenthesis a more modern spelling than is given in the books from which I quote. It may help some to determine ages and names that were in existence at the date specified, and may also reduce the number of those needing to be

grafted to the "Family Tree."

As an example we have here evidence that Benton's statement is incorrect, so far as the Herkimer family not arriving until the 1722 immigration. Here is George Herkimer. His son Johan Jost was evidently not yet 21, and his grandson General Nicholas was not born until about 1726, all of whch is consistent. Similarly, Benton argues that Rudolph Staley of Staley's Patent did not arrive until the 1722 immigration, because he was not one of the Burnettsfield Patentees; yet we now have him as "Roelof Steel," over 21 on the date specified.

John Jacob Ehl shows up as the first of his tribe apparently.

Peter Bellinger now shown to be over 21 in 1715 appeared only as sponsor at a Kocherthal record birth in 1715 from which the argument was that he was at least 15 years old when acting as sponsor. He signed deeds to land in 1782 and 1784 and lived to be over 90 therefore. He was the father in law of Adam Helmer, the famous scout, the father of Colonel Peter Bellinger, the father of "Hoffrich" Bellinger of the "Mohawk Dutch Marines," and the father in law of Lieut. Timothy Frank. Longevity in Peter's family was hereditary. Colonel Peter lived to be 87, one daughter to 96, another daughter to 110 and the son of Colonel Peter lived to 93.

Note—All the names which appear in Annals of Albany are given. Selection was made from the large number in "Colonial Laws." New York Palatines naturalized in Albany, N. Y. (Taken from Munsell's "Annals of Albany," pp. 40. 43, 45, 46, 48, and 49). At a Mayors Court held in the City Hall of Albany, Oct. 11, 1715.

The following persons, to wit.

Juryh Herck Heemmer
Petrus Van Driesen
Jan Lansingh
Claes Van Der Volgen

Jan Janse Bleecker
Peter Kneskern
Hans Jury Kast
Warnaer Deygert
Niccolas Wever
Johannis Feeck
Frederick Scheffer
Reynhaert Scheffer
Jurry Beenner
Anthony Schyet
Jacob Kop
Nicolas Korning
Jacob Weever
Christian Houys
Johannis Keyser
Hendrick Klock
Jacob Snell
Peter Feeck
Roelof Steel
Hendrick Seix
Leendert Helmer
William Schief
Paul Dinser
Johan Frederick Bell
Philips Helmer
Nicholas Schieffer
Jacob Feeck

* Did in open Court take the oaths by law appointed to be taken instead of oaths of allegiance & supremacy subscribe the test and make repeat and swear to & subscribe the abjuration oath pursuant to the directions of an act of generall assembly entituled an act declaring yt all those of foreign birth heretofore inhabiting within this colony and dying seized of any lands tenements and hereditaments shall be for ever hereafter deemed taken & esteemed to have been naturalized and for naturalizing all protestants of foreign birth now inhabiting within this colony.

To whom certificates are forthwith to be given according to the directions of ye said act.

Att a Mayors Court held at the City Hall of Albany ye 22th day of November 1715.

The following persons to witt

Adam Vroman
Evert Janze
Johan Andries Drom
Hans Pieter Heyser
Johannis Rousman
Hans Michall Brack
Pieter Vonk
Johan Coenraet Petrie
Jacob Bsheere
Peter Smith
Hendrick Nies
David Hoefler

Johan Smitt
Johan Joseph Proper
Johan Pieter Proper
Johan Fred'k Proper
Ananias Tiel
Andries Bartel
Philip Bartel
Jacob Schieffer
David Chierts
Johannis Schiets
Jacob Schoemaker
Christophel Hagedorn
Hend. Ch'l. Wiederwax
Johan And. Wiederwax
Hans Adam Schiets
Andries Vink
Frederick Kietman
Johannis Beerman
Thomas Schoemaker
Hans Jury Thomas
Frederick Bellinger

At a Mayors Court held in ye City Hall of Albany ye 3d day of January, 1715/6

The following persons to witt

Johannis Heiner
Johannis Kessler
Johannis Miller
Jacob Moussier
Johannis Jury Heyn
Baltus Annsbach
Hans Jury Moussier
Dewaeld Pryl
Christian Vink
Johannis Skans
Johan Christ Smit
Melgert Volts
Johan Hendrick Loucks
Jacob Timmerman
Jury Taxstieder
Hans Hendrick Clock
Philip Scheffer
Harme Segedorp
Christian Former
Symon Herhardt
Omy de la Crangie
Hendrick Jong
Tebald Young

At a Mayors Court held at ye City Hall of Albany the 17th day of January 1715/6

The following persons to witt

Hendrick Heydorn
Jurick Mower
Hendrick Sneyder
Coenraed Barringer
Johannis Vinger
Niccolas Smith
Coenraed Smith
Johan Adam Smith
Niccolas Smith
Hans Hendrick Hock
And. Lod'k. Casselman
Abraham Berk
Peter Smith

Samuel Muller
Philip Loucks
Michiel Heyntie
Hendrick Winter
Christiaen Lang
Mathys Coens
Johan Jurch Shmit
Johannis Wm. Pulver
Peter Clop
Hans Jurch Row
Peter Philips
Niccolas Philips
Christiaen Haver
Johan Hend. Plas
Killiaen Mincklaer
Josias Mincklaer
Coenraet Schuerman
Adam Ding
Johan Christ. Miller
Jurich Kelmer
Christ. Dederich
Jurich Emrig Scherp
Peter Stoppelbert
Niccolas Hes
Johan Wm. Shoe
Johannis Shoe
Martinus Shoe
Coenraet Ham
Johan Hend. Plas
Philips Vingler
Jury Houck
Philips Heypt
Marte Server
Hendrick Michiel
Hendrick Michiel Jun'r.
Anthony Michiel
Jonas Shinkel
Johan Hendrick Shinkel
William Rees
Claes Van Pettn
Patron Anders
Johan Jurch Muller
Johannis Leek
Daniel Janze
Jacob Best
Abraham Langer
Jacob Bayer
Johans Christman
Harma Betser
David Kesselaer
Jacob Sneyder
Johan Wm. Siemon
Johan Jacob Server
Peter Lautman
Philip Wm. Moor
Niecolas Bonnesteel
Johannis Hes
Peter Burger
Johan Casper Rouch
Johan Willem Dalis
Hendrick Coenraet
Baltus Stiever
Franz Dompsback
Jost Hend Dompsback
Ulrigh Jacobi
Firdinard Menti
Martin Tiel
Fiet Miesick
Johan Wm. Hambough
Christiaen Diederigh
Daniel Buch

Johan Hena. Buch
Enrich Bliss
Daniel Post
Johan Hend. Post
Michel Herder
Peter Betser
Willem Sneyder
Hendrick Lodwick

January 31—The following persons
(to witt)

Johan Lodoph Corning
Johannis Scholdies
Hans Jury Stomf
Johan Harme Spicker-
man
Abarham Loucks
Johan Coenraet Jefback
Uldrich Dandler
Jacob Eswine
Adam Starn
Diedrich Loucks
Philip Clom
Peter Belinger
William Nelles
Niccolas Eckhar
Johan Pieter Diegert
Marten Stiep
Hans Jury Herckhemer
Philips Bender
Johan Jacob Besharn
Johan Willem Foex
Johannis Coens
Jurch Scherts
Christian Berck
Hans Marte Weytman
Frederick Willem Leer
Hans Casper Liepe
Adam Hoft
Andries Hoft
Lodwick Wanner
Christian Nelles
Peter Waggenaer
Johan B. Sterenbergen
Adam Kleyn
Sefreen Devgert

February 14—The following persons (to witt)

Dirck Wessels Ten
Broeck
Uldrich Weyniger
Willem Linck
Johan Sneyder
Hans Gerhard Weyniger
Johannis Graet
Jacob Coens
Philip Coens
Jurich Loundert
Jurich Reyfenburger
Willem Hagedorn
Casper Ham
Hans Michiel Edich
Hans Michiel Edich Jr.
Niccolas Stickling
Johan Joest Sneyder
Jacob Kroush
Niccolas Steyger
Johannis Daet

Hans Bernhardt Daet
Jacob Cerman

February 28—The following persons (to witt)

Isabella Staats
Geertry Isabella Lydyus
Maria Adrianata Lydyus
Hendrick Meyer
Johannis Krem
Jeron Van Flyeren
Johan Pieter Lodwick
Jury Mathys
Peter Ham
Johan Adolph Warraven
Lawrence Herder

Colonial Laws, N. Y.

Vol. 1, page 858. General act of
naturalization passed July 5, 1715,
"declaring that all persons of foreign
birth hereafter inhabiting within this
colony and dying seized of any lands,
tenements or hereditaments shall be
forever hereafter deemed taken and
steemed to have been naturalized and
for naturalizing all Protestants of
foreign birth now inhabiting within
this colony."

These special acts became of no
effect if oaths were not taken and
fees paid within six months, then
nine months and later one year from
the passage of these special acts.
One of these, June 17, 1726 prescrib-
ed no time limit another passed Oct.
14, 1737 had special provisions about
removing from the colony of New
York.

"Colonial Laws," Naturalization of
Individuals

Volume 2, July 27, 1721.
Johannes Hausz (House).
October 14, 1732.
John Jacob Ell (Ehle).

Naturalization of Individuals, Colonial Laws

Volume 2, December 16, 1737.

Conrad Franck
Andreas Klebsatel
Jorg Riht Meyer
(Richtmyer)
Phlilip Schuttes
Volume 3, May 3, 1755.

John Godfrey Miller

Michael Hoffman
Jacob Tiefendorph
Hendrick Heger
Solomon Myer
Jacob Myer
Henry Bell
Jacob Miller
Jacob Abel
John Sherp (Sharp)
Michael Poltz (Folts)
Jacob Sherp (Sharp)
Michael Sherp (Sharp)
Cornelius Miller
Christopher Ring
Johan Hess
John Volmer (Fulmer)
Michael Polfer (Pulver)
Peter Polfer (Pulver)

Volume 4, July 3, 1759.

Daniel Christian Fueter
(Feeter)
John Ludwig Dunckel
Matthews Schaffer
George Kass
Lucas Vetter (Vedder)
Andreas Sneider
Nicholas Schaffer
William Gerlach
John Daniel Miller
Johannes Eigenbrood
Hermanus Eell (Ehle)
John Thomas Miller
Peter Freidrick
Gerlach Meyer
John Shauman
Felix Meyer
William Sneider
John Peter Hillegas
Frederick Franck
Johannes Eigenbrood
Martin Smith
Felix Keller
Jacob Keller
Rudolph Keller
Henry Keller
Jan Joost Koch
William Gerlach
John George Yordan
Johannes Wolgemooth
Casper Clock
Jacob Algajer (Algire)
Michael Hoffman
Carl Hoffman
Jury Hoffman

Volume 4, September 11, 1761.

Frederick Franck
Hannes Wohlgemuth
Jacob Schneyder
Ludwick Kraan (Crane)
Jorg Dieffendorf
Hannes Dieffendorf
Felix Mayer
Hendrick Dieffedorf
Jacob Mayer
Andreas Keller
Hans Geerlag Mayer Jr.
Hannes Eigenbrood

Johan Geerlag Mayer
Hendrick Hesz
Hannes Jordan junr.
Michael Sneyder
Hendrick Mayer
Casper Jordan junr.
Solomon Mayer
Joseph Mayer
Jacob Seeber
Johannes Schall
Hendrick Eckler
Andreas Dusler
Johannes Valentine Caspasus
Stephanus Frank
Johannes Ehl
Johan Hendrick Smith
Wilhelmus Smith
Godfried Shoewaker
William Seeber
George Sbrecker (Spraker)
Martin Sbrecker
Coenrood Sbrecker
Johannes Schal
William Seeber
Johan Nicholas Smith
Johannes Smith
Jacob Seeber junr.
Christian Schel
Coenraad Smith
Phillip Frederick
Augustus Eckler
Abraham Ecker
George Ecker
Jacob Sever

December 31, 1761.

George Snyder

Volume 4, March 20, 1762.

Frederick Schall
Isaac Paris
Isaac Paris Junior.
Abraham Rosekrans
Adam Kiltz
Peter Kiltz
Johannes Kilts
Johan Nekel Kiltz
Hendrick Riemesnyder
Harme Schever (Scchaffer)
John Eisenlord
Christian Young
Peter Nicholas Somner
Henrich Schneider
Jacob Fry
Jurry Fry
Philip Miller
Andries Frank
Christophel Frank
Philip Shapher
Stephen Jordan
Peter Fox
Golliep Bowman
Abraham Bowman
Johannis Joost Weeder (Vedder)

Volume 4, December 20, 1763.

Johannis Weaver
Frederick Hillecas
Henry Widerstein
Christian Schell
Johannes Schell

October 20, 1764.

Hermanus Myer
Henry Widerstein
Christian Schell
Johannes Schell

December 19, 1766.

Lawrence Schuler
Nicholas Timmerman

December 31, 1768.

Coenrad Shol
Philip Smith
John Smith
Henry Smith
Jacob Flander
Johannes Shol
Leonhart Cratser (Kretser)
Christoffel Miller
Michael Salsbergh

Volume 5, January 27, 1770.

Jacob Seber
Augustus Eckler
Conraat Smith
George Ecker
George Sharpe
Jacob Becker
Frederick Waggoner
Adam Garlogh
Peter Young
Peter Gronce (Grantz or Crontz)
William Petrie

February 1*, 1771.

John Smith
Jacob Meyars
Christian Schultz
William Shouman
Jacob Waggoner
John Smith
Adam Plank
Michael Myar
Francis Fry
Johan Adam Frank
Andreas Schough (Shoe or Shuh)
Lewis Fueter (Feeter)
Frederick Myer

Volume 5, March 24, 1772.

Michael Berringer

March 8, 1773.

Michael Warner
Jacob Waggoner
Michael Witterick (Widrig)
George Witterick
Philip Bellanger
George Ough (Ochs or Ox)
Faltin Miller (Valentine M—)
Baltus Breitenbeger
George Bower
Niccholas Keller
John Kellar Junior
Jacob Myer
Hendrick Schafer
Adam Hartman
John Eisenlord
Simon Bydeman
John Conradt Smith
Francis Fry
Jacob Myer
Leonard Kratzer
Coenradt   Hoining (Horning)
Philip Smith
Henry Smith
Samuel Millur
Jacob Flander
Johan Jost Volz

Johan Daniel Gros
Adam Dumm (Thumb or Thume)
Nicholas Dumm.
Melicher Dumm (Melchior or Matthew D.)
Henry Becker
Jacob Joran (Yerdon)
Peter Eigebrode
John Smith
Christian Graf
John Fisher

Afterthought!! Any one really interested should look over all the names given in the "Colonial Laws of New York" and follow the index which in one place is wrong, giving p. 535 where it should be p. 555. The reason for looking them over is that the name "Cognot" was discarded by me as Irish, not Palatine, and just now it appears that it might have become later "Coughnet" which united with one of the family trees of the Bellingers. In other words, a Coughnet and a Bellinger were participants in a second trial of matrimony about 100 years ago.

TRYON COUNTY MILITIA

Names of Militiamen in French and Indian War Before Revolution.
First Publication in this Form.

(By H. W Hess)

Chapter One

Believing that since the list of the names of the persons who served in the militia in the upper Mohawk valley, previous to the Revolution, will command general interest, I have collected from the reports of the state historian, the names of persons who served from 1757 to 1767 in the militia companies of Captains Petry, Dygert, Klock, Conrad Frank, Lieut. Van Alstein and Col. Jost Herkimer's Granadier company of

men to be officers in the militia, and hereby submit them for your consideration.

The first record of appointment of officers for the upper valley that I find was when Gov. William Crosby gives the "List of officers of the Militia for Albany Co. Nov. 17, 1733." "or above ye falls of ye Maquas (Mohawk) River." Capt. Johan Jurgh Kast (who drew lot 22 on north side), Lieut. John Jost Herkemer (who drew lot 36 on south side, although he seems to have lived on lot 24 in the second farm above the present stone church, Lieut. Thomas Shoemaker (who drew lot 12 on north side) and for Ensign Fredrik Starin. (Now since there was no other name on the Burnettsfield patent at this time to fit this one I assume that since the first name is shortened, that the last name is shortened also, and that this is Frederick Staring who drew lot 24 on the north side).

These four men were all located at German Flatts. If I am wrong in any of my comments I shall gladly be corrected. Now we will give the names of the men in the companies. The names are spelled as in the records, viz.

1757, Vol. IV page 130 Feb. 26, Capt. Mark Petry's return received February 26th, 1757.

Marcus petri
hanes petri
Daniel petri
John Jost petri
Dedrick Petri
fredrich herter
Adam helmer Jr
phillip helmer
Nichlas Weber Jr.
Adam hiltz
Stofel hilt
Jacob hiltz
hendrick Widersim
henrick hart
Shan Mory
Jacob hiltz Jr.
Stofel hiltz Jr.
piter Wohlleber
fridrich schot
Conrat franch
bastiahn hofman
gorg Michel franch
hanes Striwel
Joseph Ruts
Sofel fucks
Adam Stahl
Michel Itig
hanes pahn
Jacob boshor
fridrich Carl
hanes itzman
piter belinger
Conart Wals
tomas Shumacher
Stofel Schumaccher
Adam Stel
fridrich orndorf
Wilgen schot
Josep Staring
grates Mock
phillips Staring
fridrick Staring

hanes Eiseman
Melger Bell
Tomas Kesler
Joel Koch
Jacob Kesler
phillip fucks
Gotlieb Camerdiner
Warner Span
fridrich helmer Jr.
hanes Rasper
hanes Rasper Jr.
henrich Shnict
peter foltz
hanes foltz
fridrich Miller
gorg fey
Conrat Miller
John Jost Demut
Jacob fushback
Phillips Bell
Christian Snell
fredrick fronck

The above spelling is taken as the clerk of the company wrote it down in the records and are not the signaturs of the soldiers.

You will note that the date of this return is the year of the French invasion at German Flatts. This company appears to have been located on the north side of the river at German Flatts. There appears to have been an Adam Helmer Jr. and a Frederick Helmer Jr. at this date.

CHAPTER II

Company of Soffrines Deychert

1757 March 20th. By an order of Sir William Johnson, To march with my Company to Fort William Henry (on Lake George H. W. H) as Followeth, Returned home ye 29 Instant. Soffrines Deychert, Leut.

Petter Kermps
Rudolf Koch
Andreas finck
Warner Deychert
Petter S. Deychert
Jorg Snell
Nicklas Snell
Pitter Snell
Jacob Snell
Adam Snell
Beadus Koch
George Kurm
Migell Keyser
Hartwig Arrent
Johannes Keyser
Andreas Dillenbag
Johannes Raal
Didrich Sutz
Petter Sutz Jun'r.
William Dillenbag
Martin Dillenbag Ju'r.
Dittrick Dillenbag
Baltes Dillenbag
Pitter Devie
John Heckie
William Empie
Robert Gerterds
John Wallrath

Hend'k Salsman
Stofell Shultheis
Hendk Reimensneyder
George Shacke
William Laux
George Snell Jun'r.
Dewalt Merkell
William Merkell
Jacob Merkell
Hen'k Baum
Migell Franck
Adam Kills
Phillip Kills
Hen'k D. Laux
Petter Kills
Jacob Christman
George Salsman
Harman brauer
Arrent brauer
Phillip Empie
Johannes Wick
Hendrick Kremps
Martin Nistell
Johannes Shultheis
Herman Schever
Petter Howman
John Bart
John Snell Ju'r.
Christian Gethmann
John Gethman
Frittrick Empie
Adam Empie
Migell Salsmans
Jacob Dusler
Phillip fucks
Peter Weuer
Jacobus Bratt
Christian Dacchsteter
Lenart Beyer
John Beyer
George Gethman
John Schumaker
Marx Itig
Martin Wart
Christian Ruf
John Kern
William Stret
Signed, Sufferines Deygert.

Note—"Severinis Tygert" was not commissioned captain until January 5, 1758.

This was a Stone Arabia company in the 2nd battalion of militia in the Mohawk Valley under Sir William Johnson.—H. W. Hess.

CHAPTER III

Soverinus Deyger's Company

A True List of ye state of my company of Militia who has been on command at ye German Flatts, By Order of Sir William Johnson ye 24th Day of July, 1763 as Followeth, vizt.

Commissioned Officers:
Migell Keyser Lieut.
Peter S. Deyger, Ensn.
N. C. officers sergents:
William Laux
—— Suts

William Merkell
Peter Suts
Privates:
Peter Laux
William Cobernoll
George Kurn Jun.
Johnnis Keyser
Andris Finck
Joh's Koch
George Kurn
Andris Roller
Andris Dillenbag Jun.
Mardin Dillenbag
Dirck Dillenbag
Baltus Dillenbag
Christian Dillenbag Jun.
Hend'k Dillenbag, Jun.
Arnt Brower
Dirck Suts
Christian Ruf
Niccklass Charles Kind
Hardwig Arnt
Philip Kils
Ernest Becker
Dewalt Merkell
Jacob Merkell
Jorg Snell Jun.
Peter Homan
Mardin Ward
Lenart Beyer
Pertolome Shever
Joh's Hortig
Fred'k Cass
George Gettman
Christian Gettinan
Joh's Gettman
Joh's Snell
Fred'k Snell Jun.
Jacob Snell Jun.
Fred'k Empie
Joh's Empie Jun.
Nicklas Snell
Gerret Lesher
Godlieb Nestell
Phillips Empie Jun.
Joh's Shals Berger
Casper Nistle
Beadus Koch
Harman Brower
Robert Nellis
Adam Kils
Joh's Schumacher
Soverinus, Deyger, Captain

Note—Please take note of the change or spelling.

This company was out for four days with Capt. Jacob Klock's Co. on an Indian Alarm at the German Falls, from July 24 to July 28, both days included.

This company was short at this time due to there being fourteen men who did respond to the call. This list is given which shows the delinquents:

Captain Deyger's List of Delinquents
Officers and Persons Names, not appeared at the German Flatts (ye 24th Day of July 1763. H. W. H.) when was ordered by me, Soverinus Deyger, Capt. of a Company of Mi-

litia at Stonraby (Stone Arabia)
Vizt.
Wilhelmes Dillenbag Lievt.
Anthony Marx
Marden Dillenbag Jun.
George Cobernoll
Nicklass Kills
John Ercksen
Cunrath Lebber
Sweres Meselis
Joh's Lesher
Christian Lemm
Adam Empie
Thomas Williams
Soffrinus Koch Sr.
Christian Dillenbag
Signed,
                    Soverinus Deyger, Capt.
I think we ought not to condemn these delinquents too much. Note the date, July 24th. This would be during the haying time and the harvesting of winter wheat. These men were farmers and it is a tough assignment to be called out and leave your corps to rot and spoil in the field, not knowing how long you will be away. Those were strenuous days.

CHAPTER IV

A list of the Company of Captain Klock as they have been in the last Alarm to German Flats, from the 24th of July to the 28th, 1763 both days included. (The troops were called out on an Indian alarm at Burnetsfield, German Flatts).
Jacob Klock, Capt.
Nicholas Herkeman, Lieut.
Henry Nellis, Ensign.
                    Sergeants
Frederick Windecker
Jacob Feeling
Peter Gerlagh
Jacob Sever
John Pickerd
Henry Eckler
Adonia Schuyler
                    Corporals
Johannis Diefendorf
Johannis Windecker
George Klock Jun.
                    Privates
Johannis Klock
Philips Gerlagh
Charles Gerlagh
Adam Gerlagh
Adam Bellinger
Adam Young
Jacob Diefendorf
Henry Sander Jun.
Casper Zollinger
Jacob Zollinger
Solomon Meyer
Solomon Meyer Jun.
Jacob Meyer
Johannis House
John Hadcock

Johannis Sever
Severinus Sever
Henry Meyer
Peter Miller
Henry Miller
Jacob Diefendorf, Jun.
Conrad Hahn
Conrad Windecker
Bartholomew Pickerd
George Countrieman
Frederick Countrieman
Henry Windecker
Jacobus Pickerd
Conrad Zimmerman
James Grimes
James Barbazat
Dietrich Feeling
John Joost Klock
Frederick Schmid
Jacob Nellis
Henry Nellis, Jun.
Andreas Dussler
Marcus Countrieman
Henry Eckler Jun.
Henry Walrath
Jacob Walrath
Adolph Walrath
Johannis Walrath
Jacob Haberman
Martinus Sperrbeck
Christian Young
Adam Schuster
Joseph Mebie
Johan Joost Schuyler
Conrad House
Lawrence Blasius
Jacobus Meebie
Bartholomew Meebie
Johannis Schmit
Gerrit van Slyk
Marcur Petrie
Conrad Zimmerman Jun.
Jacob Zimmerman
Andreas Fort
William Pickerd
Henry Zollinger
Jacob Countrieman
Johannis Plants
Johannis Countrieman
Thomas Baxter
Eckerson Baxter
Henry Matthews
Conrad Klock
William Pease
Adam Klock
Lodovic Snyder
Frederick Gebler
Jacob Folts
George Feling
Theobald Zimmerman
Henry Zimmerman
    A list of those men who were not up in the alarm:
George Klock
Jacob Enkish
Henry Sander
Lawrence Zimmerman
Georg Zimmerman
Severinus Snell
Roger Baxter
John Baxter
Pieter Schuyler Jun.

Jacob Folts, Jun.

Gerlagh Meyer

"All the above mentioned persons have lawfully excused themselves except George Klock, who says that he is free by an act of the Assembly because he is a Miller and his son George he kept back in the Alarm till the second Day on which Day he came with the Parcel of Indians. He being asked what kept him so long answer'd that he waited for the Indians of which he was to be Commander for which Reason I think that I may fine him as ere long I intend to do." * Signed—

Capt. Jacob Klock.

It must be borne in mind that there might be many good reasons why these early settlers were lawfully unable to answer these Indian and other alarms. But continued neglect of duty and failure to answer to the call of the commanding officer of the militia generaly meant a fine.

It is surprisi..g to see how strict these wilderness soldiers were in regard to their military affairs.

CHAPTER V

Lieut. Goshin Von Alstein's Company

A true list of the Melitia Company Commanded by Lieut. Goshin Van Alstein vizt: August 8th, 1763.

Robert Flint, Lieut.
Christian Gerlach, Ens.

Serjeants:

Dewald Dychert
Adam Counterman
William Fink
Henry Shrimling

Corporals:

John Thorn
Denus Diustman
Frid'k Strobeck
George Nestle

Privates

William Merinus
Abraham Merinus
Gilbert Van Alstein
Henry Shrimling
Hermanus Ehl
Simion Brown
Peter Young Miller
Fred'k Gyesits
Nicholas Failling
Johans Ehl
Christian Ehl
Peter Selbach
Joost Cremer
John Cremer
Thomas Kesler
Jacob Braner

Adam Strobeck
Peter H. Young
Peter Sheffer
John Young
Peter Murfee
Peter Ehl
Christian Huffnagl
Severinus Dyck
Peter Dyckerd
John Meselis
Henry Warmoth
Henry Laux
Peter Laux
Jery Ecker
Joseph Warmoth
Henry Dyckerd
Thomas Killy
Henry Killy
John Wormoth
Jery Wassell
Peter Caselman
John Caselman
Severin's Caselman
William Caselman
Peter Meselis
Casp'r Jordan
Jery Jordan
John Klock
Mich'll Endler
Henry Wyl
Peter Fux
John Philipse
Abraham Wardman
Gerret Miller
Jery Pfeil
Hartman Zeller
Henry Failling
Peter Balsley
Christopher Heneman
Peter Myer
Jery Harlderffer
Christian Brown
Adam Hutmach'r
Henry Betsing'r
Godfry Rotnau'r
France Bader
John Shill
Arnold Selbach
Jacob Bratt
Isaacc Emich
Nich's Christman
Casp'r Keller
Christian Nier
Henry Seber
Adam Kurn
James Philipse
John Reber
And's Reber

I suggest that Christian Nier may be Christian Niering (Nearing). I wonder if this "Jery" is meant for Jurie i. e. George. You note the list has no name of George. Later, but no date given, Lieut. Gose Van Alstein is recommended for Captain in this Canajoharie company. His commission seems to have been dated "Nov'br. 6th, 1763." "for a Company at Canajohare whereof Ferall Wade was formerly Capt'n."

You will note that there was a senior and a junior Henry Schramling. It was this Schramling family that married into the John Frederick Hess and Catherine Nellis family and moved into Otsego county, N. Y.

CHAPTER VI

We now come to a very interesting report by Col. John Jost Herekheimer (Herkimer). This includes what he calls "The Grannadier Co." I find that this seems to be an English term. "Originally a foot soldier armed with grenades. The grenadiers were men of long service and approved courage, and only a few were attached to each regiment. Afterwards every regiment had one company of grenadiers and they retained their name even after the disuse of grenades, and were distinguished by a particular dress." Today I am told by one of our teachers, an Englishman of wide experience in teaching both here and in England, that the term now is only applied to the king's body guard called "The Grenadier Guard."

May 6th, 1767, A "reaorn" of persons names "Choesen" to be officers in the Battalion under the command of Coll'l. John Jost Herekheimer viz.

1st "The Grannadier Company".
Jost Herckheimer, Capt.
Frederick Orendorf, Leut.
Augustines Klebsatel, Leut.
Jost Schumager, Leut. (Ens.?)
George Herckheimer, Capt.
Strehebel Armstrong, Leut.
Friedrich Fux, Leut.
Jost Deygerd, Ensign
Hans Petrie, Capt.
Nicholas Weber. Leut.
Jost M. Petrie, Leut.
John Conningham, Ensign.
Daniel Petrie, Capt.
Peter Fols, Leut.
Marx Rasbach, Leut.
Georg Helmer, Ensign
Georg H. Bell, Capt.
Adam Jung, Leut.
Adam Staring, Leut.
Hans Weber, Ensign
Rudddolff Schumager, Capt.
Friedrich Schumager, Leut.
Tiederich Stehl, Leut.
Deobeld Deygerd, Ensign
Werner Deygerd, Capt.
William Conningham, Leut.
Jost Petree, Ju'r. Leut.
Diederich Petree, Ensign
Friedrich Bellinger, Capt.
Henrich Sterter, Leut.
Hans Demuth, Leut.
Peter Weber, Ensign
Peter Bellinger, Capt.
Nicolas Staring, Leut.
Jacob Bashar, Leut.
John Bellinger, Ensign
William Dygerd, Capt.
Jacob Fols, Leut.
Georg Wens, Leut.
Friedrich C. Franck, Ens'n.

Burnets Field May ye 6th, 1767., Jost Herckheimer Coll.
It will be noted that many of these men became officer in the militia in the Revolution at the beginning at least, while others if not too old served as privatts in the ranks, and others if alive and able to serve at all were in a company called the exempts.

CHAPTER VII

Captain Conrad's Company, May 8, 1767.
Officers names, commissioned all on January 17th, 1764:
Conrad Frank, Capt.
John Jost Herkermer, Lieut.
Peter Bellinger, Lieut.
George Herkemer, Ens.
Timothy Frank, Clerk.
                    Sarg't.
Fred'k Ahrendarf
Peter Bellinger
Peter Hyer
Petter Phyffer
Conrad Follmer
                    Corp's.
Mich'l Ittig
Christian Ittig
Arch'd Armstrong
Paul Sickner
                    Soldiers
Frederick Frank
Adam Staring
Dennis Clipsadel
Werner Spaun
Augustinus Hess
John Hess
Frederick Hess
Wernert Dygert
Jacob Kessleir
Johanis Kessler
Johanis Feisenman
Johanis Miller
Conrad Miller
Nicholas Staring
Joseph Staring
George Weinze
Rodolff Schumauker
Fredrick Schumaker
Andrews Weavour
Andrews Cibsadle
Deitrick Stehll
Fredrick Gettman
Jacob Ettige
Markes Ittig
Hendrick Frank
Jasob Bassor
Causper Boner
Paul Gram
Fredricg Bell
Icabod Bonney
Thomas Follmer
Joist Schyler
Peter Schyler Jun.
Nicholas Schyler
Jacob Deick
John Kesler
Michael Kesler

Jacob John Kessler
Conrad Kessler
Johanis Miller
Nich'ls Miller
John Eeiseman
Adam Nich. Staring
Fredrick Schuitte
William Schutte
Hendrick Staring
John Staring
Adam Joseph Staring
Peter Staring
John Fox
Conrad Aherndarff
Adam Steel
John Simpson
Thomas Schumaker
Nich'ls Kaissler
John Bellinger
Peter Bellinger
Fredrick Fox
John Spawn
Conrad Frank
Jacob Bell
John Ouisterhouit
Peter Wollinger
Dirck Wollinger
John Campell
Jacob Wensse
Augustus Follmer
Frd'rk Joist Schumker
Josepeh Moyer
Josepeh Moyer Jun'r.
Jacob Moyer
Rudolf Steel Jun'r.
Joist Dygert
John Frank
Christiean Peshause
John Moyer
Hendrick Frank Jun'r.
John Jacob Weavour
John Walldraut
Jacob Walldratt
George Walldratt
Fredrick Bell
Fredrick Hawk
Stoffle Trouble
Nicholas Chrissman
Hendrick Miller
Nicholas Ox
John Furgerson
Joist Cock
James Rankin
Jacob Follist
Devil Dygert
Conradd Follist
Hendrick Dygert
William Hunt
Joseph Krand
John Feildeen
John Brown

This company was located on the south side of the Mohawk at German Flatts. "Conradt Frank to be Captain of the Company w'h Peter Pellinger Commands. He being too old and unfit for service." Peter Pellinger Jr. was to be 2nd. Lieut. in Conrd Frank's Co. While this statement appears to have been made in 1762, Capt. Frank was not commismiosend until Jann. 17, 1764. Altho I have no record that Capt. Frank's Co. or Capt. Petry's Co. were called out with Capt. Klock's Co. and Capt. Deyger's Co. July 24 to 28, 1763, due to an Indian alarm at German Flatts, it would only be reasonable to suppose that they were called out, and perhaps the reason they were not mentioned in the records is because they were supposed to be on duty there at German Flatts anyway. There would be no reason for calling out the Stone Arabia and Palatine Companies to go to German Flatts and not call out the two companies there already. It will be noted that the patentees of Conrad Frank's patent and the First and Second Staley's tracts, now mostly comprised in the Town of Columbia Herkimer county, were made up of the names in this company. It will be noted also that these families inter-married to a very great degree.

CHAPTER VIII

Captain Marx Petry's Company. Bornets Field May the 9th, 1769. List of Capt. Marx Petry Compaynie.
John Petry Lieut.
Daniel Petry Lieut.
Georg Henry Bell Ens.
Fried'k P. Bellinger Cl'k
                Serg't.
Fried'k Helmer
Conrad Vols
Henry Herter
Marx Demuth .
                Corp'l
Fried'k Ad. Hellmer
Christian Riegel
Marx Raspach
Nicolaus Hils
                Soldiers
Wm. Cunigham
Andreas Cunigham
John Cunigham
Georg Dachstader
Philip Belinger
Adam Belinger
Georg Weber Jun.
Friederik Weber
Jacob Weber
Nicolaus Weber Jun.
Jacob Jacobs Weber
Peter Weber
Georg Jacobs Weber
John Demuth
Henry Weber
Nicolaus Heinry Weber
John Nic. Weber
Henry Meyer
Friederik Meyer
Marx Petry
John Christman
Jacob Christman
Friederik Helmer
Adam Bauman

Peter Bauman
Friederik Bauman
Johanes Bellinger Jun.
Nicolaus Herter
Friederik Herter
Lorentz Herter
Friederik Rieger
Christian Riegel
Georg Ludwig Smith
Peter Smith
Adam Smith
Jost Smith
Georg Smith
Nicolaus Smith
John Smith
Friederik Smith
Jost Petry
John Weber
Melchoir Thumb
Georg Hils Sen.
Georg Hils Jun.
John Kessler
Phillip Helmer
Adam Helmer
John Hellmer
Henry Hellmer
Jo'n Nicolaus Weber
Georg Weber
John Belilnger
Jost Vols
Melchoir Vols
Jacob Pfiiffer
Georg Jacob Hils
Stoffel Hils
Andre McCombs
Henry Widerstein
Friederik Dornberger
Friederik Herter
Phillip Hellmer Jun.
Georg Hellmer
Adam Friederik Helmer
Friederik Raspach
Heinry Heufer
Adam Mersh
John Schell
Friederik Weber
Georg Nellis
Jacob Bauman
Peter Vols
Christian Schell
Conrad Vols
Henry Muller
Friederik Muller
John Devy
Marx Petry Jun.
Jacob Kessler Jun.
Jost Petry Jun.
Dietrik Petry
Friederik Frank
John Hering
Jost John Petry
John Petry Jun.
Henry Rieme Schneider
John Ritter
Georg Edel

John Hogsly
Melchoir Kessler
Nicolaus Spon
Bartly Pikert
Friederik Windeker
Henry Keller
John Garter
Valentin Beyer
Friederik Kast
John Tompson
John Wolff
Caspar Hasenclever
Jacob Tynges
Michael Seitzer
Georg Bauer
Balthasar Breidenbacher
Arnold Steinwax
Heinry Berkhoff
Wm. Klein
Friederik Ayrer
Abraham Breidenbacher
John Roos
John Weisgerber
John Schad
Michael Vogt
Henry Vogt
Georg Snek Sen.
Michael Widrig
Lorentz Groninger
Georg Snek Jun.
Jacob Hiller
Georg Schieff
Jacob Berky
Georg Ogd
Lorentz Rinkel
Michael Wolf
Henry Schaffer
Georg Cronhard
Georg Brown
Nicolaus Keller
Matheas Clemons
John Nicolaus Rein
Valentin Muller
Dibold Beker
John Collsh
Peter Multer
Hieronymus Spies
Wm. Bender
Jacob Meyer
John Riema

It will be noted that these names appear as from the north side of the river at German Flatts. It will be noted also that no name of Hess or Staring appears at this date, hence I conclude that the Staring family did not move into the town of Schuyler until some time after this date.

The German Flatts Hess families staid on the south side of the Mohawk until after the Revolution except Johnnes Hess Sr. who had moved to the Harrrson Patent 1732 but his oldest son Augustinus Hess, Sr. stayed on the original Lot 31.

THE
Kocherthal Records

A TRANSLATION OF THE
KOCHERTHAL RECORDS OF THE
WEST CAMP LUTHERAN CHURCH

By J. Christian Krahmer,

October 1926

A. BAPTISMS, pages 11-66. (In original).

IN THE NAME OF JESUS

(Jesu AUSPICE)

The following records were published in the Lutheran Quarterly published at Gettysburg, Pa. and with the permisison of that paper to recopy. The translation was made from the original now deposited in the archives at Albany, N. Y. and are the property of the West Camp Lutheran Church.

Rev. Joshua Kocherthal was the pastor of the Palatines in West Camp and Schoharie. He received permission to accompany the Palatines in 1708 and came to England from the lower Palatinate, from whence in 1709 he embarked for America with ten families consisting of 41 persons. He returned to London and in 1710 accompanied the second migration. He died in 1719. His wife was Sibylla Carlotta and his children were Benigna, Sibylla, Christian, Joshua and Susanna Sibylla.

BAPTISMS

Record of children who were baptized by me, Joshua Kocherthal, the first pastor of the Germans of New York

In the year 1708, on board the ship GLOBE, the following were baptized by me:

Sept. 14th: Johann Hermann, child of Jacob and Anna Elizabeth WEBER; sponsors: W. Harmannus SCHUENEMANN, clerk on bord the ship, and Johann ROTH, constable on bord the ship.

Nov. 28th: Carolus, child of Andreas and Anna Catharina VOLCK; sponsor: Carolus CONGREVE, captain of the ship .

Total number in the year 1708..2

In the year 1709, I baptized at New York (Neo-Eboraci).

Jan. 23d: Jannicke, child of Johann Michael and Maria SCHUETZE; sponsors: Justus Falckner, Pastor of the Dutch Lutherans, and in the absence of Falckner, Daniel LUETKEN, M. D., and Jannicke, the child's aunt on the mother's side.

Febr. 23d.: Johannes, child of Johann Jacob and Elisabetha PLETTEL; Sponsors: Johannes FISCHER and Anna Marie WEIGAND.

In the same year in the colony on the Quasack Kill, in the home of Sabertand, the following were baptized by me:

July 17th: Samuel, child of Melchoir and Gertrauda SPRINGSTEIN; sponsors: Peter MIGRIGRI and his wife Letischa.

July 17th: Joseph, child of Joseph and Helena PRACTER; sponsors: Jacob
WEBER and Anna Catharina WEIGAND.

July 17th: Marla, child of Georg and Catharina SPRINGSTEIN; sponsors:
Peter JANSON and his wife Maria.

July 19th: Margretha, child of Johann and Christian   Breuen; sponsors:
Peter MAGRIGRI and his wife Letischa.

July 19th: Lydia, child of Obadias and Susanna WINTER; sponsors: Andreas
VOLCK and his wife Anna Catharina.

July 19th: Peter Samuel, child of Samuel and Emicke KANIKLI; sponsors:
Peter ROSE and Litcken HEU.

July 19th: Johannes, child of Samuel and Emicke KANIKLI; sponsors: Johann Henrich NAEHRUNG and Anna Maria WEIGAND.

July -9th: Wilhelm, child of William and Elizabeth ARSEN; sponsors: Johann FISCHER and his wife Maria.
Total   number in the year 1709..10

In the year 1710 I baptized the following on board the ship MIDFORT:

April 12th: Elisabetha,   child of Justus   Henrich and Maria   Margretha
SCHAEFER; sponsors: Johann Leonard LUED and Anna Elisabetha
CASSELMANN.

May 12th: Anna Margaretha, child of Johann Georg and Anna Maria SPON-
HEIMER; sponsors: Johann Valentin BAENDER and his wife Anna
Margretha.

June 1st: Maria Elisabetha, child of Sebastian and Maria Elisabetha LOES-
CHER; sponsors: Johann MUELIER and his wife Elisabeth.

June 1st: William, child of Johannes and Anna Apolonia GREMS; sponsor:
William FOWLES, captain of the ship.

On board the ship LEON baptized by Mr. Rohrbach:

May 2d: Anna Margretha, child of Caspar and Anna   Agatha BRENDEL;
sponsor: Anna Margretha GOEBEL.

In the same year Rev. Justus Falckner, Pastor of the Dutch Lutherans
baptized in my absence the following in this province:

In the colony on the Quasaic Kill:

April 17th: Johann Heinrich, child of Laurenz and Catharina SCHWEIT-
ZER; sponsors: Henrich RENNAU and his wife Johanna.

April 19th: Johannes, child of Jacob and Anna Elisabetha WEBER; sponsors: Michael WEIGAND and his wife Anna Catharina.

April 19th: Margretha, child of Johannes and Maria Fischer; sponsors: William SADERLAND and his wife.

At New York:

Febr. 28th: Louisa Abigail, born Febr. 26th, child of Joshua KOCHERTHAL,
at that time pastor of the church, and his wife Sibylla Charlotte; sponsors: Daniel LUETKEN, M. D., and Abigail LISPENAER.

In the same year the aforesaid Pastor baptized in my absence at New York
the following from among those who had recently arrived:

About the middle of June:

Johanna Elisabetha, child of Johann Jacob and Maria Elisabeth SCHNITT; sponsors: Johann Adolph ARTOPOEUS, Johann CHAMBORAY and his wife Barbara Elisabetha.

Johann Philipp, child of Philipp MUELLER (mother's name is not given): sponsors: Philipp ZERB and Maria Catharina BLANICK.

Anna Elisabetha, child of Abraham NEUS (mother's name not given): sponsors Johannes LAMED and his wife Anna Elisabeth.
Anna Elisabeth, child of Niclaus and Sabina HAAS; sponsors: the the parents and Anna Barbara DIPPEL.

Johannes, child of Johann Georg and Susanna KLUG; sponsors: Johann MENGIS and Anna Maria BUSCH.

In the same year, having returned to the province, I baptized the following at New York:
July 11th: Alexander, child of Johannes and Anna Margretha LORENTZ; sponsors: Alexander ROSENQUEST and Elisazetha ESWEIN.

Aug. 20th: Anna Maria, child of Dietrich and Anna Elalia HOFMANN; Sponsor: Anna Maria HOFMAN.

Aug. 21st: Anna Margretha, child of Christian and Anna Dorothea BAUCH; sponsors: Lorentz Henrich and Maria Margretha KURTZ.

Aug. 25th: Johannes, child of Benedict and Christina WENERICH; sponsor: Hananias DIEHL.

Aug. 27th: Johann Michael, child of Johann Dietrich and Anna Margretha WANENMACHER; sponsor: Michael STORR.

,ept. 3d: Johannes, child of Conrad and Anna Maria HETTICH; sponsor: Johann WIHS.

Sept. 10th: Johann Adam, child of Johann Georg and Anna Margretha SCHLEICHER; sponsors: Johann Peter HAGEDORN, Adam Michael SCHMID, and Maria Elisabetha Lucka.

Sept. 13th: Johann Henrich Valentin, child of Johann Philipp and Catharina KREISER; sponsors: Henrich MEHS and Valentin PRESLER.

Sept. 22d: Elisabeth, child of Johann and Anna Maria BERENHARD; sponsor: Elisabetha BERENHARD.

Sept 24th: Maria Margretha, child of Johannes and Anna Margretha FEEG; sponsors: Johann Jacob RISCH, Anna Maria FEEG, and Margretha KUNTZ.

Sept. 24th: Maria Sophia, child of Gerhard and Anna Maria SCHAESTER; sponsors: Johann ZECH, Maria Apollonia WUEST, and Anna Sophia KOPP.

Sept: 29th: Johann Adam, child of Johannes and Anna Magdalena ZECH; sponsor: Johann Adam LESCH.

Oct. 20th: Eva Catharina, child of Christian and Anna Maria Judith CASTELMANN; sponsors: Johann Michael WAIDKNECHT and Elisabetha MUELLER.

Oct. 22d: Elias, born July 22, 1704, child of William and Maria THIBAUX, the father being a Frenchman; sponsors: the parents.

Oct. 22d: Job, born Febr. 7, 1706, child of William and Maria THIBAUX (father being a Frenchman); sponsors: the parents.

Oct. 22d: Maria, born May 13, 1710, child of William and Maria THIBAUX, (the father being a Frenchman); sponsors: the parents.

Dec. 1st: Isaac, born Aug. 3d, child of William WEIGHT, Sr., and his wife Goodith; sponsors: Abraham von THESEN and his wife JACOBINA, and Andreas ROSE.

Dec. 3d: Henricus, born in the month of August, child of Salomon and Jannicke SCHUETT; sponsors: Hensic RISOM, and Anna RISOM.

Total number in the year 1710 32

In the year 1711:

March 6th: Robert, born March 4th, child of Henric and Anna CHISEM; sponsors: Wilhelm SCHOTT and his wife Helena.

March 25th: Jacob, child of Jacob and Maria VORST; sponsors: Wilhelm JORICK and his wife, Henrich LORENZ, Margaretha WEISHARD, and Anna Maria ZIPERLIN.

In the home of Saderland in the German colony on the Quasaic Kill:

April 17th: Anna Maria, born Oct. 24, 1710, child of Andreas and Anna Catharina VOLCK; sponsors: Johannes FISCHER and his wife.

April 17th: Georgius, born Febr. 1st child of Georg and Elisabetha LOOCK-STAD; sponsors: Georg WEIGAND and Anna Catharina VOLCK.

April 17th: William, child of Benjamin and Faemige ELSWA; sponsor: Wil-liam CLERK, and in his absence, Andreas VOLCK.

April 17th: Abraham, child of Isaac and Judith HENRICKSON; sponsors: Georg LOOCKSTAD and his wife.

April 7th: Gertraud, 3 months old, child of Georg and Catharina SPRING-STEIN; sponsor: David SPRINGSTEIN.

April 7th: Maria, child of Johann and Elisabetha BREIN; sponsors: Burck-hard MEINHARD and his wife.

April 7th: Abraham, child of Pieter and Jannicke DE BOIS; sponsors: An-dreas VOLCK and his wife.

In New York:

Jan. 3d: Anna Maria, child Ludwig and Catharina BRETSCH; sponsor: the wife of Conrad FRIEDRICH.

Jan. 7th: Johann Michael, child of Johann and Maria Margretha PLANCK; sponsors: Michael PFESTER and the widow of Conrad GERLACH.

March 28th: Christian, child of Andreas and Anna Rosina ELLIG; sponsor: Christian AIGLER.

April 8th: Andreas, child of Christian and Maria Eva AIGLER; sponsor : Andreas ELLIG.

May 1st: Johannes, child of Michael and Anna Maria PFESTER; sponsors: Jahonn PLANCK and Anna Kunigunda WANENMACHER.

In the upper German Colonies:

June 3d: Johann Wilhelm, child of Johann Bernhard and Justina LUECK-HARD; sponsor: Johann Wilhelm STUECKENRAD.

June 10th: Johann Niclaus, child of Wilhelm and Maria JORG; sponsors: Niclaus HESS, Jacob DINGS and Margretha WEISHARD.

June 10th: Anna Barbara, child of Simon and Rosina HAAS; sponsor: Anna Barbara SCHUMACHER.

June 10th: Anna Catharina, child of Johann and Gertrud GANS; sponsors: Georg Adam SCHMID, Anna Catharina PULFER, and Catharina .FULZ

June 22d: Joseph, born June 21st, child of Franz and Barbara GILLER; sponsors: Joseph REICHART and his wife Anna Maria.

June 24th: Johan David, child of Mattheus and Anna Margretha CUNTZ; sponsors: Johann BERNHARD, Johann David IFLAND, and Anna Barbara SCHUMACHER.

July 8th: Joseph, child of Gabriel and Susanna HOFFMANN; sponsors. Joseph REICHARD and his wife Anna Maria.

July 8th: Johanna Elisabetha, child Henrich and Anna Juliana REUTER; sponsors: Johanna Elisabeth WERNER and Johann HESS.

July 21st: Wilhelm, born July 19th, child of Johann Dietrich and Anna CASTELMANN; sponsor: Philip MUELLER, the sexton.

July 22nd: Philip, born July 15th, child of Johann Henrich and Elisabeth LEICH; sponsor: Philipp Peter GRAUBERGER.

July 22nd: Johann Adam, born July 21st, child of Niclaus and Anna Magdalena KOERNER; sponsors: Johann FRANCKE and Adam HERTEL.

July 24th: Johann Peter, born July 23d, child of Johann Henrich and Maria Elisabetha MANN; sponsors: Johann Peter MAURER and the wife of Peter WAGNER.

Aug. 1st: Anna Kunigunda, born July 31st, child of Michael and Elisabeth STORR; sponsor: Anna Kunigunda, wife of Dietrich WANENMACHER.

Aug. 5th: Anna Gertraut, born August 1st, child of Johann Valentin and Elisabetha Maria FALCKENBURG; sponsors: Jacob MAUCK, Gertruda KOHL, Anna Margretha HERDEL.

Aug. 8th: Appolonia, born Aug. 6th, child of Christoph and Magdalena WERNER; sponsor: Appolonia, wife of Hans Valentin FROEHLICH.

Aug. 9th: Anna Catharina, born Aug. 3d, child of Peter and Maria VOSHEL; father being a Frenchman; sponsor: Anna, wife of Johann WOODEN.

Aug. 9th: Anna Margretha, born Aug. 7th, child of Niclaus and Maria Catharina STARING, the father being a brick-maker; sponsors: Philipp PETRI, the sexton, and his wife Anna Margretha, also Anna Elisabetha (last name not given).

Aug. 10th: Maria Elisabetha, born Aug. 8th, child of Christian and Anna Gertraudt MEYRER; sponsors: Maria Christiana, wife of Johann Peter OBERBACH, Elisabeth, wife of Peter OBERBACH, Johann Georg OBERBACH.

Aug. 19th: Johanna Catharina, born Aug. 17th, child of Johannes and Anna Margretha EMMERICH; sponsors: Johann HESS and Catharina CURRING.

Aug. 23d: Christianus, born Aug. 20th, child of Bernhard and Anna Maria LISTENIUS; sponsor: Christian AIGLER.

Aug. 26th: Johann Georg, born Aug. 23d, child of Philipp and Veronica KLUMM; sponsors Anna Maria PEETER and Johann Georg SCHULTHEISS.

Aug. 26th: Jorg Ludwig, born Aug. 22d, child of Johann Georg and Anna Elisabetha SCHMID; sponsors: Jorg Ludwig KOCH and his wife Anna Maria.

Aug. 30th: Maria Magdalena, born Aug. 28th, child of Peter and Elisabetha Maria WICKHAUS; sponsors: Maria STEIN and Magdalena JUNG.

Sept. 3d: Mattheus, born Aug. 22d, child of Jacob and Maria Elisabetha HOFMANN; sponsor: Mattheus CUNTZ.

Sept. 3d: Johann Georg, born Aug. 27th, child of Johann Henrich and Anna Cecillia WIDERWACHS; sponsors: Johann Niclaus WOLLEBEN, Johann Georg ZUFELD, and Eva SCHURTZ.

Sept. 8th: Maria Catharina, born Sept. 7th, child of Abraham and Catharina LAUCK; sponsors: Johann Georg STUMP, Maria Catharina, wife of Niclaus Schaefer, and Maria CATHARINA wife of Abraham LANGRY.

Sept. 10th: Johann Peter, born Sept. 6th, child of Johann Peter and Maria Christina OBERBACH; sponsors: Peter OBERBACH, Johann Mattheus JUNG, and Anna Demuth THONIUS.

Sept. 14th: Johann Peter, born Sept. 11th, child of Conrad and Eva Margretha HOSTMANN; sponsor: Johann Peter GLOPP.

Nov. 1st: Pieter, born May 14th, child of Henrich and Wilhelmina (commonly called Williampe) BOIS; sponsor: Pieter von KLECK. This child was baptized in Poughkeepsie (Pagepsen).

Nov. 1st: Meinhard, born the middle of March, child of Hermann and Gertraud (commonly called Drincke Ohrstrohm) RAUERSEE; sponsor: Jacobus VON DE BOGARD. This child was baptized in Poughkeepsie.

Nov. 6th: Maria Catharina, child of Simeon and Anna Margretha ERHARD; sponsors: Johan Niclaus SCHAESTER and his wife Maria Catharina.

Nov. 6th: Anna Eva, child of Johann Michael and Anna Elisabetha FREYMEYER; sponsors: Melchoir VOLTZ and his wife Anna Eva.

Nov. 7th: Johannes, born October 30th, child of Henrich and Maria Margretha GLOCK; sponsor: Johannes HAYNER.

Nov. 7th: Johann Ulrich, born Oct. 26th, child of Wilhelm and Anna Maria SIMON; sponsors: Johann Ulrich BERNHARD and Eleonora Catharina, wife of David KISTLER.

Nov. 11th: Maria Catharina, born Oct. 28th, child of Henrich and Anna Margretha JUNG; sponsors: Jacob ZIMMERMAN, the wife of Jorg MATTHESEN, Maria, wife of Jacob PORSTER.

Nov. 12th: Anna Maria, born Oct. 31st, child of Johann and Anna Ursula STAHL; sponsors: Johann Peter OBERBACH, Anna Maria, daughter of Wilhelm KUESTER, Anna Elisabeth MUELLER.

Nov. 17th: Christina Elisabetha, born Nov. 8th, child of Gerhard and Anna Maria WALLRATH; sponsor: Christina Elisabetha JAEGER.

Nov. 18th: Anna Margretha, born Nov. 10th, child of Albrecht and Eva SCHREIBER; sponsors: Hans Henrich HAMMER, and the wife of Christian SITTIG.

Nov. 18th: Johanna Elisabeth Margretha, born Nov. 1st, child of Veltin and Anna Catharina KUHN; sponsors: Hermann SEGENDORST, Anna Elisabetha WIS, Anna Margretha SCHAESTER.

Nov. 18th: Johann Henrich, born Nov. 13th, child of Hartmann and Barbara Elisabeth WINDECKER; sponsor: Johann Henrich BELLINGER.

Nov. 19th: Paul, born Nov. 12th, child of Daniel and Johanna SCHAMPNOR; sponsors: Paul BUVNAT and Martha BERTRAM.

Nov. 20th: Philipp Peter, born Nov. 16th, child of Sebastian and Anna Elisabetha SPICKERMANN; sponsors: Philip MUELLER, Johann Peter HELM, Anna Elisazetha SCHAESTER.

Nov. 25th: Johann Adam, born Nov. 20th, child of Hans Jorg and Elisabetha ROEMER; sponsors: Johann Adam SOELLER and Magdalena TRAMBAUER.

Nov. 28th: Anna Maria, born Nov. 22d, child of Johann Henrich and Anna Dorothea BAST; sponsors: Johannes MUELLER, Anna Elisabetha STAHL, and Anna Julian MAUL.

Nov. 29tn: Anna Eva, born Nov. 23d, child of Johann Peter and Anna Catharina DIPPEL; sponsors: Eva Catharina MANCK, Elisabeth JUNG, Gottfrid RUEHL, Johann Balthasar KUESTER.

Dec. 2d: Johann Dietrich, born Nov. 26th, child of Albrecht Dietrich and Elisabetha MARTERSTOCK; sponsors: Dietrich CASTELMANN and Margretha WEIDKNECHT.

Dec. 9th: Ludwig, born Dec. 6th, child of Johann and Maria Catharina CUNTZ; sponsor: Ludwig BERSCHT.

Dec. 13th: Jorg Wilhelm, born Dec. 5th, child of Johann Wilhelm and Anna Margretha DIETRICH; sponsors: Jorg Wilhelm Kehl and Anna Maria Dorothea DEMUTH.

Dec. 21st: Juliana Elisabetha, born Dec. 17th, child of Johann Peter and Magdalena LASTNER; sponsors: Andreas WEIDKNECHT, Juliana MOTSCH, Elisabetha FLEGLER.

Dec. 23d: Johannes, born Dec. 20th, child of Johann Philipp and Anna Margaretha RUEGER; sponsor: Johannes MUELLER.

Dec. 26th: Johann Adam, born Dec. 10th, child of Fridrich and Anna Barbara MERCKEL; sponsors: Johann Adam FRIDERICH and his wife Regina.

Dec. 30th: Anna Maria, born Dec. 29th, child of Martin and Anna Maria STEIN; sponsors: Peter WICKHAUS and Anna Maria MUELLER.

Dec. 31st: Margreth, born November 9th, child of Wilhelm and Helena SCHOTT; sponsors: Henrich and Margretha CHISEM, in the place of these: Anna Catharina BUTT.

Dec. 31st: Anna Maria, born Dec. 26th, child of Henrich and Anna Kunigunda MEYER; sponsors: Johann SCHAESTER, Jacob BERMAN, Maria Sibylla MATHEUS, Anan Elisabetha DACHSETTER.

Total for the year 1711 68

In the year 1712:

Jan. 1st: Maria Elisabetha, born Dec. 30th, child of Conrad and Anna Elisabeth BERINGER; sponsor: Maria Elisabetha SCHLITZLER.

Jan. 4th: Johann Fridrich, born Jan. 1st, child of Philip Peter and Anna Barbara GRAUBERGER; sponsors: Fridrich MAUL and Johann FUEHRER.

Jan. 6th: Anna Catharina, born Dec. 31, 1711, child of Henrich and Anna Margretha MOHR; sponsors: Anna Sibylla Catharina KEHL, Philip MOHR, Anna Elisabetha STAHL.

Jan. 27th: Anna Eva, born Jan. 19th, child of Mattheus and Anna Veronica SCHLEMER; sponsors: Anna Louisa GESTELER, Anna Eva MENGEST, Hans Veltin FALCKENBURGER.

Jan. 27th: Johann Henrich, born (not given), child of Jost Henrich and Agnes SCHAESTER; sponsors: Elisabeth JUNG and Johann Reitz BACKUS.

Jan. 29th: Johann Bernhard, born Dec. 30th, 1711, child of Jostaph and Anna Maria REICHARD; sponsors: Johann Bernhard ZIPPERLIN and his wife Anna Maria.

Jan. 31st: Johann Henrich, born Jan. 26th, child of John Henrich and Anna Catharina KRANTZ; sponsor: Johann Henrich SCHARRMANN. (This entry is crossed out and a cross placed beneath the name of the child.)

Jan. 31st: Maria Regina, born Jan. 24th, child of Johann Melchoir and Anna Magdalena DAUSWEBER; sponsors: Johann STRAUB and his wife Maria Elisabeth, and Maria Regina FRIDRICH.

Febr. 6th: Elisabetha Ottilia, born Febr. 6th, child Johann Dietrich and Anna Kunigunda WANNENMACHER; sponsor: Elisabetha Ottilia STORR. (A cross beneath the child's name).

Febr. 10th: Johann Friderich, born Febr. 2d, child of Hieronymus and Anna Juliana WELLER; sponsors: Johann Fridrich HAEGER, Johann MUELLER and Margaretha MERTIN.

Febr. 10th: Johannes, born Febr. 5th, child of Johannes and Anna Elisabetha BECKER; sponsors: Johann STRAUB and Anna Barbara GUNTER-MANN.

Febr. 26th: Johannes, born Febr. 16th, child of Johann Wilhelm and Maria Elisabetha Catharina BRANDAU; sponsor: Johannes FRANCK.

March 12th: Johann Georg, born March 7th, child of Johannes and Anna Sibylla EBERHARD; sponsors: Johann George SPONHEIMER and his wife Anna Maria.

March 23d: Maria Margaretha (an illegitimate child), born March 15th, child of Killian (commonly called Koelin) PLANCK, a young Hollander of Albany, and Juliana, widow of Jacob JUNG; sponsors: Johann Emmerich PLIRS and Maria Margretha SCHAESTER.

March 23d: Anna Catharina, born March 23d, child of Adam and Elisabetha Catharina ECKHARD; sponsor: Anna CASTIN.

May 19th: Peter, born Jan. 4th, child of Peter and Maria JANSON; sponsors: Omyla GRANSCHE and his wife Elisabetha.

May 19th: Johannes, born March 15th, child of Andreas and Catharina VOLCK; sponsors: Johnn FISCHER and his wife Maria.

April 18th: Jannicke, born Febr. 22d, child of Rennier VON HUSUM and his wife Anna; sponsors: Volkart VON HUSUM and his wife Maria.

May 25th: Mattheus, born May 1st, child of Johann and Jannike BOND; sponsors; Mattheus GUSS and Rachel BOND.

June 1st: Jannike, born May 20th, child of John and Catharina HAAS; sponsors: Andreas BAGGS and Anna PERSCH.

June 8th: Anna Christina, born June 2d, child of Niclaus and Magdalena TROMBAUER; sponsor: the wife of Bernhard LUECKHARD, Justina.

June 11th: Andreas, born April 16th, child of Peter and Cornelia LOSTING; sponsors: Wilhelm ROOS and his wife Catharina.

July 18th: Philippus Hieronymus, born July 16th, child of Jacob STERN-BERGER; (mother's name is not given); sponsors; Philipp Peter GRAUBERGER, Hieronymus KLEIN and the wife of Rudolph CUR-RING.

July 20th: Anna Margretha, born July 8th, child of Johannes and Sibylla Catharina LEER; sponsors: Johann BECKER, Anna Margretha GER-LACH, and Maria Margretha WAGNER.

July 23rd: Johann Henrich, born July 18th, child of Johann Martin and Barbara Elisabetha NETZBACHER; sponsor: Johann Henrich CONRAD.

July 27th: Georg Henrich, born July 26th, child of Jorg Henrich and Anna Catharina STUBENRAUCH; sponsors: Henrich SCHRAMM and Anna Elisabetha EMERICH.

July 27th: Jacob, born July 24th, child of Kilian and Anna Margretha MINKLER; sponsors: Jacob SCHEDP and his wife.

July 28th: Johann Philipp, born July 26th, child of Johann Philipp and Anna Catharina FINCKEL; sponsors: Johann Philipp ZERB and Anna Maria SCHNEIDER.

July 28th: Jacob, born July 28th, child of Andreas and Maria FINCK; sponsor: Jacob KOBEL.

Aug. 3d: Johann Jacob, born July 28th, child of Johann Fridrich and Anna Maria BELL; sponsors: Johann Michael HERDER, Jacob WEBER and Anna Eva THOMAS.

Aug. 3d: Anna Margretha, born Aug. 1st, child of Jorg Martin and Sara Catharina DILLENBACH; sponsors: Jacob LOESHAAR and Anna Margretha BAUMANN.

Aug. 3d: Maria Elisabetha, born July 26th, child of Niclaus and Maria Elisabetha FELLER; sponsor: Maria Elisabetha SCHALL.

Aug. 3d: Johann Henrich, born July 20th, child of Jacob and Anna Maria KOBEL; sponsor: Johann Henrich SCHRAEMMLE.

Aug. 4th: Johann Philipp, born July 31st, child of Christoph and Johanna Elisabetha FUCHS; sponsors: Johann Ludolph CURRING and Johann Philipp FUCHS.

Aug. 8th: Johann Peter, born Aug. 1st, child of Conrad and Margretha LEIN; sponsors: Johann Peter GERLACH and his wife, and Anna Maria LISEMUS.

Aug. 10th: Anna Maria, born July 25th, child of J. Fridrich and Anna Ursula MAUL; sponsors: Christoph MAUL, Anna Barbara GRAUBERGER and Anna Maria NEUSWICH.

Aug. 10th: Johann Hermann, born Aug. 5th, child of Peter and Anna Lucia GISLER; sponsors: Johann Hieronymus WELLER, Hermann HOFMANN, and Anna Veronica SCHLEMMER.

Aug. 10th: Johann Henrich, born July 30th, child of Johann Peter and Maria Catharina SPOHN; sponsors: Henrich REITER and his wife, and Adam SPOHN.

Aug. 9th: Johann Georg, born Aug. 8th, child of Johann Peter and Elisabetha Margretha SCHMID; sponsors: Johann Georg BAENDER.

Aug. 9th: John, born July 1st, child of Albert and Maria Von LOON; sponsors: Johann ALBERTSON and Maria VON LOON.

Aug. 9th: Anna Sibylla and Anna Regina, twins, born Aug. 9th, children of Jorg and Anna Catharina ZUFELD; sponsors: Henrich WIDERWACHS and his wife, Henrich LORENTZ and his wife.

Aug. 17th: Anna Margreth, born Aug. 13th, child of Peter and Anna Catharine MAUER; sponsors: Henrich MANN and Anna Margretha MUELLER.

Sept. 4th: Maria Elisabeth, born Aug. 31st, child of Adam and Anna Margretha HERTEL; sponsors: Elisabeth Catharina BACKUS and Maria Elisabeth.

Oct. 5th: Johann Jost, born Sept. 29th, child of Daniel and Anna Maria SCHUMACHER; sponsors: Jost BERNHARD, Michael HUENSCHICK. Niclaus BASON.

Oct. 26th: Johann Eberhard, born Sept. 4th, child of Ludwig and Maria Martha LEICH; sponsor: Johann Eberhard JUNG.

Oct. 2d: Anna Magdalena Elisabetha, born Sept. 19th, child of Zacharias and Anna Elisabetha FLEGLER; sponsors: Magdalena, wife of Niclaus JUNG.

Nov. 9th: Anna Catharina, born Nov. 7th, child of Gottfried and Anna Margretha RUEHL; sponsors: Henrich STUBENRAUCH and his wife.

Nov. 10th: Johannes, born Nov. 7th, child of Bernhard and Justina LUECKHARD; sponsor: Johann EMMERICH.

Dec. 18th: Anna Catharina, born Dec. 16th, child of Johann Michel and Elisabetha EMERICH; sponsors: Wilhelm KUESTER and Anna Catharina STUBENRAUCH.

Dec. 26th: Anna Catharina, born Dec. 14th, child of Stephan and Anna Elisabetha FROEHLICH; sponsor: Anna Catharina KRANTZ.

Dec. 24th: Johann Peter, born Dec. 23d, child of Johann Reitz and Elisabetha BACKUS; sponsors: Peter MAURER, Peter GLOPP, Maria Elizabetha FRITZ.

Total number for the year 1712 51

In the year 1713:

Febr. 8th: Sebastian, born Febr. 2d, child of Gabriel and Anna Catharina HOSTMANN; sponsors: Sebastian TREBER and Magdalena ECKHARD.

Febr. 21st: Andreas, born Febr. 18th, child of Dietrich and Magdalena SUTZ; sponsors: Anna Maria RICHTER and ANDREAS RICHTER.

Febr. 24th: Maria Elisabetha, born Febr. 16th, child of Friedrich and Anna Barbara MERCKEL; sponsor: Maria Elisabetha STRAUB.

Febr. 24th: Johannes, born Febr. 18th, child of Johann Henrich and Anna Catharina KRANTZ; sponsor: Johannes STRAUB.

March 1st: Johannes, born Febr. 26th, child of Johann Valentin and Appolina FROEHLICH; sponsors: Johann EMERICH and his wife Anna Margretha.

March 4th: Niclaus, born Febr. 28th child of Mattheus and Anna BRUNCK; sponsor: Niclaus JUNG.

March 8th: Johann Hieronymus, born March 6th, child of Johann Philip and Catharina GREISLER; sponsors: Hieronymus Klein and Johann PLANCK.

March 18th: Johann Fridrich, born March 16th, child of Johann Conrad and Maria MAERTEN; sponsor: Johann Fridrich HAEGER.

April 2d: Johann Ludwig, born March 31st, child of Ludwig and Catharina BRETSCH; sponsors: Johann CUNTZ and his wife Maria Catharina.

April 7th: Johanna (commonly called HANNA), born April 3d, child of Georg Johann and Maria DECKER; sponsors: Joris DECKER and ARIANICKE DECKER.

April 8th: Anna Elisabetha, born March 25th, child of Duerck and Anna WENN, commonly called RICKART; sponsors: Fridrich MAUL, Anna Juliana REUTER and Anna Margretha EMMERICH.

March 1st: Anna Elisabetha, child of Johann Henrich and Anna Catharina SCHMID; sponsors: Adam SCHMID, Catharina Elisabeth SCHLEICHER, Anna Christina THEIS.

April 12th: Christina, child of Henrich and Annike CHISEM; sponsors: Jan CHISEM and Margreth SCHOTT.

April 19th: Benjamin, child of Johann Michael and Maria SCHUETZ; sponsors: Johann LA GRANSCHE and his wife ENTIKE.

April 19th: Anna Catharina, child of Peter and Anna Sophia Pfuhl; sponsors: Henrich SCHMID and his wife Anna Catharina.

May 17th: Anna Maria, child of Peter and Elisabetha OBERBACH; sponsors: Johann Peter OBERBACH, Anna Maria THONIUS, Anna GERTRAUD, wife of Peter SEHN.

May 24th: Jannike, born May 6th, child of Arend VON SCHAAK and his wife Maria; sponsors: Alberth VON LOON and his wife Marion.

May 31st: Jannike, born April 11th, child of Zacharias and Esther HOFMAN; sponsors: the parents and Pastor Joshua KOCHERTHAL.

Aug. 1st: Isaac, born June 23d, child of Abraham and Clara VORSTUNG; sponsors: Gabriel PRUSIE and Gertraut PRUSIE.

Aug. 2d: Anna Maria, born July 28th, child of Martin and Anna Barbara NETZBAECHER; sponsor: Maria Catharina WIDERWACHS.

Aug 23rd: Maria Justina, born Aug. 23d, child of Christian and Anna Maria Judith CASTLEMANN; sponsor: Justina LUECKHARD.

Oct. 6th: Johann Philipp, born Sept. 7th, child of Jost Henrich and Agnes SCHAESTER; sponsor: Johann Philipp WOLLEBEN.

Oct. 25th: Johann Jacob, born Oct. 9th, child of Henrich and Anna Kunigunda FEHLINGER; sponsors: Jacob BEST and the wife of Martin ZERB.

Nov. 1st: Johann, born Oct. 27th, child of Johann and Maria Margretha PLANCK; sponsor: Johann EMMERICH.

Nov. 29th: Johann Christian, born Nov. 22d, child of Johann Peter and Maria Christina OBERBACH; sponsors: Christian MEYER, Johann STAHL, Anna Christina THONUS.

Dec. 13th: Johann Peter, born Dec. 10th, child of Arnold and Anna Elisabeth FALCK; sponsors: Johann Peter SUTZ and Anna Maria BURCKHARD.

Dec. 20th: Maria Catharina, born Dec. 11th, child of Johann Henrich and Anna Maria NEUKIRCH; sponsors: Fridrich MAUL, Catharina GERYSTLER, Maria Margretha KLEIN.

Dec. 20th: Zacharia, born Dec. 12th, child of Simon and Rosina HAAS; sponsors: Zacharias FLEGLER and his wife Eve Anna Elisabetha.

Total number for the year 1713 _____28.

In the year 1714:

Jan. 3d: Hieronymus Adam, born Dec. 28th, 1713, child of Hieronymus and Anna Juliana WELLER; sponsors: Hieronymus SCHREIB, Adam HERTEL, Gertraut WEID.

Jan. 10th: Johann Christian, born Jan. 2d, child of Johann Peter and Anna Elisabetha BECKER; sponsors: Johann Veltin FALCKENBURG; Johann Christian DIETRICH, Amelia KLEIN.

Jan. 10th: Anna Margretha, born Jan. 8th, child of Adam and Anna Maria SPOHN; sponsors: Georg SCHMID and Anna Margretha SPOHN.

Jan. 18th: Johann Peter, born Jan. 10th, child of Ananias and Elisabetha DIHL; sponsors: Johann Peter HAGENDORN and Catharina STEIGER.

Febr. 14th: Susanna Margretha, born Febr. 9th, child of Peter and Anna Margretha AIGNER; sponsors: Margretha SCHRAMM, Susanna KUESTER, Mattheus SCHLEMMER, Jorg Wilhelm KAEHL.

Febr. 21st: Johann Wilhelm, born Febr. 13th, child of Christian and Anna Gertraut MEYRER; sponsors: Johann Wilhelm SCHNEIDER, Johann KLEIN, Wilhelm LERCK, Anna Maria DEMUTH.

Febr. 21st: Simon, born Febr. 16th, child of Zacharias and Anna Elisabetha FLEGLER; sponsor: Simon HAAS.

Febr. 21st: Johann Wilhelm, born Febr. 15th, child of Johannes and Maria Elisabetha STRAUP; sponsors: Johann Wilhelm BRANDAU and Anna Margretha HERDEL.

April 4th: Anna Maria, born March 29th, child of Hieronymus and Anna Catharina SCHEIB; sponsors: Veltin FALCKENBURG, Maria MARTIN, Anna Margretha HERDEL.

April 14th: Anna Eva, born April 12th, child of Johann Fridrich and Maria Barbara CONTERMANN; sponsor: Anna Catharina GERMAN.

April 16th: Anna Catharina, born March 26th, child of Johann Peter and Anna Catharina DIPPEL; sponsors: Johann LAMERT, Anna Veronica MANCK, Maria Gerdaut BUCK............

April 18th: Johann David, born April 17th, child of Joseph and Anna Maria REICHART; sponsors: Johann Bernhard ZIPPERLIN and his wife.

May 6th: Catharina Elisabetha, born April 30th, child of Johann Niclaus and Anna Magdalena KOERNER; sponsors: Catharina Elisabetha RAU and Johann Mattheus JUNG.

May 17th: Anna Elsabeth, born May 12th child of Johann and Anna Elisabetha ROSCHMANN; sponsors: Conrad BEHRINGER and Anna Agatha STAHL.

May 28th: Maria Catharina and Maria Gerdraut, born May 21st, children of Mattheus and Anna Veronica SCHLEMMER; sponsors: Conrad MARTIN, Gerdraut KEHL and Maria BORDER; Johann MANGES, Maria Margretha KLEIN and Anna Catharina SCHUETZ.

June 6th: Anna Gerdraut, born June 1st, child of Wilhelm and Anna Eva LINCK; sponsors: Johann GRAD, Gerdraut SCHUCH, Anna Margretha WINTER.

June 7th: Anna Sabina, born June 6th, child of Niclaus and Maria Sabina HAAS; sponsors: Johann Hermann SPEICKERMANN and his wife Anna Catharina.

June 22d: Elisabetha, born June 20th, child of Johannes and Anna Margretha EMERICH; sponsors: Johann HESS and his wife Catharina.

July 18th: Anna Elisabetha, born July 9th, child of Johann and Wlaburga GRAD; sponsors: Balthas STEUBER and Anna Elisabeth DUNTZBACH.

July 24th: Johann Wilhelm, born July 17th, child of Johann and Elisabetha PLASS; sponsors: Johann Wilhelm SCHNEIDER and Magdalena PHILIPP.

Aug. 1st: Anna Maria, born July 19th, child of Johann and Maria Barbara BRICK; sponsor: Anna Maria WINTER.

Aug. 1st: Marcus, born July 30th, child of Samuel and Elisabetha LUN; sponsor: Marcus BELLINGER.

Aug. 1st: Dorothea, born July 27th, child of Johann Conrad and Anna Barbara DIESTENBACH; sponsors: Jorg MAURER and his wife Dorothea.

Aug. 18th: Johann Wilhelm, born Aug. 13th, child of Clemens and Gertraut LEHMAN; sponsors: Johann Wilhelm LEHMAN and Anna Maria KLEIN.

Aug. 20th: Jo! nn Fridrich, born Aug. 16th, child of Henrich and Anna Juliana REUTER; sponsors: Johannes STAHL and Fridrich MAUL.

Sept. 5th: Sophia, born Aug. 28th, child of David and Anna Catharina HUPFER; sponsors: Gerhard HORNING and his wife Sophia.

Sept. 5th: Anna Catharina, born Sept. 1st, child of Peter and Anna Catharina Sibylla HAMM; sponsors: Niclaus SCHMID and Anna Cathrina ROHRBAUCH.

Sept. 15th: Johann Samuel, born Sept. 10th, child of Henrich and Anna SCHNEIDER; sponsors: Samuel MUELLER and his wife Anna.

Sept. 19th: Johann Wendell, born Sept. 15th, child of Jacob and Margretha ESSWEIN; sponsors: Johann Wendel PULVER and Justina, wife of Theobald SCHERER.

Sept. 20th: Anna Margretha and Anna Maria, twins, born Sept. 18th, children of Kilian and Anna Margretha MUENCKLER; sponsors: Jerg DEMUTH and Anna Maria DOPF; Jerg SCHAESTER and Anna Maria MATTHES.

Sept. 26th: Joahnnes, born Sept. 21st, child of Andreas and Elisabetha RICHTER: sponsors: Johann FUEHRER, Heinrich MOHR, Christina OBERBACH.

Sept. 26th: Johann Henrich, born Sept. 21st, child of Conrad and Anna Elisabzetha BEHRINGER; sponsors: Johannes ROSCHMANN and his wife Anna Elisabetha.

Oct. 7th: Anna Catharina, born Sept. 26th, child of Peter and Catharina DRECHSLER; sponsors: Jacob GERMAN and his wife Anna Catharina.

Oct. 17th: Anna Catharina, born Oct. 13th, child of Johann Philip and Anna Catharine GREISSLER; sponsors: Catharina Elisabetha RAU, Apolonia FROEHLICH, Johann Philipp HELLER.

Oct. 21st: Anna Elisabetha, born Sept. 2d, child of Adam and Anna ECKHARD; sponsor: Anna Elisabetha LAMBERT.

Oct. 21st: Anna Maria, born Sept. 18th:, child of Jerg and Anna Catharina ZUFELD; sponsors: Peter DIPPEL and Anna Maria ZIPPERLIN.

Oct. 21st: Anna Margretha, born May 12th, child of Johann Philipp and Anna Margretha WOLLEBEN; sponsors: Veltin and Anna Margretha CAPUTZGIN.

Oct. 24th: Johann Wilhelm, born Oct. 18th, child of Johann Wilhelm and Anna Margretha TALES; sponsors: Johann Niclaus HAAS, Johann Wilhelm HAMBUCK, Maria Catharina SEGENDORST.

Oct. 31st: Rudolph, born Oct. 1st, child of Rudolph and Janike DETEUTSCHER; sponsors: Gabriel PRUSTI and Gertraut PRUSTI.

Nov. 2d: Johann Jacob and Anna Magdalena, twins, born Oct. 29th, children of Johann Henrich and Magdalena BRAUCHLER; sponsors: Jacob GERMAN and Anna Catharina MUELLER.

Nov. 7th: Susanna Margretha, born Nov. 5th, child of Niclaus and Anna Margretha BOHNENSTIHL; sponsor: Susanna Margretha SCHNEIDER.

Nov. 7th: Georg Andreas, born Oct. 26th, child of Niclaus and Maria Barbara MICHEL; sponsors: Georg THAETER, Johann Andreas BARTHEL, Elisabetha BARTHEL.

Nov. 28th: Johann Hieronymus and Agnes, twins, born Nov. 24th, children of Johann Valentin and Elisabetha Maria FALCKENBURG; sponsors: Hieronymus KLEIN, Johann Wilhelm KUESTER, and Catharina SCHREIB, Christian DIETRICH, Anna Elisabeth BECKER, Agnes DIETRICH.

Dec. 20th: Johanna Maria Sophia, born Dec. 17th, child of Albrecht Dietrich and Elisabetha MARTERSTOCK; sponsors: Gottfrid WULSTEN, Sr., and his wife and Maria Barbara TESTU.

Dec. 26th: Anna Maria Catharina, child of Sebastian and Anna Elisabetha SPICKMANN; sponsors: Adam Spoon and his wife, Niclaus OHMICH and his wife, and Anna Elisabetha LAUX.

Total number for the year 1714 _____49

In the year 1715:
Jan. 2d: Johann Heinrich, born Dec. 29th, child of Veit and Maria Catharina MOESSIG; sponsor: Henrich HEYDORN.

Jan 2d: Philipp Henrich, born Dec. 28th, child of Philipp Wilhelm and Christina MOOR; sponsors: Henrich MOOR, Philipp LAUNERT and Catharina SPEICKERMANN.

Jan. 4th: Johann Fridrich, born Jan. 1st, child of Johann Wilhelm and Elisabetha BRANDAU; sponsors: Fridrich STREIT and Elisabetha KRANTZ.

Jan. 10th: Eva Maria, born Jan. 9th, child of Adam and Anna Margretha HERTEL; sponsors: Hieronymus WELLER and Maria KLEIN.

Jan. 10th: Anna Maria Dorothea, born Nov. 10, 1714, child of Valentin and Susanna WOLLEBEN; sponsors: Joseph REICHART and his wife, Carl NAEHER and his wife, Dorothea CAPUTZ.

Febr. 22nd: Johann Daniel, born Febr. 13th,, child of Bernhard and Justina LUECKHARD; sponsors: Johannes FUEHRER and Daniel BESTUH.

Febr. 26th: Gertraut, born Febr. 18th, child of Arnold and Anna Elisabeth FALCK; sponsors: Niclaus RAU and his wife Gerdraut.

Febr. 26th: Johann Henrich, born Feb. 19th, child of Johannes and Anna Ursula STAHL; sponsors: Fridrich MAUL, Henrich REUTER, Anna HARTMANN.

Febr. 27th: Catharina, born Febr. 18th, child of Philipp and Gerdraut HAUPT; sponsors: Bernhard NOLL and Bernhard SCHMID.

Febr. 27th: Johann Peter, born Febr. 25th, child of Balthasar and Anna Maria AMSTACH; sponsor: Johann Peter SCHMIDT.

Febr. 6th: Johann Henrich, born Jan. 30th, child of Johann Conrad and Maria Elisabeth MAERTEN; sponsors: Hieronymus WELLER, Heinrirch SCHRAMM, Catharina SCHAIB.

Febr. 13th: Anna Maria, born Jan. 22d, child of Johann Wilhelm and Anna Gerdraut SCHNEIDER; sponsors: Johann PLASS, Anna Maria BITZWIG, Maria Catharina BITZER.

Febr. 13th: Maria Margretha, born Febr. 3d, child of Martin and Elisabeth ZERB; sponsors: Maria Margretha BARTHEL, Henrich WIDERWACHS, Maria Margretha FREHD.

Febr. 13th: Johannes, born Jan. 17th, child of Peter and Elisabetha Margretha SCHMID; sponsors: Johann ROSCHMANN and his wife.

Febr. 27th: Anna Margretha, born Febr. 17th:, child of Martin and Anna Ursula WEIDMANN; sponsors: Philipp LAUNERT and his wife.

March 6th: Johann Mattheus, born March 1st, child of Johann REICHART, (commonly called Reitz) and Elisabetha Catharina BACKUS; sponsors: Johann Mattheus JUNG and Sophia HORNUNG.

March 13th: Peter, child of Salomon and Anna Maria SCHUETT; sponsors: Johann Peter SCHMID and Anna Catharina ROHRBACH.

March 31st: Johann Wilhelm, born March 26th, child of Hieronymus and Anna Juliana WELLER; sponsors: Georg Wilhelm KEHL, Johann Henrich TESCH (or YESCH) and Anna Catharina HEIL.

April 3d: Johann Wilhelm, born Jan. 31st, child of Frantz and Barbara KELLER; sponsors: Johann Jacob KAPUTZKI and his wife.

April 3d: Johann Georg, born Nov. 9th, 1714, child of Johann Michel and Anna Maria WAEGELIN; sponsor: Johann George BRIGEL.

April 3d: Johann Adam, born March 22d, child of Justus Henrich and Agnes SCHAESTER; sponsors: Johann Adam FRIDRICH and his wife Regina.

April 10th: Johann Peter, born April 3d, child of Christian and Anna Maria Judiths CASTELMANN; sponsors: Johann Peter BURCKHARD and Andreas ELLICH.

April 14th: Johann Emerich, born March 28th, child of Conrad and Maria Salomo SCHAUERMANN; sponsors: Johann Emerich PLIEST and his wife.

April 18th: Jerg Philip, born April 14th, child of Jerg and Anna Maria SCHAESTER; sponsors Philip CUNTZ and Georg DEMUTH.

April 18th: Maria Catharina, born (not given), child of Michel and Anna Maria BRACK; sponsors: Johann ROSCHMANN and Maria Catharina DRUM.

April 18th: Maria Barbara, born April 13th, child of Latzarus and Anna Margreth DORN; sponsors: Conrad SCHMID and Maria Barbara HEYDORN.

April 24th: Anna Maria, born April 19th, child of Johann and Anna Catharina HESS; sponsor: Anna Margreth BURCKHARD.

April 26th: Anna Maria, born April 22d, child of Niclaus and Anna Catharina OHMICH; sponsors: Jerg THAETER and his wife Anna Maria.

June 6th: Johannes, born April 15th, child of Antoni and Gerdraut KRAEMER; sponsor: Johann Henrich SCHARMANN.

June 26th: Rennalt, born April 26th, child of Zacharias and Ester HOFFMAN; sponsors: Andreas ELLICH and Benigma Sibylla KOCHERTHAL

July 6th: Maria Elisabetha, born July 1st, child of Johann Henrich and Anna Catharina KRANTZ; sponsors: Johann STRAUP and his wife Maria Elisabetha.

July 24th: Anna Elisabetha, born July 21st, child of Johannes and Anna Eva MENGES; sponsors: Mattheus SCHLEMER and Anna Elisabetha, wife of Peter BECKER.

Aug. 14th: Anna Elisabetha, born July 30th, child of Johannes and Anna BERNHARD; sponsors: Elisabetha HASTMANN and Henrich SCHAESTER.

Sept. 9th: Catharina Elisabetha, born Sept. 2d, child of Johann Mattheus and Anna Veronica JUNG; sponsors: Christoph MAUL, Elisabetha JUNG, Eva Catharina MANCK.

Sept. 18th: Frantz, born Sept. 4th, child of Lorentz and Regina HENRICH; sponsors: Frantz KELLER and his wife Barbara.

Sept. 25th: Anna Margretha, born Sept. 21st, child of Clemens and Gertraud LEHMANN; sponsors: Philipp MUELLER and his wife Anna Margretha.

Oct. 2d: Anna Margretha born Sept. (day not given), child of Martin NETZBACHER, (mother's name not given); sponsors: Johann KUHLMANN and Anna Margreth ESCHENREUTER.

Oct. 16th: Johann Georg, born Oct. 9th, child of Johan Peter and Maria Christina OBERBACH; sponsors: Jerg OBERBACH, Johann Wilhelm SCHNEIDER, Anna Catharina WEID.

Oct. 16th: Anna Catharina. born Sept. 24th, child of Philipp and Anna Margretha LAUNERT; sponsors: Jerg LAUNERT and his wife Anna Catharina.

Oct. 23d: Johann, born Sept. 16th, child of Isaac and Annika SPOOR; sponsors: Peter THONUSEN and Margretha THONUSEN.

Oct. 30th: Johann, born Oct. 19th, child of Wendell and Christina Elisabetha JAEGER; sponsors: Johann BERURER and Johann Werner SCAESTER.

Oct. 30th: Anna Christina, born Oct. 24th, child of Abraham and Anna Catharina LAUCK; sponsors: Philipp Wilhelm MOOR and his wife.

Nov. 10th: Christina, born Nov. 10th, child of Johann and Maria Margretha PLANCK; sponsor: Pastor Joshua KOCHERTHAL.

Nov. 13th: Johann Peter, born Nov. 5th, child of Christian and Anna Gerdraut MEYER; sponsors: Peter BITZER, Johann Georg SCHNEIDER, Anna DEMUTH.

Dec. 3d: Catharina Elisabeth, born Nov. 26th, child of Henrich and Anna Margreth MOOR; sponsors: Johann Hermann HARTMANN, Anna Catharina ROHRBACH, Anna Elisabetha LAUX.

Total for the year 1715 45

In the year 1716:

Jan. 1st: Johann Wilhelm, born Dec. 30th, child of Niclaus and Anna Elisabeth LAUX; sponsors: Johann Wilhelm HAMBUCH, Sebastian SPICKERMAN, and the wife of Ulrich WENIGER.

Jan. 8th: Anna Benigma, born Dec. 28th, child of Johann Henrich and Anna Maria NEUKIRCH; sponsors: Veltin FROEHLICH and Benigma Sibylla KOCHERTHAL.

Jan. 16th: Johannes, born Jan. 12th, child of Peter and Anna Catharina MAURER; sponsors: Reichart BACKUS and his wife Elisabetha Catharina.

The following children, 26 in number were baptized in Schoharie:

Jan. 21st: Christina Elisabeth, born Nov. 1, 1715, child of Henrich and Christina SIXT; sponsors: Andreas FINCK, Christina FUX, Elisabeth SIXT.

Jan. 21st: Johann Henrich, born Sept. 26th, child of Jacob and Anna Barbara SCHNEIDER; sponsors: Henrich SIXT, Johann CHRISTMANN, Dorothea SCHUMACHER.

Jan 21st: Susanna, born Jan. 1st, child of Peter and Anna Magdalena GLOPP; sponsor: Susanna SCHUTZ.

Jan. 21st: Johann Henrich, born Dec. 4th, child of Jerg and Anna THOMAS; sponsors: Henrich FREY and his wife.

Jan. 21st: Anna Maria Clara, born Sept. 2d, child of Adam and Anna Catharina KLEIN; sponsors: Johann Peter THOMAS, Jerg HERCHEMER, Ann Maria BAENDER.

Jan. 22d: Johann Jacob, born Dec. 2d, child of Jerg and Maria Catharina MATTHEUS; sponsors: Jacob WEBER, Peter BELLINGER, Anna Maria IFLAND.

Jan. 22d: Niclaus, born Jan. 7th, child of Henrich and Maria Kunigunda FEHLING; sponsors: Niclaus RUHL and his wife.

Jan. 22d: Johann Georg, born Oct. 15th, child of Hartmann and Barbara Elisabetha WINDECKER; sponsors: Johann Georg BAENDER and his wife.

Jan. 22d: Johann Henrich, born Oct. 30th, child of Henrich and Anna Kunigunda MEYRER; sponsors: Henrich FREY and his wife.

Jan. 22d: Anna Dorothea, born Nov. 13th, child of Johann Georg and Anna LAST; sponsors: Christian BAUCH and his wife.

Jan. 22d: Anna Maria, born Dec. 29th, child of Henrich and Anna Maria ZELLER; sponsors: Johann SCHAEFER and his wife.

Jan. 22d: Anna Gerdraut, born Dec. 14th, child of Johann Just and Cordula PETRI; sponsor: Anna Gerdraut PETRI.

Jan. 22d: Anna Catharina, born Jan. 1st, child of Veltin and Anna Catharina CUN; sponsor: the daughter of Niclaus FELLER.

Jan. 22d: Anna Catharina, born Nov. 21st, child of Johann and Anna Margretha KESTLER; sponsors: Johann Just SCHNELL and Anna Catharina GROSTER.

Jan. 22d: Anna Margretha, born Dec. 18th, child of Johann Peter and Anna Maria FEEG; sponsors: Johann Georg LAST and his wife, and Anna Maria FEEG.

Jan. 22d: Johann Georg, born Jan. 29th, child of Johann and Elizabeth MOOR; sponsors: Johann Georg RUED and Anna Margretha SCHAESTER.

Jan. 22d: Johann Niclaus, born Jan. 19th, child of Henrich and Anna Catharina SPOHN; sponsors: Johann Niclaus WOLLEBEN and Anna Margretha LAND.

Jan. 24th: Johann Adam, born Dec. 28th, child of Johann Dietrich and Maria Catharina LAUX; sponsors: Adam STARRING and his wife.

Jan. 24th: Johann Gottfrid, born Dec. 27th, child of Leonhard and Elisabetha HEMLER; sponsors: Gottfrid RUEHL and his wife.

Jan. 24th: Johann Michael, born Sept. 27th, child of Johann Ludwig and Agnes Barbara WANNER; sponsors: Johann Michael ITTICH and Maria Christina MENDES.

Jan. 24th: Anna Elisabetha, born Jan. 16th, child of Martin and Catharina STUPP; sponsors: Johann Jacob MERCKEL and Elisabetha SCHULTHEIS.

Jan. 24th: Johann Henrich and Anna Margreth, twins, born Jan. 24th, children of Henrich and Anna Margreth JUNG; sponsors: Conrad SCHEUTZ and Ottilia WEBER, Jacob WEBER and Anna Margretha ZIMMERMAN.

Jan. 24th: Maria Catharina, born Sept. 28th, child of Johann Adam and Anna Maria STARRING; sponsors: Dietrich LAUX and his wife.

Jan. 24th: Jerg Adam, born Dec. 14th, child of Johann Martin and Anna Maria SEIBERT; sponsors: Jerg Adam OEMICH, Jerg LANDGRAST and his daughter Anna Elisabetha.

Jan. 24th: Anna Maria, born Dec. 30th, child of Johann Peter and Elisabetha Barbara KNIESTBERG; sponsor: Anna Maria BAENDER.

Febr. 12th: Johannes, born Febr. 3d, child of Johann Fridrich and Anna Ursula MAUL; sponsors: Johannes STAHL, Johann NEUKIRCH and Juliana REUTER.

March 4th: Rebecca, born Febr. 13th, child of Richart and Anna WENN; sponsors: Arnold FALCK and his wife Anna Elisabeth.

March 4th: Anna Elisabetha, born March 1st, child of Johann and Anna Margretha WULFEN; sponsors: Adam SPOHN and his wife Anna Maria.

March 29th: Maria Eva, born March 23d, child of Adam and Anna Maria SPOON; sponsors: Wilhelm LEHMANN and his wife Maria.

March 30th: Anna Elisabetha, born March 17th, child of Johann Niclaus and Magdalena TROMBAUER; sponsors; Arnold FALCK and his wife Elisabetha.

April 1st: Johann Fridrich, born March 29th, child of Johann Peter and Anna Margretha AIGNER; sponsors: Valentin FUEHRER, Fridrich SCHRAMM and Anna Maria KUESTER.

April 29th: Anna Maria, an illegitimate child, born April 27th, 1715, child of Jan, a negro from Martinique, and Maria Catharina, daughter of Henrich ZOLLER of Etzbach, district of Hachenburg; sponsor: Anna Maria PFESTER.

May 21st: Elisabetha Margretha, born May 7th, child of Johann Niclaus and Anna Barbara MICHEL; sponsors: Susanna Margretha FORSTER, Elisabeth TRAUT and Peter HAGENDORN.

May 25th: Anna Sophia, an illegitimate child, born April 18th, child of Dorothea, widow of Jerg SCHAESTER; sponsors: Andreas ELLICH and his wife Anna Sophia.

June 24th: Maria Elisabeth, born June 18th, child of Hieronymus and Anna Catharina SCHEIB; sponsors: Maria KLEIN, Elisabeth HERDEL and Peter BECKER.

June 24th: Johannes, born March 8th, child of Philip and Catharina MUELLER; sponsors: Henrich KRANTZ and his wife.

June 25th: Johann Fridrich, born May 27th, child of Carl and Anna Constantia NEHER; sponsors: Johann Fridrich MEYER and his wife Barbara.

June 15th: Anna Elisabetha, born June 9th, child of Johann Wilhelm and Anna Maria SIMON; sponsors: David KISTLER and Anna Elisabeth SCHMID.

June 18th: Jacob, born June 7th, child of Jan and Cornelia VOSBURG; sponsors: Peter VOSBURG and Gertraud VOSBURG.

July 27th: Anna, born July 20th, child of Johannes and Anna Margreth EM-
ERICH; sponsors: Johann Valentin FROEHLICH and his wife
Apollonia.

July 29th: Anna Margretha, born July 23d, child of Jerg and Anna Catharina
ZUFELD; sponsors: Bernhard NOLL, Anna Margretha REISDORST.

Aug. 5th: Maria Magdalena, born July 7th, child of Jerg and Anna Maria
TAETER; sponsors: Jacob KAPUTZGI and his wife Anna Magdalena.

Aug. 14th: Jacob, born Aug. 12th, child of Johann Fridrich and Maria Barbara CONTERMANN; sponsors: Jacob GORMANN and his wife An-
na Catharina.

Sept. 11th: Johann Georg, born Sept. 4th, child of Hermann and Margretha
HUMMEL; sponsors: Richart ORMEN, Johann Georg SCHNEIDER
and Anna Maria DEMUTH.

Sept. 14th: Amilia, born Sept. 4th, child of Peter and Anna Margreth SUTZ;
sponsors: Johann Martin BURCKHARD and AMELIA KLEIN.

Sept. 16th: Maria Christiana, born Sept. 11th, child of Peter and Elisabeth
OBERBACH; sponsors: Mattheus SCHLEMMER, the wife of Johann
Wilhelm SCHNEIDER, Anna Christina TONNIUS.

Oct. 14th: Elisabetha, born Sept. 20th: child of Andreas FRANTZ and Sibylla CONTERMANN; sponsor: Gerdaut KRAEMER.

Oct. 16th: Anna Juliana, born Oct. 10th, child of Peter and Anna Elisabeth
BECKER; sponsors: Anna Juliana WELLER, Anna Eva MENGES,
Hieronymus SCHEIB.

Nov. 18th Johann Georg, born Nov. 9th, child of Peter and Anna Lucia
GISTLER; sponsors: Johann MENGES, Georg Wilhelm KEHL, Anna
Catharina SCHEIB.

Nov. 25th: Johann Peter, born Nov. 10th, child of Bernhard and Justina
LUECKHARD; sponsors: Peter BURCKHARD and Amilia KLEIN.

Dec. 2d: Anna Elisabetha, born Nov. 26th, child of Mattheus and Anna Veronica SCHLEMMER; sponsors: Elisabeth Magdalena OBERBACH
Anna Juliana WELLER and Henrich SCHRAM.

Dec. 16th: Johann Heinrich, born Dec. 9th, child of Hieronymus and Anna
Juliana WELLER; sponsors: Henrich SCHRAM, Mattheus SCHLEM-
ER, Elisabeth OBERBACH.

Total number for 1716 56

In the year 1717:

Jan. 6th: Johann Bernhard, born Jan. 3d, child of Veltin and Apollonia
FROEHLICH; sponsors: Bernhard LUECKHARD and his wife Justina.

Jan. 7th: Daniel, born Dec. 23d, 1716, child of Albrecht Dietrich and Elisabetha MARTERSTOCK; sponsors: Daniel DESTUH and his wife Barbara.

Jan. 7th: Eva, born Dec. 21, 1716, child of Fridrich and Anna Barbara
MERCKEL; sponsor: Eva MUELLER.

Febr. 10th: Anna Margretha, born Febr. 1st, child of Philipp and Veronica
KLUMM; sponsors: Philipp MOHR, Anna Catharina LUTT, Anna
Margretha DOLEST.

Febr. 24th: Johannes, born Febr. 8th, child of Cornelius and Aliken WARM-
ER; sponsors: Jan WARMER and his wife.

April 14th: Johann Georg, born April 4th, child of Hermann and Maria Catharina SEGENDORF; sponsors: Johann Henrich CONRAD, Johann Georg LAUNERT, Margreth SCHNEIDER.

April 14th: Anna Catharina, born April 7th, child of Johann and Maria Barbara LEICK; sponsors: Johann HOENER and his wife Anna Catharina.

April 29th: Anna Margretha, born April 14th, child of Veltin and Susanna WOLLEBEN; sponsors: Joseph REICHART and his wife and Anna Margretha CAPUTZGI.

April 28th: Johann Peter, born April 19th, child of Adam and Anna ECKHARD; sponsors: Johann Peter DOPF and Anna Catharina DIPPEL.

May 19th: Johann Jacob, born May 14th, child of Johannes and Maria Elisabeth STRAUP; sponsors: Jacob SCHUMACHER and his wife.

The following children, 18 in number, were baptized in Schoharie:

June 6th: Johann, born Febr. 8th, child of Johann and Anna Margretha LOEHN; sponsor: Johann CAST, Commissioner.

June 6th: Johann, born Febr. 5th, child of Johann and Anna Margretha KESTLER; sponsors: Johann MUELLER and Gertraut HETTMANN.

June 6th: Johann Georg, born March 17th, child of Jacob and Anna Catharina BOESHAAR; sponsors: Johann George STUMP and his wife.

June 6th: Johann Fridrich, born May 14th, child of Georg and Anna Elisabeth DACHSTETTER; sponsors: Fridrich SCHAESTER and his wife.

June 6th: Johann Adam, born May 17th, child of Theobald and Maria Catharina JUNG; sponsors: Johann Just LAUX, Johann Adam KOPP, Catharina FREY.

June 6th: Gertraut, born Apr. 16th, child of Henrich and Christina SIXT; sponsors: Georg SEYBOLD, Gertraut CHRISTMANN and Gertraut HETTMANN.

June 6th: Anna Elisabeth, born April 19th, child of Joseph and Anna Elisabeth SAVOY; sponsors: Johann Michel MEYSER and Anna Elisabeth SIXT.

June 6th: Ottila Helena, born May 9th, child of Johann and Sibylla Catharina LEER; sponsors: Johann Adam WALLRATH, Magdalena ECKHARD, and Ottilia CURRING.

June 6th: Conrad, born May 10th, child of Georg and Maria Catharina MATTHEUS; sponsors: Conrad WEISSER, Conrad SCHUETZ, and Anna Maria BELL.

June 7th: Johann Gottfrid, born April 26th, child of Johann Peter and Elisabetha Barbara KNIRSTBERG; sponsors: Johann Gottfrid FIDLER and his wife.

June 7th: Johann Wilhelm, born May 11th, child of Bertram and Maria Christina ENDTERS; sponsors: Jerg BAENDER, Johann Wilhelm SCHESET, and Elisabeth FIDLER.

June 7th: Anna Margretha, born March 17th, child of Georg and Anna Elisabeth HAUCK; sponsors: Johann KRAEMER and his wife.

June 7th: Anna Catharina, born March 25th, child Johann and Anna Catharina HESS; sponsor: Anna Catharina CONRAD.

June 7th: Maria Dorothea, born March 23d, child of Ludwig and Anna Barbara WANNER; sponsor: Maria Dorothea STEHL.

June 9th: Johann born June 4th, child of Johann and Anna Maria SCHES-TER; sponsors: Johann ZOELLER and his wife.

June 9th: Anna Catharina, born May 25th, child of Niclaus and Anna Dorothea Margretha RUEHL; sponsors: Johann ZOELLER and his wife.

June 9th: Maria Elisabetha, born June 1st, child of Henrich and Anna Margretha OHRENDORF; sponsors: Martin BARDORF and Maria Elisabeth WALBORN.

June 10th: Maria Catharina, born June 9th, child of Johann Adam and Margreth BAUMANN; sponsors: Johann Henrich SPOHN and his wife.

Jan. 31st: Anna Margreth, born Nov. 13th, 1716, child of Johann and Anna Margretha KEYSER; sponsors: Henrich JUNG and his wife. This child was baptized by the low-German (Niderteutschen) Pastor of Albany, P. v. DRIESEN.

June 16th: Margreth, born May 16th, child of Wiensan and Elsgen BRUSCHI; sponsors: Peter TONESE and Margretha KURTZ.

June 16th: Henrich, born May 22d, child of Benjamin and Gertraud REES; sponsors: Andreas REES and Catharina REES.

July 7th: Johann Philipp, born June 26th, child of Adam and Anna Catharina HOF; sponsors: Philip Wilhelm MOOR, Johann Balthas LUTT and Elisabeth HEMER.

July 7th: Agnes, born June 29th, child of Antoni and Margreth SCHNEIDER; sponsors: Agnes DIETRICH, Maria Catharina SEGENDORF, and Johann Christian DIETRICH.

July 7th: Andreas Christian, born June 18th, child of Pieter CHRISTIAN of Madagascar, and his wife Elisabeth; sponsors: Andreas ELLICH and his wife Sophia.

July 14th: Maria Barbara, born June 23d, child of Johann Reichart and Elisabeth Catharina BACKUS; sponsors: Johann Veltin SCHESTER and Maria Barbara MEYER.

July 28th: Johann William, born July 22d, child of Fridrich and Anna Maria SCHRAMM; sponsors: Johann Balthasar KUESTER and Catharina SCHRAMM.

Aug. 4th: Anna Christina, born July 26th, child of Christian and Anna Gerdraut MEYER; sponsors: Christina TONIUS, Anna Elisabeth JUNG, and Johann MENGES.

Aug. 11th: Johann Niclaus, born July 21st, child of Johann Philipp and Catharina Elisabeth FELLER; sponsor: Johann Niclaus RAU.

Aug. 18th: Anna Elisabeth, born Aug. 10th, child of Michael and Magdalena HOENIG; sponsors: Johann STAHL and Elisabeth DUNTZBACH.

Sept. 15th: Johann Wilhelm, born Sept. 7th, child of Andreas and Anna Sophia ELLICH; sponsors: Johann Wilhelm LEHMANN and his wife.

Oct. 6th: Gottfrid Sebastian, born Oct. 4th, child of Jan and Anna Margreth WULTSEN; sponsors, Godfrid Sebastian WULTSEN, Benigma Sibylla KOCHERTHAL.

Oct. 13th: Anna Maria, born Sept. 17th, child of Carl and Anna Constantia NOECHER; sponsors: Joseph REICHART and his wife Anna Maria.

Oct. 13th: Johann Henrich, born Oct. 4th, child of Veltin and Anna Margretha BAENDER; sponsors: Johann Henrich SCHAESTER and his wife Agnes.

Nov. 17th: Anna Christina Elisabeth, born Nov. 8th, child of Johann Wilhelm and Elisabeth Catharina BRANDAU; sponsors: Elisabetha KRANTZ, Anna Christina STREIT and Jan BERTSCH.

Dec. 12th: Anna Elisabeth, born Dec. 8th, child of Clemens and Gerdraut LEHMANN; sponsors: Niclaus SCHMID, Anna Margretha WOLST.

Dec. 15th: Eva Catharina, born Dec. 9th, child of Henrich and Anna Juliana REUTER; sponsors: Anna Catharina MAUL and Anna Eva and David MUELLER.

Dec. 22d: Johann Wilhelm, born Dec. 13th, child of Johann Henrich and Anna Catharina KRANTZ; sponsors: Jerg Wilhelm KEHL, Peter OBERBACH and Elisabeth Catharina BRANDAU.

Total number for 1717 _____47

In the year 1718:

Jan. 11th: Gerdraut, born Jan. 6th, child of Johann and Anna Eva MENGES; sponsors: Peter GISTLER, Anna Gerdraut MEYER and Gerdraut KEHL.

Jan. 12th: Michael, born (date not given), child of Latzarus and Anna Margreth DORN; sponsors: Michel WERNER and his wife.

Jan. 20th: Anna Kunigund, born Jan. 11th, child of Johann Jacob and Maria Catharina ZERB; sponsor: Anna Kunigunda WINTER.

Febr. 2d: Margreth, born Jan. 12th, child of Arend VON SCHAACK and his wife Maria; sponsors: Peter BURCKHARD and Benigna Sibylla KOCHERTHAL.

Febr. 9th: Johannes, born Jan. 11th, child of Georg and Anna Maria THAETER; sponsors: Johann Michael WAEGELIN, and his wife.

March 2d: Maria, born Febr. 13th, child of Johann Conrad and Anna RITSCHER; sponsors: Henrich REUTER and Ursula MAUL.

March 8th: Johann Conrad, born March 4th, child of Peter and Amalia BURCKHARD; sponsors: Conrad HANTI (or MAEUTI), Mattheus SCHLEMMER and Gerdraut KEHL.

March 16th: Maria Elisabeth, born March 6th, child of Adam and Anna Maria SPOHN; sponsors: Niclaus SCHMID and Maria Elisabeth MUELLER.

March 30th: Sophia Magdalena, born March 22d, child of Christian and Anna Maria Judith CASELMANN; sponsors: Andreas ELLICH and his wife Sophia, and Magdalena SUTZ.

April 13th: Eva Maria, born April 8th, child of Johann Mattheus and Anna Veronica JUNG; sponsors: Andreas ELLICH, Anna Maria DEMUTH, and Maria Christina OBERBACH.

April 27th: Johann Henrich, born March 15th, child of Ananias and Elisabetha DIHL; sponsors: Johann Lorentz HENRICH and his wife Regina.

April 27th: Johann Peter, born March 15th, child of Johann and Maria Barbara DOPF; sponsors: Peter DOPF and Christina UHL.

Inasmuch as some of our government officials have made inquiry concerning the growth and progress of the German colonists, and also concerning the number of children baptized, I have looked over these records and I am herewith giving the number of them by yars:

1. 1708_____ 2
2. 1709 _____10
3. 1710 _____32
4. 1711 _____68

```
5.  1712 ................................................................................51
6.  1713 ................................................................................28
7.  1714 ................................................................................49
8.  1715 ................................................................................45
9.  1716 ................................................................................56
10. 1717 ................................................................................47
11. 1718 ................................................................................12
                                                         —
Total  number .................                ...........................................400
```

May 4th: Elisabetha Catharina, an illegitimate child, daughter of Dorothea SCHAESTER, a widow; sponsors: Peter MAURER and Elisabeth MARTERSTOCK.

May 7th: Jann, child of Abraham DOBUS; (date of birth, name of mother and names of sponsors not given.

May 11th: Dietrich, born May 10th, child of Niclaus and Magdalena TROMBOUR; sponsors: Dietrich SUTZ and his wife.

June 2d: Susanna Catharina and Maria Catharina, twins, born May 8th, children of Johan Peter and Elisabeth SCHMID; sponsors: Susanna Catharina LUDWIG and Maria Catharina MOESIG.

Aug. 10th: Catharina (date of birth not given), child of Georg and Catharina SPRINGSTEIN; (names of sponsors not given).

Aug. 26th: Johann Balthasar, born Aug. 26th. child of Peter and Anna Margreth AIGNOR; sponsors: Johann Ralthasar KUESTER and the wife of Veltin FALCKENBURG.

Oct. 5th: Elisabetha, born Sept. 28th, child of Johann Christian and Margretha MUELLER; sponsors: Bastian LESCHER and Elisabetha KUN.

Nov. 30th: Anna Margretha, born Nov. 20th, child of Fridrich and Anna Urschel MAUL; sponsors: Dietrich SUTZ and Anna Margretha EMERICH.

Dec. 14th: Johann Henrich, born Dec. 5th, child of Fridrich and Anna Maria SCHRAMM; sponsors: Peter EIGNER, Henrich VOESS and Christiana VOESS.

Total number for the year 1718 22

In the year 1719:

Febr. 1st: Maria Barbara, born Jan. 28th, child of Balthasar and Anna Maria ANSPACH; sponsors: Henrich SCHAESTER and Anna Maria PROPERT.

Febr. 1st: Anna Catharina, born Jan. 25th, child of Andreas and Catharina Appolonia SCHUERTZ; sponsors: Jerg SCHUERTZ and Anna Catharina, daughter of Peter PHILIPP.

Febr. 1st: Johann Henrich, born Jan. 26th, child of Niclaus and Eva SCHMID; sponsors: Jacob SCHAESTEH, Henrich SCHNEIDER and Susanna SCHNEIDER.

Febr. 1st: Philipp, born Jan. 23d, child of Philip and Anna Margretha SCHMID; sponsors: Philip MOHR and Anna Maria, wife og Dietrich SCHNEIDER.

Febr. 1st: Anna Maria, born Jan. 29th, child of Johann Christian and Anna Maria DIETRICH; sponsors: Abraham LANG and his wife, and the wife of Fridrich RAU.

Febr. 1st: Veronica, child of Jacob ESSWEIN; (date of birth and mothers name not given); sponsor: Anna Maria SCHNEIDER.

Febr. 2d: Anna Margretha, born Nov. 3d, child of Georg and Anna Margretha SALTMANN; sponsors: Johann Fridrich ZIPPERLIN and Anna Margretha BACKUS.

Febr. 6th: Johannes, born Jan. 22d, child of Just Henrich and Agnes SCHAESTER; sponsors: Johann Reitz BACKUS and his wife.

Febr. 7th: Lorentz, born Febr. 6th, child of Niclaus and Anna Catharina OEMICH; sponsors: Lorentz THAETER and the wife of Johann LAMERT.

Febr. 20th: Elisabetha, born Febr. 16th, child of Johann Fridrich and Barbara MERCKEL; sponsors: Johann KLEIN and his wife.

March 15th: Maria Elisabetha, born March 9th, child of Johannes and Maria Elisabetha STRAUP; sponsors: Fridrich STREIT, Elisabeth HERDEL and Catharina KUHLMAN.

March 15th: Peter, born March 8th, child of Hermann and Anna Margretha HUMEL; sponsors: Johannes SCHNEIDER and Eva SCHUH.

March 30th: Susanna Catharina, born Febr. 1st, child of Veit and Maria Catharina MOESSIG; sponsors: Henrich LUDWIG and his wife.

March 30th: Anna Elisabetha, born March 17, child of Conrad and Maria Apollonia WUEST; sponsors: Johann LERCK and Anna Elisabetha ZERB.

March 12th: Johannes, born March 5th, child of Niclaus and Magdalena TROMBOUR; sponsors: Johannes EMERICH and his wife Margretha.

March 19th: Maria Christina, born March 17th, child of Albrecht Dietrich and Elisabeth MARTERSTOCK; sponsors: Wilhelm BRANDAU and wife, and Christina BRUNCK.

April 26th: Fridrich, born April 18th, child of Hieronymus and Anna Catharina SCHAIB; sponsors: John Fridrich HAEGER, Fridrich SCHRAM, and Christina VOESS.

May 14th: Johannes, born May 7th, child of Johannes and Margreth EMERICH; sponsors: Wilhelm LEHMANN and his wife.

May 14th: Catharina, born May 10th, child of Christian and Anna Gerdraut MAYER; sponsors: Sibylla Catharina KEHL and Hieronymus WELLER.

JESUS THE FOUNDER AND PRESERVER OF HIS CHURCH
(JESU, ECCLESIA SUAE AUCTORE ET CONSERVATORE)

B. A LIST OF FIRST COMMUNICANTS, pages 81-86.
(CATALOGUS NEO-COMMUNICANTIUM).

By whose admission to communion with us the membership of our church has been increased. May you, dear reader, unite with me in the sincere prayer that all these will be and remain true and living members of the Church.

From among our own young people the following partook of holy communion with us for the first time:

The following persons united with our church from other denominations:

EDITOR'S NOTE— For each date the names in the first column will appear in the first paragraph, and those in the second column will be given in the second paragraph.

March 27, 1709, when holy communion was administered at New York: Anna Maria WEIGAND.

At the communion service in the colony on the Quasaic Kill, April, 1710: Maria FISHER.

At the communion service conducted by Daniel Falckner, in my absence, about the middle of June 1710:
Johannes ENGEL, formerly a member of the Episcopal Church.
At the second communion service conducted by Daniel Falckner in the month of June 1710.
Johannes Peter EIMER, Martin RAUSCHER, Johann Reitz BACKUS, Elisabetha Magdalena STEIS, Anna Catharina HOSTMANN.
All of these were formerly members of the Episcopal Church.

At the communion service, conducted by myself in New York, July 19, 1710:
Johannes WINTER, Johann Heinrich NUESS, Johann Conrad ..FRIDE-RICH, Johann Bernhard ZIPPERLIN, Anna Margretha DOERNER, Anna Magdalena RUSCH, Anna Maria FUCK, Anna Gertruda VOLLBART, Anna Elisabetha HEYPERT, Anna Magdalena SEXER, Maria Elisabetha WALBUER, Maria Margretha LAUX, Maria Barbara ECKHARD, Maria Catharina CORHOF, Maria Barbara SCHMID.
Anthon KRAEMER, Johann MOHR, Johann CONNRATH; wife of Jacob STERNBERGER, wife of Johann Henrich POELER, wife of Johann BERG, wife of Daniel GOETTEL, Anna Elisabetha ROSCHMAN, wife of Johann Georg MAUER, Anna Margreth RECKFEL. All of these were formerly members of the Episcopal Church.

At the communion service which I conducted at New York, Sept. 26, 1710:
Johann Michael RUED, Johann Peter RUED, Sebastian TREBER, Johanna Elisabetha PLANCK.

At the communion administered by me in the new colony of Germans, April 30, 1711:
Johann Philipp BRAUN, Johann Georg ZEH, Johann Adam OEMICH, Andreas BARTHEL, Johann Philipp THAIS, Barthas LUTT, Susanna Gerdraut MICHEL, Maria Jacobina HUPFER, Barbara SCHUMACHER, Maria Catharina STUEBER.
The following from Episcopalian parentage:
Johann Georg WINTER, Maria Catharina WINTER, Margretha BRUCKER.
Sibylla WARNO, Maria Catharina OBER, formerly members of the Episcopal Church.

June 24th, 1711:
Johann Niclaus WOLLEBEN.
Anna Margretha ESCHENREITER, formerly Episcopalian.

At the communion service held March 23, 1712, in Queensberg:
Philip Balthasar BARTHEL, Bartel MULLER, Johann Georg ECKHART, Andreas PFEISTER, Johann Heinrich SCHASTER, Dietrich DEMUTH, Johann Georg RAU, Johann Jacob ZERB, Peter LANDMANN, Johann Georg LOSCHER, Maria Barbara PROPERT, Catharina FEG, Maria Gerdraut HAGENDORN, Anna Catharina HAUPT, Margaretha Elisabeth SCHASTER, Anna Catharina WUST, Catharina Elisabetha BARDORST (ORF), Maria Elisabeth MANNICH, Anna Christina RAUSCH, Elisabetha LOSCH, Anna Margaretha SCHAESTER, Anna Albertina TAUS, Anna Christina GOCKEL, Anna Catharina HAS, Sophia Elisabeth Margaretha MERTZ.

June 16, 1712, in Newtown:
Johann Daniel WORMS, Johann Peter TOBICH, Johann Balthasar KUSTER, Johann Lampert STERNBERGER, Maria Elisabeth WEERICH, Margaretha LEIN, Anna Maria DEMUTH, Catharina STREIT, Anna Maria STREIT.
Ursula STREIT, Maria Magdalena WERNER, formerly of the Episcopal Religion.

Easter, 1713, at New Town:
Johann Georg SCHMID, Johann Georg WENNERICH, Johann Martin BURCKHARD, Andreas GUNTERMANN, Johann Michael SCHAUER, Anna Barbara LISTENUS, Christina ARNOLD.

October 25, 1713, at Queensberg:
The wife of Martin ZERB, formerly of the Episcopal Church.

February 7, 1714, at Schoharie:
Johann Ludwig CASTELMANN.

Easter, 1714, at New Town:
Johann Georg KREYSTLER, Johann Fridrich DEMUTH, Anna Barbara RICHTER, Anna Margretha BACKUS, Maria Gerdraut HECKMANN. At Queensberg: Johann Georg BAUNERT, Johann Peter LAUX, Jurg Adam ZUFELD, Andreas WIDERWACHS, David SCHURTZ, Conrad LÖSCHER, Johann Christian BERG, Susanna Margretha FORSTER, Elisabeth HASSMANN.

April 3, 1715, at Rheinbeck:
Valtin SCHAESTER.

Easter, 1715, at Queensberg:
Johann Niclaus STEIGER, Johann Henrich MICHEL, Johann Adam SCHMID, Johann Mattheus LAUER, Johanna Maria BECK, Anna Elisabeth STUBER, Anna Elisabeth SCHMID, Maria Catharina SCHMID.

January 22, 1716, in Schoharie:
Philipp MOOR.
Jan. 24, 1716:
The daughter of Gerhard SCHASTER.
Ulrich BRUCKHARD, formerly of the Episcopal Church.
February 16, 1716, at New Town:
Anna Sibylla SCHASTER.

October 14, 1716, at Rheinbeck:
Anna Catharina EBERT, Anna Maria DIPPEL.
The father of the following is Reformed:
Anna Margaretha KAPUTZGIN, Anna Dorothea KAPUTZGIN.

St. Stephan's Day, 1716 at Kingsberg:
Anna Gerdraut WUST, and Kunigunda WINTER, whose father and mother are Episcopal.
April 14, 1717, at Kingsberg:
Fridrich RAU, Elisabetha MERTZ, Maria Catharina ROSCHMANN.
April 29, 1717, at Rheinbeck:
Amalia, wife of Georg SALTZMANN, whose parents were Dutch Reformed.

Easter 1717, at New Town:
Niclaus SCHMIDT, Johannes GREYSLER, Catharina Susanna KUSTER, Christiana Clara MULLER.

Finis.

C. MARRIAGES, pages 137-154.
IN THE NAME OF JESUS
THE HEAVENLY BRIDEGROOM OF OUR SOULS.
(JESU CAELESTI NOSTRARUM ANIMARUM SPONSO).
A RECORD OF THE MARRIAGES PERFORMED
DURING THE PASTORATE OF
JOSHUA KOCHERTHAL
THE FIRST PASTOR OF THIS COLONY OF GERMAN
LUTHERANS

In the year 1709:
1. July 19th: In the colony of the Quasaic ill: Johann FISCHER, widower, and Maria HILL, daughter of the late Carolus HILL, of Stonetown in New England.

2. Sept. 21st: Georg LOOCKSTAD, born in Mechlin, Mecklenburg, and Elisabetha PLETTOL, widow of the late Jacob PLETTOL.

In the year 1710:

3. July 9th: Johann Philipp ZERB, of Kettenbach, commune of Minister, and Maria Catharina STEIBER, from the commune of Hachenburg.

4. July 19th: Johann GANSS, of Roemershausen, commune of Blanckenstein, near Giessen, and Gertrauda SCHMIDT, widow of the late Niclaus SCHMID, from the commune of Hachenburg.

5. July 25th: Johann KRANTZ, widower, from the commune of Isenburg, and Anna Catharina SCHAARMANN, daughter of Heinrich SCHAARMANN, from the commune of Isenburg.

6. July 26th: Johann Michael WAEGELIN, of Bohnfeld in Creichgau, and Anna Maria HARTMANN, widow of the late Conrad HARTMANN.

7. July 27th: Johann Wilhelm SIMON, widower, of Neuwied, and Anna Maria MUELLER, widow of the late Johann Georg MUELLER, of Mastenbach in the commune of Neuburg.

8. July 27th: Johann HANOR, widower, of Birsen, commune of Ostenbach, and Catharina MUSTIRR, daughter of Johann Jacob MUSTIRR, of Steinfort in Erichgau.

9. July 27th: Johann Hermann SPEICHERMANN, widower, from the neighborhood of Otterberg, and Anna Catharina MERTZ, widow of the late Johann MERTZ.

10. Aug. 1: Peter SCHMID, widower of Soetzwich, commune of Isenberg, and Elisabetha Margretha COBLENTZER, daughter of the late Johann Peter COBLENTZER, from the neighborhood of Bingen.

11. Aug. 15th: Zacharias FLEGLER, widower, of Wertheim in Franconia, and Anna Gertrauda HUEN, daughter of the late Dietrich HUEN, of Wallbruehl in the commune of Berg.

12. Aug. 22d: Johann Paul REITSCHAFT, of Dueren, district of Pfortzheim, commune of Durlach, and Anna Maria KRAUS, widow of the late Johann Jacob KRAUS, of Simmern in the Palatinate.

13. Aug. 24th: Johann Heinrich POELER, of Altzheim on the lower Rhine, and Susanna CLOTTER, widow of the late Johann Paul CLOTTER, of Borckheim, near Weinheim in the Palatinate.

14. Aug. 29th: Johann Georg BORNER, widower, a carpenter, of Grosstain commune of Astach in Wuerttemberg, and Maria Barbara DAUSWEBER, daughter of the school teacher Johann Melchoir DAUSWEBER.

15. Aug. 29th: Carl NAEHR, widower, a tanner, of Brickenfeld in Westerich, and Maria Apollonia MATTHES, daughter of the late Peter MATTHES, of Eckerswell, near Zweibruecken.

16. Aug. 31st: Johann Heinrich SCHMID, a carpenter, of Nieder-Malmenach, on the Rhine, principality of Hessia and Anna Catharina SCHLEICHER, daughter of Johann Georg SCHLEICHER, of Erbenheim, commune of Nassau.

17. Sept 5th: Albrecht Dietrich MARTERSTOCK, widower, of Lamsheim, commune of Neustadt in the Palatinte and Elisabetha RUEBENICH, widow of the late Mattaeus RUEBENICH, of Sittern, near Birckenfeld, Westerich.

18. Sept. 5th: Just Henrich SCHAESTER, widower, of Hochspeur, earldom of Hartenburg, and Agnes BACKUS, widow of the late Sebastian BACKUS, of Roth near Bingen.

19. Sept. 5th: Johann KEYSER, of Unter-Oetisheim, Wuerttemberg, and Margretha HOERNER, daughter of the late Ludwig Ernst HOERNER, of Unter Oetisheim, Wuerttemberg.

20. Sept. 12th: Johann SCHULTHEIS, a tailor, of Gahgraebler near Kreuznach and Anna Barbara RAUTENBUSCH, widow of the late Johann RAUTENBUSCH, of Emmerich, in the Palatinate.

21. Sept. 27th: Ludwig SCHMID. widower, of Michelbach, near Giessen, Hessen-Darmstadt, and Elisabetha BECKER, widow of the late Johann Michael BECKER, of Kreuznach in the Palatinate.

22. Sept. 27: Abraham LOUCK, of the commune of Epstein, Darmstadt, and Anna Catharina BECKER, daughter of Johann Henrich BECKER, of Weerheim, commune of Dillenburg.

23. Sept. 27th: Christian HAUSS, widower, a carpenter, of Alten-Staeden, near Wetzler, duchy of Solm and Anna Catharina BECKER, widow of the late Johann BECKER, of Duernberg, near Dietz, commune Schaumburg.

24. Sept. 27th: Peter PFUHL, widower, a cabinetmaker, of Nieder-Rammstock, Darmstadt, and Anna Sophia BOHL, widow of the late Lastar BOHL, of Maller near Coblenz.

25. Oct. 10th: Johann MINCKLER, widower, of Parthenheim, commune Alzey, in the Palatinate, and Anna Elisabetha ESSWEIN, widow of the late Thomas ESSWEIN, of Haert, commune Germersheim.

26. Oct. 16th: Engelbertus WOLLBACH, widower, of the commune Neustadt, Marck-Brandenburg, and Anna Barbara DIPPEL, daughter of the late Philipp DIPPEL, of Flammborn, commune Alzey, Palatinate.

27. Oct. 25th: Johann Adam SOELLN ER, widower, a miller, of Eppingen, Palatinate and Anna Maria BAUMANN, widow of the late Henrich BAUMANN, of Upstatt, near Brustel, commune Speyer.

28. Nov. 1st: Mattheus BRINCK, widower, a blacksmith, of Andel, earldom of Veldenz and Anna WORMSER, widow of the late Sebastian WORMSER, of Bubach, commune Lichtenberg, county of Zweibruecken.

29. Nov. 20th: Johann CRUMP, a gardner, of Bristol, England, and Maria Agnes LAUR, daughter of the late Arnold LAUR, of Gebler, near Kreuznach in the Palatinate.

30. Dec. 10th: Henrich SCHARRMANN, widower, of Fishborn, near Hanau, earldom Isenburg, and Anna Catharina HELMER, widow of the late Antonius HELMER, from the vicinity of Giessen, Darmstadt.

31. Nov. 29th: John Dietrich WANNENMACHER, of Leheim, Darmstadt and Anna Kunigunda Kornmann, of Leheim, Darmstadt.

In the year 1711:

32. Jan. 9th: Joseph REICHART, wido wer, of Kirchberg, commune Marbach, duchy of Wuerttemberg, and Anna Maria TREBER, widow of the late Johann TREBER, a wheelwright, formerly of Woellstein, commune Kreuznach.

33. Jan. 23d: Antoni KRAEMER, widower, of Altzheim on the lower Rhine, and Gertrauda ELSAESSER, widow of the late Paul ELSAESSER, of Fishborn, earldom Isenburg.

34. Febr. 13th: Johann Melchoir DAUSWEBER, widower, a school teacher, of Burschel, commune Marbach, Wuerttemberg, and Magdalena SCHAUER, widow of the late Michael SCHAUER, of Mastenbach, in Erichgau.

35. Febr. 20th: Johann Henrich SPOHN, step-son of the furrier Philip MUELLER and Maria Catharina WOLLEBEN, daughter of the late Wallrath WOLLEBEN, formerly a citizen of Bacharach on the Rhine.

36. Febr. 27th: Johann Bernhard ZIPPERLIN, widower, blacksmith, of Unter-Oetiswein, Wuerttemberg, and Anna Maria REICHARD, daughter of the late Hans REICHARD of Kirchberg, commune Marbach, duchy of Wuerttemberg.

37. Febr. 27th: Martin STEIN, of Langensalza, in Thuringia, and Anna Maria BLAST, widow of the late Adam BLAST, of Alt-Zabern in the Palatinate.

38. March 6th: Adam BAUMANN, widower, a butcher, of Bacharach on the Rhine, and Anna Margretha KUGEL, widow of the late Johann KUGEL, Unter-Oetisheim, commune Maulbronn, duchy of Wuertterberg.

39. May 11th: Herman SCHUENEMANN, of Hamburg, a captain of the North German people, and Elisabetha MUELLER, daughter of the late Georg MUELLER, of Hamburg.

40. March 12th: Zacharias FLEGLER, of Wertheim in Franconia, and Anna Elisabetha SCHULTZ, widow of the late Georg SCHULTZ, of Darmstadt.

41. June 26th: Georg Ludwig LEICH, widower, of Bernsfeld, Darmstadt, and Maria Martha EMMERICH, widow of the late Johann Peter EMMERICH, of Neustadt on the Hard.

42. June 26th: Thomas EHMANN, widower of Schornbach, Wuerttemberg, and Elisabetha LAUCK, widow of the late Jacob LAUCK, of Nurstatt, Darmstadt.

43. July 10th: Johannes FRANCK, widower of Altzheim on the lower Rhine, and Magdalena STREIT, widow of the late Ludwig STREIT, of Westhofen, commune Alzey, in the Palatinate.

44. July 24th: Johann EBERHARD, widower, of St. Johann, near Kreuznach, margraviate Baden, and Sibylla GIESSER, daughter of the late Johann GIESSER, of Ober-Moschel-Landsberg, commune Zweibruecken.

45. Aug. 29th: Johann HESS, a blacksmith, of Bleichenbach, in the earldom Hanau, and Anna Catharina CURRING, daughter of Ludolst CURRING, of Hellstein, earldom Isenburg.

46. Sept. 5th: Christoph BELLROSS, of Schwerin, duchy of Mecklenburg, and Maria Ottila BALL, daughter of the late Johann BALL, of Magenheim, commune Alzey, in the Palatinate.

47. Sept. 10th: Henrich HEIDORN, widower, of Gelhausen, near Hanau, and Elisabetha HUMBEL, widow of the late Jerg HUMBEL, formerly a citizen of Mossbach in the Palatinate.

48. Sept. 11th: Gabriel HOSTMANN, widower, of Woellstein near Kreuznach, and Anna Catharina BATZ, widow of the late Fridrich BATZ, of Auerbach in Hessia-Darmstadt.

49. Sept. 12th: Johann Peter GLOPP, a tailor, of Horn, commune Simmern, in the Palatinate, and Anna Magdalena LUTZ, widow of the late Johann Christoph LUTZ, of Klingen-Minster in the Palatinate.

50. Dec. 4th: Johann BEER, widower, of Dicksem, commune Oppenheim Palatinate, and Magdalena HAUG, widow of the late Lucas HAUG, formerly a citizen of Lichtenberg, commune Zweibruecken.

51. Dec. 18th: Johann Michael EMERICH, of Delkenheim, commune Epstein Darmstadt, and Elisabetha KRANTZ, widow of the late Conrad KRANTZ, of the commune Zigenheim in Hessia.

52. Dec. 31st: Christian HABER, of Salzberg, commune Homburg, Hessen-Cassel, and Anna Gertraud WERNER, daughter of Michael Werner, of Rheinfels on the Rhine.

In the year 1712:

53. Jan. 3d: Johann Adam SUELLER, widower, of Eppingen, commune Brockheim, Palatinate, and Elisabetha BURCKHARD, widow of the late Johann BURCKHARD, formerly a citizen of Ober-Mopstatt in the Wetter :u, earldom Isenburg.

54. Jan.. 3d: Philip PETRI, widower, sexton of Sinn, commune Nassau-Dillenburg, and Anna Elisabetha MUELLER, daughter of the late Johann MUELLER, of Mattern-Muehl, commune Nassau-Dillenburg.

55. Dec. 2d: Johann Adam STARRING, son of Johann Niclaus STARRING, of Wensheim, commune Alzey, in the Palatinate, and Anna Maria LIFENIUS, widow of the late Bernhard LIFENIUS.

In the year 1713:

56. Febr. 10th: Adam SPOHN, son of the late Werner SPOHN, sexton at Manweiler, commune Kaiserslautern, and Anna Maria SCHMID, daughter of Henrich SCHMID, a citizen of Newtown.

57. Febr. 24th: Joerg Martin DILLENBACH, widower, and Anna Elisabetha CASTELMANN, daughter of Johann Dietrich CASTELMANN.

58. April 7th: Johann FUEHRER, widower, a citizen of Newtown, and Anna Maria RICHTER, widow of the late Andreas RICHTER, of Newtown.

59. Nov. 3d: Clemens LEHMAN, step-son of Johann Henrich SCHMID, a citizen of Newtown, and Anna Gertraud WOLF, daughter of the late Bertram WOLF, formerly a citizen of Gershofen, commune Doerdorst, earldom of Runckel.

In the year 1714:

60. Jan. 31st: Peter CHRISTIAN, of Madagascar, servant of Master John von Loon, and Anna Barbara ASMER, widow of the late Philipp ASMER, formerly a citizen of Langen on the mountain-road (Bergstrasse); the marriage ceremony was performed after the consent of his Master had been obtained and written attestation thereon given, and after previous proclamation of the banns thrice repeated.

61. March 31st: Frantz FINCK, son of the late Johann Adam FINCK, of Trarbach, commune Birckenfeld and Elisabetha Barbara FEEGEN, daughter of Johann FEEGAN, of the commune Oberstein in the Palatinate.

62. Sept. 21st: Ephraim ROOS, son of Wilhelm ROOS of Claverack and Margretha BREHJIS, daughter of Christoph BREHJIS, of Rulphilanc Kill, near Livingston Manor.

63. Sept. 28th: Duerck WENN, commonly called RICHART, residing on Catskill Bay, and Anna ONDERLING, of New York.

64. Sept. 28th: Johann Mattheus JUNG, son of the late Jerg Hans JUNG, of Gernheim, commune Stromberg, Palatinate, and Anna Veronica MANCKEN, daughter of Master Jacob Mancken, of Urbach, commune Neuwied.

65. Oct. 26th: Jerg DEMUTH, son of the late Alexander DEMUTH, formerly a citizen of Runckel on the Lahn, and Margretha DOPF, daughter of Peter DOPF, of Metter, comune Zweibruecken.

66. Oct. 28th: Georg SCHAESTER, son of the late Jacob SCHAESTER, formerly a citizen of Oferdingen, commune Tuebingen, duchy of Wuerttemberg, and Anna Maria MATTHES, daughter of the late Peter MATTHES, 'of Eckersweilen, commune Lichtenberg, district of Zweibruecken.

67. Nov. 2d: Johann Jacob CUNTZ, son of Mattheus CUNTZ, citizen of Bischmisen, earldom of Nassau-Saarbruecken, and Susanna MICHEL, daughter of Henrich MICHEL, formerly a citizen of the commune Weisenheim, district of Zweibruecken

In the year 1715:

68. Jan. 11th: at Rhinebeck: Carl NAEHER, widower, of Brickenfeld, commune Trarbach, Palatinate, and Anna Constantia REICHART, daughter of Joseph REICHART, of the commune Marbach, duchy of Wuerttemberg.

69. April 26th: Jerg THAETER, son of the late Johann THAETER, formerly a citizen of Lehnberg, commune Giglinger, duchy of Wuerttemberg, and Anna Maria MEYER, daughter of the late Johann Fridrich MEYER, formerly a citizen of Rohrbach, near Sintzen, baronate Vennig.

70. May 9th: Andreas ELLICH, widower, of Neckar-Burcken, commune Mossbach, in the Palatinate, and Anna Sophia HORNUNG, widow of the late Gerhard HORNUNG, citizen of Newtown.

71. June 7th: Johann Georg LAUNERT, son of the late Philipp LAUNERT, citizen of the earldom Ustingen, and Anna Catharina SCHNEIDER, daughter of Johann Dietrich SCHNEIDER, formerly a citizen of the earldom Hachenburg.

72. Sept. 19th: Andreas Frantz CONTERMANN, son of Johann Fridrich CONTERMANN, of Entzberg, commune Maulbronn, duchy of Wuerttemberg, and Sibylla SCHARRMANN, daughter of Johann Henrich SCHARRMANN, of Fischborn, commune Isenburg.

73. Oct. 25th: Christian MUELLER, son of the late Johann Georg MUELLER, formerly a citizen of Elgard, commune Neuwied, and Maria Margretha SCHISTER, daughter of Philipp SCHISTER, formerly a citizen of the commune Isenburg.

74. Oct. 27th: Robert WIHLER, son of Edwart WIHLER 'of Kinderhook, and Catharina HEYL, daughter of the late Johann Wilhelm HEYL, formerly of Williamsdorf, duchy of Nassau-Siegen.

75. Nov. 1st: Johann Peter SUTZ, son of Johann Dietrich SUTZ, formerly a citizen of Bellheim, commune Geimensheim, Palatinate, and Anna Margretha BURCKHARD, daughter of the late Johann BURCKHARD, formerly a citizen of Ober-Magstatt, earldom of Isenberg.

76. Nov. 1st: Leonard FEEG, of Schoharie, son of the late Johann FEEG, formerly a citizen of Oberstein, duchy of Nassau-Siegen, and Anna' Catharina SCHUTZ, daughter of the late Conrad SCHUTZ, formerly a citizen of Langen-Sellweck, earldom of Isenburg.

77. Nov. 2d: Anthonious SCHNEIDER, son of Dietrich SCHNEIDER, formerly a citizen of the commune Hachenburg, and Margretha DIETRICH, daughter of Christian DIETRICH, formerly a citizen of the earldom Neuwied.

In the year 1716:

78. Jan. 24th: in Schoharie: Johann Jacob BECKER, son of the late Johann BECKER, formerly a citizen of Darmbach, earldom of Runckel, and Maria Elisabetha LAUX, daughter of Johann Just Laux, formerly a citizen of Weiber, earldom of Runckel.

79. May 29th: Johann PLANCK, widower, of Dausenach, commune Nassau, and Anna BRUNCK, widow of the late Mattheus BRUNCK, of Newtown.

80. June 20th: Peter SCHMID, widower, residing at Hunterstown, but hailing from Boerstein, earldom Isenburg, and Elisabetha BARTHEL, daughter of Henrich BARTHEL, of Hunterstown, formerly of the commune Epstein, duchy of Darmstadt.

81. June 25th: Philipp Henrich CUNTZ, son of Mattheus CUNTZ, of Queensberg, formerly of Bischmusen near Saarbruecken, and Maria Elisabetha MAEMIG, daughter of Ferdinand MAEMIG of Ansberg, formerly of Wollbergshofwen, near Cologne, commune Neuburg.

82. June 26th: Adam HERTEL, widower, of Georgetown, formerly of Liferspach, near Heppenheim, on the mountain-road (Bergstrasse), and Gertraud WAID, widow of the late Johann WAID, formerly of Wallwig, duchy of Nassau-Dillenburg.

83. Aug. 31st: Johann Henrich CONRAD, widower, of Ashausen, duchy of Nassau-Siegen, and Anna Gertraud SEEGENDORF, daughter of Adam SEEGENDORF, of Hermansdorf, commune Neuwied.

84. Sept. 18th: Johann Philipp FELLER, son of Niclaus FELLER, of Guntersblum, earldom Leinig-Hartenburg, and Catharina Elisabetha RAUH, daughter of Niclaus RAUH, of Oppenheim, in the Palatinate.

85. Nov. 13th: Rev. Johann Fridrich HAEGER, High-German Pastor in Kingsberg, and Anna Catharina ROHRBACH.

86. Jan. 3d: Johann Michel BRACK, of Kllein-Odenbach, commune Meistenheim, district of Zweibreucken, and Anna Maria SCHLEY, daughter of Johann Michel SCHLEY, formerly a citizen of Hettenbach, Rhenish Earldom.

87. Febr. 12th: Fridrich SCHRAMM, son of Henrich SCHRAMM, formerly a citizen of Woellensdorf, duchy of Siegen, and Anna Maria KUESTER, daughter of Johann Wilhelm KUESTER, formerly a citizen of Langen-Goens-Hestein, duchy of Darmstadt.

88. June 4th, in Schoharie: Conrad BECKER, son of the late Sebastian BECKER, formerly a citizen of ALTZHEIM on the lowert Rhine, commune Altzheim, in the Palatinate, and Sabina MATTEUS, daughter of the late Henrich MATTEUS, formerly a citizen of Duerheim, commune Altzheim, Palatinate.

89. July 2d: Johann Wilhelm HAUBUCH, widower, of Nieder-Biber, commune Neuwied, and Anna Catharina LUTT, widow of the Johann Peter LUTT, formerly a citizen of Wald-Lebersheim near Bingen, earldom Schromburg.

90. July 29th: Jan von NORDSTRANDT, widower, residing with Jacob HOCHDIHL, near Rhinebeck and Belicka CAUJUN, widow of the late Fransa CAUJUN and residing with Henrich CHISEM.

91. Nov. 5th: Johann Peter BURCKHARD, son of the late Johann BURCKHARD, formerly a citizen of Ober-Mockstatt, in the earldom of Isenburg, and Anna Amalia KLEIN, daughter of Hieronymous KLEIN, formerly a citizen of Flommersfeld, in the earldom of Sehinsch-Hachenburg, near Neuwied.

In the year 1718:

92. Febr. 6th: Georg SALZMANN, widower, of Stollberg, in the Upper Lausitz, electorate of Saxony, and Anna Margretha KAPUTZGI, daughter of the late Johann Jacob KAPUTZGI, formerly a citizen of Erbelheim on the Rhine, duchy of Darmstadt.

93. Dec. 5th: Johann Georg SCHNEIDER, son of Johann Wilhelm SCHNEIDER, of Nieder-Elsten, commune Hachenburg, and Anna Catharina THONIUS, daughter of the late Stephan THONIUS, of Wolferlingen, commune Hachenburg, and the step-daughter of Jerg OBERBACH.

In the year 1719:

94. Febr. 24th: Peter LANDMANN, son of Peter LANDMANN, of Stockheim, commune Litting-Isenburg, and Johann Elisabetha PLÁNCK, daughter of Johann PLANCK, formerly a citizen of Dausenau, commune of Nassau.

J. CHRISTIAN KRAHMER

JESUS THE RESURRECTION AND THE LIFE

Record of all High Germans of this colony who died since my arrival and during my residence at Newtown, on the west side of the Hudson. I either was present at the death of these persons and officiated at their funrals, or I was notified of their decease.

In the year 1713:

1. The child of Adam HERTEL.
2. Adam SOELLER.
3. Dec. 6th: Sibylla Charlotta KOCHERTHAL.
4. The child of Arnold FALCK.

In the year 1714:

1. Aug. 22d: Child of Hieronymus WELLER.
2. Aug. 25th: Child of Clemens LEHMAN.

In the year 1715:

1. Jan. 21st: Mattheus BRUNCK, drowned.
2. March 9th: Child of Johann Reitz BACKUS.
3. March 17th: Johann Quirinius JUNG.
4. March: 20th: Wife of Andreas ELLICH.
5. March 30th: Child of Jacob MANCK.
6. April 9th: Gerhard HORNUNG.
7. Nov. 10th: Child of Johann PLANCK.
8. Nov. 15th: Wife of Johann PLANCK.
9. Dec. 8th: Child of Johann PLANCK.
10. Dec. 23d: Niclaus JUNG, drowned.

In the year 1716:

1. Febr. 26th: Daughter of Johann FUEHRER.
2. March 21st: Wife of Adam HERTEL.
3. Oct. 27th: Wife of Johann PLANCK.
4. (Not given): Child of Dorothea SCHAESTER.

In the year 1717:

1. Sept. 1st: Child of Bernhard LUCKHARD.
2. Sept. 16th: Johann Fridrich CONTERMANN.

In the year 1718:

1. March 23d: Elisabetha BURCKHARD, widow, age, 56 years.
2. Aug. 26th: Johann Balthasar Aigner, child of Peter AIGNER, age 1 day.

E. JESUS WILL REPAY. (Jesu Retribuente).

A list of articles which were obtained from time to time for the furtherance of our work and for the maintenance of church parsonage and schools, either voluntarily contributed and bequeathed by pious, Godfearing souls from pure and unselfish motives, or provided for and secured in some other way. Pages 221-222.

In the year 1708:

At my, Pastor Kocherthal's humble petition to their royal majesties, Queen Anne and Prince George, a bell, weighing 113 lbs., was donated for use in connection with our church services.

The following articles were procured by me and paid for from the proper funds:

A pewter chalice and paten for the administration of Holy Communion, for five shillings sterling, or according to current value, 7 and ½ shilling.

In the year 1710:

This Church Record for which 6½ shilling were paid to H. Bredfort.

For a small bell, weighing 42 lbs., 52 shilling sterling, current value 3 pounds 18 shillings, were paid.

For a second pewter set of chalice and paten for the administration of Holy Communion here in New York, 7½ shilling were spent and for pewter basin, 3 shilling, total 10½ shilling.

For a round iron (rund Eisen) for preparing bread for Holy Communion, 2½ shilling were paid.

Maria Margretha, wife of Just Henrich Schaster, bequeathed upon our death-bed a white linen cloth for use upon the altar or table at the divine services.

In the year 1715:

Elisabetha, wife of Albrecht Dietrich Marterstock, also donated a white linen homespun cloth for use at the church services.

Anna Margretha, wife of Adam Bertold, donated a white cloth for use at church services; this was done in the month of December 1715.

In the year 1716:

Anna Maria Reichart donated a pewter basin for the administration of Holy Baptism.

In July, 1716, Anna Juliana, wife of Henrich Reuter, donated a printed chalice cloth for use at church services.

THE W. C. BERCKENMEYER ENTRIES
in the
KOCHERTHAL RECORDS

F. These entries are found on pages 77-80 and are as follows:

In the year 1725 during the Advent season there were baptized by me, W. C. Berckenmeyer, Lutheran Pastor at New York:

Nov. 25th: Maria, child of Friderich (Reformed) and Maria (Lutheran) SCHRAM; sponsor: Hieronymus KLEIN.

Nov. 25th: Anna Margareta, child of Friderich and Eva Dieterich; sponsors: Hans Wilhelm Dietrich, the grand-father, and his wife Anna Margareta.

Nov. 28th: Johann Bastian, 6 weeks old, child of Andreas and Anna Barbara WIEDERWACHS; sponsors: Johann Bastian LOSCHER, the father-in-law (socer) and Anna Sibilla MULLER, the step-mother (noverca).

Nov. 28th: Maria Margaret, born Nov. 27, child of Johannes BERNARD, commonly called SPIELMANN, and his wife Anna Eulalia; sponsors: Johann Smith SAALBACH, commonly called HANNEMANN, and his wife Maria Margareta.

Nov. 28th: Johann Jacob, 2 months old, child of Jurgen Henrich SCHERP, (Reformed), and his wife Anna Barbara; sponsors: Jacob SCHERP, the grand-father, and Anna Maria SCHERP, the grand-mother.

Nov. 28th: Maria Barbara, 8 days old, child of Jacob and Catharina ZERBER; sponsors: Johannes LEITZ and his wife Maria Barbara.

Nov. 28th: Robert, 3 weeks old, child William LOINER, an Englishman, and his wife Abigail; sponsor: James KERNICK.

Nov. 28th: Catharina, 7 weeks old, child of Friderich and Catharina RAU; sponsors: Michael RAU and Elsie SCHNEIDER.

Nov. 28th: Johann Hermann, 4 weeks old, child of Johann Jacob and Christina BEST; sponsors: Hermann BECKER, the father-in-law, (socer) and Catharina BECKER.

Nov. 28th: Johann Wilhelm, 7 weeks old, child of Georg Kilmer (Reformed), and his wife Eva Margareta, Lutheran; sponsor: Johann Wilhelm KUNZ.

Nov. 28th: Johannes, 8 days old, son of Johann and Elisabeth RUSMANN; sponsors: Johann Jost PROPPER and his wife Anna Elisabeth.

Total number baptized in 1725, 11.

In the year 1726:

Jan. 23d: Johannes Peter, born Jan. 18th, child of Peter and Catharina HAM, both Reformed; sponsors: Johann Peter PHILIP and his wife Catharina.

Jan. 23d: Johannes Peter, born Dec. 31, 1725, child of Justus Adam and Christina SCHMID, both Reformed; sponsors: Peter PHILIP and his wife Magdalena.

Jan. 24th: Johannes and Anna Elisabeth, twins, about 6 weeks old, children of Johann Peter BURCKHARD and his wife Amalia, Reformed; sponsors: Johann Hermann REUTER and his wife Anna Juliana for the boy, and Johann Jacob MAUL for the girl.

March 9th: Gertrudt, born Febr. 23d, child of Johann Matthias and Anna Veronica JUNG, both Reformed; sponsors: Elisabetha KLEIN, Wilhelm SCHMID, Gertrud FALCKENBURG.

March 9th: Henrich, born March 5, child of Balthasar and Christina KIEVER; sponsors: Henrich FEES and his wife Christina.

(The remaining entries on page 78, 6 in number, are scarcely discernible; and inasmuch as they have been made with a different kind of ink and in a different hand-writing and, apparently, are not a part of the W. C. Berckenmeyer entries, I did not attempt to translte them. J. C. K.)

In the year 1726, on October 12th, I, W. C. Berckenmeyer, baptized the following at Newtown:

1. Margareta, born July 21, child of Daniel and Catharina WORMS; sponsors: Hans Willem DIETERICH and his wife Margrete.

2. Anna Maria, born June 15th, child of Friderich and Anna Catharina STREID; sponsors: Paul SMID and Anna Margareta MAUL.

3. Anna Maria, one and one half month old, child of Valentin and Catharina FUHRER; sponsors: Friderich and Anna Maria SCHRAMM.

In the year 1727, on June 14th I again (presumably at the same place) baptized:

1. Johannes, born June 8th, child of David and Margrete MULLER; sponsors: Johannes and Anna Sibilla EBBERT.

2. Margaret, born April 29th, child of Jurg Jan and Margrete DECKER; sponsors: Willem VAN ORDE and his wife Temperans.

In the year 1728, on Jan. 24th, I conducted services at Kiskatom and baptized the following:

1. Catharina, born Dec. 12th, child of Balthasar and Christina KIEVER; sponsors: Catharina EMMERICH (the mother of the child acting in her place), and Hermannus BEHR.

2. Maria, two months old, child of Peter and Mattie BURGARD; sponsors: Friderich MAUL and Maria KLEIN.

3. Liesabeth, born Oct. 7th, child of Nicklas and Liesabeth BRANDAU; sponsors: Hannes BRANDAU and Liesabeth REUTER.

4. Maria, three months old, child of Friderich and Eva DIETERICH; sponsors: Jurge Willem KOHL and Maria Margreta GRAAD.

5. Catharina, born Nov. 19th, child of Christian and Margareta DIETERICH; sponsors: Catharina SCHUT and Hans Jurge ELIG.

May 2, 1728, I baptized the following in the church:

Lisabeth, born some time in February, child of Anna Margareta SCHEFF, who participated in the confessional and communion service; she was employed by Ernst WYNSCOP and his son Johannes is presumably the father of the child; sponsors: Georg Wilhelm KOHL and his wife Gertrud.

2. Anna Maria, born April 4th, child of Clement and Gertrud LEMAN; sponsors: Andreas EICHLER and Anna Maria SCHEF.

3. Wilhelmus, born April 23d, child of Wilhelm and Maria Elisabeth SCHMID; sponsors: Johann Wilhelm BRANSAN and Anna Maria OBERBACH.

September 21, 1728, I baptized:

1. Margaretje, born Febr. 5th, child of Nicklas and Anna Elisabeth SCHMID of Kiskatom; sponsors: Willem LEMAN and his wife Maria Eva.

2. Henrich, born Febr. 18th, child of Valentin and Catharina FUHRER; sponsors: Henrich SCHRAM and his wife Margareta.

In the year 1729, on April 26th, I baptized:

1. Johann Adam, born March 20th, child of Johann and Anna Margareta WOLF; sponsors: Adam SPOON and his wife Anna Maria.

2. Jannetje, born March 18th, child of Hendrick and Gebje KORB (Kort?); sponsors Hannes EMMERICH and Jannetje WENNE.

3. Catharina, born March 12th, child of Michael and Anna Maria RAUW; sponsors: Wilhelm WAMBACH and his wife Catharina.

4. Gabriel, born April 3d, child of Gerrit and Gertrud DECKER; sponsors Gabriel GRAAT and his sister Greetje GRAAT.

5. Anna Catharina, born March 29th, child of Friderich and Eva DIETERICH; sponsors: Gabriel GRAAT and Maria Cathrina DIETERICH.

March 11th, 1729, I baptized at Kiskatom:

Johannes, born Jan. 10th, child of Jan Matthias and Anna Verornica JUNG; sponsors: Johannes SCHEFFER and Maria Elizbeth SCHMIDT.

THE END

LONDON DOCUMENTS

The Names, Trades, etc., of the German Protestants to be settled in New York.

We are indebted to Pascoe Williams of Albany for the following additional names to the Kocherthal Records. These were secured in the State Library at Albany. The list gives the names of the party who came to England with Rev. Kocherthal from the lower Palatinate in Germany in 1708. It will be noted that the German feminine ending of "in" is added wherever the name of a wife or daughter occurs. The list was dated June 28, 1708.

Names	Trades	Conuttion of Life	Male Fem.	Year
1.				
Lorens Schwisser	Husbandman	Married	M	25
Anna Catharina Schwisserin		Wife	F	26
Johanna Schwisserin		Child	F	*
2.				
Henry Rennau	Stockingmaker	Married	M	24
Johanna Rennauin		Wife	F	26
Susanna Liboscha		Sister, unm	F	15
Maria Johana Liboscha		Sister, unm	F	10
Lorenz Rennau		Child	M	2
Heinrich Rennau		Child	M	**
3.				
Andreas Volck	Husbandman	Married	M	30
Ana Catharina Volckin		Wife	F	27
Maria Barbara Volckin		Child	F	5
Georg Hieronymus Volck.		Child	M	4
Anna Gertrauda Volckin		Child	F	1
4.				
Michael Weigand	Husbandman	Married	M	52
Ana Catharina Weigandin.		Wife	F	54
Ana Maria Weigandin		Child	F	13
Tobias Weigand		Child	M	7
Georg Weigand		Child	M	5
5.				
Jacob Weber	Husbandman	Married	M	30
Anna Elisabetha Weberin..		Wife	F	25
Eva Maria Weberin		Child	F	5
Eva Elisabetha Weberin ..		Child	F	1
6.				
Jacob Pletel	Husbandman	Married	M	40
Ana Elisabetha Pletelin		Wife	F	29
Margaretha Pletelin		Child	F	10
Anna Sara Pletelin		Child	F	8
Catharine Pletelin		Child	F	3
7.				
Johannes Fischer	Smith	Married	M	27
Maria Barbara Fischerin....		Wife	F	26
Andreas Fischer		Child	M	***

Names	Trades	Condition of Life	Male	Fem	Year
8.					
Melchoir Gulch	Carpenter & Joiner	Married	M		39
Ana Catharine Gulchin		Wife		F	43
Magdalena Gulchin		Child		F	12
Heinrich Gulchin		Child	M		10
9.					
Isaac Turck	Husbandman	Unmarried	M		23
10.					
Josua Kocherthal	Minister	Married	M		39
Sibylla Charlotta Kocher-thal		Wife			39
Benigna Sibylla Kocher-thal		Child		F	10
Christian Joshua Kocher-thal		Child	M		7
Susanna Sibylla Kocher-thal		Child		F	3

* 8 Months.
** 5 months.
*** one half month.

JOSHUA VON KOCHERTHAL

The following sketch of the career of Rev. Joshua Kocherthal was prepared by Rev. Herman F. Vesper, of St. John's Lutheran Church, Canajoharie, N. Y. The devotion and courage of Joshua Kocherthal and his part in the settlement of the Mohawk Valley should not be overlooked. Descendants of the Palatines will appreciate the scholarly contribution which follows: The publisher of this series feels indebted to Rev. Vesper for his contribution.

Twenty-one years after the close of the devastating Thirty Years' War (1618-1648), there was born at Landau on the left bank of the Rhine River, in what is now Rhenish Bavaria, Joshua Kocherthal, the man who directed the first Palatines to America. His family name was apparently derived from the beautiful valley through which the river Queich flows, for in his later church records he styles himself: "Josua of the valley of Concord, commonly called Kocherthal." Where he obtained his theological education is not known, for though the Reformation was formally introduced into the Palatinate by the Elector-Palatine, Frederick H., in 1546, and Lutheran professors taught theology at Heidelberg until 1560, from that year on the Calvinists were in power, and the Heidelberg Catechism of 1562 made final the cleavage from Lutheranism. However, Kocherthal became a Lutheran pastor and ministered to his fellow believers at a time when persecution, plunder, and pillage ravaged the Rhine countries and laid waste whatever had survived the horrible devastation of the Thirty Years' War.

In 1668 war again broke out, and in 1673 Louis XIV of France began his marauding expeditions for the purpose of extirpating the heretics. Destructive raids laid waste the Palatine countryside, and this ruthless pillage continued until 1668 when the French King himself entered the land "to make it a wilderness," as he declared. As a youth of twenty years Kocherthal heard of the burning of Heidelberg and Manheim and in May of 1689 news reached him that Speyer and Worms had been set on fire. The villages, towns and farms of the Rhine regions were pillaged and burned, their inhabitants tortured, ravished or slain. Few escaped the country, and those who survived were spared further horrors when, in 1705, England, Holland, Sweden and Prussia intervened and threatened reprisals unless this inhuman carnage ceased. The War of the Spanish Succession (1701-1713) followed, but it touched only lightly the already devastated country.

Added to the horrors of war, there came further to harass the unfortunate Palatines the unusually severe winter of 1708-09. Vineyards and orchards were blasted by the cold, birds froze on the wing, fires failed to warm the shivering populace. Furthermore, oppressive ecclesiastical regulations made still more unbearable the life of these "poor Palatines." Kocherthal's powers of resistance to oppression and his influence over the sorely tried people of his own faith must have been considerable. But their circumstances had become intolerable, and their only salvation lay in migrating to other lands. Kocherthal had long entertained the idea of leading a group of his co-religionists to lands across the sea. He is said to have gone to London as early as 1704 for the purpose of negotiating such a transportation of Palatines. In 1706 he published a pamphlet in which he recommended South Carolina as a favorable site for German colonization.

Kocherthal went to Frankfort-on-the-Main in January, 1708, to obtain from a Mr. Davenant, a British resident, passes and money for a trip to England. Davenant made the consent of the Elector-Palatine a condition of such assistance, and when his permission was not forthcoming, Kocherthal, with some 50 to 60 Germans, left in March for London by way of Holland. Queen Anne was apprised of their extreme poverty and granted them each a shilling a day toward their subsistence. This royal example of benevolence inspired others to come to the aid of the refugees and soon their physical needs were sufficiently satisfied. Pastor Kocherthal was beginning to evince his great abilities as a colonizer and as a born leader of this distracted company of exiles. He now petitioned the Queen to permit them to sail for one of the British colonies in North America. "We humbly take leave to represent," he writes to the London Board of Trade, "that they are very necessitous and in the utmost want, not having at present anything to subsist themselves; that they have been rendered to this by the ravages committed by the French in the Lower Palatinate, where they lost all they had." This request was eagerly entertained and discussed by the royal counsellors and the London Board of Trade.

England desired to extend her frontiers in the New World, and there she also sought for raw materials with which to fit out her royal Majesty's ships. Concluding, therefore, that these homeless and distressed, though "honest and laborious" Palatines might profitably be engaged in the manufacture of naval stores, such as ship masts, tar and pitch, the Board of Trade resolved to transport them to the islands of Jamaica and Antigua. However, after more mature consideration, it was determined to send them to New York.

On April 28, 1708, permission was granted Kocherthal and his 53 Palatine refugees to sail for America. They were to be naturalized as British citizens before their embarkation, and they were to make the voyage with the newly appointed Governor of the Province of New York, Lovelace, on her Majesty's transport "Globe." Negotiations dragged on into the summer. On June 22, 1708, Queen Anne signed an agreement according to which her government would supply the colonists with foodstuffs for one year and with the necessary agricultural implements. In addition to these provisions her Majesty granted Pastor Kocherthal twenty pounds sterling and 500 acres of land toward the endowment of a German Protestant church. On August 25, 1708 the Palatines were made "denizens of the kingdom" by a special act of naturalization.

Finally, about the middle of October, the "Globe" was ready to cross the Atlantic with the first Palatine refugees on board, a voyage of no less consequence to the colonization of the future American Republic than that of the "Mayflower" 88 years before. Scant justice has been done by our historians toward these hardy Rhinelanders, who, robust in body and strong in heart and soul, accustomed to hardship, poverty, and toil, conscientious and honest toward God and man, were willing rather to face the unknown but peaceful American wilderness than political, economic and religious degradation in the war wasted lands of Europe.

Students of the European history of this period are wearied by the spectacle which the petty, fanatical, cruel and self seeking monarchs, electors, princes and ecclesiastics present. The common man's rights were ruthlessly trampled upon, the peasants, craftsmen, artisans and merchants saw lands, properties and fortunes ruined. Religious fanaticism was stirred to ceaseless activity and wanton cruelty by unscrupulous Jesuits who gained the ear of such tyrants as France's Louis XIV and John William, Elector of the Upper Palatinate. Lutherans and Calvinists longed for peace, liberty and self-expression in a new world, and they were ready, heart rending as it might be, to tear themselves away from all that had meant home and fatherlnd to them, in order that they might live in peace, establish homes and families, worship God unmolested and enjoy benevolent government, at least, to a degree unknown in Europe.

On such a quest Kocherthal and his compatriots crossed the mighty ocean. For eleven long weeks the "Globe" was at the mercy of wind and wave. Yet the Palatines were comforted   and encouraged by good Captain Congreve and their faithful pastor. The latter preached to them and administered the sacrament. He baptized the babies who were born on board ship. He counselled with Governor Lovelace concerning the administration of the future colony and the division of the land. In this official the Palatines possessed a warm friend.

At last the shores of America were sighted and the "Globe" sailed into the harbor of New York. Then, after casting anchor off Manhattan Island so that the new governor might land and attend   to certain formalities the little ship entered the mouth of the river discovered by Hendrick Hudson a century before. For sixty miles the voyage continued up the lordly stream, the first signs of Winter already visible on both banks. With the close of the year their arduous sea journey also drew to its close. On New Year's Day, 1709, the vessel anchored at the confluence of Quassaic Creek with the river, a pleasant site on the western shore. Here Kocherthal and 53 emigrants, including his wife, Sibylla   Charlotta,   and their three children, landed. It was necessary to build rude huts for shelter from the wintry cold, and the ambitious men, young and sturdy and skilled, lost no time in taking their axes and hammers to hand. Their average age was between 25 and 40, only one was 52, and among them were vineyard keepers, carpenters, smiths,   weavers, cabinet makers and masons. These doughty pioneers named the district Newburgh (Neuburg)after a city in the Upper Palatinate. It contained 2,190 acres which had been assigned to them by royal decree, but the deed to this land came into their possession only in 1719 through the so-called "German Patent." Before the Summer of 1709 Governor Lovelace had died, and as Kocherthal had not yet received the deed to this land, and the colonists were in need of further help from the Crown, he sent a petition to England, dated June 29, 1709, asking for a free passage to London. He proceeded to New York with his family and, leaving wife and children there, sailed back to England on behalf of the colonists. During his absence his daughter, Louisa Abigail   was born.   Dominie Justus Falckner,   the first Lutheran pastor to be ordained in America, ministered to the Palatines while Kocherthal was abroad.

Pastor   Kocherthal   reached London safely, but discovered   that thousands of German refugees had migrated to England since his departure the year previous. The Queen, Parliament, the Board of Trade, and Londoners in general, hardly knew what to do with all the "poor Palatines" who sought asylum in their domains. Hundreds of tents had been erected on the Black Heath in London for these homeless people, others were hospitably received into British homes, but their number increased daily until they came to be regarded as a menace to the peace of the realm. The majority demanded to be transported to other countries under the rule of the British Crown, such as Ireland, Jamaica and the American continent.

Dominie Kocherthal stood in the good graces of Queen Anna, who recognized his talents as a land agent and colonizer. She acceded to his wishes and ordered that 3,000 Palatines be sent to America with him and with Robert Hunter, the successor of Lovelace as Governor of New York. The vessels left London in January, 1710, Kocherthal sailing on H. M. S. "Medford." For six months this fleet of sailing ships with their precious human cargo was tossed about on the briny deep. At least one ship was wrecked, and 470 emigrants died during the perilous voyage, while 250 succumbed to a fever after landing at New York on June 14. Of their quarantine on Nutten (now Governor's) Island, and of their subsequent settlement on both sides of the Hudson above Newburgh this sketch need not go into detail. The "tar period", through which Gov. Hunter and the Palatines passed, is one of the sad chapters in British Colonial history. Its consequence was the migration to and the settlement of the Schoharie and Mohawk Valleys and parts of Pennsylvania.

From London Kocherthal returned in June, 1710, his mission resulting in better conditions for the Palatines on the Quassaic. A church was built on the "glebe" designated for religious purposes. The Queen donated a bell, and Kocherthal set to work to build up his New World parish. Three villages were established on the western side of the river, Georgetown, Elizabethtown and Newtown. Across the Hudson were Annsbury, Haysbury, Queensbury, and Hunterstown, each one under the supervision of a "listmaster," who was appointed by Hunter because of his individual integrity and qualities of leadership. Kocherthal ministered to these pioneer colonists most faithfully and conscientiously. During the first months of 1711 he made New York his residence, but later in that year he came to his "upper colonies", as he called them, and made his abode on the west side of the river near Newburgh. He organized a Lutheran congregation at West Camp, the site of Newtown, in that year. But his ministerial duties and activities were not confined to one parish, nor even to the Hudson Valley settlements. After 1713 he journeyed across the Catskills or by way of Albany to the Palatine colonies in the Schoharie Valley. Often Dominie Haeger of the Reformed faith undertook the trip with him. Here, too, he held services, administered communion, baptized infants, catechized the young, and united in marriage those who sought his pastoral services. His church records which have been preserved, testify to the genuine piety, the customary German thoroughness, the conscientiousness and sincerity, the scholarship and orthodoxy, which distinguish this true servant of God and friend of man. No better leader and spiritual guide could those pioneer settlers have had in those trying times. With his devoted people he remained true to his religious convictions and principles and by precept and example he inculcated standards of character that distinguish the Palatine to this day.

For ten years Joshua von Kocherthal labored among his countrymen, ever intent upon their material and spiritual welfare. His interest in the Glebe on the Quassaic never abated and for this church land he desired to obtain clear, incontestable title. It was June 18, 1718 when he directed a petition to Governor Hunter in which he requested him to grant him, his heirs and assigns a suitable portion of the Glebe for their support. On the following eighth of October certain Palatines sent a counter petition to the Governor, asking that these 500 acres of Glebe land be assigned to some other Lutheran pastor The reason was that Kocherthal had not lived there for nine years. and one of the conditions of the Queen's grant specified that the minister must reside upon this land. Kocherthal, relying upon his personal influence with the Queen, and convinced that this misinterpretation of the royal grant warranted another trip to England, made preparations to return to London. But his unexpected death intervened to nullify his plans. At West Camp on St. John's Day, December 27, 1719, Kocherthal suddenly sickened and died. A longer journey than the one to England was his to undertake, and that when he was but fifty years of age. The rigors and privations of pioneer life would not permit men to become old. They were simply worn out before the Biblical allotment of "three score years and ten." And so at West Camp they laid to rest the worn and weary body of the man who had done more for them than any other individual. We do not know who officiated at the obsequies of this noble servant of God. For five years no regularly called pastor served in this parish, but in September, 1724, Daniel Falckner, "pastor at Millstone and in the mountains of the Raritan" made entries in the church record. He was succeeded in the following year by Dominie William Berkenmeyer, whose entries are recorded from 1725 to 1730.

But the Glebe question was not settled with the death of Kocherthal. The Commission of the Council of the Province convened soon after to consider the two petitions. Generously they granted to Kocherthal's widow and to her three children "the whole 250 acres to them and to their assigns forever." To the counter petitioners the Commission granted "500 acres of land for the maintenance and support of a Lutheran pastor forever." For a term not to exceed seven years these lands might be rented, but these rentals and profits "shall be impropriated to the maintenance of such Lutheran minister and his successors forever, and to no other use whatever; and it being granted for a pious intent, you may cause the quit-rent to be reserved for the said Glebe land, be the yearly rent of one peppercorn, if the same be legally demanded, which nevertheless is humbly submitted." Thus the terms of the provincial authorities.

Kocherthal's wife, Sibylla Charlotta, was also born in 1669. She accompanied him from Germany to London and across the sea in 1708 with their three children, all born in the Palatinate. She, too, died at an early age, departing this life on December 16, 1713 at West Camp, aged 44 years. She died six years before her husband, and she did not live to see her oldest daughter Benigna Sibylla, who was born in 1698, married to Dominie Berkenmeyer of Loonenburgh on the Hudson. Christian Joshua was born in 1701. He was appointed one of the listmasters on the eastern side of the river and died in 1731. In 1705 was born Susanna Sibylla. She became the wife of William Hurtin, a goldsmith, residing in Bergen County, New Jersey. Louisa Abigail was born in New York on February 26, 1710. She too, was married to a goldsmith, John Brevoort of New York. Peter Lynch, a New York merchant chose Kathalina, the youngest daughter to be his wife. It was she who inherited her mother's interest, for Kocherthal's wife had died six years before the patent was granted to the original settlers. Later the brother's interest fell to Louisa Abigail.

In the year 1742 the three surviving daughters ordered a brown stone tablet to be placed over the grave of their parents at West Camp. The inscription translated from the German reads:

"Know, O traveler,
under this stone rests,
beside his Sibylla Charlotta,
a genuine traveler,
of the High-Germans in America,
their Joshua,
And a pure Lutheran preacher of the same
in the east and west side
of the Hudson river.
His first arrival was with L'd Lovelace
1707-8, January 1
His second with Col. Hunter
1710, June 14
Brought his journey to England to end.
His heavenly journey was
on St. John's Day, 1719
Do you wish to know more?
Seek in Melanchton's Fatherland
Who was Kocherthal
Who Harschias
Who Winchenbach
B. Berkenmeyer   S. Huertin   L. Brevoort
M D C C X L I I.

THE GRAVEYARD

The following records from the graveyard at Stone Arabia and the lists from the Congregational Register kept by the first resident pastor in Schoharie, Rev. Peter Nicholas Sommer, are taken from the pamphlet "Lutheran Trinity Church of Stone Arabia," written by Rev. Andrew Dillenbeck, D. D., and published by the Church in 1931.

W E WISH we need not speak of this. Shamefully has it been neglected for nearly a century. Pigs and cows have overrun it for years. Tombstones are broken and fallen. An orchard was planted in it years ago and the trees are old and dying. Something should be done. In it are buried one pastor, Rev. Philip Jacob Groz, A. M., and at least one pastor's wife, Mrs. Anna Margretha Ries, wife of the first resident pastor of the Church together with many other ancestors of the present members of the congregation.

In 1914, a list was made of the tombstones with their inscriptions, which we incorporate in this history, here and now:

1. JOHN STRAYER, died 24 Oct. 1800 aged 56 years.
2. PETER REAS, died 6 Feb. 1825 aged 60 years. (A son of Rev. Ries without a doubt).
3. CATHARINE VAN SLYKE, died 7 July 1866, aged 39 years, 4 mos. and 14 days.
4. MALACHI POTTER, died 11 April 1848, aged 69 years and 5 mos. (This is an error, we think, on the part of the transcriber, since there were no Potters connected with the Church, and since the transcriber notes a headstone and footstone next to this one, with illegible inscriptions but which appear to the transcriber as "Bauder").
5. GEORGE BAUDER, died 21 Jan. 1858, aged 85 years.
6. MARGARET KLOCK, wife of George Bauder, died 15 May 1858, aged 82 years.
7. MARIAH M., daughter of Benjamin and Lany PANGBURN, died 13 Aug. 1851, aged 4 years, 9 mos., 29 days.
8. HENRY LASHER, JR., died 13 July 1878, aged 87 years, 9 mos. and 26 days.
9. NANCY, wife of Henry LASHER, died 28 Dec. 1858, aged 62 years and 2 days.
10. ANGELINE, wife of Walter LASHER, died 28 March 1859, aged 19 years, 8 mos., 2 days. Also an infant daughter Angeline, born 18 March 1859, died 17 July 1859.
11. SUSANNAH, wife of Jacob SARFASS, died 22 March 1844, aged 60 years.
12. LANY KLOCK, wife of Michael M. BAUDER, died 22 April 1838, aged 76 years 4 mos., 28 days.
13. MICHAEL M. BAUDER, died 28 Dec. 1822, aged 60 years. 11 mos., 14 days.
14. MICHAEL WICK, died 13 March 1886, aged 95 years, 9 mos. and 6 days.

15. Catharine, wife of Michael WICK, died 22 August 1860, aged 62 years, 5 mos. and 22 days.

16. Reverend PHILIP JACOB GROZ, A. M. Late pastor of the Evangelical Lutheran Congregation of Stone Arabia and Palatine. Born in Wurtembergh, Germany, who after thirty years' labor in the Lord's vineyard, was in the 62nd year of his age on the first day of December, 1809 sud-denly called to our ....

17. JACOB HARTMAN, son of J. and Lydia Ann STOVER died 27 August 1840, aged 1 year, 10 mos., 25 days.

18. BENJAMIN, son of Joseph and Margaret ENGLAND, died 21 June 1837, aged 9 years.

19. CATHARINE, daughter of same parents, died 13 May 1839, aged 2 years, 3 mos., 21 days.

20. LAWRENCE son of same parents, died 15 April 1854, aged 6 years, 4 mos., 20 days.

21. KATHERINE EMPIE, wife of John F. Empie, died 14 August 1820, aged 56 years, 4 mos., 8 days.

22. CATHARINE, wife of Daniel A. LIPE, born 10 Oct. 1796, died 29 August 1837.

23. MARY ANN LIPE, born 3 Sept. 1820, died 29 April 1835.

24. MARIA LIPE, born 25 Jan. 1836, died 15 Oct. 1831.

25. JAMES LIPE, son of Daniel and Catharine Lipe died 8 Oct. 1830, aged 4 years, 3 mos., 12 days.

Many of the stones legible in 1914, have disappeared altogether or are now illegible.

Congregational Register of Stone Arabia and Cani-schohare

(Names set in from the margin are the names of the children)

(   )
John Wolfgang Berlet
Anna Barbara Berlet
   Catharina
   Magdalena
   Eva
   Johan Gotlieb
   Anna Margretha
   Andreas Besinger

Ludwig Casselmann
Margretha
   Johann Dieterich
   Johannes
   Conrad
   Joh. Jacob
   Anna
   Elisabet
   David
   Elisabet
   Sophia
Johan Wilhelm Casselmann
Anna Margretha Casselmann
   Anna Margretha
   Anna Maria
   Anna Magdalena
Elisabet Crems
Joh. Dewi

Wilhelm Emche
Andreas Frenck
Christina Frenck
   Eva
   Catharina
Robert Dewig
Cathar. Dewig
   Catharina
   Henrich
   Anna Maria
Anna Margreta Fuchs
Margaretha Frey
Margaretha Frey
Nic. Hertzinger
Maria Sibylla Hertzinger
Johannes Hess
(   )hannes
(   ) Kayser
(   )arertha Kayser
(   )na
(   )ns
(   )ab Barbara
(   )han Michel
   Elisabet
   Joh. Jurgen
Johannes
(   )istian Nellis
(   )m Nellis

Anna Dewi
( )
Elisabet Dillenbach
Christian
Anna Maria
Wilhelm
Elisabet
Martinus
Joh. Dieterich
Joh. Baltasar
Joh. David
Henrich Dillenbach
Anna Margareta Dillenbach
Christian Dillenbach
Anna Maria (............)
Johannes Dillenbach
Magdalena Dillenbach
Maria Elisabet
Johannes Emche
Elisabet Emche
Friederich
Adam
Johannes
Anna Maria
Philip Emche
Philip
Conrad
Johannes
Adam
Margreta
Nicolas Stenzel
( ) Sutz
Peter Wagner
Johan Peter
Maria Elisabet
Anna Barbara Walrath
Christina von der Wercken

Wilhelm
Adolph
Anna Elisab
Johannes
Ludwig
Henrich
Maria
Anna Margareta
Elisabet
( )old Pickert
( )harina Pickert
( )diah Portman
( )rgen Resener
( )aria Catherina Resener
( )
Johannes Schultz
Johan
Maria Elisabet Barbara
Johan Jacob Schultz
Johan Christopher Schultz
Henrich Six
Christina Six
Elisabet
Henrich
Johannes
Johan Jurgen Saltzmann
Henrich
Maria Dorothea
Magdalena
Michel
Maria
Anna Maria
Julianna
Elisabet
Christina
Jurgen Saltzmann
Catharina Elizabet Saltzmann

The following appear as members "At the Fall" the first members of the present Manheim Church (Lutheran):

( ) Baumannen (this a female, note the feminine "en" ending).
Leonhard Baier and his wife
Catharina Barsen and her mother
Johan Jurgen Cast, Senior
Johan Jurgen Cast, Junior
Gertrude Cast
Elisabet
Conrad
Friederich
Maria Catharina Contz
Jurgen Dachstater
Johan Leonhard
Andres Deeck
Dieterich Demuth

Johannes Eiseman and his children
Eva Ittichs
Andreas Klebsettel
Johannes
Augustinus
Johan Jost
Anna Cunigund Meier
Gustavus Osterod
Andreas Pfeiffer
Anna Margreta Rils
Werner Schafer
Johan Adam Schafer
Barbara Weber
Nicolas Wohlleben

Rev. Sommer's Register of Baptisms Performed at Cani-scohare and Stein Raby, 1743-1750.

MARIA ELIZABETH born 2 July 1743, baptized 17 July 1743. Parents ANDREAS BESINGER, MARIA ELIZABETH BESINGER. Sponsors, Johannes Emche and his wife Elisabet.

ELISAZET, born 22 Aug. 1743, baptized 11 Sept. 1743. Parents, GERHARD MISSELIS, CATHARINE MISSELIS. Sponsors, Elisabet Teicher and Thomas Killy.

ANNA MARIA, born at Stein Raby 8 January 1744, baptized 22 January 1744. Parents, JOHANNES EMCHE and ELISABET EMCHE. Sponsors, Severinus Teicher and his wife.

JACOB, born at Stein Raby, 31 December 1743, baptized 22 January 1744. Parents FRIEDERICH SCHNELL and ANNA MARIA SCHNELL. Sponsors, Jacob Schultz and his wife.

CATHARINA, born at Cani-scohare, baptized at Stein Raby. Born 26 December 1743, baptized 22 January 1744. Parents, HENRICH DILLENBACH and ANNA MARGRETHA. Sponsors, Peter Wagner, Junior, and Elisabet Dillenbach.

ANNA MAGDALENA, born at Stein Raby 20 January 1744, baptized 22 January 1744. Parents, JOHAN WILHELM CASSELMANN and MARGRETHA CASSELMANN. Sponsors, Miss Anna Magdalena (............) and Miss Anna Elisabeth Walrath and Johannes Casselmann.

JOHAN JACOB, baptized at Cani-scohare, baptized 13 August 1744. Parents, JACOB CHRISTMANN and CATHARINA CHRISTMANN. Sponsors, Johan Jacob Fehling and Magdalena. (No record of birth).

JOHAN CHRISTOPH, born at Cani-scohare, 12 August 1744, baptized 21 August 1744. Parents HENRICH ECKLER and MARGARETA ECKLER. Sponsors, (   ) Jung and his wife Margaretta Jung.

B(   ), a little girl born at the River 23 July 1744, baptized 22 August 1744. Parents JAMES DILLEN and MARGRETH. Sponsors Joh(   ) von Evern and Jannetje von E(   ).

ELISABET, born at Stein Raby (   ) December 1744, baptized 18 February 1745. Parents, ADAM LAUTZ and CATHARINE ELISABET LAUTZ. Sponsors, Wilhelm (   ) and his wife (   ).

(   ) a little girl born at Stein Raby (   ), baptized 18 February 1745. Parents, ANDREAS BESINGER and MARIA ELISABET. Sponsors, (   ) and his wife.

JURGEN, born April (   ) baptized June (   ) 1745. Parents, JURGEN SALTZMANN and CATHARINA ELISABET SALTZMANN. Sponsors, (   ) and his wife.

(   ) a little girl born at Caniscohare June ...., baptized 18 June 1745. Parents, GUSTAVUS OSTEROD and ANNA MARIA. Sponsors, Utilia Schumacher and Johan Friederich Hess.

LUDWIG, a bastard, born at the Fall. Born (   ), baptized 17 June 1745 of CATHARINA (   )UNTERMAN. Sponsors, Jon(   ) (   )ewi.

JOHAN HENRICH, baptized 3 July 1746 at Stone Arabia. Parents, DEWALD TEICHER and CUNNIGUNDA. Sponsors, Henrich Dillenbach and (   ) Cramer (birth date not given).

ADAM, born at Stone Arabia, 27 May 1747, baptized 7 June 1747. Parents ADAM LAUTZ and CATHARINA ELISABET. Sponsors, Nicholas Fehling and Elisabet Schnell.

N. B.—A child baptized of ANDR. FINCK.

BAREND FREY baptized 26 February 1749.

N. B.—A child baptized (   ) KILLY.

N. B.—A child baptized of (   ) RESENER.

HENRICH, born at Stone Arabia 1 September 1749, baptized 3 September 1749. Parents, JOH. CHRISTIAN DILLENBACH. Sponsors, Henrich Saltzman and his wife.

MATTHEUS, born at Stone Arabia 23 August 1749, baptized 3 September 1749. Parents, JOHANES WARMUTH. Sponsors, William Warmuth and his wife.

PETER, born at Stone Arabia, 28 September 1749, baptized 30 September 1749. Parents, DANIEL von ANTWERPEN.

A son, baptized at Stone Arabia 1 October 1749 of CHRISTOPHER SCHULTZ.

A little girl of HERMAN HAUS, baptized 1 October 1749.

A little boy of JURGEN HAUS, baptized 9 October 1749.

A little boy of Mr. WOHLGEMUTH, baptized 9 October 1749.

JOHAN PHILIP of PHILIP EMCHE, baptized 10 October 1749.

MAGDALENA of HENR. DILLENBACH, baptized 10 October 1749.

ANNA, baptized 17 June 1750, of WILHELM GERLACH.

JOHAN NICOLAS, baptized 17 June 1750, of ADAM JUNG.

THE OLD CHURCH AT SCHOHARIE

Built 1772 and used as a fort during the Revolution. Loaned by N. Berton Alter, of Nelliston, pres ent owner of the Simms collection of cuts. This illustration first ap peared in the Frontiersmen of New York, Vol. 2, page 64.

Palatine Heads of Families

FROM

Governor Hunter's Ration Lists

June, 1710 to September, 1714

Compiled from the Records in London and Presented to the Descendants of the Palatines by

BOYD EHLE, C. E.

Historians in general and descendants of the Palatines in particular have long felt a desire for a more complete list of those Palatine emigrants who settled in New York and along the Hudson under the patronage of Queen Anne of 1710. Documentary History of New York, Vol. III gives a census of those in New York, also those in West Camp but no mention is made of those in East Camp although it is known that there were unlisted settlements on the east side.

During the summer of 1931 Mr. Boyd Ehle through his London agents caused a search of the records there with the result that the ledger accounts of Governor Hunter were consulted and all the names of heads of families drawing rations were copied. Mr. Ehle has arranged them in alphabetical order and indicated their place of residence by the symbols to be found following the name in cases where residence is known as follows:

E.—East Camp, Soldiers in Canadian Exposition of 1711.
W.—West Camp.
N.—New York City.
These locations are from the census reports in Doc. Hist., Vol. 3. Those not designated are presumed to have been residents of East Camp. No census of this camp has been discovered, but by eliminating those of known location the balance must belong to East Camp.
This kindly service on the part of Mr. Ehle is duly acknowledged by the Enterprise and News on behalf of the descendants of the Palatinate. Surely no kindlier service can be imagined and not only those living today but those who will follow will find reason to be grateful for the thoughtfulness of Mr. Ehle in preserving the precious knowledge for the descendants.

London Letter

The letter accompanying the Ration Lists from the London compilers will be of interest and is here given:

Colonial Office Class 5

Vols. 1230-1231.

(Badly classified—1731 is first in point of order).

These two folio volumes, clearly written and bound in undressed calf are the statement of Gov. Hunter's account against the Government for the subsistence to the Palatines 1710-1713 each having the certificates and the seal of New York in red wax.

as noted in Dr. Andrew's Guide." The first is the Journal or account book, No. 1231, the other (1230) is the ledger, each name being posted up in alphabetical order. Both these show the number drawn for by the heads of families or the recipient thus:—2 adults 2 young (i. e. under 10 years); 3 adults 1 young; 1 adult, as the case may be

Vol. 1231

This journal, as it is called is divided under the following headings:
p. 1. "New York 30 June 1719.
"The Palatines hereafter named for themselves and their families Subsistence, Debtors to the Queen's most Sacred Majesty . . . for 4 days subsistance distributed . . . from 27 June to this day at the rate of 6d

for persons above 10 years of age and 4d per diem for children under 10 years . . . .

(Then follows names and sums of money to cash).

p. 4 New York 1st July 1710. Similar heading for 4 days 28 June to this day.

p. 10 New York 4th July 1710. Similar heading 4 days 1st July to this day.

p. 14 New York 4th August 1710. Similar heading 26 days 10th July to this day.

p. 29 New York 4 October 1710. Similar heading. 61 days 5th August to this day.

p. 45. Mannor of Livingston 31 December 1710 The Palatines hereafter named for themselves and their families subsistance debtors to the Queens most Sacred Majesty for Subsistance distributed to the said Palatines from the time of their several arrivals at this place and ye other side Hudson River (the first being ye 6 October) to this day make 89 days. . .

p. 55 Mannor of Lovingston 25 March 1711 . . . for 84 days from 1 January 1711.

p. 66 Mannor of Livingston 24 June 1711 . . . 91 days from 26 March.

p. 78 Mannor of Livingston 29 September 1711 . . . 97 days from 25 June abating 14 days during which time they had little or no provision.

p 91. Mannor of Livingston 24 December 1711 . . . 86 days from 30 September.

p. 103. New York 24 December 1711 . . . from 5th October 1710 at New York to 5 October last . . N. B. Those families charged with small sums were sent up to the Settlement last fall, others with large sums were subsisted at New York in the spring following and not sent up till April and May. And the remainder being Widows and Orphans have been subsisted to this time.

p. 117. Mannor of Livingston 25 March 1712 . . . for 92 days from 25 October 1711 to this time.

p. 129 New York 25 March 1712 . . 172 days from 6 October 1711 to this day.

p. 130 Mannor of Livingston 24 June 1712 . . . 91 days from 26 March.

p. 143 Mannor of Livingston 13 September 1712 . . . 81 days from 25 June.

A few names added under heading "New York."

p. 155 (no place given) 23 September 1713 for unequal time subsistance from 13 September 1712 to this day.

p. 156 The book is then apparently made up 27 August 1714 and certified and sealed 2 September 1714.

Palatine Heads of Families

Location (N), New York city.

(E), East Camps, Columbia Co., N. Y.

(W), West Camps, Ulster Co., N. Y.

Abelman, Johan Peter, (N).
Anspach, Johann Balthasar (E).
Anthess, Conrad (his widow).
Arnold, Jacob, (W).
Arthopeus, Johan Aloph
Asmer, Philip
Baches, Agnes
Bahr, Johannes, (N)
Bahr, Jacob (widow)
Ballin, Anna Catherin
Barthel, Henrich
Barthelin, Anna Dorothea
Barthin, Anna
Bason, Nicolas
Bast, Johann Henrich
Bast, Jacob, (E)
Bast, Georg
Battorfin, Anna
Batzin, Anna Catherin, (N)
Bauch, Christian, (E)
Baum, Mathias (son of Johan Jost)
Bauman, Adam
Baumannin, Anna Margaretha
Baumarsin, Anna Maria
Bayerin, Anna Margretha
Beck, Adreas Friderich
Becker, Peter, (W)
Becker, Johan Friderick, (W)
Beckerin, Maria
Beckerin, Elizabetha, Sr., (W)
Beckerin, Elizabetha Jr.
Beckerin, Anna Catharina
Beckerin, Anna Dorothea
Beckerin, Magdalena
Bellin, Elizabetha
Bellinger, Niclaus
Bellinger, Johannes
Bellinger, Marcus, E)
Bellinger, Henrich, (E)
Bellinger, Elizabetha
Bender, Georg, (E)
Bender, Valentin, (W)
Bender, Peter, his widow
Benderin, Anna Maria, (N)
Berck, Christian
Berg, Johannes
Berg, Abraham
Bergman, Andreas, (E)
Beringer, Conrad
Berleman, Johannes
Berner, Georg Ludwig
Bernhart, Johann Jost
Bernhart, Johann Jost
Bernhard, Johannes, (E)
Bernhard, Ulrich, (E)
Bertin, Gerhard Berter and Anna
Bertram, Jacob
Betzer, Herman, (E)
Beyer, Johan Jacob
Beyerin, Susanna
Bierman, Johannes
Blass, Johannes, (E)
Bohler, Johan Henrich
Bohm, Henrich

Bollin, Sophia
Bonn, Franz le Febure
Bonnenstiel, Niclaus
Bonroth, Pohannes, (E)
Borne, Jacob
Borsch, Ludwig
Borst, Jacob
Boshaar, Jacob
Boshaar, Johann Jacob
Bousche, Daniel
Brackin, Anna Catharina
Brack, Johan Michael
Brandaw, Wilhelm, (W.)
Brandorff, Jost
Braun, Johann Jost
Braun, Johann Paul
Brendel, Caspar
Bressler, Valentin, (N)
Bretter, Anthoni
Bregel, Georg, (E)
Brillin, Anna Margretha
Brillemannin, Helena, (N)
Bronnwasser, Anna Gertrude
Brong, Mattheus, (N)
Bruchle, Henrich
Bruyere, Susanne
Bruyere, Jeanne, (N)
Boff, Johann Georg
Buck, Martin
Brucher, Ulrich
Burckhard, Johannes
Bouche, Daniel
Busch, Daniel, Sr., (E)
Borsch, Elizabeth

Capulscher, Joann Jacob
Cast, Johannes
Castner, Johann Conrad
Castner, Johann Peter
Champanois, Daniel
Christman, Hanns
Christmannin, Elizabeth
Chevenius, Bernhard
Conrad, Henrich, (E)
Conradin, Anna

Dachstatter, Georg, (E)
Dahles, Johan Wilhelm, (E)
Danler, Ulrich
Dannemarcker, Christoph, (N)
Darrey, Conrad
Dather, Lorentz
Datt, Johann Bernhard
Dansweber, Melchoir, (N)
Deffer, Daniel, (N)
Demuth, Jacob, (N)
Demuthin, Anna Catharina
Demuthin, Anna Maria, (W)
Demuthin, Agnes
Deubig, Johann Paul
Dietrich, Johann Jacob, (N)
Dietrich, Johann Wilhelm
Dietrich, Christian
Dietrichin, Anna Elizabetha, (W)
Drerenbach, Conrad and his mother Anna
Diewel, Johannes, (N)
Diewel, Johann Peter, (W)
Deuchert, Werner, (E)
Dill, Annanias
Dill, Wilhelm, (E)
Dillin, Anna Clara

Dillenbachin, Barbara and son Martin, (E)
Dilteyin, Catharina
Dinant, Peter
Dings, Jacob, (E)
Dorn, Lazarus
Dorner, Johannes, (N)
Dorner, Jacob
Dornheiser, Jacob
Dontzbachin, Anna Elizabetha
Dontzbach, Franz
Dopff, Johan Peter, (E)
Diaurh, Ludwig, his widow
Drechsler, Peter
Dreuthin, Catharina
Dreuthin, Elizabetha
Drumm, Andreas
Drumbaur, Niclaus
Duntzer, Paulus

Eigenbrodt, Elizabeth
Eberhard, Johannes, (W)
Eckling, Johann Georg
Eckhard, Adam
Eckhard, Niclaus, (E)
Eckhardin, Gertrude, (W)
Ehemann, Tomas,(W)
Ehlig, Andreas, (N)
Eigler, Christian
Elasser, Paul

Emichen, Johan Ernst
Emich, Johan Niclaus
Emmerich, Johannes
Emmerich, Johan Michael, (W)
Emrichin, Anna Maria, (W)
Engel, Johannes, (N)
Engelin, Maria Elizabetha
Engelbert, Johan Peter
Engesbrucher, Niclaus
Engelsbrurger, Tilleman
Enners, Bertram
Erbin, Catharina, (N)
Erckel, Bernhard, (N)
Erhard, Simon
Eschenreuter, Henrich
Eschoffin, Catharina
Eschideins, Thomas, his widow
Ess, Jacob, (E)
Esswein, Jacob
Eygner, Peter, (W)
Eygnerin, Jeremia
Faeg, Peter
Faeg, Johannes, (E)
Fahling, Henrich, (E)
Falck, Arnold, (N)

Falckenburg, Johann Wilhelm, (W)
Fasius, Valentin
Fasius, Johannes
Feller, Niclaus, (E)
Fewersbach, Dietrich, (N)
Fiddler, Gottfriend, (W)
Fills, Wilhelm Philip
Fills, Philip
Finck, Johann Wilhelm
Finck, Frantz, (E)
Finck, Andreas
Finckin, Magdalena
Foltz, Melchoir
Finckel, Johan Phillip
Fischer, Peter
Fischer, Sebastian

Fluger, Zacharias
Forster, Johan Georg
Franck, Johannes, (W)
Fred, Johan Georg
Freil, Christopher
Frey, Henrich
Freyerin, Barbara
Freymeyer, Michael
Friderick, Conrad, (N)
Friderick, Hanns Adam, (W)
Frillin, Maria Elizabeth
Fritz, Johann Wilhelm
Frolich, Stephan, (W)
Frolich, Valentin
Fucks, Johann Christoph, (E)
Fucks, Johann Philip
Fucks, Johann Peter, (N)
Fuhrer, Johannes
Funck, Peter
Fuhrman, Jacob

Gieserin, Sibilla
Galdach, Anna Maria, (N)
Gantz, Johannes
Gebelin, Anna Margretha
Georg, Johann Anthoni
Georg, Johann Wilhelm, (E)
Georgin, Anna Elizabetha
Gerlach, Peter, (N)
Gerlach, Johann Christ, (W)
Gerlachin, Otilla
German, Jacob
Gesinger, Henrich, (N)
Getel, Daniel, his widow
Getmannin, Barbara
Giesler, Peter, (W)
Glump, Philipp
Getmannin, Maria Barbara
Glock (Klock), Henrich
Goldman, Conrad, (E)
Gondermann, Johann Friderick
Grad, Johannes
Grauberger, Philipp Peter
Graw, Gerlach, his widow
Grawsin, Anna Maria
Greisler, Johann Philipp, (N)
Gresserin, Maria Elizabetha
Griffon, Marie
Griot, Jean
Grucko, Arnold
Gruco, Johann Peter

Hammin, Gertrude
Haas, Simon
Haas, Niclaus
Haber, Christian, (E)
Hahn, Johann Georg
Hagedorn, Peter
Hagedorn, Johann Peter, (E)
Hager, Johann Friderick
Hagerin, Maria
Haintz, Urbanus
Hambuch, Johann Wilhelm, (E)
Hamer, Johann Henrich, (E)
Hamm, Peter
Hamm, Conrad
Harter, Johann Niclaus
Harter, Johann Michael
Hartman, Johann Hermann
Hartman, Peter
Hartmanin, Anna Maria
Hartwig, Caspar, (N)

Hartel, Adam, (W)
Hasel, Wilhelm
Haselin, Johan Henrich
Hassman, Dietrich
Haupt, Philipp
Haugh, Lucas, his widow
Haug, Plaichard
Haus, Johann Christian
Hayd, Niclaus, (E)
Hayd, Johan Jost
Hayd, Peter, (E)
Haydin, Maria Cunigunda
Hayer, Henrich
Hebmann, Michael, (N)
Heel, Jacob
Heydelberg, George Jacob
Heyner, Johannes
Heytersbach, Niclaus, (N)
Helmer, Philipp, (W)
Helmer, Peter
Hemmerle, Anna Barbara
Henneschield, Michael, (N)
Henrich, Lorentz
Herman, Jost
Herner, Ludwig Ernest
Hertzel, Jacob
Hertzog, Henrich, his widow
Hess, Johannes
Hers, Niclaus
Hefferick, Johannes
Heffick, Johannes Conrad
Heusen, Johan Peter
Heydin, Anna Maria
Heydorn, Henrich
Hildebrand, Anna Catharina
Hirchemer, Georg
Hoff, Johan Adam
Hoff, Andreas
Hofferlin, Anna Maria
Hoffin, Margaretha
Hoffmann, Gabriel
Hoffman, Herman, (N)
Hoffmann, Jacob
Hoffmann, Conrad
Hoffmann, Heinrich, (E)
Hoffmannin, Anna Eva
Hoffmannin, Anna Catharina
Homburger, Thomas
Honingen, Michael
Horne, Johan
Horne, Caspar
Hornich, Niclaus
Horning, Gerhard
Hothenrothin, Veronica
Huckin, Barbara
Huls, Christoph
Hummel, Georg
Hummel, Herman
Huner, Benedict
Huppert, David, (E)
Hussmann, Johann Adam
Hussam, Herman

Iffland, Johann David
Ingold, Ulrich
Ittich, Johann Michael

Jacobi, Ulrich
Jager, Wendel
Jager, Christian
Jamin, Peter

Jung, Johann Eberhard
Jung, Peter
Jung, Henrich, (E)
Jungin, Maria
Jung, Johannes, (N)
Jungin, Anna Elizabeth
Jung, Theobald
Jungin, Juliana
Jungens, Niclaus, (N)

Kabsin, Anna Sibilla
Kahl, Johann Wilhelm
Kamer, Johann Wilhelm, (E)
Kang, Johan Peter
Kaschelin, Anna Margretha
Kasselmann, Christian, (N)
Kasselmann, Dietrich
Kast, Johann Georg
Kayser, Johann Wilhelm, (W)
Kayser, Johann Matheus, (E)
Kayserin, Maria
Kasin, Eva Catharina
Keller, Christian, his widow
Keller, Frantz, (N)
Kercherin, Anna Maria
Kessler, Johannes, (E)
Kesselerin, Anna Maria
Kefler, Henrich
Kieffer, Johan William
Kiesler, David
Kirtzenberg, Elizabetha
Klapperin, Anna Agatha
Kleinin, Helena
Kleins, Peter, his widow
Klein, Hyeronimus, (N)
Klein, Johannes
Klein, Johann Jacob
Klein, Johan Herman
Klein, Henrich
Klein, Adam
Klapp, Peter
Klotter, Henrich
Klotterin, Susanna and Caspar
Klug, Johan Georg
Knab, Ludwig
Kneibin, Helene Sophia
Kneskern, Hans Peter, (E)
Kobel, Jacob, (E)
Koch, George Ludwig, (E)
Koch, George Ludwig, (E)
Kocherthal, Joshua, (W)
Kohlmeyerin, Catharina
Kolsch, Anna Eva
Kolsch, Johan Henrich
Konig, Marcus
Kopff, Jacob
Kornmann, Peter Jacob, (N)
Korn, Johann Henrich
Korner, Niclaus, (W)
Krafftin, Anna Ursula
Kramer, Johannes
Kramer, Anthoni, (W)
Kramer, Anna Maria & Michael, (N)
Krantz, Johann Henrich, (W)
Krantz, Conrad
Krembs, Johannes
Kugel, Johannes
Kuhlmer, Johannes
Kuhlmann, Georg, (W)
Kuhn, Johann Jacob, (E)
Kuhn, Samuel, (E)

Kuhn, Conrad & Valentin, (E)
Kuhn, Valentine, (E)
Kohner, Benedict, (N)
Kundy, Matheus, his widow
Kuntz, Jacob, 1st
Kuntz, Jacob 2nd.
Kuntz, Johannes, (W)
Kuntz, Mathias
Kuntz, Matheus
Kurtz, Johan Christoph
Labach, Johannes
Laib, Johann Caspar
Lahmeyer, Johannes
Lambertin, Elizabetha, (N)
Lamet, Johannes
Lancker, Johannes
Lampmann, Peter
Landgraff, Georg
Langin, Magdalena
Langer, Abraham, (E)
Lantin, Anna Catharina
Lappin, Agnes
Lauck, Johan Jacob, his widow
Lauck, Abraham
Laucks, Johann Niclaus, (E)
Laux, Philipp, (E)
Laux, Johan Philipp
Laux, Johan Jost
Laux, Johannes
Laux, Georg
Laux, Dietrich
Laux, Johann Dietrich
Lawer, Peter
Lehemann, Wilhelm
Lehr, Johannes, (W)
Leicht, Henrich, (N)
Leicht, Ludwig, (N)
Leick, Johannes
Lein, Conrad, (N)
Lenckin, Maria Catharina, her son
Lepper, Philipp Hermann his widow
Lesch, Balthasar
Lescherin, Magdalena
Leyer, Johannes, (E)
Lickard, Bernhard, (N)
Lincken, Johan Wilhelm
Linsin, Apolonia, (N)
Lorentz, Johannes, (N)
Loscher, Sebastian
Lohin, Anna Catharina
Lucas, Georg
Lucas, Francois
Ludwig, Johann Henrich
Lutzin, Magdalena
Lutzin, Anna Barbara
Madebachin, Elnora
Maisinger, Conrad
Maisinger, Sebastian & Niclaus
Manck, Jacob, (W)
Mann, Henrich, (W)
Marterstock, Albrecht Dietrich, (W)
Martin, Johann Conrad
Marvin, Maria Magdalena
Mathesin, Ann
Mattheus, Johann Martin
Matheus, Andreas
Matheus, Georg, E)
Matheus, Henrich, (E)
Maul, Johann Friderich, (N)
Maul, Johannes & widow, (N)

Maul, Christoph
Mauer, Georg
Mauer, Johan Georg
Mauer, Peter, (W)
Mauser, Johan Georg
Mausin, Eva
May, Christoph, his widow
Mayin, Otillia
May, Peter
Mengelin, Anna Maria, (N)
Menges, Johannes
Mentgen, Ferdinand
Merckel, Frederick, (W)
Mertzin, Anna Catharina
Mess, Henrich
Messerin, Anna Margretha, (N)
Meyer, Christian, (W)
Meyer, Henrich
Meyer, Friderick
Meyer, Henrich
Meyerin, Elizabeth
Meyin, Meyin, (N)
Meyin, Barbara
Meysenheim, Anna Gertrud
Michael, Hans Henrich
Michael, Johan Georg
Michael, Niclaus
Milch, Johan Eberhard
Milges, Johan Wilhelm
Minckler, Kilian
Mittler, Johannes
Mohin, Maria, (N)
Moor, Henrich, (W)
Moor, Johan Christ
Moor, Philipp Wilhelm
Morellin, Anna Eva, (N)
Motsch, Johannes
Muller, Adam
Muller, Johann Christoph
Muller, Johann Wilhelm
Muller, Johannes, 1st.
Muller, Johannes, his widow
Muller, Johannes, 2nd.
Muller, Adam
Muller, Philipp, 1st., (W)
Muller, Philipp, 2nd.
Muller, Philipp, 2nd., his wiodw
Muller Johann Conrad
Muller, Johann Wilhelm
Muller, Johann Henrich
Mullerin, Christina
Muller, Samuel
Muller, Johann Georg, (E)
Mullerin, Catharina, (N)
Mullerin, Anna Maria
Mullerin, Anna Margretha
Mullerin, Anna Margretha
Musinger, Jacob
Musig, Johan Jost
Musig, Viet, (E)

Neff, Georg Friderick, (N)
Nehr, Carl, (E)
Nelles, Johan Georg, (E)
Nellesin, Maria Elizabeth
Nelles, Johan Wilhelm, (E)
Nerbel, Johan Georg
Ness, Georg Wilhelm, his widow
Netzbackes, Johan Martin, (E)
Newkirch, Johan Henrich, (N)

Netthaber Quiriness
Neiss, Abraham, his widow, (N)
Noll, Bernhard
Nollin, Anna Margaretha

Oberbach, Peter (W)
Oberbach, Georg
Oberbach, Johann Peter
Oberer, Johan Jacob his widow
Oberin, Anna
Off, Jacob, (N)
Ohrendorff, Henrich

Pach, Daniel, his widow
Peter, Philipp
Peterin, Anna Gertrude
Petri, Gertrude
Petri, Johan Jost, (E)
Pfeffer, Michael, his widow, (N)
Pfeiffer, Severin, his child
Pfeiffer, Henrich, his widow
Pfuhl, Johan Peter
Philips, Peter
Planck, Johannes, (N)
Plies, Emerich
Poffner, Johannes Paul
Proppert, Johann Jost
Prunet, Paul
Pulver, Johan Wilhelm

Rabel, Daniel
Rainault, Peter
Rainault, iPerre
Rauch, Niclaus
Raudenbusch, Johann, his widow
Rauscher, Martin
Rausch, Caspar, (E)
Raw, Niclaus
Rawin, Anna Joh & Georg
Reich, Balthasar
Reichard, Joseph, (W)
Reiffenberg, Johann Georg, (E)
Reinbold, Matheus, (E)
Reisdorff, Johannes
Reitzbackes, Johannes, (W)
Reitschuff, Johan Paul, (E)
Reuther, Henrich
Rickardt, Conrad
Richter, Andreas, (N)
Riclausin, Christina
Riedtin, Anna Catharina
Riedt, Johann Leonhard
Riegel, Christoph
Riehl, Gottfried, (W)
Rietich, Johann Peter
Rietichin, Amalia
Reisch, Jacob, (E)
Ritznig, Johannes
Rohrbachin, Anna Elizabeth
Romsch, Christian
Romer, Georg, (N)
Roos, Andreas, (W)
Roschmann, Johannes, (N)
Rosenbaum, Bernhard
Rosenweig, Agnes Gertrude
Rothin, Anna Catherin, (N)
Rouch, Friderich
Rues, Ludwig
Ruffner, Thomas
Ruger, Johann Philipp
Ruhl, Niclaus

Salbach, Johannes
Salbach, Johann Edmund
Saxin, Anna Gertrude
Saxin, Anna Maria, (N)
Schaff, Wilhelm, (E)
Schaffer, Friderich, (E)
Schaffer, Johannes
Schaffer, Joseph
Schaffer, Georg, (W)
Schaffer, Reinhard, (E)
Schaffer, Johann Werner, (E)
Schaffer, Jacob, (W)
Schaffer, Jost Henrich
Schaffer, Gerhard, (E)
Schaffer, Johann Niclaus
Schafferin, Elizabeth
Schafferin, Maria Elizabetha
Schafferin, Maria Margretha, (N)
Schaib, Hyeronimus, (W)
Schaid, Anthon
Schantz, David
Schawerin, Magdalena
Schawerman, Conrad, (E)
Schellin, Anna Margretha
Schellin, Anna Gertrude
Schenckel, Jonas
Schenckelberg, Christina
Scherl, Jacob
Scherer, Johann Theobald
Scherer, Ulrich, his widow
Schermann, Henrich, (N)
Schienck, Michael
Schlicherin, Anna Margretha
Schieffer, Philipp, (E)
Schleumer, Mathias, (W)
Schley, Johann Peter
Schmidt, George Adam
Schmidt, Adam, his widow
Schmidt, Johann Adam
Schmiden, Elizabetha
Schmidt, Johann Georg, (E)
Schmidt, Georg Volbert & Adam
Schmidt, Henrich, Sr., (N)
Schmidt, Henrich, Jr.
Schmidt, Johann Henrich, (E)
Schmidt, Ludwig, (E)
Schmidt, Martin
Schmidt, Johann Wilhelm
Schmidt, Niclaus
Schmidt, Peter, (E)
Schmidt, Valentin
Schmidt, Ulrich
Schmidin, Gertrude
Schmidin, Anna Barbara
Schmidin, Margretha, Adam & Michael, (N)
Schneiderin, Catharin & Peter
Schneider, Jacob
Schneider, Henrich
Schneider, Jacob
Schneider, Johannes 1st, (E)
Schneider, Johannes 2nd, (N)
Schneider, Johann Wilhelm, Sr., (N)
Schneider, Johann Wilhelm, Jr.
Schneider, Johann Dietrich
Schneider, Johann Wilhelm, (E)
Schnell, Jacob, (E)
Schottin, Anna Maria
Schramm, Henrich
Schreiber, Albertus

Schremle, Henrich, (W)
Schuch, Johann Wilhelm
Schuch, Johannes, (E)
Schucherin, Anna Catharin
Schultheis, Johannes, (E)
Schultheis, Johann Georg
Schultheisin, Anna Barbara
Schultzin, Anna Elizabetha
Schumacher, Jacob
Schumacher, Thomas, (E)
Schumacher, Daniel, (N)
Schumacherin, Anna Eva
Schunemann, Hermann
Schuppmann, Herman
Schultz, Michael & Andreas, (E)
Schultz, Johann Adam
Schutz, Adam
Schutz, Philip, 1st
Schutz, Catharina & Philipp 2nd, (W)
Schwalb, Johannes, (E)
Schwedin, Anna Elizabetha, (W)
Schwitzler, Henrich
Segendorff, Johann Adam, (E)
Seibs, Henrich, his widow
Sein, Johann Peter, (E)
Selher, Johann Adam
Seuberb, Johann Martin
Sex, Henrich, his widow, (E)
Sibelin, Anna Getha
Signer, Johannes, his widow, (N)
Simendinger, Ulrich, (N)
Simon, Philipp, his widow
Simon, Wilhelm
Simonin, Anna Margretha
Simonin, Maria Magdalena
Sittenich, Christian, (E)
Spanheimer, Johann Georg, (W)
Speder, Johannes
Speichermann, Sebastian
Spickermann, Johann Herman
Spies, Peter, (E)
Spoon, Henrich
Spuler, Jacob
Stahl, Henrich
Stahl, Johannes
Stahl, Rudolph, (E)
Stahl, Joseph
Stayger, Niclaus
Stayger, Stephen
Stambuchin, Anna Margretha
Staringer, Niclaus
Stein, Martin
Sterenberger, Jacob, (N)
Stier, Jost
Stockelin, Anna Maria
Stoppelbein, Peter
Storr, Michael, (N)
Straub, Johannes, (W)
Streithin, Magdalena, (W)
Streith, Christian, (N)
Stickhauser, Balthasar
Stubenrauch, Georg Henrich, (W)
Stuber, Henrich Balthasar, (E)
Stuber, Jacob
Stuckrad, Johann Wilhelm, (N)
Stumpff, Johan Georg
Stupp, Martin
Sutz, Johan Dietrich

Taschen, Hubert
Theis, Johan Philipp, (E)

Thiel, Adolph
Thomas, Henrich
Thomas, Andreas
Thomas, Henrich Peter
Thomas, Johann Georg
Taberin, Anna Maria
Trillheuser, Johannes, (N)
Uhl, Carol
Uhl, Henrich
Ulrich, Johannes Elias
Umbertro, Valentin
Vandeberg, Cornelius
Velten, Johann Wilhelm
Vogt, Simon, (N)
Volbert, Jacob, his widow
Vollandin, Anna Regina
Wagner, Johann Christ
Wagner, Peter
Walrath, Gerhard
Walborn, Johan Adam, (E)
Wallrath, Henrich Conrad
Wannemacher, Dietrich, (N)
Wannemacher, Peter
Wanner, Ludwig
Warembourg, Maria
Warno, Jacob, (E)
Weber, Henrich
Weber, Valentin
Weber, Niclaus, (E)
Weber, Jacob, (E)
Weber, Wigand
Weberin, Otillia
Wegle, Michael
Weydknecht, Andreas, (N)
Weidschopff, Johann Peter
Weillin, Catharina
Weis, Stephan
Weis, Mathias
Weisborn, Georg
Weiser, Johann Conrad, (E)
Weisin, Susanna, (N)
Weller, Hyeronimus, (W)
Wendelin, Anna Juliana
Wennerich, Balthasar, (N)

Wennerich, Benedict
Werner, Michael
Weydin, Gertrude
Wickhausen, Peter, (N)
Widerwachs, Henrich, (E)
Wies, Melchoir
Wilhelm, Paul
Wilhelm, Anthony, his widow
Wilhelm, Niclaus, his widow
Windecker, Hartman, (E)
Winniger, Ulrich
Winther, Henrich, (E)
Wisener, Johannes
Wittman, Johan Martin
Wittmachin, Maria Catharina
Wolleben, Peter, (W)
Wohleben, Philipp, (W)
Wohleben, Christoph
Wohleben, Valentin, (W)
Wohleben, Michael
Wohleben, Anna Catharina
Wolbach, Engelbert
Wolbert, Niclaus
Wolffin, Anna Gertrude
Wolffin, Maria Clara
Wolffin, Maria Catharina
Wormbs, Christian
Woschel, Peter Anthoni
Woschel, Augustin
Wulffen, Gottfried
Wurhmserin, Anna, (N)
Wust, Conrad
Zangerin, Johannes, (N)
Zehe, Johannes, (E)
Zeller, Johann Henrich
Zeller, Johannes, (E)
Zerbe, Philipp, (E)
Zerbe, Martin
Zimmerman, Johan Jacob
Zipperle, Bernhard
Zufeld, Johan Georg
Zwickin, Veronica, (N)
847 names.

(THE END)

A Review of the Food List
By Boyd Ehle

Dear Editor:

While your appreciation of the Hunter food list of the Palatines properly weigh its key value for the family names of a large number of Mohawk valley descendants, its full value can only be realized by careful study to eliminate errors in spelling and in Anglacising the German names as well as to reconcile the list of names with the changes that have followed in the spelling with the pasage of more than two centuries. Full data of these changes and errors are not available and any attempt to now cover the subject would be futile. However the necessity for discrimination, to encourage and to make a beginning the following instances of variations from the list are noted:

List   Variations

Bauman–Bowman
Barnhard–Barnhart
Beyer--Baer--Behr
Boshaard–Boshart
Brach–Brock
Braun–Brown
Busch–Bush
Cast--Kast
Christman–Cristman--Chrisman
Dachstatter–Dagsstatter-- Dockstader
Deuchert--Deichert--Dygart
Dillenbach--Dillebag--Tillebagh--Dillenbeck
Echard–Eacker–Aker
Fahling–Fehling–Failing
Fischer--Fisher
Franck--Frank
Frolich--Fraley--Fraleigh
Friderick–Frederick
Fucks--Fox
Gerlach–Garlob–Garlock
Giesler–Geesler–Keesler
Conderman–Conterman–Contryamn
Glock--Klock
Harter–Herter
Hartwig–Hartwick
Hayd–Haight
Henrich--Henry
Hirchemer–Herkomer--Herkimer
Hoffman–Huffman
Horne–Horn
Huls–Hultz
Ittich–Ittig
Jager–Yager

Jung–Young
Kasselman–Casselman
Kayser–Kaiser--Keyser
Kneskern--Knieskern
Koch--Cook
Kolsch–Kolesch
Krembs–Crems–Gramps
Laib–Lipe
Lancker–Leniger
Laucks--Laux--Loucks
Manck–Mang
Meyer–Mayer--Maier
Muller–Miller
Nehr--Neher
Nelles--Nellis
Noll–Knoll
Petri–Patrie–Petrie
Pfeiffer--Piper
Reichard–Richard
Rouch–Rauch
Shawerman--Showerman
Scherer–Shearer
Scherman--Sherman
Sprecher–Spraker
Schienck–Schenck
Schmidt--Smith
Schneider--Snyder
Schnell–Snell
Schultheis–Shults
Schumacher--Shoemaker–Schoonmaker
Salzman--Saltsman
Suts--Suits
Seybert–Seibert--Sibert
Spoon–Spohn
Staringer--Staring–Starin
Stompff--Stumf
Thiel–Tiel–Teall
Wagner–Waggoner
Wannemacher–Wannemaker
Zehe–Zeh
Zimmerman--Timmerman
Zeller–Zoller

The list also enables some corrections to be made in local history that Hendrick Frey came with the Palatines in 1709 instead of in 1689 as stated by Simms in his Frontiersmen. This correction is also confirmed by the London List. It is also noted that Herkimers appear in this 1709 emmigration which is a correction to Benton's History of Herkimer county. The Zollers also appear in the 1709 list which is a variation from the family tradition.

It will be noted that many family names have "in" added which is merely the German way of indication of female members of the family and does not indicate another family.

Yours truly,
BOYD EHLE.

LIST OF SCHOLARS AT THE FREE SCHOOL, JOHNSTOWN. NO DATE GIVEN. PROBABLY IN 1769

Richard Young
Peter Young
Hendrick Young
Richard Cotter
Hendrick Rynnion
James Mordon
Daniel Cammel
Samuel Davis
Reneir Vansiclan
Jacob Veder
Randal M'Donald
John Foilyard
Peter Runnion
Peter Potman
Jacob Doran
David Doran
Jeromy Doran
Adam M'Donald
Abraham Boice
Adam M'Donnald
Caleb M'Carty
Hendrick Collinger

Jacob Servos
John Servos
John Miller
James M'Gregar
George Binder
Christian Rider
Bernard Rider
Simeon Scouten
Francis Bradthau
John Everot
Sarah Connor
Leny Rynnion
Betsey Garlick
Baby Garlick
Rebecca Vansiclan
Caty Cammel
Caty Garlick
Mary M'Intyre
Peggy Potman
Eve Waldromm
Leny Waldroff
Margaret Servos
Catharine Servos

Males and Female —45.

Documentary History of New York, Vol. 4, page 416

MOHAWK SCHOOL AT FORT HUNTER

Began to Open School April ye 17th, 1769.

Augt. 28th 1769. A List of The Indians Children belonging to the Free School at Fort Hunter near the Mohawk River in the County of Albany and Province of New York with their Tribes.

Bear Tribe David, David, Abraham, John, Jacob, Peter, Joseph, Adam, Brant, Kreenas, Johannes, Peter, Nellithe Nellithe (Females)..............15
Wolf Tribe Thomas, Paul, Jacob, John, Daniel, Catharine, Susanna, Catharine. (Females) ....8.

Turtle Tribe Isaac, Joseph, Daniel, Jacob, Thomas Christianna, Catharine. (Females)........7.

Total 30.

Pr. Me Colin Mc(Leland) Schoolmaster.

Sr. According to your Direction I have sent your Honour this List.

LIST OF PALATINES IN 1709

COPIED FROM THE MANUSCRIPT IN LONDON, ENGLAND

Palatine Emigrants Into England to June 20, 1709
Copies of notes taken at British Museum.
The original lists are in C. O. 388:76, D. 57-70.

1. List taken at St. Catherines May 6, 1709, 852 persons.
2. List taken at Walworth, May 27, 1709, 1193 persons.
3. List taken at St. Catherine's June 2, 1709, 1745 persons.
4. List taken at St. Catherine's and Deftford June 15, 11, 1709.

Note—In the following son or sons and daughters or daughters followed by figures denote that the head of the family was married and had that number of children of the ages noted. The abbreviations Ref., Luth., Cath. refer to their religion. Segregation of occupation or trade is made.

Note—Second immigration to New York sailed January 10, 1710 had a few of these listed here.

BOARD OF TRADE MISCELLANEOUS
Vol. 2, D. 57

LEGEND

Hs. V.—Husbandman and Vinedresser.
Hus.—Husbandman.
Hrd.—Herdsman.
*—Unmarried.

A

Adeler, Henry, weaver, age 41, son 12, R.
Anke, Joseph, miller, age 28, R.
Andrew, Benedict, smith, age 40, son 1½, L.
Albrecht, James, Hs. & V., age 26, Luth.

B

Bergleuchter, Anton, tanner, age 24, R.
Belle, Jacob, Hrd., age 20, son 1½, C.
Bauer, Cristina, unmarried, age 23, R.
Bettinger, Anna Cristina*, age 60.
Bien, John, weaver, age 24, Bap.
Boos, John Henry*, tailor, age22, son 1, daughter 5, L.
Bruchly, John Henry, weaver, age 38, sons 4-2, R.
Buchler, John, butcher, age 48, daughters 16-12-11, L.

Blesinner, Daniel, Hs. & V., age 27, daughters 4-1 3 mos.
Bakell, Philip, Hs. & V., age 53, son 10, daughters 12-8-6-6-½..
Berg, Frederick, Hs. & V., age 32, son 3, daughter 1, L.
Bolker, Charles, Hs. & V., age 25, R.
Bollon, Cristoff, Hs. & V., age 26, son 4, daughter 2-1½, Ref.
Buff, George, Hus., age 28, daughter 1, L.
Becker, Gerhard, Hus., age 38, son ½, daughter 5, R.
Brectsch, Lorentz, Hs. & V., age 26, R.
Bauman, Michael, Hs. & V., age 37, daughter 8, R.
Bertsler, Adam, Hs. & V., age 30, sons 8-4, daughter 1, L.
Bahr, John, Hs. & V., age 38, sons 8-6-3, Ref.
Bauer, George, smith, age 40, L.
Bauer, Christian, carpenter, age 30, sons 8-6 daughters 10-4-1, R.

C

Clemens, Gerhard, Hs. & V., age 28, sons 5-1½, Baptist.
Closterbeker, Hs. & V., age 31, son 6, daughters 4-1, L.
Catherine, servant maid, unmarried, age 36, R.

D

Dixon, David (Englishman), Hs. & V., age 40, son 10, Ref.
Durck, John Adam, Hs. & V., age 36, son 10, daughter 12-2, Cath.
Daun, George, Hs. & V., age 35, daughter 2, C.
Daninger, Jacob, Hs. & V., age 38, sons 6-1, daughter 10, L.
Drechsler, John Peter, Hs. & V., age 28, son 1, L.
Du Bois, Abraham, tobacco planter, age 38, sons 13-9-3, daughter 7, R.
Durbecker, Hus., age 26, daughter 2, R.
Degen, Felix, smith, age 23, R.
Dieterich, John*, saddler, age 44 son 2,C.
De Rockeford, Peter, butcher, age 38, sons 12-10, daughters 15-3, R.

E

Ends, Matthew, Hs. & V., age 50, son 20, Ref.
Engelsbreucher, Nicol, Hs. & V., age 57, daughter 15, Ref.
Erkel Bernhard, Hs. & V., age 33, Ref.
Ebert, Hartman, Hs. & V., age 30, Ref.
Ende, John Philip am, Hs. & V., age 35, son 9 mo., daughter 3, L.
Eyeach, John Valentine, wheelwright, age 22, L.
Escherich, John, miller, age 37, L.
Emichen, Ernst, Hs. & V., age 55, sons 9-6-5-1½, L.
Eschelmans, Anna*, age 37,, son 16, Bap.

F

Faubel, John, age 30, daughters 1-½, Luth.
Frey, Conrad, Hs. & V., age 61, sons 17-4, daughters 25-19.
Fahman, Jacob, Hs. & V., age 34, daughters 7-5, R.
Friede, Cathrina, unmarried, age 30, R.
Fodder, John, Hus., age 38, sons 9-4, daughter 1, R.

G

Garrinot, Peter, Hs. & V., age 37, Cath.
Gnaed, Benedict, Hs. & V., age 60, son 24, daughter 25, Ref.
Gerhardt, John George, Hs. & V., agr 41, sons 12-2, daughters 16-14-8-6, Ref.
Gaisell, George, Hs. & V., age 42, sons 6-1, C.
Glaents, John, Hs. &V., age 46, son 18, R.
Goebell, Paul, Hus., age 59, son 23, daughter 25, L.
Gring, Jacob, Hus., age 26, daughter 1 R.
Guthzeit, William*, carpenter, age 29, son 3, daughter 2, L.
Gruendner, Matthew, smith, age 33, R.
Goth, Henry, miller, age 30, R.

Galattic, John Jacob, shoemaker, age 32, son 12, daughter 6, R.
Gessinger, Henry, carpenter, age 28, L.
Galathe, Jacob, carpenter, age 75, R.

H

Humacher, Nicolas, Hs. & V., age 33, son 6, daughters 4-1, Ref.
Hoblar, Abraham, Hs. & V., age 32 , son 6, daughter 1, Ref.
Haun, Andrew, Hs. & V., age 50, sons 17-11-11-8-4, daughters 13-14, Luth.
Hornigh, John George, Hs. & V., age 38, sons 8-2, daughters 12-10, Ref.
Hirzeach, Martin, Hs. & V., age 56, sons 24-14, daughters 21-18, Ref.
Herman, Valentine, Hs. & V., age 34, sons 7-½, Luth.
Helfert, Peter, Hs. & V., age 49, Ref.
Heidmer, Peter, Hs. & V., age 30, daughters 6-2½, 3 mos, L.
Herman, Peter, Hs. & V., age 28, son 6-2 and 4 mos., daughter 1 mo, R.
Hass, John, Hs. & V., age 52, sons 16-11, daughters 9-3, R.
Harlaender, Conrad, Hs. & V., age 30 ,sons 4½-3 C.
Hoffart, John Adam, Hs. & V., age 27, L.
Hesse, John, Hs. & V., age 40, daughters 7-4, R.
Harman, Daniel, Hs. & V., age 25, sons 2, daughters 4, R.
Herman, Jacob, Hs. & V., age 28, L.
Hassmer, John, Hs. & V., age 25, R.
Herman, Niclas, Hs. & V., age 52, R.
Hecky, Peter, Hs. & V., age 26, R.
Hocky, Andres, Hs. & V., age 22, R.
Hartman, John George, Hus., age 40, son 9, C.
Hobscher, Andres, Hus., age 50, son 22, daughters 13-9-8-5, Bap.
Harman, Niclas, Hus., age 52, R.
Hagder, John, Hus., age 27, R.
Hebenstreit, John Jas., locksmith, age 30, R.
Heffen, Bartin, smith, age 30, R.
Hohenstein, Christian, shoemaker, age 37, sons 4-1, daughter 6, C.
Heyde, Peter, carpenter, age 28, son 1½, R.
Hagenbeck, Frederick, carpenter, age 30, sons 3-6, C.
Haki, John George, mason, age 30, daughters 9-5-4, C.
Henich, Lorentz, cooper, age 48, son 2½, daughter 1 3 mo., R.
Hoffstaeter, Philip, book binder, age 19, R.
Hirtzbach, Anton Hs. & Vr., age 36, sons 10-8-5, daughter 4, Ref.

J

Jacobi, John Thomas, Hus., age 38, sons 13-9, daughter 1, L.
Jalethc, John Wm., Hus., age 30, son 6½, daughter 12, R.

K

Kaff, Bazar, Hs. & V., age 36, sons 14, 12-3 mos., Cath.
Kliein, Michael, Hs. & V., age 28, daughters 6-½, Luth.
Kueffer, John, Hs. & V., age 38, daughters 3-1, Ref.
Klein, Peter, Hs. & V., age 42, son 2½, daughter 3 mos., C.
Klein, John Jacob, Hs. & V., age 25, son 4, R.
Klein, John, Hs. & V., age 55, 14-6, C.
Klug, George, Hs. & V., age 37, son 1½ R.
Klacmer Ludwig, Hs. & V., age 37, sons 3-4, daughters 6-4, L.
Kaldaver, Valentine, Hs. & V., age 34, sons 6-1, daughters 14-9-3, C.
Kuhner, Jacob, Hs. & V., age 30, sons 10-8-6, daughter 2, L.
Koll, Henry, Hs. & V., age 30, daughters 6-3½, Baptist.
Kolb, Arnold, Hs. & V., age 28, Bap.
Kinfeller, Frederick, Hus., age 37, son 5, daughter 12, R.
Kuhlwein, Philip, Hus., age 26, R.
Keyser, George Frederick*, smith, age 40, daughters 7-5, L.
Koenig, John Adam, tailor, age 30, L.
Kirchofen, Francis Ludwig, carpenter, age 37, R.

Klein, Michael*, sister in law of, unmarried, age 20, R.

L

Lang, Philip, Hs. & V., age 35, son 13, daughter 3, C.
Lauber, Jacob, Hs. & V., age 37, daughters 7-6-2, Ref.
Le Pas, John, Hus., age 47, daughters 20-18, R.
Le Ferro, Abram*, Hus., age 50, son 7, daughter 20, R.
Leucho, Lewis, smith, age 54, son 22, L.
Lup, Henry, miller, age 28, sons 11-9-6, daughter 8, R.
Lucas, Frances, weaver, age 46, sons 17-11, daughters 18-8-6-5-3, R.
La Forge, John Wm.*, miner, age 50, R.

M

Machtig, Jacob, schoolmaster, age 40, sons 11-6, daughters 13-12, Ref.
Mendingen, John, age 40, Hs. & V., sons 5-2, Ref.
May, David, Hs. & V., age 24, Ref.
Mesner, Sylvester, Hs. & V., age 45, son 14-5, daughter 23-7, R.
Meyer, Henry, Hs. & V., age 41, daughters 5-½, Ref.
Mayer, Hartman, Hs. & V., age 38, son 9, daughters 7-4, R.
Moor, John, Hus., age 25, R.
Moor, Austin, Hus., age 22, R.
Moor, John Wm., Hus., age 18, R.
Mendon, Jacob, shoemaker, age 22, R.
Mason, Niclas*, weaver, age 46, son 17, R.
Meyers Henry, sister in law of, unmarried, age 42, R.
Muller, Daniel, baker, age 50, R.
Muller, John Jacob*, shoemaker, age 42 sons 13-12-10-8-6-4, dau. 15, R.
Mueller, Valentine, Hs. & V., age 23, R.
Martins, Gertrud*, age 42, son 9, R.

N

Nagel, John, Hs. & V., age 40, daughters 9, R.
Notzel, Rudolf, Hus., age 38, daughters 8-7-2, R.
Neidhofer, John Quirinus, carpenter, age 42, son 8, daughter 20-17, L.

O

Obender, Samuel, Hs. & V., age 35, daughter 2, R.
Oberhaltzer, Mark, Hus., age 45, sons 10-8-3, daughters 6-1, Bap.

P

Penning, Daniel, baker, age 22, L.
Pelle, Peter*, Hus., age 24, R.
Presler, Valentine, Hs. & V., age 40, sons 6-4-1-½, daughters 10-8, Cath.
Pfeiffer, John Jacob, Hus., age 42, son 8, daughter 3, R.

R

Rohrbach, Christian, Hs. & V., age 34, daughter 3 mos., Ref.
Reuling, Jacob, Hs. & V., age 28, daughter 1, L.
Rath, John, Hs. & V., age 29, son 2, daughter 6 days, R.
Rheime, John am, Hs. & V., age 30, C.
Rauscha, George, Hs. & V., age 24, L.
Riedels, George*, motherin law, age 50, L.
Raths, Jane*, age 50, Cath.
Rose, Anna*, age 53, son 9, daughter 17-4, R.
Rose, Catherine*, age 24, daughter 1½.
Ruabner, Anton, Hs. & V., age 30, sons 5-3-4, daughter 2-½, L.
Rudolff, John, Hs. & V., age 14, L.
Reiser, John Peter, cooper, age 40, sons 14-12-8-6-1½, C.
Rebell, Jacob, miller, age 30, R.

Rider, Niclas, weaver, age 38, R.
Roherluth, George Adam, weaver, age 45, sons 12-9, daughters 17-14, Bap.
Riedell, John George, tailor, age 30, sons 1, daughters 5, L.

S

Shaver, John Adam, Hs. & V., age 35, sons 8-5, daughter 2, R.
Schletzer, Jeremy, Hs. & V., age 53, sons 7-5, daughters 13-9 3 mos., L.
Schaeffer, John Conrad, Hs. & V., age 23, R.
Schuctz, John, Hus., age 46, daughters 6-4-3-1½, R.
Schrager, Andrese, Hus., age 53, daughters 23-20, Bap.
Stacnler Peter*, Hus., age 24.
Schlingluff, John, Hrd., age 30, sons 20-15-11, R.
Smith, Henry, butcher, age 53, sons 22-19-12-6, daughter 15, L.
Schlottenhofer, Christian, shoemaker, age 38, sons 6-1, R.
Schaeffer, John, carpenter, age 44, sons 14-10-2-5days, daughters 8-6, R.
Srhaeffer, John, mason, age 26, son 1, R.
Seibert, Conrad, Hs. & V., age 31, daughters 1-½, R.
Schneider, John Michael, Hs. & V., age 24, son 10, daughter 1½, L.
Schneider, Philip, Hs. & V., age 36, sons 10-3, daughter 3 mo., C.
Smith, Jacob, Hs. & V., age 51, sons 14-10, daughter 4, L.
Schmitzer, John Martin, Hs. & V., age 26, son 1, C.
Schaeffer, Joseph, Hs. & V., age 38, son 10-3, daughter 14-12-8-6, R.
Seibert, Martin, H. S., age 35, son 2, daughter 4, R.
Schwangel, John, Hs. & V., age 40, son 12, daughters 4-2-1, L.
Spusniar, Jacob, Hs. & V., age 30, son 1, R.
Shawartze, John, Hs. & V., age 32, son 1, 9 mos., daughter 7, R.
Schwartz, Matthias, Hs. & V., age 33, sons 11-4 daughter 8,Luth.
Showneiss, John, Hs. & V., age 48, sons 1-½, daughters 14-12, Ref.
Smith, John, Hs. & V., age 47, sons 7-5-3-1, daughters 24-17-16-13-11-9, Luth.
Shawk, Peter, Hs. & V., son 1, daughter 1½, Luth.
Schoen, Maria Cathrina*, age 38, sons 10-8-4, daughter 1½, Cath.
Schwaegerin, Apollonis*, age 50, R.
Stutz, John Eberhard, cooper, age 44 sons 7-8 daughter 5, L.

T

Thor, Conrad am, Hs. & V., age 30, daughters 1-½, C.
Trombauer, Nicolas, Hs. & V., age 33, son 6, daughter 5-3-4, C.
Thereux, Daniel, Hs. & V., age 44, son 6, daughter 2, R.
Thomas, John George, Hus., age 50, son 7-2, daughter 5.
Trumph, John Michael*, Hus., age 48, son 18, R.
Truat, John, brewer, age 40, sons 10-6, R.
Turch, Caspar, student Divinity, age 35, single, Ref.
Tanner, Catherine*, age 35, daughter 6, Cath.

V

Vogt, Abraham, Hs. & V., age 50, son 12, daughters 16-18-7-4, R.
Vogt, John, Hs. & V., age 25, son 2, R.
Volweider, Jacob, Hs. & V., age 27, Baptist.

W

Wismar, Jacob, Hus., age 50, son 20, daughter 22, Baptist.
Wandel, Arthur (Leibengur), Hs. & V., age 53, son 28, Ref.
Wagner, John, Hs. & V., age 43, sons 10-8, daughters 12-5-3, Ref.
Wenig, Peter, Hs. & V., age 26, daughters 1½, L.
Weyner, Henry, Hr. & V., age 40, sons 8-4, daughter 12, L.
Weitzell, John Hs. & V., age 29, sons 1½-3 mos., L.
Weinrich, Hs. & V., age 40, sons 7-5-3, daughter 15, L.
Warner, Christoff, Hs. & V., age 33, son 1, L.
Weber, John Engel, carpenter, age 46, daughters 20-18-13-8-4, L.
Weber, John Jacob, carpenter, age 26, L.

Winter, Maria Cathrina*, age 50, daughter 20, Cath.
Warambour, Mary*, age 56, sons 24-23-19-17, daughters 22, R.
Wagner, Mary Elizabeth, unmarried, age 24, R.
Wentzen, Peter, Hus., age 25, R.
Willich, Peter, smith, age 30, daughters 5-2, R.
Walter, John George, weaver, age 45, sons 12-9½, daughters 17-7, R.

Z

Zimmerman, John Wolff, smith, age 53, sons 20-16, daughters 22-18-11-5, L.
Zinkhan, Conrad, Hrd., age 37, son 1 3mo., daughter 1 3mo-4, R.
Zaitz, John Peter, smith, age 30, R.
Ziegler, Michael, weaver, age 25, L.
Zitel Jacob, Hus., age 25, R.
Zeber, John, Hs. & V., age 46, sons 18-4, daughters 11-8, R.
Zeisler, Lorentz, Hs. & V., age 40, sons 6-3, daughter 1, R.

Such as entered their names last.

No. of
the family   Names

   4   Johan Lang
   5   Eberhard Stuts.
   4   Benedict Pens
   1   Johannes Bohm
   1   Philip Denias
   1   Christoph Albenz
   1   Gottlieb August Lichtnegger
   1   Jacob Graeff whose parents live in Pennsylvania, a boy 10 years
      of age.
   1   George Klug, his sister and son, a boy 15 years of age.

Second List of Palatines

List taken at Walworth, May 27, 1709, 1193 Persons.

SECOND LIST

Vol. 2 B 64. The Second List of 1193 Palatines Lately come over from Germany into this Kingdom taken at Walworth 27th of May, 1709

A

Ade, John, Hs. & V., age 56, sons 17-5, daughters 15-6, L.
Arm, David, Hs. & V., age 52, sons 21-13-8, daughters 17-6-2, R.
Aman, John, tailor, age 27, R.

B

Bauer, Christian, Hs. & V., age 28, son 1, R.
Becker, Frederick, Hs. & V., age 23, L.
Baltz, John Philip, Hs. & V., age 18, L.
Buehler, John, Hs. & V., age 53, daughters 20-14-1, R.
Bernard, John George, Hs., also carpenter, age 36, sons 5-1, daughters 3, L.
Bach, John, Hs. & V., also gardener, age 37, son 7, daughters 13-11, C.
Bauman, Michael (Beukman?), Hs. & V., age 24, R.
Bonus, Julius, Hs. & V., age 31, sons 15-6-2, R.
Bush, Christian, Hs. & V., age 16, L.
Bush, Philip, Hs. & V., age 26, sons 15-10, daughters 8-3½, L.
Bonden, John, Hs. & V., age 34, daughters 5-3-1.
Bogenman, Jacob, Hs. & V., age 30, sons 2 1½, R.
Benus, John Jacob, Hs. & V., also mason, age 45, sons 14-12-8-7, dau. 11, L.
Buco, Jacob, Hs., age 28, son 5, daughters 3-1, R.
Bason, Nicol, Hs., age 34, sons 6-4, R.
Balmus, Nicol, Hs., age 28, son 3, daughter 2, L.
Blaum Herman, Hs., age 50 son 6, daughter 12, R.
Brunn, John Tiel, Hs., age 35, daughters 3 mos., C.
Busch, Caspar, Hs., also hunter, age 22, daughter 2, L.
Boehm, John Martin, Hs., age 30, L.
Boltz, George, Hs., age 50, sons 13-7-4, R.
Beck, John Jacob, Hs., age 50, son 18, daughters 20-13-10-8-6, L.
Bergman, Abraham, Hs., age 46, son 10 daughters 19-16-14-7, L.
Bash, Daniel, Hs., age 45, son 5, daughter 18, R.
Bauer, Elias, smith, age 23, R.
Barrabam, Jacob Wolf, tailor, age 34, daughters 4-2, R.
Becke, Ephraim, linen weaver, age 32, sons 4-3, L.
Bastian, Andreas, linen weaver, age 21, C.
Bishop, Ludwig, mason and stone cutter, age 19, L.
Baehr, Tobias, cooper and brewer, age 45, sons 11-9-6-3, daughter 14, R.
Bruder, Valentin, cooper and brewer, age 25, R.
Beck, John, mech. apprentice, age 22, L.
Biece, Mary Lucas*, age 52, daughters 25-14, sons 18-11-8, R.
Bingerin, Elizabeth*, age 24, daughter 2, R.

Barrabam, Anna Clara*, age 23, R.
Barba, Anna*, age 18, C.
Bertram, Hs. & V., age 21, R
Bessern, Dorothea*, age 25, L.

C

Cunitz John, Hs. & V., age 33, sons 15-5, daughter 1, C.
Conradt Martin, Hs. & V., age 45, sons 9-6, daughters 13-3, L.
Caslman, Christian, Hs. & V., age 37, son 2, L.
Cramer, Christian, Hs. & V., age 24, L.
Crass, Philip, Hs. & V., age 50, son 12, daughters 18-13-7-2, C.
Casselman, John, Hs., age 49, sons 10-3, daughters 19-13-½ L.
Codd, John, carpenter, age 26, L.
Clanenberg, Conrad butcher, age 38, L.
Crukot, Arnold, cooper and brewer, son 2, R.
ᴗauer, Jacob Mitter, linen weaver, age 40, sons 5-3, daughter 1, L.

D

Dietrich, John Peter, Hs. & V.,, age 35, son 8, daughters 5-15 mos., L.
Diestel, Peter Daube, Hs. & V., age 24, R.
Dunger, John, Hs., age 20, C.
Depper, Lobonus, Hs., age 41, sons 16-1½, daughters 12-4, C.
Duerr, Peter, Hs., also carpenter, age 37, son 4, daughters 8-2, R.
Debald, Francis, Hs., age 30, sons 7-5-3, R.
Debald, Conrad, Hs., age 27, son 2, daughters 8-5-4, R.
Daul, John Michel, Hs., age 22, L.
Duester, John, Hs., age 34, sons 9-3-½, daughter 6, R.
Daniel, tailor, age 24, R.
Diebolt, John Georg, tailor, age 20, R.
Dufin, Peter, linen weaver, age 53, R.
Dalem Lambert, carpenter, age 27, daughter 5, C.
Dietz, John Peter, carpenter, age 26, C.
Dinant, Peter, cooper and brewer, age 59, sons 11-9-7-6, R.
Dinkelin, Appolonia*, age 80, L.
Dresin, Gertrud*, age 30, C.

E

Emich, Paulus, Hs. & V., age 30, L.
Eckstedt, John George, Hs. & V., ag e 22, C.
Eyler, John Conradt, Hs., age 30, R.
Erhardt, John Simon, Hs., age 46, sons 6-3, daughter 8, R.
Eckart, Balzar, Hs. & V., age 23, son 2, C.
Ellenberger, George, cooper and brewer, age 45, son 15, R.
Eberhard, John, Hs. & V., age 30, sons 16-14-12, daughter 6, C.
Eck, Valentin, linen weaver, age 50, sons 16-10-7, daughters 12-5, C.
Ernmoch, Anna Eve*, age 44, sons 21-18, C.

F

Fuhrar, John, Hs. & V., age 40, sons 13-6, daughters 8-1-, C.
Frick, Henrich, Hs. & V., age 30, L.
Fusz, John, Hs. & V., age 30, son ½, daughters 6-3, R.
Frey, Henrich, carpenter, age 27, daughter ½, R.
Fisher, Simon, Hs., age 30, C.
Fuhrman, John Michel, Hs., age 47, daughters 13-7-4, L.
Fuss, Andreas, Hs., age 34, sons 9-6, daughters 11-3, R.
Fink, Andres, Hs., age 34, son 9, R.
Fischbach, John, Hs., age 35, sons 10-1, daughter 3, L.
Frederick, Wendel, tailor, age 50, son 8, daughters 18-4-½, L.
Friel, William, Hs. & V., age 50, son 8, daughter 13, L.
Fink, John Godfred, tailor, age 44, sons 18-10, L.

Frauch, Georg, linen weaver, age 30, sons 5-2, R.
Fleger, Zacharra, carpenter, age 36, sons 8-4, daughter 1, L.
Fuehrer, John Jacob, carpenter, age 26, C.

G

Geiger, David, Hs. & V., age 50, sons 2-3-10, daughters 5-4, R.
Gerby, John Michael, Hs. & V., age 29, son 7, daughter 3, R.
Gemelk, Michel, Hs., age 30, son 1, L.
Graeff, Henry, Hs., age 44, son 4, daughters 12-6, L.
Garter, John (Englishman), mason and stone cutter, age 40, R.
Guthman, Maria Barbara*, age 22, C.

H

Henckel, John George, Hs. & V., age 38, C.
Heidman, Gerhard, Hs. & V., age 20, L.
Hartbeck, Mathew, Hs. & V., age 30, C.
Hust, Jacob, Hs. & V., age 52, son 18, R.
Harnish, John, Hs. & V., age 24, son 2, R.
Hepman, Melchoir, Hs. & V., age 53, daughters 17-12-8, L.
Helwig, Henrich, Hs. & V., age 27, son 3, R.
Herber, John Jacob, Hs., age 18, L.
Helm, John Adam, Hs., age 44, C.
Holtzschuch John Jacob, Hs., age 31, daughters 16-4, L.
Habig, Conrad, Hs., age 50, sons 24-21, daughter 16, L.

Heischer John, Hs., also lineweaver, age 30, son 5, daughter 6, L.
Herman, Sebastian, smith, age 23, L.
Haber, Bartel, linen weaver, age 20, son 9 mos., daughters 11-6-4, L.
Hero, Henrich, linen weaver, age 33, son 8, daughter 5, R.
Hodell, Michael, Hs. & V., age 34, daughters 6-3, R.
Hach, John Peter, Hs. & V., age 60, son 20, R.
Hach, John, Hs. & V., age 30, son 14, R.
Holzer, John Hs. & V., also hunter, age 40, son 3, C.
Hartzog, Caspar, Hs. & V., age 34, sons 7-4, R.
Hartwig, Caspar, baker, age 38, sons 5-4, daughter 7, R.
Hahn, Johan Martin, Hs. & V., age 30, C.
Hermichel, Henrich, mason and stone cutter, age 46, son 5, daughters 9-2, R.
Hartung, Caspar, carpenter ,age 25, L.
Hartman, John Georg, cooper and brewer, age 28, son 1, L.
Hofman, Gabriel, turner, age 40, R.
Hatteman, Ulrich, turner, age 40, sons 10-4, daughters 9-5-2, Menonite.
Hertzog, Jacob Andreas, Hs. & V., age 38, sons 14-10-8, daughters 5-4, L.
Helm, Peter, laborer, age 30, sons 15-11-9-5-4 3 mos, daughter 7.
Hartwegin, Anne Elizabeth*, age 22, L.

I

Imberger, Andres, Hs. & V., age 22, L.

J

Jacky, Ulrich, linen weaver, age 31, R.
Jung, Abraham, a shoemaker, age 18, R.
Jacob, Christian, Hs. & V., age 34, sons 8-5-2, R.
Jordan, Conrad, Hs. & V., age 21, R.
John, Christoph, carpenter, age 33, L.
Jung, John, butcher, age 28, R.   ?
Jung, Jacob, tanner, age 25, R.
Jacob, John, apothecary, age 21, L.

Jungin, Elizabeth*, age 46, sons 24-12, daughters 19-6, L.

K

Klein, Jacob, Hs. & V., age 24, L.
Klessin, Maria*, age 24, L.
Kennel Samuel Hs., age 25, son 1 1-4, R.
Kuehn, Matthew, Hs. & V., age 34, son 2, C.
Keyser, Matthew, Hs. & V., age 38, daughter 12, R.
Krebs, John, Hs. & V., age 29, son 4, C.
Krebs, Peter, Hs. & V., age 35, sons 4-2, L.
Keyser, John Michel, Hs., age 46, sons 14-6, daughters 11-3.
Kraut, John George, Hs., age 28, R.
Kieser, John Adam, Hs., age 29, R.
Klingelstein, Nicol, Hs., age 36, sons 7-3, daughters 5-1, R.
Koener, Wolf, Hs., age 30, sons 4-2, L.
Kennleiter, John, Hs., age 38, sons 6-2, daughter 4, L.
Kuehn, Conrad, Hs., age 40, sons 14-11-8-2, R.
Kuntze, Nicol, wheelwright, age 33, sons 8-7-4, daughter ½, R.
Korman, John Jacob, wheelwright, age 50, son 20, daughter 19, L.
Kertner, Peter, wheelwright, age 46, sons 11-8-5, R.
Kopf, John, smith, age 30, C.
Krebsin, Salome*, age 50, R.
Kleus, John, tailor, age 24, daughter ½, R.
Kleus, Carl, tailor, age 16, R.
Korn, George, Hs. & V., age 50, daughter 7, L.
Kopf, Henrich, Hs. & V., age 38, son 12, daughters 10-7-5, R.
Kroen, John George, Hs. & V., age 38, daughter 2, R.
Klaus, Henrich, Hs. & V., age 36, daughters 7-2.
Keller, John, Hs. & V., age 28, son 2, C.
Keller, Nicol, Hs. & V., age 24, R.
Keller, John Jacob, Hs. & V., age 24, son 5, L.
Kless, Henry, a shoemaker, age 37, sons 6-1, daughters 10-8-4, L.
Kauffer, Daniel, linen weaver, also shoemaker, age 27, L.
Kling, John Conrad, baker, age 22, L.
Korman, John Peter, baker, age 37, son 5, daughter 1, R.
Kremmeln, Solomon, mason and stone cutter, age 23, R.
Kleinsin, Gertrud*, age 48, son 14, daughters 11-8, R.
Keiferin, Barbara, age 21, R.
Koesenn, Anna Catharine*, age 18, C.
Koernerin, Maria*, age 24, R.

L

Lambert, John, Hs., age 65, sons 11-8, daughters 13-9, C.
Lutz, John, Hs., also carpenter, age 35, sons 8-6-3, daughter 3 mos., C.
Ludorf, Conrad, Hs., age 19, R.
Lutz, John Adam, wheelwright, age 22, L.
Ludwig, John, tailor, age 35, sons 10-1, daughter 5, R.
Liebhan, John, tailor, age 36, son 12, C.
Ludolph, John, linen weaver, age 31, sons 5-3, daughter 7-½, R.
Lutz, John George, Hs. & V., age 49, son 3, daughters 14,10-8, R.
Lang, John, Hs. & V., age 49, sons 17-12-6, daughters 18-6.
Langhein, Christoph, Hs. & V., age 25, R.
Lorentz, Peter, Hs. & V., age 50, son 10, daughters 16-14-11, L.
Lutz (Lut), John Pete, Hs. & V., age 29, son 11, daughter 3-½, L.
Lut, Anton, Hs. & V., age 28, C.
Lescher, Sebastian, Hs. & V., age 40, sons 20-14-10-8-6, daughters 15-12-4-1, L.
Lorentz, John, Hs. & V., age 39, son 2, daughters 14-12-10-5-5, R.
Lickel, Daniel, Hs. & V., age 24, R.
Lash, Jacob, Hs., age 46, daughters 23-18, L.
Lutz, Cristoph, cooper and brewer, age 36, R.
Licktherin, Anna Maria*, age 30, son 2.

Licktherin, Margaret*, age 50, R.

M

Moor, Cleman, Hs., age 33, sons 6-2, daughters 8-4, R.
Minglen, Kilian, Hs., age 36, son 9, daughter 11-7, R.
Muntrian, Paul, Hs., age 38, sons 8-6-4, C.
Moret, Jacob, Hs., age 45, daughters 18-13-11, R.
Murin, Peter, Hs., age 30, son 5, daughter 20, R.
Muller, John Ludiger, smith, age 22, R.
Muschel, Jacob, tailor, age 25, son½, L.
Moritz, John Philip, schoolmaster, daughters 25-27, R.
Muller, Valentine, Hs. & V., age 32, son 6, L.
Mattern, William, Hs. & V., age 30, son 4, L.
Mattern, John George, Hs. & V., age 40, sons 14-4-1, daughters 20-17-8, L.
Misemer, Daniel, Hs. & V., age 28, son 3, daughters 5-1½, L.
Misner, Valentine, Hs. & V., age 23, sons 3-1, L.
Meurer, John Quirimus, age 53, sons 25-17, daughters 26-24, L.
Meyer, John Joseph, Hs. & V., age 24, son 1, R.
Muller, Henrich, Hs. & V., age 48, sons 24-16-12, daughters 18-9, C.
Martin, Matthew, Hs. & V., age 50, sons 11-5, daughter 18-12, C.
Martin, Thomas, baker, age 24, L.
Marx, Matthew, baker, age 23, C.
Muller, John Jacob, baker, age 30, son 1, daughter 1, R.
Meister, Jacob, mason and stone cutter, age 24, R.
Mueller, John Nicol, carpenter, age 22, C.
Mueller, Jacob, carpenter, age 37, sons 14-10-4, daughters 6-3, C.
Muller, John, miller, age 24, L.
Matthew, John, cooper and brewer, age 37, sons 3-5, daughter 11, C.
Milbert, John Martin, cooper and brewer, age 40, son 13, daughter 11-2, L.
Mehder, John Henry, cooper and brewer, age 28, R.
Mueckel, Ulrich, turner, age 36, son 3-1, R.
Mutten, Anna Maria*, age 50, R.
Meyer, John George, Hs. & V., age 28, C.
Muschelin, Anna Maria*, age 50, son 16, R.
Melkin, Anna Margaretha*, age 22, L.
Mueller, Peter, Hs. ,age 36, son 3, daughter 10, L.
Margareth, Elizabeth*, age 20, L.

N

Neubauer, Andrew, Hs. & V., age 37, son 19, daughters 6-4, L.

O

Oster, Arnd, Hs., age 24, C.
Otsenberger, John Peter, Hs. & V., age 40, daughter 1, C.
Oberitter, John George, Hs. & V., age 37, son 5, daughters 10-2, C.
Obermullerin, Mary Catherine*, age 30, R.

P

Pfadheucher, Marcel, Hs., age 52, daughters 30-22, L.
Pfadheucher, Hans Henrich, Hs., age 27, sons 13-3, daughter 4, L.
Petri, Henry, tailor, age 20, R.
Peter, John Hs. & V., age 38, daughter 2.
Paular, Andreas Jacob, tailor, age 20, R.
Peters, Henrich, Hs. & V., age 24, R.
Port, Justus, Hs., age 30, daughters 8-2, R.
Philip, George Thomas, mason and stone cutter, age 40, L.
Pazerin, Sarah*, age 36, son 2, L.

R

Riesenbucher, aMttheus, Hs., age 27, sons 4-2, daughter 7, L.

Richter, John Andres, Hs., age 46, son 14, daughters 17-7-3, L.
Rose, John Christoph, Hs., age 45, sons 16-12-9-7-3-1 day, daughter 2, L.
Roth, John Peter, Hs., age 29, sons 3-1½ L.
Ruehl, John Peter, Hs., age 20, L.
Rendel, John Peter, Hs., age 43, daughter 2, L.
Rufenacht, Benedict, Hs., age 46, son 9, daughters 13-11-6-3 mos., R.
Riet, John George, Hs., age 50, sons 20-18-16-14-7, daughters 22-12-10, L.
Rinner, Hans Hanrich, schoolmaster, sons 20-4, daughters 14-11-9-6, R.
Richardt John, Hs. & V., age 46, sons 14-3, daughters 19-12-9-6, R.
Ritwell Jacob, Hs. & V., age 22, L.
Rauch, John Jost, Hs. & V., age 49, son 8, daughter 18, L.
Roth, John, Hs. & V., age 24, L.
Richard, Peter, Hs., age 34, sons 13-1, daughters 5-3.
Riesenburn, John, carpenter, age 37, C.
Rudolf, John, saddler, age 20, R.
Rheinhold, John Georg, silversmith, age 27, L.
Rockeln, Elizabeth*, age 77, L.
Reichardin, Anna Barba*, age 20, C.

S

Schmotzer, John Jacob, baker, age 33, son 4, daughter 12, L.
Stephen, John, mason and stone cutter, age 36, son 2, C.
Semter, John, carpenter, age 38, son 2, R.
Schueler, Franciscus, carpenter, age 42, C.
Selner, John Adam, miller, age 51, daughters 5-2, L.
Schuch, John Peter, miller, age 32, daughters 12-10, C.
Stein, John, miller, age 44, C.
Schultheis, John, cooper and brewer, age 26, son ½, L.
Schmiedel, Segmund, silversmith, age 24, R.
Schultheis, Esther Susanna*, age 46, sons 20-9, daughters 11-6-4, L.
Steigerin, Cristina*, age 60, R.
Schaker, Susanne*, age 70, R.
Schutmeyen, Charlotte*, age 26, C.
Siegler, John Conrad, tailor, age 20, R.
Stoll, John, tailor, age 16, C.
Shaefer, Georg, tailor, age 18, R.
Schertz, Michael, tailor, age 18, C.
Schaar, Daniel, age 24, R.
Schwartz, Christian, linen weaver, age 36, R.
Schanne, Justus, schoolmaster, age 34, sons 4-15 mos., Luth.
Schmidt, John George, Hs. & V., age 30, son 4, daughter 2, R.
Smidt, Frederick, Hs. & V., age 30, son 4, L.
Shwygart, Frederick, Hs. & V., age 34, sons 6-3-1½, daughters 7-4, L.
Stauch, John Peter, Hs. & V., age 44, sons 12-9-2, daughter 5, R.
Sternberger, John Jacob, Hs. & V., age 29, sons 10-7-6, daughter 9, L.
Schneider, Bernard, Hs. & V., age 48, sons 18-16, daughters 11, L.
Schmidt, John William, Hs. & V., age 54, sons 4-3, daughters 8-6, L.
Sprosser, Anton, Hs. & V., age 23, C.
Spanheimer, George, Hs. & V., age 45, daughters 11-9-7-1, R.
Stoppelbein, Peter, Hs. & V., age 24, son 5-2 months, R.
Scherz, Jacob, Hs. & V., age 24, son 5, daughter 2, R.
Stambach, John Jacob, Hs. & V., age 28, R.
Seitz, John Dietrich, Hs. & V., age 36, son 14, daughters 10-3, R.
Spingler, Caspar, Hs. & V., age 43, sons 11-3, daughters 12-3, C.
Schwegars, John Henrich, Hs., age 38, sons 6-1, L.
Schreckenberg, John Henrich, Hs., age 28, daughter 3, L.
Schombert, John Jacob, Hs., age 36, son 3, R.
Sigmund, John Michel, baker, age 27, son 1, R.
Schaeffer, Andreas, Hs. also carpenter, age 42, son 13, daughter 15-7, R.
Schaeffer Henry, Hs., age 43, sons 20-17, daughter 14, R.
Schmidt, Caspar, Hs., age 58, sons 16-14-6-3, daughters 27-24-10-7, C.
Schaefer, John Henry, Hs., age 35, son 9, daughter 4, R.

Schnell, Matthew, Hs., age 48, C.
Seyfried, John Jacob, smith, age 23, L.

T

Turbell, Anton, Hs., age 40, son 12, daughters 9-4, L.
Tiel, Bernard, Hs. & V., age 40, sons 13-10-2, daughters 18-11-6-4, R.
Thal, Philip, Hs., age 45, sons 20-3, daughters 10-7-3, R.
Trep, John Jacob, butcher, age 28, R.
Tibold, Isaac, cooper and brewer, age 48, R.
Teake, Jacob, turner, age 50, sons 20-16, L.

U

Umbach, John George, Hs., age 35, daughters 7-5, R.
Unstat, Valentin, smith, age 22,, L.
Ulrich, Cristof, tailor, age 30, son 2, daughters 7-3, L.

V

Vonder Sabelgaul, John Leonhard, wheelwright, age 28, daughter 2, C.
Vogel, John, Hs. & V., and carpenter, age 47, son 6, daughters 7-3, L.
Vreel, John Nicol, Hs. & V., age 29, daughter 3, R.
Vogelsperrer, Joachim, mason and stone cutter, age 30, C.

W

Wille, Henrich Georg, Hs., age 36, sons 9-7, daughter 2, L.
Wentz, John George, Hs., age 30, son 4, daughter 6, L.
Wordman, John, Hs., age 40, sons 10-5, daughters 13-½, R.
Woolhand, Engelhard, Hs., age 26, R.
Weber, John Adolf, smith, age 18, R.
Weber, John Philip, smith, age 18, L.
Wolf, John Michel, smith, age 27, L.
Wentzel, John Georg, tailor, age 20, L.
Weibel, John Jacob, Hs. & V., age 36, daughters 10-6-315 mos., L.
Werbel, John Wilhelm, Hs. & V., age 23, L.
Weber, John George, Hs. & V., age 34, son 1, R.
Werner, Michael, Hs. & V., age 50, daughter 14, L.
Wilmar, Ulric, Hs. & V., age 53, son 16, R.
Waldman, Leonard, Hs., age 36, son 5, daughters 3-1½, L.
Weber, John Caspar, baker, age 20, R.
Windeberger, John Jacob, baker, age 35, sons 12-3, daughters 10-5, L.
Winhofer, John Georg, mason and stone cutter, age 28, C.
Wambach, Nicol, carpenter, age 36, sons 12-8-5-2, C.
Wagner, Andreas, laborer, age 37, sons 6-3, C.
Weiss, Mary*, age 34, R.
Weiss, Magdalena*, age 30, R.
Weritsen, Anna Catherine*, age 27, C.
Weberin, Eva*, age 22, R.
Welkin, Maria*, age 30, R.
Wunderich, Christina*, age 21, C.

Z

Zwick, Matthew, Hs., age 35, sons 11-6-5, daughter 13, L.
Zeiter, John George, Hs. & V., age 38, son 8, daughter 12, L.
Ziegler, Henrich, Hs. & V., age 50, sons 3-4, R.

Men 311, women 263, sons 323, daughters 296, total 1193.
(This is the second installment of the London List of Palatine immigrants.
Another list will appear in an early issue.)

Third List of Palatines

List taken at St. Catherine's, June 2, 1709, 1745 persons

VOL. 2, NO. D 68

Paltaine at St. Catherins, June 2, 1709

A

Abel, Michael, Hs. & V., age 29, son ½, daughter 3 C.
Alberts, Jacob, tailor, age 20, R.
Albert, John, smith, age 23, R.
Aldenuess, Philip, linen weaver, age 43, sons 9-4, daughter 7, L.
Altrater, Johan Valentine, Hs. & V., age 24, R.
Altheimer, Johan Georg, Hs. & V., age 40, sons 13-10-8-6-4, daughter 11, L.
Altheim, Anna*, age 64, L.
Alman, Simon, cooper & brewer, age 25, L.
Andrus, Michel, butcher, age 30, dau. 2, R.
Andelin, Catherin*, age 50, C.
Anweiler, John, Hs. & V., age 27, son 1, L.
Appel, Christian, Hs. & V., age 37, daughters 6-3, C.
Appelin, Elizabeth*, age 30, C.
Apfel, Johan Jacob, Hs. & V., age 21, C.
Artus, Isac, linen weaver, age 43, R.
Aschenburg, William, butcher, age 40, daughter 3, L.

B

Bauer, John, smith, age 22, L.
Bay, Wedell, shoemaker, age 38, sons 9-4, daughters 13-5-3, L.
Bast, Nicol, smith, age 50, sons 23-21-2, dau. 18-15-13-12-8, R.
Baehr, Frederick, Hs. &V., age 29, sons 4-2, C.
Bargman, Andreas, carpenter, age 32, L.
Barrabam, Ezechias, tailor, age 0, R.
Baker, Michael, Hs. & V., age 32, son 6, daughter 4, R.
Bauer, Thomas, Hs. & V., age 40, sons 14-12-10-8-6, daughters 19-16-13-9, C.
Becker, Hendrick, Hs. & V., age 53, sons 20-19-15-11, dau. 22-18-16-13, C.
Becker, Peter, Hs. & V., age 28, R.
Becker, Michel, smith, age 24, L.
Becker, Anton, Hs. & V., age 30, son 5, daughter 7, C.
Beck, Conrad, tailor, age 53, C.
Beckart, Conrad, Hs. & V., age 30, sons 10-18 mos., daughter 4, C.
Bell, Johan Engel, Hs. & V., age 27, R.
Benler, Henry, cooper & brewer, age 30, R.
Beisser, John, Hs. & V., age 50, sons 30-20, daughters 18-11, R.
Benter John Just, Hs. & V., age 23, son 2, L.
Beckman, Michel, Hs. & V., age 26, son 1, daughter 7, C.
Bergin, Anna*, age 25, R.
Bellerin, Mary*, age 21, R.
Beker, Paulus, Hs. & V., age 42, son 14, daughters 14-12.
Bergman, Johan Jost, Hs. & V., age 32, son 4, daughter 8, C.
Berger, Veit, Hs. & V., age 36, son 3, daughter 4, C.
Belz, Leonhard, Hs. & V., age 20, C.
Bertshy, Rudolph, carpenter, age 24, R.
Beydelman, Johan Michael, Hs. & V., age 40, sons 7-5, daughter 9.

Big, John, Hs. & V., age 36, sons 16-8, L.
Big, John, linen weaver, age 24, R.
Bischoff, George Henrich, Hs. & V., age 28, daughters 6-2, L.
Biel, Adolf, shoemaker, age 32, R.
Bloss, Conrad, Hs. & V., age 33, sons 8-6-2, daughters 2 mo., L.
Black, Nicol, carpenter, age 25, R.
Blank, Cassran, mason & stone cutter, age 28, C.
Boehm, Frantz, Hs. & V., age 44, sons 12-7-3, daughters 20-18-5, R.
Boller Philip, Hs. & V., age 36, sons 11-9-7, daughters 4-2½, R.
Boef, Johan, Hs. & V., age 41, sons 6-2, daughter 4, C.
Bodin, Mary*, age 50, daughters 24-22-12, R.
Bode, John George, Hs. & V., age 20, R.
Bohne, Francis, Hs. & V., age 39, sons 10-9, daughter 5, C.
Boef, William, Hs. & V., age 70, C.
Boher, Andrew, Hs. & V., age 40, R.
Boering, Michael, Hs. & V., age 30, son½, R.
Bruch, Michel, cooper & brewer, age 27, L.
Braun, Lucas, cooper & brewer, age 32, son 1, daughter 6, R.
Braun, John Debauld, Hs. & V., age 58, son 3 mos., R.
Brummer, Johan, Hs. & V., age 40, sons 7-1, C.
Brandlin Caspar, Hs. & V., age 42, son 4, daughter 6 mos., C.
Braun, Sebastian, Hs. & V., age 48, son 10, daughters 12-5, R.
Bredhauer, Israel, Hs. & V., age 43, sons 6-1, daughters 9-3, L.
Brauch, Johan Valentine, Hs. & V., age 34, sons 6-5 daughter 1, L.
Braun, John, Hs. & V., age 39, sons 12-9-4-1, daughters 7-5-3, L.
Brugerin Mary*, age 19, L.
Braun, Andrew, Hs. & V., age 26, sons 3-1½, daughter 5, C.
Burded, Johan, Hs. & V., age 16, R.
Buss, Johan Jacob, carpenter, age 25, L.
Bundersgell, George, hunter, age 36,, sons 4, daughters 9-7-2, C.
Bucholtz, John, surgeon, age 30, L.
Bunderskeil, Andreas, Hs. & V., age 40, sons 14-7, daughters 10-7, C.
Bungart, Jacob, Hs. & V., age 51, son 15, C.
Bungart, Matthew, Hs. & V., age 24, daughters 4-1, C.
Bungart, William, Hs. & V., age 26, sons 4-2, C.
Bucheberger, Johan Nicol, Hs. & V., age 53, sons 11-9-5-9 mos., dau. 9, L.
Bubeheiser, John Adam, Hs. & V., age 57, son 20-15-13-12-4 dau. 21-19-15-12-8, R.
Burder, Magdalena*, age 22, R.
Busch, Herman, Hs. & V., age 54, son 4, daughter 24, L.
Burge, Arnold, Hs. & V., age 24, R.

C

Cays, John Brill, shoemaker, age 45, sons 18-7, daughters 15-11, R.
Carp, John, smith, age 50, sons 14-2, daughters 22-17-7, L.
Catherin, Anna*, age 16, C.
Carten, John, brickmaker, age 46, sons 20-14-11, dau. 9-6-2, L.
Christhiles, George, miller, age 28, son 15 mo., C.
Charton, Hendrich, Hs. & V., age 32, daughters 19-6—4, 18 mos., C.
Clos, Peter, Hs. & V., age 28, C.
Clother, John Paul, Hs. & V., age 46, sons 18-7, daughters 9-4, L.
Clemen, Bastian, Hs. & V., age 44, sons 21-16-7, daughters 10-8, R.
Clemen Valentine, Hs. & V., age 20, son 18 mos., R.
Closs, Peter, Hs. & V., age 50, sons 20-11-8, daughters 24-13, R.
Closin, Mary*, age 30, L.
Claude, Francis, Hs. & V., age 22, R.
Conradt, Christoph, tailor, age 18, R.
Conrad, Matthew, carpenter, age 21, C.
Corrier, Carl, tailor, age 31, C.
Conrads, Conrad, Hs. & V., age 36, daughters 10-1, C.

Creaner, Philip, Hs. & V., age 35, C.

D

Dales William, Hs. & V., age 36, sons 4-1, daughter 6, R.
Dales, Catherine*, age 25, R.
Derding, Conrad, Hs. & V., age 30, L.
Debald Martin, Hs. & V., age 30 son 10, daughter 8-2, R.
Derding, Conrad, Hs. & V., age 30, L.
Dienes, August, baker, age 26, C.
Dietrich, Bernhard, carpenter, age 24, L.
Diggart, Andreas, Hs. & V., age 30, son 5, R.
Dittmar, David, mason & stone cutter, age 22, L.
Dietz, William, linen weaver, age 33, daughter 1, R.
Diess, butcher, age 30, C.
Dietrich, Jacob, linen weaver, age 44, sons 18-12-2, dau. 15-12-10-6, R.
Dolmetsch, Johan, Hs. & V., age 30, sons 12-9-6, daughters 2-6 mos., L.
Dorry, Conrad, carpenter, age 36, C.
Dorniger Caspar, Hs. & V., age 36, son 4, daughter 10, R.
Doettel, John, shoemaker, age 32, C.
Dorn, Lazarus, Hs. & V., age 48, sons 14-7, daughters 10-9-6-18 mos.-3 mos., R.
Drummer, Gerard, Hs. & V., age 24, R.
Dres, Catherine*, age 19, C.
Drap, Lorentz, carpenter, age 50, sons 13-9-3, daughters 10-8-4, C.
Du Bray, Peter, butcher, age 19, R.
Du Bray, John, brickmaker, age 26, sons 4-2, R.
Durrin, Catherin*, age 30, C.
Dungel, Matthew, Hs. & V., age 33, C.
Dungel, Matthew, Hs. & V., age 33, C.

E

Eacheroeder, Hendrick, carpenter, age 46, son 18, L.
Ebelman, Jacob, Hs. & V., age 36, R.
Ebeling, Johan, Hs. & V., age 25, sons 14-10, daughters 8-1, C.
Eckhard, Balzar, Hs. & V., age 60, daughters 21-18, C.
Eckhard, Johan Jacob, Hs. & V., age 24, R.
Egler, Christian, mason & stone cutter, age 28, son 2, dau. 8-7-4, R.
Eich, Martin, shoemaker, age 29, sons 11-4, daughters 14-6-3-1, C.
Eisern, Anton, carpenter, age 30, daughter 5, C.
Emmel, John, Hs. & V., age 36, daughter 4.
Emerich, Peter, Hs. & V., age 36, daughter 5, R.
Engelman, John Adam, Hs. & V., age 37, son 2, daughters 8-6, L.
Engel, Martin Hs. & V., age 36, sons 13-10-2, daughter 5, C.
Engel, Johan Rupert, Hs. & V., age 42, sons 21-17-14, daughter 12, C.
Engels, Anna Mary*, age 60, R.
Estich, Paul, Hs. & V., age 21, R.
Eyfel, Helkert, Hs. & V., age 13, R.
Ehrenwein, John, carpenter, age 30, daughter 2, C.
Eydicker, John, carpenter, age 23, C.
Eydecker, Michel, tailor, age 16, C.
Eyler, Johan, Hs. & V. age 50, sons 15-3-3 mos., daughters 12-10-8-4, R.
Erbs, Johan Henry, Hs. & V., age 25, sons 6-4-3 mos., R.
Ekern, Anna*, age 44, son 9, L.
Ehrlich, John, cooper & brewer, age 25, R.
Eyfelin, Christina*, age 20, C.
Eschenbrender, Wolf, Hs. & V., age 40, C.
Eybach Reinhard, Hs. & V., age 50, sons 20-16, daughter 25, R.
Ebrecht, John, Hs. & V., age 40, daughters 5-2, R.
Edian, Sebastion, Hs. & V., age 32, daughter 2, L.

F

Faber (Taber), Ebert, turner, age 20, L.

Falck, Arnold, Hs. & V., age 32, sons 6-2, C.
Falkenburg, Valentin, Hs. & V., age 38, sons 7-2, R.
Fechter, Martin, Hs. & V., age 40, son 6, daughter 18-15-10-3-1 and 6 mos., L.
Feller, Johan, Hs. & V., age 45, sons 4-2, daughters 12-9, R.
Feldnacht, Johan, Hs. & V., age 37, sons 3-½, C.
Fischerin, Margretha*, age 55, C.
Fischerin, Margaretha*, age 55, C.
Fishers, Margaretha*, age 24, C.
Fink, John Adam, Hs. & V., age 24, daughter 1, C.
Finkin, Ursula*, age 46, son 9, daughter 19, C.
Fisher, John, tailor, age 23, son 3, L.
Flor Johan, Hs. & V., age 46, son 23, daughter 25, R.
Flor, Peter, Hs. & V., age 25, C.
Flor, Johan, Hs. & V., age 36, sons 8-4, daughter 9, C.
Fohrer, John, tanner, age 60, sons 20-18, C.
Fohrer, John, Hs. & V., also tanner, age 60, sons 20-18, C.
Fohrer, John, Hs. & V., age 25, daughter 2, C.
Fosterin, Anna*, age 20, R.
Friedrik, Nicol, cooper & brewer, age 60, sons 25-21-, dau. 17-15, L.
Freund, Johan, Hs. & V., age 46, sons 26-24, daughters 19-17-14, R.
Frank, Johan Martin, schoolmaster, age 27, L.
Fritzin, Johan, Hs. & V., age 36, L.
Frank, Michel, cooper & brewer, age 20, C.
Frantz, Conrad, cooper & brewer, age 20, R.
Friesen, John Riccas, Hs. & V., age 27, son 2, daughter 3-3 mos., C.
Fuchsin, Margareth*.
Fuchsin, Mary*, age 22, L.
Fuchs, John Bernhard, smith, age 39, sons 9-5-2, daughter 7, C.
Fuhrman, Johan   Mathew, Hs. & V., age 32, L.

G

Gam, Jacob, Hs. & V., age24,R.
Gaus, Nicol, shoemaker, age 23, L.
Geldmacherin, Sabina*, age 21, L.
Geschwind, Johan, Hs. & V., age 35, son 7, daughter 5-3-1, C.
Gedert, Johan, carpenter, age 26, L.
Gedel, John Peter, Hs. & V., age 27, son 9 mos., R.
Geney, Jacob, Hs. & V., age 50, sons 2-20, daughters 18-16-14-11-7, C.
Gerger, Jacob, mason & stone cutter, age 31, C.
Gerhard, Peter, carpenter, age 32, C.
Gerhard, Valentine, Hs. & V., age 38, daughters 13-11-6-9-1, R.
Gersner, Balzar, Hs. & V., age 28, L.
Gesch, Godfried, linen weaver, age 37, son 3, L.
Geyer, Johan David, Hs. & V., age 34, son 4, daughters 12-9-2, L.
Giessiebel, John Michel, smith, age 28, dau. 2, L.
Giess, Fredick, butcher, age 42, son 4, dau. 10-2, R.
Glaser, Dietrich, mason & stone cutter, age 26, son 4, dau. 6-½, C.
Glasin, Margaretha*, age 21, C.
Glass, Valentine, Hs. & V., age 25, C.
Glass, William, Hs. & V., age 36, sons 8-5, daughters 3-3 mo., C.
Glaser, Georg, Hs. & V., age 47, son 5, daughter 9, L.
Gnaedig, John, carpenter, age 40, sons 11-5, daughter 1, C.
Goerher, Sebastian, Hs. & V., age 23, son 1, R.
Goedel, Jacob, hunter, age 60, sons 20-16-14, dau. 10-4-2, L.
Goff, Mary*, age 38, R.
Graehl, Lorentz, Hs. & V., age 27, son 1 L.
Graef, Johan, Hs. & V., age 27, L.
Grosman, Johan, Hs. & V., age 26, son 2, daughters 8-6, C.
Gresman, Henry, wheelwright, age 28, L.
Greylach Urban, Hs. & V., age 50, daughter 18, L.
Grisn, Frederick, Hs. & V., age 23, L.

Graef, Georg, carpenter, age 30, son ½, daughter 1, L.
Graf, Philip Leonhardt, Hs. & V., age 48, son 15, daughters 18-12-9-4, R.
Gross, William, Hs. & V., age 24, son 4, daughter 18 mos., R.
Gross, Frederick, Hs. & V., age 36, son 3, daughter 1, L.
Gross, Joachim, Hs. & V., age 25, L.
Guth, Johan, Hs. & V., age 36, sons 10-6, daughter 11, C.
Gusman, Peter, Hs. & V., age 40, sons 8-7-1, C.

H

Haas, Elizabeth*, age 21, R.
Haas, Nicol, Hs. & V., age 44, sons 7-4-1, daughter 10, L.
Hack, Conrad, Hs. & V., age 80, sons 16-9, R.
Hafer, Peter, carpenter, age 23, L.
Haub, Christoph, Hs. & V., age 20, L.
Handwerker, Daniel, Hs. & V., age 28, R.
Handwerker, Peter, Hs. & V., age 24, R.
Hargart, Johan Nicol, Hs. & V., age 30, sons 14-½, daughter 8, L.
Habel, Jonas, baker, age 24, R.
Hamel, John, baker, age 66, son 26, R.
Hanson, Bernhard, linen weaver, age 32, sons 12-4, daughters 9-1, C.
Halgarde, Peter, mason & stone cutter, age 24, C.
Hach, Peter, linen weaver, age 35, daughter 2, R.
Hardtz, John, cooper & brewer, age 30, C.
Hartman, Conrad, Hs. & V., age 45, daughter 4, L.
Hartman, Conrad, Hs. & V., age 30, son 7, daughters 4-½, C.
Hayn, Jacob, Hs. & V., age 40, son 16, daughters 12-7-18 mos., C.
Hay, Eva*, age 30, R.
Heumacher, John Jacob, Hs. & V., age 30, sons 3-2, C.
Hamerkin, Johan Jacob, Hs. & V., age 45, son 13, daughters 11-7-2, R.
Herbener, Henrich, Hs. & V., age 40, son 10, daughters 6-3, L.
Hess, Jeremy, Hs. & V., age 34, sons 7-5, daughter 2, L.
Hess, Andrew, tanner, age 24, R.
Hess, Frederick, Hs. & V., age 42, son 2, daughters 11-7, R.
Heck, Bastian, Hs. & V., age 40, son 6, daughters 8-4, L.
Heineman, Johan Henrich, Hs. & V., age 28, son 5, daughters 7-1, C.
Hehrman, Johan Just, Hs. & V., age 30, C.
Hep (Hess?), Johan Jacob, Hs. & V., age 28, daughters 6-4, L.
Hesper, Simon, Hs. & V., age 30, L.
Hessel, William, Hs. & V., age 22, R.
Heisterback, Nicol, shoemaker, age 52, son 3, daughters 7-5, R.
Helfer, Christop, Hs. & V., age 40, sons 8-2, daughter 6, L.
Herman, Schweikhart, Hs. & V., age 40, sons 19-6, daughter 4, C.
Hecht, Caspar, Hs. & V., age 50, sons 24-11-9-7-2, daughters 27-18, L.
Henrich, Johan James, Hs. & V., age 23, L.
Hermes, Johan, Hs. & V., age 27, daughter 2, C.
Herbst, John, locksmith, age 46, son 5, daughter 3, C.
Herzin, Margaretta*, age 50, sons 16-10, daughters 14-7, C.
Herman, Philip, cooper & brewer, age 25, L.
Herling, Conrad, miller, age 28, L.
Henzelin, Mary*, age 23, C.
Henzelin, Eva*, age 21, C.
Helles, Henry, Hs. & V., age 25, R.
Henniger, Johan Adam, Hs. & V., age 24, L.
Herman, Conrad, Hs. & V., age 23, R.
Hey, Anna*, age 18, R.
Heyd, Nicol, linen weaver, age 24, C.
Heyn, Paul, Hs. & V., age 39, sons 8-3, daughter 11, L.
Heil, Matthew, Hs. & V., age 30, R.
Henrich, Caspar, wheelwright, age 24, C.
Heins, Johan Valentine, Hs. & V., age 33, daughters 10-3, L.
Heins, Adam, Hs. & V., age 22, L.

Herber, Caspar, tailor, age 48, L.
Hitschke, John, Hs. & V., age 30, son 4, daughter 1, R.
Hill, Balzar, Hs. & V., also carpenter, age 43, sons 16-14-10, daughters 18-7, C.
Hill, John William Hs. & V., age 40, son 1, daughters 5-4, R.
Hill, Johan, Hs. & V., age 90, R.
Hill, Johan, Hs. & V., age 24, C.
Hildebrand, Johan, Hs. & V., age 50, son 11, daughter 15, L.
Hillig, Andreas, Hs. & V., age 26, son 2, L.
Hirt, Stephen, schoolmaster, age 42, sons 13-10-7-3, L.
Hornberg, Christian, Hs. & V., age 18, R.
Hop, Christian, Hs. & V., age 35, L.
Holtzlaender, Albert, Hs. & V., age 40, sons 5-½, daughters 14-9-4, C.
Hollander, Melchoir, weaver, age 20, L.
Horst, Walter, tailor, age 39, son 5, daughters 9-3, L.
Hochappel, John, linen weaver, age 43, sons 23-16-10, dau. 12-4, R.
Hoechat, Burckard, Hs. & V., age 27, sons 5-3 mos., L.
Hofman, Henry, miller, age 33, dau. 6-3-1, L.
Hoffman, Matthew, Hs. & V., age 20, C.
Hoffman, Catherine*, age 24, C.
Hop, Michel, Hs. & V., age 26, L.
Hofferling Henrich, Hs. & V., age 54, son 24, daughters 22-21-18, C.
Huhm, Matthew, Hs. & V., age 20, R.
Hunold, Seyfert, Hs. & V., age 38, sons 16-14-12-3 and 6 mos., daughters 9-5, L.
Huntin, Jane*, age 60, son 30, C.
Hup, Margaretha*, age 30, son 8, daughters 11-6-4, R.
Huber, Hs. & V., age 30, son 13, daughter 10-7, L.
Huper, Ludolf, carpenter, age 24, C.
Huberin, Christina*, age 21, R.
Hubnerin, Margaret*, age 20, C.

I

Igelsbach, Wendal, Hs. & V., age 45, sons 4-2, daughters 6-6 mos., R.
Isler, Nicolas, mason & stone cutter, age 48, sons 15-8-6, dau. 5-1, R.

J

Jagerin, Elizabeth*, age 70, R.
Jacger, Peter, Hs. & V., age 23, C.
Jaegerin, Mary*, age 18, C.
Jahnin, Elizabeth*, age 19, C.
Jocobi, Johan, baker, age 45, sons 18-12-11-6-2, daughters 15-8-½, C.
Johan, Johan Michel, Hs. & V., age 18, L.
Jordan, Henry, Hs. & V., age 36, sons 11-9, daughters 5-3, C.
Jungin, Elizabeth, age 45, R.
Jung, Johan, Hs. & V., age 32, son 9, daughter 1, C.
Jung, Adam, Hs. & V., age 17, R.
Jung, Johan, Hs. & V., age 18, R.

K

Kahl, Margaretha*, age 21, R.
Kast, John George, Hs. & V., age 30, son 8, daughters 6-4-2, L.
Kaul, Matthew, cooper & brewer, age 50, sons 16-14-10-8, dau. 5-2, R.
Kaul, Francis, Hs. & V., age 36, daughter 2, L.
Keyserin, Anna*, age 30, C.
Kemmer, Peter, cooper & brewer, age 28, L.
Kegelman, Leonhard, carpenter, age 35, son 9, daughter 6, R.
Kern, Francis, linen weaver, age 30, sons 17-9, dau. 6-2, C.
Keinin, Rose*, age 50, son 19, R.
Keselbach, John, Hs. & V., age 40, son 12 daughters 1-5, C.
Kehler, John Simon, Hs. & V., age 42, son 6, daughter 2-2 mo., R.
Keller, Jacob, Hs. & V., age 35, sons 12-10-8-5, daughters 5-2, R.

Kesler, Johan Peter, Hs. & V., age 21, L.
Kirches, Paul, cooper & brewer, age 23, C.
Kirschner, Philip, Hs. & V., age 28, sons 5-2, daughter 2, L.
Klein, Jacob, Hs. & V., age 48, son 20, L.
Klein, Johan William, Hs. & V., age 42, son 18, daughter 24-20, C.
Klein, Johan Michael, Hs. & V., age 40, sons 11-9-7-5, daughter 4,, C.
Klein, Ludwig, Hs. & V., age 18, R.
Kloetter, John, baker, age 29, son 1, R.
Klitten, George, Hs. & V., age 27, son 2, C.
Knaub, Johan Cristoph, Hs. & V., age 30, son 2, daughter 1, R.
Knichel, John, carpenter, age 27, L.
Knecht, Michael, Hs. & V., age 50, daughters 21-18-15,12, C.
Knochl, Herman, Hs. & V., age 24, C.
Kniddelmeyer, Caspar, carpenter, age 25, C.
Knut, Nicol, Hs. & V., age 32, son 9, C.
Kolbe, Francis, Hs. & V., age 36, sons 20-14-10-7, daughter 15, C.
Koehler, Jacob, linen weaver, age 54, sons 16-10-½, dau. 18-14-12-10-4, L.
Koch, Martin, Hs. & V., age 28, L.
Kohl, Johann, Hs. & V., age 24, R.
Koch, Johan, Hs. & V., age 22, L.
Koster, Dietrich, mason & stone cutter, age 36, son 11, daughters 6-3, L.
Koerner, John Nicol, Hs. & V., age 50, sons 6-3, daughters 9-4, R.
Koenig, Justus, Hs. & V., age 36, son 7, daughter 12 R.
Kossing, Anthony, Hs. & V., age 30, L.
Koster, Henry, carpenter, age 51, sons 17-13, daughters 10-6, L.
Kraut, John Peter, Hs. & V., age 38, son 1, daughters 10-7-4, R.
Kraus, John George, Hs. & V., age 62, L.
Kraus, John Michel, miller, age 50, sons 24-6, L.
Kraemer, John, baker, age 30, daughter 2, C.
Kraft, Matthew, shoemaker, age 37, sons 12-6, daughters 8-2, C.
Kraft, Valentine, Hs. & V., age 40, sons 6-4, daughters 16-9-2, L.
Krochner, John, mason & stone cutter, age 40, son 18, C.
Kreisher, Ludwig, linen weaver, age 24, L.
Kuehlman, John, Hs. & V., age 50, daughters 20-12-9-7-2, R.
Kuml, Johan Peter, Hs. & V., age 40, s ons 20-16-12-10-5, daughter 18, C.
Kuhn, Peter, Hs. & V., age 24, R.
Kusferin, Eva*, age 25, son 8, daughter 6, C.
Kuth, Peter, Hs. & V., age 26, R .
Kuntz, Philip, carpenter, age 22, R.
Kuhn, Henry, Hs. & V., age 53, son 8, daughter 10, L.
Kuenstler, Henry, Hs. & V., age 36, son 5, daugther 2, R.
Kurtz, Johan, Hs. & V., age 41,   son 8, daughter 13, C.

L

La Mothe, Daniel, shoemaker, age 30, son 4, daughters 9-1, L.
Land, Philip, Hs. & V., age 24, C.
Land, Anton, linen weaver, age 26, daughter 1, C.
Lang, Christian, carpenter, age 37, son 5, daughters 11-9-2, C.
Lauber, Johan, Hs. & V., age 30, daughters 9-6-3, C.
Langin, Elizabeth*, age 22, C.
Laurmanin, Eva*, age 22, R.
Lanbegeier, Gottlieb, baker, age 26, L.
Laurer, Matthew, Hs. & V., age 23, L.
Lauer, Agnes*, age 20, C.
Laurentz, Nicol, Hs. & V., age 40, sons 15-11-5, daughter 8, R.
Lambreht, Georg, hunter, age 44, sons 20-16-14-7, dau. 17-9, L.
Lerner, Matthew, shoemaker, age 50, son A, daughter 8, R.
Lesch, Balzar, Hs. & V., age 38, sons 14-8-2, daughter 9, L.
Leonhard, Johan Peter, Hs. & V., age 24, daughter ½, C.
Leyser, Christoph, Hs. & V., age 56, sons 24-14-11, daughter 20, L.
Lepert, Matthew, Hs. & V., age 24, R.
Lescherin, Magdalen*, age 34, son 18, R.

Lemp, Conrad, Hs. & V., age 36, son 7, daughter 3, R.
Lehrers, John Philip, Hs. & V., age 30, daughter 13, R.
Leach, John, baker, age 25, sons 10-6-4-5 days, L.
Legoli, John, figure maker, age 26, son 1, R.
Leinweber, Johan, Hs. & V., age 36, son 14, daughter 9, R.
Lentz, Henry, Hs. & V., age 40, sons 1-9-2, C.
Lichte, John, shoemaker, age 40, daughters 5-2, R.
Liebler, John, tailor, age 19, C.
Lipper, Johan Jacob, Hs. & V., age 30, sons 13-8, daughter 1, C.
Lieborn, Ludwig, Hs. & V., age 30, daughter 2, L.
Lindeman, Justus, carpenter, age 26, R.
Lorentz, Michael, Hs. & V., age 48, sons 20-18, daughter 15, C.
Lopp, Jacob, mason & stone cuter, age 40, son 7-1 mo., dau. 5-4, L.
Los, Adam, mason & stone cutter, age 21, L.
Los, John, mason & stone cutter, age 40, son 7, daughter 11, C.
Loss, Jacob, Hs. & V., age 25, L.
Loucks, Philip, Hs. & V., age 28, R.
Lobwasser, Anton, Hs. & V., age 41, son 7, C.
Lunch, Caspar, mason & stone cutter, age 37, daughters 7-2, L.
Ludwig, Johan, Hs. & V., age 54, sons 20-25, daughters 12-10, R.
Luetz, John George, Hs. & V., age 30, daughter 2, R.
Lutz, Hs. & V., age 40, sons 7-2, daughtr 10, R.
Lutz, Anna Mar*, age 20, C.
Lutz, Peter, Hs. & V., age 27, son 2, daughters 8-5, R.

M

Manke, George, wheelwright, age 20, L.
Mathes, Johan, Hs. & V., age 33, sons 15-10, daughter 12, C.
Maul, Johan Henry, Hs. & V., age 48, son 5, daughters 13-11-4-½, R.
Mauer, John Jacob, Hs. & V., age 22, C.
Martin Nicol, Hs. & V., age 51, son 21, R.
Mandersel, John Peter, Hs. & V., age 24, C.
Mathes, Henry, Hs. & V., age 42, sons 8-6-1, daughters 13-10-6, R.
Master, Lambert, mason & stone cutter, age 50, son 25, daughter 15, C.
Marry, David, butcher, age 40, sons 10-2, dau. 8 days, R.
Mahler, Bastian, linen weaver, age 24, C.
Mattheus, Hs. & V., age 23, son 1, C.
Margreth, Elizabeth*, age 18, C.
Madler, Michel, Hs. & V., age 38, sons 11-7-4, daughter 18, L.
Mara, Peter, cooper & brewer, age 24, C.
Mathesin, Anna*, age 53, daughters 23-20-18, R.
Manderset, Mary*, age 26, C.
Margaretha, Anna*, age 15, L.
Mallot, Catherina*, age 20, C.
Mank, Jacob, Hs. & V., age 39, daughters 17-9-3, R.
Martin, Adam, Hs. & V., age 36, son 3, daughters 7-5, R.
Mehden, Martin, potter, age 42, sons 10-7-4, daughters 14-7, C.
Meyer, Egidy, potter, age 22, C.
Meyer, Nicol, Hs. & V., age 33, daughters 10-5-½, R.
Meyer, Johan, Hs. & V., age 29, sons 7-3, daughter 4, L.
Meyfart, Jacob, Hs. & V., age 12, R.
Merich, George, Hs. & V., age 53, sons 20-15-5, L.
Mensen, Conrad, Hs. & V., age 54, L.
Mehs Paul, Hs. & V., age 24, C.
Merstallen, Henry, Hs. & V., age 41, sons 10-5-1, daughters 7-6, L.
Menges, John, carpenter, age 35, sons 9-3-3 mos., R.
Metz, Andrew, carpenter, age 40, sons 10-5-2, daughters 13, R.
Metz, George, carpenter, age 28, L.
Meyer, Henrich, Hs. & V., age 43, son 11, daughter 13, L.
Meyer, Jacob, Hs. & V., age 32, son 2, L.
Mey, Cristoph, Hs. & V., age 35, daughter 3, R.

Mey, John Peter, Hs. & V., age 38, daughters 7-5, C.
Mentz, Anton, Hs. & V., age 28, son 8, daughter 6, C.
Meyerin, Barbara*, age 60, daughter 18, L.
Meyerin, Barbara*, age 60, daughter 18, L.
Meyschin, Jane*, age 36, daughter 2, L.
Meyshin, Anna*, age 30, daughter 2, L.
Meyer, Jacob, cooper & brewer, age 20, L.
Metzger, Philip, cooper & brewer, age 40, sons 13-10-7-3 mo., daughters 9-4, L.
Merden, Cristoph, cooper & brewer, age 40, sons 8-3 mo., daughters 12-6, R.
Meier, Paul, miller, age 43, sons 12-7, daughters 13-8-½, L.
Meyerin, Elizabeth*, age 30, L.
Meyer, Thomas Hs. & V., age 44, son 1, daughter 10, R.
Medke, Daniel, Hs. & V., age 41, son 15, daughters 14-13-3, L.
Meyer, Johan, Hs. & V., age 25, L.
Merket, Peter, linen weaver, age 38, son 4, R.
Meiss, Henry, smith, age 38, son 3-3 mo., R.
Menges, John, mason & stone cutter, age 32, L.
Mick, John Hs. & V., age 23, R.
Midler, Juliana*, age 21, R.
Miller, Philip, linen weaver, age 23, R.
Mick, Frederick, Hs. & V., age 65, sons 23-18, daughters 28-26, C.
Michel, Otto Henry, Hs. & V., age 30, son 1, C.
Mick, Henry, Hs. & V., age 35, sons 9-5 daughters 12-7, R.
Molendueck, Herman, Hs. & V., age 50, daughters 19-12, R.
Mohr, Cristoph, Hs. & V., age 40, L.
Molsberger, Philip, Hs. & V., age 30, daughter 4, R.
Mohr, Johan, Hs. & V., age 38, son 10, L.
Michel, Henry, weaver, age 38, daughter 6, L.
Muuer Caspar, Hs. & V., age 42, sons 12-10, C.
Middler, William, Hs. & V., age 12, R.
Munkenast, Joseph, mason & stone cutter, age 27, C.
Mulleker, Francis, mason & stone cutter, age 30, son 1, C.
Mueller, George, mason & stone cutter, age 26, L.
Munchofer, Philipp, butcher, age 36, C.
Mungesser, Philip, miller, age 27, son 6, daughter 15 mo., L.
Muller George Philip, Hs. & V., age 36, sons 11-6, daughters 8-5-1, L.
Musier John Jacob, Hs. & V., age 54, sons 24-12-9-3, daughters 21-18, R.
Muench, Cristoph, Hs. & V., age 26, L.
Muhler, Philip Vonder, Hs. & V., age 51, sons 19-18 ms., dau. 22-17-14-13-11-7, R.
Muster, Lambert, Hs. & V., age 50, son 25, daughter 15, C.
Mullerin, Mary*, age 30, daughters 8-6, R.
Mullerin, Mary*, age 30, sons 8-6, R.
Muelerin, Susana*, age 32, R.
Muller, Adam, cooper & brewer, age 36, son 8, daughters 12-6, R.
Muserin, Anna*, age 24, L.
Mullerin, Margaretha*, age 23, C.   ?
Muench, Peter, Hs. & V., age 24, L.

N

Nactigall Johan Conrad, Hs. & V., age 26, son 2, daughter 5, L.
Naegler, Jacob, mason & stone cutter, age 30, R.
Nakhan, William, Hs. & V., age 38, daughters 5-6 mos., R.
Nabigt, John, carpenter, age 50, son 9, daughter 6, L.
Naser, Johan Michael, Hs. & V., age 48, sons 20-12, daughters 18-6, L.
Nellesin, Anna Eve*, age 50, son 16, daughter 11, R.
Neuman, Ludwig, Hs. & V., age 37, sons 12-9-6, daughters 9-6, R.
Neumeyer, John August, Hs. & V., age 35, son 3, daughters 12-8-6, C.
Neckes, Bartin, shoemaker, age 31, L.
Neio, Andrew, shoemaker, age 30, L.
Neuss, Andrew, Hs. & V., age 27, C.
Nilius, Johan, Hs. V., age 34, sons 11-13, daughters 12-6-3 mo., C.

Nick, Johan Jacob, Hs. & V., age 15, L.
Niedermeyer, Andrew, Hs. & V., age 43, son 6, daughters 11-9-5 C.
Noll, Daniel, Hs. & V., age 22, R.
Noset, Susana*, age 60, C.
Nonin, Elizabeth*, age 60, R.
Noll, Bernhard, carpenter, age 47, R.
Nuentzeberger, Dietrich, Hs. & V., age 51, sons 17-13-10-8-4, daughters 19-15, C.
Nuckland, Arnold, schoolmaster, age 42, sons 11-9-5-3-4, daughter 9, L.

O

Ortminger, Nicol, Hs. & V., age 34, sons 7-5, daughters 3-1, C.
Ott, William, Hs. & V., age 24, R.
Ozeberger, Mary*, age 18, C.

P

Paul, Gerhard, Hs. & V., age 52, sons 24-11, daughters 27-18-10-8-6, R.
Paul, Johan, Hs. & V., age 22, R.
Paul, John Daniel, Hs. & V., age 59, daughters 36-33-30-20, R.
Petisht, Hs. & V., age 50, sons 14-9-12, daughters 6-1, C.
Petri, Jacob, tailor, age 42, sons 16-10, daughters 19-15-12-5, L.
Petisht, Johan Dietricht, Hs. & V., age 36, daughter 4, C.
Petri, Andrew, saddler, age 39, daughters 9-6-4, R.
Petit, Johan Jacob, Hs. & V., age 50, R.
Penner, Henry, Hs. & V., age 30, sons 6-4, daughters 3 mos., R.
Petri, Nicol, Hs. & V., age 38, s on 7, daughters 10-18 mos., L.
Pfeifer, George, miller, age 57, son 19-5, L.
Pfiz, Joseph, miner, age 33, sons 6-2, L.
Pfiz, Jacob, miner, age 30, L.
Port, John, carpenter, age 23, C.
Phillips, Jacob, wheelwright, age19,L.
Pisch, Benedict, Hs. & V., age 55, son 3, daughter 6-2, C.
Pliss, John, Hs. & V., age 35, sons 8-3, daughter 11, L.
Proebstel, George, Hs. & V., age 40, son 7, daughter 11, C.
Puppelritter, Christian, Hs. & V., age 43, son 5, daughters 20-10-12, C.

Q

Quint, Anton, Hs. & V., age 36, sons 4-3, daughter 3, C.
Quriea, Francis, Hs. & V., age 50, sons 8-4-3, C.

R

Rab, Kilian, shoemaker, age 47, sons 10-7-2, R.
Rabenegger, Nicol, Hs. & V., age 20, C.
Rautebusch, Johan, Hs. & V., age 30, daughter 3, L.
Reckart, Justus, Hs. & V., age 53, L.
Reck, Jacob, Hs. & V., age 50, son 20, daughters 16-14, C.
Rehm, Anton, linen weaver, age 41, son 3, daughter 2, C.
Rentel, Johan Nicol, Hs. & V., age 46, sons 16-12, daughter 5, L.
Reidman, Martin, mason & stone cutter, age 24, C.
Reichard, Caspar, Hs. & V., age 24, sons 3-1, C.
Reichard, Henry, Hs. & V., age 25, R.
Reif, John Peter, baker, age 64, R.
Reinhard, Henry, Hs. & V., age 28, son 2, L.
Reiser, Michel, cooper & brewer, age 24, R.
Reisdorf Johan, Hs. & V., age 34, son 1, daughter 4, C.
Reisenberger, Lorentz, Hs. & V., age 46, son 2, daughters 9-6, R.
Rhod, Jacob, surgeon, age 44, son 8, daughter 2, C.
Rhode, Philip, linen weaver, age 34, son 2 mo., dau. 19-14-4, R.
Rhode, Johan Juste, Hs. & V., age 28, sons 3-1, daughter 5, R.
Ringer, John Thiel, linen weaver, age 24, L .
Ritz, John, Hs. & V., age 40, son 10, daughters 6-18 mos., C.

Roeger, Dietrich, mason & stone cutter, age 32, C.
Roethgen, Nicol, shoemaker, age 20, R.
Roethgen, Peter, mason & stone cutter, age 27, son 1, R.
Rohn, Johan, Hs. & V., age 45, sons 20-18-16-12-8, daughters 14-5-2, L.
Ropf, George, locksmith, age 38, L.
Rosmanin, Catherin*, age 54, daughter 20, L.
Rosenthal, Johan, Hs. & V., age 30, L.
Rosbach, Peter, Hs. & V., age 28, R.
Rottenflohn, John, carpenter, age 36, son 7, daughter 10, C.
Rufel, John Nicol, Hs. & V., age 49, sons 17-12-5, daughters 21-19-7, L.
Ruhl Jacob, Hs. & V., age 42, sons 22-12, daughters 17-16-10, C.
Ruhl, John Caspar, Hs. & V., age 25, L.
Ruhl, Daniel, smith, age 24, R.
Ramp, Nicol, Hs. & V., age 37, sons 13-5, daughters 10-2 R.
Rufer, Peter, mason & stone cutter, age 19, R.
Rufner, Thomas, carpenter, age 28, L.
Rup, George, Hs. & V., age 18, R.
Rup, Margaretha*, age 16, R.
Rup, Johan, Hs. & V., age 52, daughters 23-20, L.
Rutigin, Elizabeth*, age 60, C.

S

Sarburger, Agust, Hs. & V., age 36, son 2, daughter 5, R.
Sarburger Johan, Hs. & V., age 25, daughters 3-1, R.
Sarburger, Wenceslag, Hs. & V., age 43, sons 9-7, daughters 13-2, R.
Schautz (Schantz), Johan, Hs. & V., age 63, son 7, daughter 20, R.
Schaeffer, Philip, Hs. & V., age 36, son 10, daughter 2, C.
Schaeferin, Elenore*, age 45, L.
Schaffer, John, linen weaver, age 29, sons 4-2-3 mos., daughter 5, C.
Schaefer, John Andreas, Hs. & V., age 42, sons 11-7-1, daughters 12-4-4, L.
Schaffer, Lorentz, Hs. & V., age 28, R.
Schaeffer, Gerhard, Hs. & V., age 30, sons 6-3-1, C.
Schaeffer, Matthew, Hs. & V., age 40, son 8, R.
Schaeffer, John Peter, Hs. & V., age 34, L.
Scheur, Peter, smith, age 22, C.
Scheider, John George, Hs. & V., age 28, son 11, daughter 6, L.
Scherer, Ebald, Hs. & V., age 20, R.
Scherer, Jost, linen weaver, age 76, R.
Schmaleberger, Cill, Hs. & V., age 26, son 2, C.
Schellenberger, Catherine*, age 34, son 1, daughter 5, R.
Schenkelberger, Johan Jacob, Hs. & V., age 36, son 3, daughters 12-18-16-1, C.
Schesman, Valentin, mason & stone cutter, age 25, R.
Schiefer, Johan, Hs. & V., age 42, sons 9-5-3, daughter 18 mos., L.
Schlick, Martin, carpenter, age 36, C.
Schleyer, Johan, Hs. & V., age 40, daughters 8-4-1½, C.
Schloemer, Mattheas, Hs. & V., age 38, son 3 mo., daughters 8-3, R.
Schlecht, John, carpenter, age 25, daughter 2, R.
Schlosser, John, Hs. & V., age 54, daughters 14-8, C.
Schmid, Christine*, age 60, R.
Schmif, Nicol, Hs. & V., age 45, sons 11-6, daughter 3, C.
Schmid, Barbara*, age 22, son 2, R.
Schmidt, Eva Mary*, age 17, C.
Schmidt, Nicol, Hs. & V., age 30, son 2, daughters 4-6 wks., C.
Schmidt, Matthew, miller, age 30, sons 5-3, C.
Schmid, Bernhard, Hs. & V., age 27, L.
Schmid, Christian, Hs. & V., age 22, R.
Schmidt, Nicol, smith, age 46, sons 18-9, daughters 9-12-10, L.
Schmid, Caspar, carpenter, age 27, L.
Schmidt, Henry, mason & stone cutter, age 48, sons 19-15-6, daughters 21-15, R.
Schmidt, Michael, Hs. & V., age 50, sons 18-7, daughters 20-14-4, L.
Schmidt, Andrew, Hs. & V., age 47, son 4, daughters 20-14-11-7, L.

Schmidt, Daniel, Hs. & V., age 33, son 2, daughter 4, R.
Schmidt, Peter, weaver, age 36, son 8, daughters 12-10-3-½, R.
Schmidt, Michel, wheelwright, age 55, sons 23-21-12-8, dau. 25, L.
Schmidt, Johan, Hs. & V., age 34, son 1, daughter 9, R.
Schmidt, Caspar, Hs. & V., age 50, sons 18-13-11, daughter 20, R.
Schneide, Conrad, Hs. & V., age 33, daughters 8-5, R.
Schnidt, John Jacob, Hs. & V., age 25, son 9 mos., L.
Schnell, Matthew, Hs. & V., age 43, sons 17-13-10-5, daughter 7, L.
Schneider, Johan, Hs. & V., age 30, son 7, L.
Schneider, John, Hs. & V., age 29, son 2 mo., L.
Schneider, Joachim, turner, age 41, dau. 13-11-4, R.
Schneider, Conrad, carpenter, age 30, son ½, daughter 3, L.
Schneiderin, Margaretha*, age 30, daughter 7, R.
Schoepf, Thomas, mason & stone cutter, age 40, son 6, R.
Schomberger, Georg, butcher, age 31, R.
Schreiner, Martin, Hs. & V., age 20, C.
Schraeblin, Rudolf, linen weaver, age 30, sons 3-9 mos., daughters 6, R.
Schreiber, Albert, Hs. & V., age 26, R.
Schrer, Ulrich, Hs. & V., age 30, sons 10-8, R.
Schuch, Nicolas, Hs. & V., age 24, daughters 4-1½, R.
Schuch, Anna Catherine*, age 64, R.
Schum, John George, Hs. & V., age 35, L.
Schwing, Jacob, Hs. & V., age 23, R.
Schweitzer, Michael, Hs. & V., age 28, sons 2-6 months, L.
Schwan, John, linen weaver, age 25, L.
Schwartz, George, carpenter, age 44, daughters 13-6 -3-1 mo., R.
Schwart, Jane Jacob*, sons 13-9, daughters 7-14-2, R.
Schwartz, Elizabeth*, age 40, sons 13-9, daughters 7-2, L.
Schweitzer, Christoph, Hs. & V., age 23, L.
Scnerer, Peter, smith, age 26, L.
Sex, Philip, Hs. & V., age 53, sons 20-5, daughters 16-13-18 mos., L.
Seip, John Peter, Hs. & V., age 27, daughter 2, R.
Seyfare, Johan Valentine, Hs. & V., age 44, son 17, R.
Seiffart, John, Hs. & V., age 43, son 13, daughters 10-8-2, L.
Seelingerin, Margaretha*, age 54, R.
Shiles, William Christ, Hs. & V., age 35, daughters 10-8-5-2, C.
Shiles, Dominic Christ, Hs. & V., age 76, son 18, C.
Shiler, Matthew, shoemaker, age 36, sons 6-4-1, daughter 7, C.
Shezinger, John, smith, age 37, son 5, C.
Sharnigk, Andrew, Hs. & V., age 26, son 4, daughter 2.
Simon, Philip, Hs. & V., age 25, R.
Sickin, Cecelia*, age 26, son 6, R.
Simon, Nicol, Hs. & V., age 14, R.
Slacyrin, Elizabeth*, age 23, daughter 5, R.
Slott, Ulrich, linen weaver, age 43, sons 17-9, daughter 11, C.
Smith, Philip, Hs. & V., age 42, sons 13-8, daughters 11-9 mos., R.
Sonnenhofin, Mary*, age 60, R.
Spad, Ludwig, carpenter, age 30, C.
Spader, Simon, tailor, age 20, R.
Sprehd, Ignatius, Hs. & V., age 28, son 3, C.
Specht, Johan, Hs. & V., age 31, son 5, daughter 4-½, C.
Spengeler Frederick, Hs. & V., age 53, sons 20-11, R.
Spengler Frantz, Hs. & V., age 30, R.
Spanknebel, Peter, tailor, age 19, R.
Spielman, John, shoemaker, age 33, C.
Spiess, Werner, Hs. & V., age 50, sons 11-5, daughters 14-9, R.
Stock, Johan Henrich, Hs. & V., age 33, L.
Stiebel, Johan, Hs. & V., age 36, sons 6-1 mo., daughters 8-4-2, L.
Stork, John Henry, Hs. & V., age 45, sons 20-18-8-6, daughters 12, L.
Strassberger, Frederick, Hs. & V., age 26, son 3, R.
Steinbacher, Philip, smith, age 30, son 2, L.
Stick, Herman, Hs. & V., age 40, son 14, daughter 8, C.

Steinhauer, Christian, Hs. & V., age 46, son 6 mo., dau. 25-22-19-16-4, C.
Sturteweg, Caspar, Hs. & V., age 24, R.
Stricksheiser, Balzar, cooper & brewer, age 45, son 9, dau. 13-5, R.
Straub, John, Hs. & V., age 26, L.
Strauch, Johan, Hs. & V., age 30, son 2, L.
Streit, Ludwig, Hs. & V., age 42, sons 8-6, daughters 5-3-6 mos., C.
Stieb, John Reinhard, Hs. & V., age 48, sons 12-9, daughters 23-18, L.
Stieb, John Peter, Hs. & V., age 45, sons 5-3, daughter 9 mos., L.
Stuetz, John, Hs. & V., age 35, sons 13-6, daughters 11-3, C.

T

Tagin, Catherine*, age 30, L.
Tanner, Urban, cooper & brewer, age 33, dau. 6-4-3-1.
Tauflin, Catherine*, age 20, R.
Tag, Francis Hendrick, Hs. & V., age 47, son 9, daughter 11, L.
Ternbach, Justus, Hs. & V., age 18, R.
Teiss, Peter, Hs. & V., age 25, R.
That, Bernhard, cooper & brewer, age 45, son 6, daughter 2, L.
Thurdoerf, Frederick, Hs. & V., age 24, R.
Theis, Thomas, mason & stone cutter, age 30, son 1, C.
Thomas, Mattheus, Hs. & V., age 42, son 4, daughters 11-8-3 mos., R.
Thomas, Francis, Hs. & V., age 28, son 2, C.
Tiel, Johan, Hs. & V., age 22, C.
Tielman, Johan, Hs. & V., age 30, C.
Tieffenthaler, George, Hs. & V., age 18, L.
Traut, Johan, Hs. & V., age 20, C.
Trip, Matthew, mason & stone cutter, age 30, son 2, dau. 4, C.
Tragsal, Jacob, mason & stone cutter, age 43, son 15, dau. 13-11-3, C.
Trausch, John, mason & stone cutter, age 18, L.
Tresanus Johan, Hs. & V., age 45, sons 20-4, daughters 22-16, C.
Tulges, Conrad, Hs. & V., age 36, sons 8-4, daughters 6-½, C.

U

Ulrich, Johan, Hs. & V., age 28, R.
Umbauer, Adam, tailor, age 20, R.

V

Valpert, Jacob, Hs. & V., age 40, sons 8-4, daughter 10, R.
Vier, Jacob, carpenter, age 26, L.
Villonger, Johan, Hs. & V., age 30, R.
Volker, Henry, Hs. & V., age 32, L.
Voodrauer, Matthew, carpenter, age 34, sons 15-9-8, daughters 4-1, C.
Volk, Peter, shoemaker, age 29, sons 6-5-1, L.
Volk, Oswald, shoemaker, age 27, L.
Vogt, Daniel Hs. & V., age 46, sons 7-2, daughter 1, C.
Vogt, Johan, Hs. & V., age 63, sons 15-8, daughter 10, R.
Volkerin, Margareth*, age 20, L.
Von Rheim, Christian, Hs. & V., age 23, L.
Volpertin, Margaretha*, age 45, daughter 26, R.

W

Wagner, Conrad, smith, age 46, sons 15-12-11-9, daughters 7-5, L.
Wagner, John, Hs. & V., age 46, sons 6-2, C.
Wagner, Wendel, Hs. & V., age 36, sons 11-4, daughters 9-1 mo., L.
Wagner, Ernset Ludwig, Hs. & V., age 40, sons 16-13-10-6-3, daughter 10, L.
Wagner, Valentine, Hs. & V., age 48, son 7, daughters 13-10 C.
Waldman, Balzar, mason & stone cutter, age 24, L.
Walter, Jacob, potter, age 16, R.
Walter, Philip, Hs. & V., age 21, sons 6-3-1, R.
Walter Adam, Hs. & V., age 50, sons 15-12-4, daughters 6, C.

Walter, John Jacob, Hs. & V., age 41, son 7, daughter 10, R.
Walter, Rudolf, linen weaver, age 28, sons 15-8, R.
Wann, Francis, Hs. & V., age 30, son 3, daughter 5, R.
Wannenmacher, Henry, tile maker, age 64, son 20, C.
Warnon, Jacob, tailor, age 40, son 1, daughter 4, C.
Webber, Martin, Hs. & V., age 34, daughters 3-9 mos.
Weber Philip, Hs. & V., age 60, son 20, C.
Weber, Michel, mason & stone cutter, age 50, sons 18-13, C.
Weber, Henry, Hs. & V., age 52, sons 16-8-6, daughters 2-6 mo., R.
Weber, Valentin, tailor, age 31, son 2, R.
Weber, Henrik, Hs. & V., age 32, sons 13-10-1, daughter 7, R.
Wegman, Mattheus, Hs. & V., age 35, sons 11-9-6 mos., daughters 13-7-6-3, R.
Wehn, Christian, Hs. & V., age 54, daughter 22, R.
Wentzel, Lorentz, Hs. & V., age 29, daughters 10-8-6-4-1, L.
Weichel, Frederick, weaver, age 30, son 2, R.
Weidmanin, Elizabeth*, age 21, R.
Weigel, Valentine, Hs. & V., age 43, sons 11-4, daughters 7-6, C.
Weitz, John, Hs. & V., age 35, sons 6-1, daughter 8, L.
Weimar, Simon, Hs. & V., age 40, sons 10-8 , daughter 5, L.
Weiss, George, miller, age 20, R.
Weiss, Philip, shoemaker, age 44, son 20. daughters 18-11-9-7-4, L.
Weiss, Johan, Hs. & V., age 26, son 3, daughter 2, R.
Weiler, Andrew, shoemaker, age 45, sons 7-5-½, R.
Weiler, Johan, Hs. & V., age 32, R.
Weimar, Simon, mason & stone cutter, age 30, C.
Weinman ,Andreas, Hs. & V., age 30, son 2, daughters 10-6, L.
Wellerin, Anna*, age 38, sons 7-2, R.
Wendels, Johan Peter, schoolmaster, age 42, son 10, daughter 3, L.
Wenzel, Anna Mary*, age 50, L.
Wentz, Balzar, Hs. & V., age 24, L.
Wenzelin, Anne*, age 47, C.
Werner, Henry, Hs. & V., age 24, R.
Westhofer, Johan Jacob, Hs. & V., age 30, son 2, R.
Wezel, Georg, Hs. V., age 14, C.
Wezel, Jacob, Hs. & V., age 12, C.
Wickhart, Conrad, baker, age 31, sons 4-2, daughter 6, L.
Wickert, Melchoir, carpenter, age 21, L.
Wickart, William, linen weaver, age 23, L.
Wickel, Johan, Hs. & V., age 38, R.
Wiennegar, Ulrich, Hs. & V., age 41, son 7, daughter 11-4, C.
Wiesenegger, Caspar, tailor, age 24, L.
Wilmart, Hs. & V., age 35, sons 10-5, daughters 13-8-5, C.
Winter, Henry, Hs. & V., age 40, sons 13-6, daughters 14-11, C.
Winter, Melchoir, saddler, age 42, son 5, C.
Witschager, Magdalene*, age 25, C.
Wipt, Johan Jacob, Hs. & V., age 27, son ½, L.
Wolf, John George, Hs. & V., age 37, sons 7-2, daughters 10-4, L.
Wolf, Peter, Hs. & V., age 28, R.
Wolf, Conrad, carpenter, age 32, son 1, R.
Wolff, Johan, Hs. & V., age 28, L.
Wolfee, Peter, mason & stone cutter, age 30, C.
Wolfskeil, George, Hs. & V., age 28, L.
Wolfschlager, Melchoir, carpenter, age 28, C.
Wollehe, John, baker, age 35, sons 8-5, daughters 10-4-1, R.
Wrikedy, Philip, Hs. & V., age 30, son 7, daughter 1, C.

Z

Zacharias, Lorentz, tailor, age 47, sons 12-10, daughters 23-21-14-5, L.
Zeg, John, Hs. & V., age 42, sons 1-6-½, C.
Zeltnerin, Ursula*, age 20, R.
Zeller, John, cooper & brewer, age 23, L.

Zeber, Joseph, Hs. & V., age 30, C.
Zentgram Johan Hendrich, Hs. & V., age 37, sons 8-2 mo., daughters 10-6, L.
Zimmerman, Matthew, mason & stone cutter, age 38, sons 9-6, R.
Zick, Conrad, mason & stone cutter, age 21, C.
Zink, Rudolf, Hs. & V., age 44, sons 22-17-14, daughter 19, R.
Zinger, Nicol, schoolmaster, age 40, sons 12-6, daughters 9-3, R.
Ziegler, Nicol, Hs. & V., son 7, daughters 23-15-9, R.
Zinckin, Elizabeth*, age 26, son 2, daughters 6-3, L.
Zweiler, Philip, Hs. & V., age 44, sons 12-5, daughter 15 C.
Zwinger, George Peter, Hs. & V., age 40, sons 21-2, C.
Zimerman, Caspar, Hs. & V., age 28, L.

Fourth List of Palatines

List taken at St. Catherine's and Deftford June 15, 11, 1709

FOURTH LIST

Vol. 2, No. D69 and D 70.   Public Record Office, London
List of Poor Palatines who arrived at St. Catherines June 11th, 1709, Taken
June 16

A

Auten, Paulus, Hs. & V., age 39, sons 17-9-6-3, daughter 12, C.
Alten, John, Hs. & V., age 56, daughters 23-22-9-4, C.
Arnold, Philip, Hs. & V., age 30, daughters 5-3, C.
Arlott, Francis, tailor, age 22, C.
Albiget, William, shoemaker, age 34, L.
Adam, Jacob, shoemaker, age 24, L.
Andoit, Samuel.
Albin, Engel*, age 63, L.

B

Baehr, Nicol, Hs. & V., age 52, son 18, R.
Biederman, John, Hs. & V., age 48, R.
Bork, Henrich, Hs. & V., age 50, daughters 20-12-4.
Becker, John, Hs. & V., age 30, daughters 3-1, C.
Bork, Matthes, Hs. & V., age 40, sons 13-11-2, daughters 10-8-5, C.
Borr, Matthes, Hs. & V., age 45, son 21, daughter 18, C.
Baum, Abraham, Hs. & V., age 34, sons 14-12-3-1, daughter 16.
Brandau, William, baker, age 30, son 3, R.
Buntz, Nicol, Hs. & V., age 30, son 16, daughters 14-8, C.
Brathecker, Justus, Hs. & V., age 44, daughters 18-11-9-3-1, R.
Batz, Frederich, Hs. & V., age 28, sons 5-3, daughter 8, L.
Boll, Caspar, Hs. & V., age 40, daughter 4, L.
Brunwasser, Herman, Hs. & V., age 31, son 1, L.
Binhammer, Barthel, Hs. & V., age 42, sons 6-1, daughters 10-3, C.
Bachler, Michel, Hs. & V., age 47, son 5, daughters 12-10-7, R.
Balzar, Jacob, Hs. & V., age 40, sons 9-6, daughter 15, C.
Beyer, Thomas, Hs. & V., age 28, daughters 6-4-2, L.
Busch, Daniel, Hs. & V., age 65, R.
Berger, John, Hs. & V., age 45, sons 16-14-8, daughters 20-10, R.
Borkes, Herman, Hs. & V., age 25, son 15 mo., R.
Baum, Frederik, Hs. & V., age 45, son 14, daughters 21-19-15, C.

Bestel, Jacob, Hs. & V., age 33, C.
Becker, John, Hs. & V., age 26, daughter 1½, C.
Braun, Nicol, Hs. & V., age 60, sons 20-15-11, daughters 17-18-1, R.
Becker, John, Hs. & V., age 28, L.
Bellesheim, Peter, Hs. & V., age 27, son 1, C.
Bartel, Henrich, Hs. & V., age 45, sons 17-14-9, daughters 20-6, L.
Biss, Nicol, Hs. & V., age 20, C.
Baus, Nicol, Hs. & V., age 24, R.
Busch, Justus, Hs. & V., age 24, R.
Burger, Caspar, Hs. & V., age 26, C.
Beckart, Christian, Hs. & V., age 26, C.
Baum, Frederick, cooper, age 45, son 14, daughters 21-19-15, C.
Buch, Henry, cooper, age 49, son 17, daughters 24-16-12-3, C.
Blatz, Andreas, carpenter, age 32, son 2, daughter 5, L.
Buchsel, Augustin, carpenter, age 50, sons 25-22-20-16-12-8-1, R.
Bauer, Cristoph, carpenter, age 21, L.
Besler, Francis, mason, age 46, sons 18-16-7, C.
Beus, Jacob, mason, age 30, sons 6-1, C.
Brill, Michel, linen & cloth weaver, age 21, C.
Bless, Conrad, linen & cloth weaver, age 29, R.
Boset, Daniel, linen & cloth weaver, age 59, son 14-5, da. 21-19-13-11-9-1 mo., R.
Bart, Henrich, linen & cloth weaver, age 54, son 22, daughters 18-16-14-12, R.
Brozis, Anton, tailor, age 33, son 1, daughter 4, C.
Brenner (Bronner), Balzar, baker, age 20, L.
Buerger, John, baker, age 55, son 12, daughter 20, C.
Bakus, Ferdinand, Hs. & V., age 31, son 4, daughter 2, C.
Berchtold, Jacob, miller, age 44, sons 18-15-12, daughter 4, R.
Brain, Barba*, age 40, son 18, daughters 12-4, R.
Baum, Sarah*, age 50, R.
Blasig, Maria*, age 46, son 26, C.
Bork, Elizabeth*, age 20, C.
Bauman, Mary*, age 30, L.
Barba, Anna*, age 22, R.

C

Creuts, Matthes, Hs. & V., age 40, sons 18-7-6-2, daughters 9-4, C.
Creuts, John, Hs. & V., age 36, son 13, daughters 10-7, C.
Coblentzer, John, Hs. & V., age 38, son 5, daughter 2, R.
Christman, John, Hs. & V., age 41, sons 7-5, daughters 9-2, Menon.
Crabbacher, Peter, Hs. & V., age 28, son 2, L.
Cleman, Peter, Hs. & V., age 17, C.
Christ, John, Hs. & V., age 20, C.
Closs, Simon, mason, age 26, daughter ½, C.
Carat, John, mason, age 16, R.
Cobel Jacob, miller, age 27, son½, C.
Crausin, Catherine*, age 52, daughters 24-16, R.
Creuzin, Elizabeth*, age 48, sons 15-13, daughters 19-17-11-8, L.
Clossmanin, Margaretha*, age 40, daughter 19, C.

D

Doenny, Martin, Hs. & V., age 44, son 6, daughter 16, C.
Dietrich, Nicol, Hs. & V., age 46, sons 17-10-5-2, daughters 18-15-7, C.
Drosel, William, Hs. & V., age 36, R.
Durr, Philip, Hs. & V., age 27, L.
Daul Henry, Hs. & V., age 50, sons 21-7-5, daughters 17-14-12-9, L.
Daniel, Anton, Hs. & V., age 40, sons 17-12-6-1, daughters 18-8-4, C.
Dressel, John, Hs. & V., age 32, daughter 1, C.
Dewick, Francis, Hs. & V., age 22, R.
Deller, Jacob, smith, age 22, L.
Decker, John, shoemaker, age 29, son½. C.
Dunckel, Andreas, miller, age 38, son 3, daughters 8-1, C.

Dunckel, John, miller, age 26, C.
Daubin, Barba*, age 60, L.
Dumbacher, Catherine*, age 20, R.

E

Engel, William, Hs. & V., age 27, C.
Engler, Peter, Hs. & V., age 30, son 5, daughter 2, C.
Eckman, John, shoemaker, age 36, daughter 4.
Eschweilen, Thomas, Hs. & V., age 34, daughters 10-6, R.
Eschwein, Jacob, Hs. & V., age 41, son 15, daughters 7-1, R.
Eilen, Henry, Hs. & V., age 38, sons 12-8-3, C.
Ess, Jacob, Hs. & V., age 49, daughter 1, C.
Eberhard, Michel, Hs. & V., age 44, sons 21-12-8, daughter 13, R.
Ehresman, Michel, Hs. & V., age 46, son 20, daughters 22-13-7, R.
Engel, John, Hs. & V., age 36, daughters 10-6-3, C.
Emmel, Christoph Hs. & V., age 27, son 7, daughter 3, R.
Ermitter, Francis, Hs. & V., age 35, son 7, daughters 5-2, C.
Ehrenbach, Michel, Hs. & V., age 27, C.
Erlenbach, George, tailor, age 53, son 6, daughters 16-8, R.

F

Fritz, Nicol, Hs. & V., age 54, sons 20-14-13-9, daughters 15-12-2, C.
Fushs, John, Hs. & V., age 30, sons 4-1, L.
Fischer, Peter, Hs. & V., age 36, daughters 5-2, R.
Froebus, George, Hs. & V., age 39, son 18, daughters 20-12, R.
Fuchs, George, Hs. & V., age 40, son 12, daughters 17-10-8-6, C.
Fritz, John, Hs. & V., age 30, sons 7-2, daughters 8-5, C.
Fehling, Henry, Hs. & V., age 24, R.
Faber, Adam, Hs. & V., age 30, R.
Friede, Nicol, Hs. & V., age 21, C.
Frantzberg, John, cooper, age 24, L.
Forster, George, linen & colth weaver, age 39, daughters 14-10-7-6, L.
Forster, Nicol, tailor, age 22, R.
Ferry, John C., shoemaker, age 23, C.

G

Graner, Jacob, Hs. & V., age 60, R.
Gro, George, Hs. & V., age 40, son 2, daughters 7-5, L .
Gro, Philip, Hs. & V., age 30, sons 6-5-3-1, L.
Gesher, Conrad, Hs. & V., age 26, sons 2-½, L.
Guck, John, Hs. & V., age 35, daughter 3, C.
Gross, Dietrich, Hs. & V., age 27, C.
Getman, Caspar, Hs. & V., age 36, sons 16-14-8-5, daughters 6-5-2, L.
Gross, William, Hs. & V., age 56, sons 12-9, daughter 5.
Gebel, Henrich, Hs. & V., sons 12-10, daughters 14-2, L.
Giss, Jost, Hs. & V., age 39, sons 12-10-3, daughter 5, C.
Geibel, Peter, Hs. & V., age 17, R.
Gamben, John, Hs. & V., age 24, R.
Ganter, Christian, cooper, age 50, son 4, daughters 20-1, R.
Gerser, Henry, carpenter, age 36, sons 7-4, daughters 13-10, L.
Gruber, Matthes, joiner, age 46, sons 14-12-10-4, daughter 1, C.
Gibstein, Martin, shoemaker, age 33, C.
Ganglet, John, baker, age 28, daughter 4 mo., L.
Gerlach, Conrad, huntsman, age 49, sons 7-5, daughters 16-1, R.
Guidi, Philip, surgeon, age 40, daughters 3-1, C.
Ganglof, Magdalena*, age 60, L.

H

Hank, Bleigart, Hs. & V., age 46, son 7, daughter 4, R.
Heffrich, Henrich, Hs. & V., age 50, sons 19-16, R.

Herzel, Adam, Hs. & V., age 44, daughter 14, L.
Herman, Justus, Hs. & V., age 41, daughters 14-7, L.
Hofman, Philip, Hs. & V., age 30, son 1, L.
Herman, Sebastian, Hs. & V., age 26, R.
Heibel, Bernhardt, Hs. & V., age 40, son 8, daughters 14-3-1, R.
Hodel, Isaac, Hs. & V., age 36, son 3 mo., R.
Hedgen, Conrad, Hs. & V., age 42, son 17, R.
Hupfer, David, Hs. & V., age 30, daughters 12-9, R.
Hern, John, Hs. & V., age 37, sons 7-5, daughters 2, R.
Hagadorn, Peter, Hs. & V. age 60, sons 24-22-15, daughters 17-11, L.
Hilles, Nicol, Hs. & V., age 40, son 10, daughters 16-3-5, R.
Heins, John Adam, Hs. & V., age 33, son 6, L.
Heins, Nicol, Hs. & V., age 24, L.
Herich, Jost, Hs. & V., age 50, sons 16-11-7, daughters 18-12-5, C.
Hauch, Lucas, Hs. & V., sons 22-16-13-9-3-8 da., daughters 13-12-9, R.
Huhn, Henry, Hs. & V., age 40, R.
Heller, Wolf, Hs. & V., age 26, L.
Henning, Andreas, Hs. lb V., age 38, C.
Hohenfeld, Lorenz, Hs. & V., age 22, C.
Hensel, Valentin, Hs. & V., age 20, C.
Heiden, Jacob, cooper, age 44, son 1, R.
Hoges, Michel, wheelwright, age 26, C.
Hohn, Michel, smith, age 31, son 4, daughters 10-4, L.
Herman, Sebastian linen & cloth weaver, age 36, C.
Heddesheimer, Henry, tailor, age 22, R.
Hag, Caspar, tailor, age 20, L.
Horsbach, Dietrich, shoemaker, age 36, son 6, daughter 1, C.
Hen, Henrich, shoemaker, age 40, sons 13-11-9-6, daughter 2 L.
Horning, Gerhard, bricklayer, age 40, daughters 6-2, R.
Has, Henry, bricklayer, age 26, son 3, daughter 1, L.
Hibig, Anne*, age 50, sons 29-24-23, daughter 26, R.
Hillis, Catherine*, age 28, daughter 2, R.
Hausen, Eve*, age 24, C.
Hofman, Sophia*, age 18, L.
Heins, Eva*, age 24, L.
Haasin, Engel*, age 22, C.

J

Johan, Nicol, Hs. & V., age 32, sons 13-9-7, daughters 6-1, L.
Jung, Nicol, carpenter, age 21, L.
Julius, Henrich, joiner, age 21, L.
Jager, Carl, miller, age 36, son 7, daughter 4, R.
Jakoettin, Mary*, age 24, R.
Jakoettin, Anne*, age 20, R.

K

Kochin, Elizabeth*, age 55, L.
Khidy, Catherine*, age 30, R.
Krutsch, Margaretha*, age 24, C.
Kaefer, Casimir, Hs. & V., age 23, L.
Kesler, George, Hs. & V., age 40, sons 14-10-6-3, C.
Klein, Philip, smith, age 45, sons 9-7, daughter 4, R.
Krutsch, John, Hs. & V., age 40, son 2, daughters 8-6-4, C.
Keusel, Jacob, Hs. & V., age 44, sons 7-1½, daughters 13-11, L.
Kurtz, George, Hs. & V., age 37, son 12, L.
Kintig, John, Hs. & V., age 45, sons 12-10, daughters 17-16-6, R.
Krenig, John, Hs. & V., age 40, son 6, daughter 11, R.
Kuhns Conrad, Hs. & V., age 44, son 24, daughter 20, L.
Kauer, John, Hs. & V., age 27, daughters 7-6-3, C.
Kessler, Caspar, Hs. & V., age 64, son 20, daughter 25, C.
Kulpfaber, Jacob, Hs. & V., age 26, daughters 4-2, R.

Kludy, George, Hs. & V., age 22, R.
Kirsch, Adam, cooper, age 28, son 6, daughters 2-3 mo., C.
Klein, William, carpenter, age 26, L.
Kless, John, carpenter, age 28, daughter 3, C.
Koerner, John, joiner, age 33, L.
Klein, Adam, wheelwright, age 28, R.
Kerber, Nicol, smith, age 50, son 3 mo., C.
Kesler, Nicol, linen & cloth weaver, age 24, L.
Keller, Jacob, Hs. & V., age 58, son 4, R.
Knauer, Zacarian, Hs. & V., age 26, L.
Kuehn, Herman, Hs. & V., age 55, son 26, daughters 28-18, C.
Kolhaus, Lucas, linen & cloth weaver, age 40, son 3, daughters 11-8, C.
Kuhn, Peter, linen & cloth weaver, age 24, L.
Klein (Lang), Moritz, tailor, age 30, sons 8-6, daughters 10-4-1, C.
Kummer, John, schoolmaster, age 40, sons 9-1, daughters 8-6, R.
Klepper, Conrad, bricklayer, age 33 sons 9-2, daughter 5, C.
Kuhlbrunner, Caspar, baker, age 23, R.
Krantz, Conrad, Hs. & V., age 23, daughter 1, R.
Krinin, Mary*, age 24, L.

L

Ludwig, Henry, Hs. & V., age 40, sons 18-10, L.
Lang, Wolf, Hs. & V., age 30, son 1, daughters 6-3, C.
Lutz, John, Hs. & V., age 33, sons 10-7-3, daughter 14, R.
Lakeman, Isaac, Hs. & V., age 36, son 10, daughters 7-4, R.
Lorentz, Dierich, Hs. & V., age 34, sons 12-3, C.
Linnenbaum, Peter, Hs. & V., age 50, sons 20-3-1, C.
Linnenbaum, Christoph, Hs. & V., age 26, daughters 4-2, C.
Leich, Simon, Hs. & V., age 34, son 6, daughter 1½, L.
Lerne, Matthes, Hs. & V., age 42, sons 15-12-2, daughters 14-8, C.
Leophard, John, Hs. & V., age 38, sons 7-3, daughters 14-12-7, C.
Lenacker, Peter, Hs. & V., age 36, sons 14-9-6, daughters 14-12-10-7-2, C.
Leasch, Burchard, cooper, age 28, L.
Leis, Mathes, cooper, age 38, sons 12-½, daughters 18-16-11-8-7, C.
Liset, Philip, carpenter, age 24, R.
Luich, Kostman, carpenter, age 36, sons 22-8, R.
Liris (Siris), Michel, Hs. & V., age 40, son 3 mo., daughters 12-11-10-4, L.
Ledig, Nicol, Hs. & V., age 25, son 2 wk., daughter 18 mo., R.
Lechner, Michel, Hs. & V., age 40, sons 14-3, C.
Leib, John, Hs. & V., age 45, son 10, daughters 14-6 mo., R.
Ludwig, Anton, tailor, age 28, son 2, daughter 6, C.
Leilling (Salling), Francis, tailor, age 16, C.
Lucerni, Abraham, baker, age 27, R.
La Dour, John, blazier, age 18, C.
Lisin, Eve*, age 45, son 12, daughter 10, R.
La Force, Barbara*, age 20, C.
La Force, Anna*, age 18, C.
Leich, Catherine*, age 30, L.

M

Morheiser, Nicol, Hs. & V., age 26, son 7, daughter 2, C.
Matthes, Lorentz, Hs. & V., age 75, son 24, L.
Meyer, Henry, Hs. & V., age 43, son 4, daughter 6, R.
Mueller, Henry, Hs. & V., age 34, sons 4-3, daughter 1, R.
Mitwig, Gennanus, Hs. & V., age 54, son 18, daughter 14, C.
Mohr, Augustin, Hs. & V., age 36, sons 13-4-2, daughter 6, C.
Mueller, Peter, Hs. Ib V., age 45, sons 18-6-4, C.
Metz, Sebastian, Hs. & V., age 36, son 18, daughters 15-7, L.
Mumenthal, Jacob, Hs. & V., age 48, R.
Mullen, Gerhard, Hs. & V., age 35, son 7, C.
Mullen, Michel, Hs. & V., age 26, son 2, daughter 1, L.

Michel, Nicol, Hs. & V., age 30, L.
Margaret, Peter, carpenter, age 50, son 24, C.
Metz, Simon, carpenter, age 33, son 4, daughters 7-2, C.
Mauer, George, mason, age 32, L.
Moor, David, mason, age 36, R.
Mey, John, mason, age 36, son ½, daughters 8-6-4, C.
Meyer, George, smith, age 19, L.
Michel, John, smith, age 42, C.
Muller, Anton, linen and cloth weaver, age 56, R.
Mueller, Jacob, Hs. & V., age 50, son 6, daughter 14, R.
Mess, Abraham, Hs. & V., age 34, daughters 14-2.
Maur, John, Hs. & V., age 36, sons 13-11-10-8, daughter ½.
Metzger, John, Hs. & V., age 32, daughter 1½, C.
Mutz, Friederik, Hs. & V., age 22, C.
Mueller, Martin, Hs. & V., age 32, sons 8-6-5, daughter 2, R.
Mansbeil, Caspar, Hs. & V., age 33, son 5, L.
Meyer, Adam, Hs. & V., age 30, C.
Mengel, Wendel, Hs. & V., age 27, son 3, daughters 5-2 da., R.
Maus, Michel, linen & cloth weaver, age 24, C.
Maus, Reinhard, linen & cloth weaver, age 18, C.
Merzel, Jacob, tailor, age 30, L.
Munster , Peter, shoemaker, age 30, sons 9-4, daughters 8-6, L.
Maus, Dietrich, bricklayer, age 30, sons 9-6, daughter 3 mo., C.
Matthes, Mareus, weaver, age 88, daughter 24, R.
Matthas, George, weaver, age 32, son 3, R.
Michel, Henry, weaver, age 38, sons 8-5, daughters 10-1, L.
Meyer, Barthol, age 50, daughters 14-3-6-5, L.
Meiss, Barthal, glazier, age 26, L.
Meyer, Henry, brickmaker, age 43, son 4, daughter 6, R.
Meyer, Henry, herdsman, age 31, sons 7-4-2, C.
Mueller, Peter, miller, age 45, sons 15-14-7, daughters 19-3, R.
Martin, Peter, miller, age 33, son 1, daughter 7, C.
Meyerin, Delia*, age 21, C.
Mosenheim, Mary*, age 23, L.
Meyerin, Margaretha*, age 23, R.
Mayer, Paulus, Hs. & V., age 18, C.
Mussel, Barba*, age 24, L.

N

New, Wencelag, smith, age 20, C.
Nuss, Ludwig, Hs. & V., age 46, daughters 15-12-10, R.
Nusbaum, John, shoemaker, age 46, sons 13-9-6-2, daughters 17-13, Mennon.
Nutzberger, Matthes, butcher, age 56, son 3, daughters 18-12-7, L.

O

Oudenbecker, John, Hs. & V., age 18, C.
Omes, Peter, Hs. & V., age 21, C.
Oberdubbel, Jacob, Hs. & V., age 35, sons 4-2, daughter 11, C.
Ostwald, John, tailor, age 44, sons 14-3, daughters 22-6, L.
Osewald, Adelia*, age 28, son 8, C.

P

Peder, Nicol, Hs. & V., age 40, sons 16-15-9-2, daughter 8, C.
Peters, John, Hs. & V., age 19, R.
Pfuhl, Peter, joiner, age 48, sons 10-5-1, daughters 12-5, L.
Peter, Jacob, Hs. & V., age 22, R.
Pommer, Bongraf, Hs. & V., age 45, son 17, daughter 14, C.
Propfer, Justus, Hs. & V., age 30, sons 7-4, daughter 9, L.
Puner, Wendel, Hs. & V. age 30, sons 5-2, C.
Pfalzer, Henry, shoemaker, age 36, sons 5-2, daughter 10, C.

Pitty, Jacob, brickmaker, age 50, daughters 18-10, R.

R

Riegel, Christian, Hs. & V., age 20, L.
Reuter, Nicol, Hs. & V., age 25, C.
Reuter, Ludwig, Hs. & V., age 14, C.
Rosing, Matthes, carpenter, age 23, C.
Roll, Sost, smith, age 26, C.
Rappell, John, Hs. & V., age 32, daughter 4.
Resch, Adam, Hs. & V., age 50, sons 17-11-6, daughters 19-18.
Rosbach, Peter, Hs. & V., age 40, sons 12-7, L.
Rennersbacher, Christian, Hs. & V., age 24, R.
Reishardt, Christian, Hs. & V., age 32, son 3, daughter 4, R.
Rink, Melchoir, Hs. & V., age 42, son 16, daughter 10, R.
Ritter, Jacob, Hs. & V., age 31, sons 10-5-½, L.
Rup, Peter, Hs. & V., age 42, sons 20-16, daughters 14-12-2, R.
Roemer, John, Hs. & V., age 26, son 1, daughter 3, C.
Reuter, Ludwig, Hs. & V., age 32, R.
Reichardt, Valentine, Hs. & V., age 18, L.
Rock, Jacob, linen & cloth weaver, age 40, R.
Reichard, Henry, tailor, age 15, C.
Regel, Matthes, schoolmaster, age 40, son 2, C.
Rasor, Frederick, schoolmaster, age 29, L.
Reid, Nicol, shoemaker, age 34, son 13, daughter 10, L.
Roth, Andreas, baker, age 24, L.
Reuter, Henry, huntsman, age 34, daughters 4-2, C.
Rose, Cristoph, glazier, age 35, L.
Reichman, Anne*, age 43, son 9, daughters 6-3, C.

S

Schnick, Michel, Hs. & V., age 22, L.
Schuster, Peter, Hs. & V., age 40, C.
Schoemacher, Michel, cooper, age 24, L.
Schummer, John, carpenter, age 20, C.
Siffer, Bastian, carpenter, age 21, R.
Schmidt, Peter, carpenter, age 39, son 10, daughters 14-5-2, C.
Strosser, Daniel, carpenter, age 60, son 12, R.
Scheyer, John, carpenter, age 30, son 3, R.
Schmidt, Carl, smith, age 36, sons 10-9-7-4, daughter 1, L.
Schantz, Peter, smith, age 20, L.
Schezel, Jacob, carpenter, age 39, L.
Son, Elias, joiner, age 21, L.
Schmidt, Christian, smith, age 18, R.
Stein, William, smith, age 23, C.
Scheuer, John, Hs. & V., age 35, C.
Schueler, Peter, Hs. & V., age 46, son 7-1, daughters 20-14-5, C.
Sontag, Francis, Hs. & V., age 36, sons 5-1, daughters 13-5, C.
Schunger, Theobald, Hs. & V., age 38, sons 13-11-5, daughter 2, C.
Schmidt, Caspar, Hs. & V., age 30, son 2, R.
Schoepfer, George, Hs. & V., age 32, R.
Schnorr, Nicol, Hs. & V., age 50, son 12, daughters 22-17, L.
Steiner, Michel, Hs. & V., age 50, C.
Schutz, Martin, Hs. & V., age 22, son½, C.
Stengel, Philip, Hs. & V., age 54, L.
Schales, Peter, Hs. & V., age 38, daughters 15-12-4, L.
Schmidt, Peter, Hs. & V., age 33, sons 12-10, daughters 14-2, R.
Schaefer, Zerben, Hs. & V., age 40, son 12, C.
Seip, Michel, Hs. & V., age 23, L.
Speicherman, Herman, Hs. & V., age 46, son 16, daughter 18, L.
Schwed, Jacob Hs. & V., age 42, sons 18-13-8, daughters 10-5-4-3 mo, C.
Stegen, Nicol, Hs. & V., age 58, sons 7-3, daughters 14-12, L.

Schleicher, George, Hs. & V., age 40, son 3, daughters 19-17-1, L.
Salbach, John, Hs. & V., age 52, daughters 17-14, L.
Sahlbach, Edmund, Hs. & V., age 21, L.
Stott, Dietrich, Hs. & V., age 31, daughter 4, C.
Schaefer, Andreas, Hs. & V., age 50, sons 27-24-17, daughter 20, L.
Sorg, Matthes, Hs. & V., age 54, son 4, daughters 10-7, C.
Sperling, Peter, Hs. & V., age 47, sons 10-8-4, daughters 18-16-14, L.
Schintzerling, John, Hs. & V., age 41, daughters 12-8-4, R.
Schreiner Simon, Hs. & V., age 36, sons 4-2, daughters 12-10-8, C.
Schmidt, Nicol, Hs. & V., age 19, R.
Schmidt, Nicol, Hs. & V., age 36, son 12, R.
Sottig, Herman, Hs. & V., age 40, sons 11-1, daughters 14-9-5, C.
Schneider, Ulrich, Hs. & V., age 34, sons 14-1, R.
Schmidt, Adam, Hs. & V., age 36, daughters 13-10-8, C.
Schmidt, John, Hs. & V., age 35, son 8, daughters 3-3 mo., C.
Staut, Grin, Hs. & V., age 30, R.
Schmids, Henry, Hs. & V., age 60, sons 15-12.
Schenkel, John, Hs. & V., age 44, son 10, daughters 13-8-5, R.
Schmidt, John, Hs. & V., age 35, son 8, daughters 3-3 mo., C.
Schmidt, Arndt, Hs. & V., age 30, son 10, daughter 3, R.
Schumacher, Bartel, Hs. & V., age 41, sons 11-6, daughters 17-14-8, L.
Scherner, John Michel, Hs. & V., age 39, sons 7-3, daughters 18-16-14-8, L.
Schmidt, George, Hs. & V., age 53, sons 22-20-2, daughters 18-16-14-8, L.
Stoss, John, Hs. & V., age 40, sons 10-1, daughters 16-3, C.
Saar, John, Hs. & V., age 50, sons 20-18-5-5-2, daughters 14-9, C.
Son, Philip, Hs. & V., age 30, L.
Schwab, Philip, Hs. & V., age 20, C.
Seibel, Valentin, Hs. & V., age 22, R.
Seibel, George, Hs. & V., age 20, R.
Singerin, Anne*, age 20, L.
Schinkin, Cristina*, age 24, L.
Schaeds, Anne*, age 20, R.
Schreibin, Margaretha*, age 24, C.
Shoemaker, John, baker, age 37, R.
Schellin, Magdalene*, age 22, R.
Schmidt, John Peter, tailor, age 19, L.
Schmidt, Peter, tailor, age 19, L.
Schmidt, John, baker, age 23, son 3, C.
Schwab, Conrad, baker, age 20, L.
Schoenwoif, John, locksmith, age 23, R.
Schnick, Michel, miller, age 22, L.
Schaeflin, Henry, miller, age 49, son 15, C.
Sheffen, Elbot*, age 40, son 10, daughter 5, L.
Schmidin, Gertrud*, age 30, daughter 3, C.
Seibelin, Cristina*, age 56, R.
Segbin, Appolonia*, age 50, sons 24-18-9, C.

T

Tieffenbach, Anna*, age 74, R.
Themer, John, Hs. & V., age 36, sons 15-11-8-6, daughter 1, L.
Tachfletter, George, Hs. & V., age 30, son 3, L.
Thiel, John, Hs. & V., age 50, daughters 18-12, L.
Tiel, Herman, Hs. & V., age 26, daughter 2, L.
Tieffenbach, Conrad, cooper, age 50, daughters 11-4-1, R.
Tiel, Jacob, cooper, age 24, L.
Thalheimer, Nicol, carpenter, age 27, daughters 3-1, L.
Tiel, Ananias, wheelwright, age 36, sons 5-1, L.
Tielman, Conrad, Hs. & V., age 30, sons 8-6-1½, daughter 9, C.

U

Ulrich, Elias, Hs. & V., age 46, son 2, daughters 13-2½, R.

V

Vogt, Elizabeth*, age 48, C.
Valentin, John, Hs. & V., age 56, sons 14-3, daughters 16-8, C.
Volkhart, John, Hs. & V., sons 20-18-15, daughters 13-12, L.
Valentins, Velten, Hs. & V., age 20, C.
Volks, Arnold, Hs. & V., age 32, sons 9-1, daughters 13-4, C.
Vorbeck, John Hs. & V., age 56, daughter ½, C.
Vogt, Henry, Hs. & V., age 25, C.
Valentin, Henry, Hs. & V., age 20, C.

W

Wieser, Jacob, linen & cloth weaver, age 53, son 16, R.
Walten, John, tailor, age 20, R.
Wremmar, John, tailor, age 18, C.
Wegrauch, Valentin, hatter, age 38, sons 7-2, daughters 11-9, L.
Weisgerber, John, saddler, age 45, C.
Wirs, Frederick, brickmaker, age 39, daughters 8-6-2, L.
Walrat, William, miller, age 23, C.
Weisrockin, Catherine*, age 47, daughter 18, R.   z
Wilhelm, Jane*, age 28, R.
Wilhelm, Paul, Hs. & V., age 30, R.
Wicked, Bernhard, Hs. & V., age 36, sons 11-5-½, daughter 8, C.
Wilmar, Anton, Hs. & V., age 40, son 13, L.
Wolpert, Nicol, Hs. & V., age 30, son 10, daughter 4, C.
Wind, Peter, Hs. & V., age 41, sons 21-8-7-2, daughter 18, C.
Walter, Caspar, Hs. & V., age 44, sons 21-16-12-8-4, daughters 18-14-12-6, L.
Weber, Dietrich, Hs. & V., age 42, son 1, daughter 15, C.
Wend, Henry, Hs. & V., age 38, sons 15-2-5, daughter 10, L.
Wilhelm, John, Hs. & V., age 40, C.
Wenckel, Henry, Hs. & V., age 23, R.
Weber, Sebastian, carpenter, age 30, R.
Weber, Henry, carpenter, age 24, R.
Wadenspfhut, Jacob, carpenter, age 32, sons 3-1, L.
Weller, John, linen & cloth weaver, age 49, C.
Wingart, John, Hs. & V., age 46, sons 18-13-11-8-6, B.
Wiehelm, Mathes, Hs. & V., age 40, sons 23-15-11, R.
Wagnerin, Catherine*, age 20, C.
Wiedmacher, Catherine*, age 24, R.

Z

Zerbst, Philip, figuremaker, age 25, L.
Zerbst, Martin, Hs. & V., age 34, sons 11-8-4-2, L.
Zepp, Leonhardt, Hs. & V., age 44, sons 20-19-8, daughter 17, R.
Ziegler, Andreas, cooper, age 40, son 14, daughters 3-1, R.
Zerbst, Conrad, Hs. & V., age 39, R.
Zolker, Balzar, Hs. & V., age 70, R.
Zerbst, Peter, Hs. & V., age 50 son 25, daughters 28-27-25-23-14, C.

Abstract of the Fourth List of 1745 Palatines that Arrived June 11, 1709

Men	338
Wives	331
Widows	16
Unmarried Men	92
Unmarried Women	29
Sons above 14 years	122
Daughters above 14 years	127
Sons under 14 years	351
Daughters under 14 years	339
Total	1745

An Abstract of the Three Lists of Palatines Who Came from Germany May 1-June 10, 1709

Men	940
Wives	903
Widows	73
Unmarried Men	292
Unmarried Women	77
Sons above 14 years	257
Sons under 14 years	1016
Daughters above 14 years	247
Daughters under 14 years	970
	4775
Fourth List	1745
Total here now June 26, 1709	6520

Further Classification of London List By Occupation

	1st	2nd	3rd	4th	Tot.
Hs. and V.	113	113	456	262	944
Hus.	32	83			115
Hrd.	3			1	4
Wheelwrights	1	5	5	3	14
Smiths	11	9	15	12	47
Saddlers	1	1	2	1	5
Millers	5	4	9	10	28
Bakers	2	10	11	11	34
Brewers	1	12			13
Butchers	3	3	8	1	15
Clo. & lin. wea.	8	15	27	15	65
Tailors	3	19	18	16	56
Shoemakers	5		20	12	37
Stocking wea.	1		2	3	6
Tanners	1		2	3	6
Carpentrers	8	14	44	22	88
Joiners	3			5	8
Masons	2	9	36	7	54
Coopers	3			12	15
Bookbinders	1				1
Miners			2		2
Schoolmaster	3	5	3		11
Coop. & Br.			23		23
Turners	4	2			6
Laborers		2			2
Silversmiths	2				2
Hunters		3	2		5
Wool weav.		2			2
Potters		3			3
Tilemakers		1			1
Brickmkr.		2	3		5
Surgeons		2	1		3
Figuremkrs.		1	1		2
Locksmith		2	1		3
Hatters			2		2
Glazers			3		3
Bricklayers			4		4

By Religion

	1st	2nd	3rd	4th	Tot.
Luth.	55	132	243	132	562
Ref.	125	145	282	140	692
Cath.	25	63	258	177	523
Bap.	9			1	10
Menonite		1		2	3

PRISONERS OF WAR

Individuals Captured During the Colonial and Revolutionary War as Shown by The Correspondence of Gov. Clinton and Others.

List of English Prisoners Delivered to
Col. Schuyler, Colonial Documents
Vol. 10, Page 881-883
Montreal the first 9ber, 1758.

Ammen, Jeremie
Aste, John
Arforder, Thomas
Arter, Phillipe
Ahesener, John
Bayde, George
Browford, Carpenter
Benham, John
Brown, Thomas
Bachoren, Piter
Chapman, Rufus
Crus, Lous
Claland, Epham
Drick, Fastery
Emerson, Thomas, Sergeant
Els, Stoful
Fangran, William
Galik, Joseph
Guilas, Arman
Gregorie, William
Grille, Frederick
Hontz, Ezekel
Halmey, Phillippe
Hall, John
Ingel, Fattel
Jacques, Jermi
Lake, John
Lorge, Jacob
Michel, Thomas
McDogul, Hugh
Neles, Henry
Night, David
Philippe, Daniel
Parent, John
Pilo, Phillippe
Petry, John Jost, Militiaman
Petry, Joste, Magistrate
Parker, Isaac
Raik, George
Rayde, Arten
Rodjer, Amos
Rochester, Mikael
Robertds, Benjamin
Reliquen, Peter
Raiford, John
Semeth, Louis
Semelon, Joseph
St. Clair, John
Sanade, Garet
Sile, John

Stuard, Malcom
Severence , Matthiew
Sansworth, Ebenizer
Scribner, Samuel
Sanswood, William
Stall, Thoby
Staver, Nicolas
Slix, Georges
Stille, John
Tetman, Joseph
Tipaul, Mikael
Timoth, George
Vickerre, Joseph
Wedge, James
Woods, Georgus
Wiver, John
Wader, Armant
Will, Frederick

WOMEN

Almer, Slelaine
Petry, Delias
Petry, Marie
Wiver, Marie

CHILDREN

Arter, Marie
Balligneur, Marguerite
How, William
How, Josia
How, Peter
Lorge, Lisette
Petry, Anne
Petry, Marie   x
Petry, John Joste
Petry, Elizabeth
Wiver, Marguerite

Names of women and children not included in the change, whom the Marquis de Vaudreuil has been so good as to send back.

Almer, Marguerite
Arter, Elisabet
Anglich, Marie
Armer, Anne
Andrews, Isabel
Askener, Anne
Broterton, Anne
Branon, Sara
Carik, Suyanne
Flelius, Ledia
Hix, Ister
Moon, Marguerite
McQueen, Marguerite
Piters, Sarah
Rill, Marguerite
Rodjer, Eleonard

Timothy, Delia

Nord, Marie

List of prisoners who are going up rom Quebec to Montreal to contribite to the exchange intended by he General:

Officers

Mess. Schuyler, Col of the New Jersey Regiment.

Martin, Captain-Lt. of Artillery

Polman, Captain-Major in the New England Regiment.

Stakes, Surgeon Mj. in said Regiment.

Thorne, Ensign in Blakeneys Regiment.

Webb, Ensign in the New Jersey Regiment.

Soldiers

Chappy, Moses

Colens, Matthieu

Dogwendes, Jacob

Dolavert, Samuel

Frayer, Daniel

Hamilton, William

Johnson, Alex

Robertson, John

Robert, Nathanel

Ware, John

Sailors

Brarate, Thomas

Carr, Michael

Malson, Adam

Rotner, Solomon

Stonevert, John

Thompson, John

Warton, William

Laborers and Others

Pourner, Patrick

Lock, Jonathan

Lock, Daniel

Stynes, Thomas

Symonton, Matthew

Eston, Abel

Thomas, Negro servant to Mr. Schuyler (not a prisoner).

A child whose name is unknown.

Johnson, Silvanis

Women

Bruler, Barberry, widow

How, Miss

Hamilton, Miss

Scott, Elizabeth

Williams, Elizabeth

List of English who are absent at Mr. Schuyler's departure and of those who go in their stead, viz.

Names of English Absent

Benham, John

Drich, James

Gregorie, William

Grill, Frederick

Ingrel, Fallet

Sanade, Jaret

Tarin, John

Names of English Delivered to M. Schuyler in Their Stead

Binyem, John

Brown, John

Bams, John

Crabb, Theodore

Felk, Cornelius

Mauholand, Denis

Tite, George

Catalogus Serius Adventorum ex Palatinatu ad Rhenum

Peter Rose, Cloth weaver, married, m. 34; Johanna Rosin, wife, f. 45.

Maria Wemarin, husbandwoman, widow f. 37; Catharina Wemarin, child, f. 2.

Isaac Feber, husbandman and vineyard, married m. 33 ; Catharina Feber wife, f., 30; child Abraham Feber, child m. 2.

Daniel Fiere, husbandman, married, m. 32; Anna Mair Fiere, wife, f., 30; Andreas Fiere, child, m. 7; Johannes Fiere, child, m. 6.

Ex Holsatia

Herman Schuneman, Clerk, unmarried, M. 28.

In index additional names to be sent to New York, no dates given. Taken from Documents relating to Colonial History, page 53, Vol. 5.

(Note—We are indebted to William Brinkman of Altamont, N. Y. for assistance in preparing the following lists.—Ed).

A list of persons captured by the British and Indians in the Mohawk Valley, Tryon County, N. Y., in the year 1780 in the War of the Revolution:

Clinton Papers Vol. VI, pages 724-27

Ayrer, Jacob taken April 3, 1780 not in arms.

Ayrer, George

Bell, Diedrick

Bettinger, Christina, 7 years, child of Martin Bettinger.

Brown, George

Brooner, Jacob, aged 63

Bellinger, John Jost, son of Col. Bellinger.

Bost, Elizabeth, 20 years.

Brooner, Jacob, 63 years, father.

Brooner, Frena, 13 years, daughter of Jacob Brooner.

Ball, wife of Samuel Ball.

Biggs, Hannah, Abigail and Esther daughters of Honestill Biggs taken

from Skeensborough 1780.
Becker, Lieut. Tebalt
Chr istman, Frederick
Casselman, Peter taken latter end of
July
Davis,, a daughter of the late Jost
Davis.
Duer, wife of John Duer.
Demot, George
Demot, Nicholas
Davis, Peter
Davis, Henry
Dornberger, Frederick.
Duer, John
Deline, Benjamin
Dennis, Jacob
Dubois, men of Col. Dubois regiment
of Levies
Demot, Capt. Mark, taken in arms
Oct|, 1780.
Dockstadder, George taken in arms
Oct. 1780.
Eccles, Jacob, 7 years, son of Henry
Eccles, Jr.
Elder, Sarah of Pennsylvania.
Easeman, Stephen
Friesleman, Catharina, 30 years, wife
of Christian Friesleman.
Friesleman, Margaret, 1 0years, child
of Christian Friesleman.
Friesleman, Elizabeth, 8 years, child
of Christian Friesleman.
Friesleman, Anna, 1 year, child of
Christian Friesleman.
Frank, John taken June 8, 1778 not in
arms.
Forbes, son of Jacob Forbes.
Failing, Jacob, taken Aug. 1780.
Forrer, Rudolph
Forrer, Adam
Frank, Lawrence, taken Sept., 1778
not in arms.
Forenboss, John
Forenboss, Nicholas
Ferry, Rudolph
Furry, Adam
Garter, John
Garter, John, taken not in arms April
3, 1780
Gymitz. Mary, 17 years, daughter of
Frederick Gymitz.
Garter, two sons of John Garter.
House, Christiner, 16 years, child of
the widow of Henry House.
House, Elizabeth, 11 years, child of
the widow of Henry House.
House, Conrad, 7 years, child of the
widow of Henry House.
House, Elizabeth, 21 years, wife of
Hanyose House.
House, Christiner, 4 years, child of
Hanyose House.
House. Jacobus, 6 mos., child of Han-
yose House.
House, Maria Elizabeth, 17 years,
daughter of George House.
House, Conrad, 15 years, son of Adam
House.
Haverman, Adam. 10 years, son of Ja-
cob Haverman.

Heppely, Jacob
Hakeney, Samuel
Riegel, Frederick
Helmer, John
Hyser, Rudolph
Hauss, John
Hyser, Jacob
Herder, Nicholas
Hansen, Peter, taken in November or
December, 1778.
Helmer, Johannes taken April 3, 1780,
not in arms
Ittig, Jurry
Keller, Jacob, 10 years, child of Solo-
mon Keller.
Kreemer, Conrad, 13 years, son of
Godfrey Kreemer.
Kring, a son of John Kring.
Keyser, two sons of John Keyser.
Klock, Lieut. Jacob
Klock, Jost
Klock, Jost
Klock, Jacob
Keeler, Leonard E.
Keyser, John, Capt. of militia
Kessler, Mark
Keller, Nicholas
Lapton, Daniel
Lighthall, Michael
Lighthall, Francis
Lawyer, Coenradt taken Oct. 16, 1780
Lambert, Jacob, 11 years, son of Peter
Lambert.
Lambert, John F., 7 years, son of Pet-
er Lambert.
Lepper, Mary, 24 years, wife of Fred-
erick Lepper.
Lepper, Frederick, 1 year, child of
Frederick Lepper.
Lones, Margaret, 24 years, wife of
John Lones.
Lones, Margaret, 5 years, child of
John Lones.
Lones, Martinus, 3 years, child of
John Lones.
Lones, Cathrina, 6 months, child of
John Lones.
Lawyer, Conradt, son taken Oct. 16,
1780.
Lapton, 3 or 4 sons of Daniel Lapton.
Miller, Matheus,
Maetener, John
Makley, Susanah, 7 years, child of
Phelix and Catharine Mackley.
Mackley, Anna, 3 years, child of Phe-
lix and Catharine Mackley.
Miller, Eve, 25 years, wife of Theo-
nessius Miller.
Miller, Catharina, 2 years, child of
Theonessius Miller.
Meyer, Eve, 5 years, child of Joseph
Meyer.
Mydrig, Jacob
Neller, John
Ogd, George
Pikert, Bartholomew
Piper, Peter
Piper, Jacob
Passage, Henry
Picker, Bartle taken April 3, 1780

Rasbach' wife and son of Frederick Rasbach.
Rabold, George
Rymer Schnyder, Henry
Seber, John, 8 years, child of John Seber.
Shnyder, Mary, 14 years, daughter of Jacob Shnyder.
Shnyder, Rachael, 9 years, daughter of Jacob Shnyder.
Sleyfer, Elizabeth Rush, 23 years, wife of Paulus Rush Sleyfer.
Schreibner, Rebecca, 25 years, wife of Stephen Schriebner.
Schrieber, Elizabeth, 7 years, child of Stephen Schrieber.
Schrieber, Abram, 4 years, child of Stephen Schrieber.
Schriebner, Maria (Maxia), 1 year, child of Stephen Schriebner.
Schneck, Barbara, 37 years, wife of George Schneck.
Schneck, Margaret, 13 years, child of George Schneck.
Schneck, Christina, 9 months, child of George Schenck.
Snouts, George, 50 years, father.
Snouts, John, 10 years, son of George Snouts.
Steed, Maria, 19 years, wife of John Steed.
Steed, John, 1 year, son of John Steed.
Staring, wife and two sons and four daughters of John Staring.
Street, son aged 12 of John Street.
Sitz, Maria, 7 years, daughter of Baltus Sitz.
Shell, Mark
Schaffer, Henry
Seiffert, John
Snouts, George, age 50.
Shell, Henry
Sheffer, Henry
Steinwax, Tebalt
Staring, Henry
Shoemaker, John
Shoemaker, Christopher
Staring, Jacob
Street, John n
Tobias, Frederick
Van Slyck, Jacob
Van Slyck, Jacobus
Van Slyck, Gerard taken April 3, 1780, not in arms
Windecker, son of Frederick Windecker.
Woolendorf, Cathrina, 20 years, wife of Daniel Woolendorf
Walls, Margaret, 13 years, daughter of Jacob Walls.
Windecker, Frederick
Wolleber, John Nicholas

In the Caughnawaga District. Tryon County Taken May, 1780

Fonda, Adam
Hansen, Barent
Kennedy, Samuel
Myers, Joseph
Sammons, Frederick

Terwilliger, Hermanny

In Harpers Field Taken April 7, 1780

Brown, Doctor
Brown, David
Brown, Solomon
Brown, John
Drake, Capt. Joshua
Duggan, James
Harper, Capt. Alexander
Hendry, Lieut. John
Lamb, William
Lamb, William, Jr.
Newman, Joseph, not in arms
Patchin, Isaac
Patchin, Freegift
Thorp, Esaray
Vrooman, Capt. Walter

DESTRUCTION OF HERKIMER

Col. Bellinger's Report to Governor Clinton on the Destruction of German Flatts, N. Y.

German Flatts, Sept. 19. 1778.

May it please your Excellence. I humbly beg to lay our distresses open to your Excellency. On Thursday the 17th instant about six in the morning the enemy attacked Fort Dayton on the north side of the German Flatts and burned and destroyed all the houses, barns and grain and drove a great number of horses and horned cattle away with them. The church fort, together with two houses is all that is left on that side and they had two men killed and one wounded. The enemy tried to take Fort Dayton but they kept them off. On the south side of the river they began about six miles above Fort Herkimer and burned all the houses, barns and grain quite down to the church at Fort Herkimer they tried to set fire to the barn but we sallied out with what men we could spare and kept them from destroying any more homes. We have built in our district four garrisons and have none but my regiment to guard them and a few rangers. I sent out a scout of the rangers, nine men, three days before this happened. They met the enemy at Major Edmonston's place at the head branch of Unadilla river, the enemy attacked them and drove them into the river. They have killed two of the rangers and scattered the rest. One of them came in the night before the Flatts was attacked. And immediately I wrote per express to Col. Klock and another to be signed by him, to be sent to the nearest place for assistance as the enemy was within in nine miles of us when the rangers saw them last. In my letter to Col. Klock I begged him for God's sake to assist us with men and if he had marched his men on directly, he might have been at the Flatts before we was attacked and if he had sent 200 men we might in all probability have saved a great many houses and a great deal of grain and creatures. But alas we could get no assistance. Several times this summer we have intelligence that they intended to destroy this place and I have wrote to General Stark in Albany for assistance but could get none and once I wrote to your Excellency but I imagine you did not receive it. Our case is really very hard as the enemy threatens us yet. Therefore I am obliged to be thus throublesome to Your Excellency to desire the favor of a reinforcement, otherwise I cannot pretend to keep the inhabitants here any longer. I have given orders to the A. D. C. of issues at Fort Dayton to supply those who have lost their effects with provision as they was crying to me for bread. But if your Excellency does not approve of it I hope you will send me orders how I must behave in the said affair. After the enemy had finished the destruction of the Flatts they went off about noon. In the afternoon I sent an express again to Col. Klock desiring him to send to Col. Alden at Cherry Valley that if he would turn out with about 400 men and strike across to the creek at Unadilla where I was certain they would come up with the enemy they might have recovered most part of the plunder again but as far as I can learn they did not mind it. I had a great deal of trouble I can assure your Excellency to keep the inhabitants from moving off on the account of having no assistance. I was obliged to threaten them that I would take their effects from them. But as the place is mostly destroyed I have prevailed on them to wait till I have orders from your Excellency how to behave in our distressed circumstances. But if there is no reinforcement comes up I shall not be able to hinder them from moving off. I here send your Excellency an account of the damage done by the enemy on both sides of the river. They burned 63 dwelling houses, 57 barns with grain and fodder, 3 grist mills, 1 sawmill and they have taken away with them 235 horses, 229 horned cattle, 269 sheep and they killed and destroyed a great number of hogs and they have burned a great many out houses.

I hope your Excellency will take our circumstances into consideration and grant us a reinforcement sufficient to hinder the enemy from utterly ru-

ining of us. So relying entirely on your Excellency I beg leave to subscribe myself your Excellencies most obedient humble servant.

PETER BELLINGER, Colonel.

To His Excellency, George Clinton, Esqr.

SUFFERS AT GERMAN FLATTS

Vol. 4, Pages 340-345

A return of the refugees or inhabitants of the German Flatts who were burned off and lost their effects by the enemy. All above 16 years old are allowed one pound of bread and one pound of beef and all under 16 years old half a pound of bread and half a pound of beef per day.

Bellinger, Frederick, 7 above, 1 under.
Bersh, Ludowick, 2 above, 1 under.
Bellinger, John, 3 above, 1 under.
Bauman, Jacob, 2 above, 4 under.
Bauman, Adam, 5 above, 2 under.
Bauman, Frederick, 2 above, 1 under.
Bell, Dorothy, above 1, under 2.
Bell, Mary, 1 above, 3 under.
Bell, Jacob 2 above.
Bersh, Margaret, above 1, under 4.
Bonny, Ichabod, 3 above, 3 under.
Cline, William, above 2, under 5.
Christman, Jacob, 2 above, 5 under.
Casler, John, 2 above, 4 under.
Christman, John, Jr., 2 above, 3 under.
Cunningham, William, 2 above, 6 under.
Christman, Nicholas, above 2, under 1.
Campbell, Ludowick and John above 4, under 3.
Clapsattle, Barbary, above 3, under 7.
Cunningham, Barbara above 1, under 3.
Dornberger, Frederick, 1 above, 7 under.
Demuth, John, 3 above, 2 under.
Dochsteder, George 4 above.
Folts, McLeod, 2 above, 1 under.
Folts, Joseph, 2 above, 5 under.
Folts, Conrad, 4 above, 2 under.
Frank, Eve, 1 above, 5 under.
Frank, Stephen, 2 above, 1 under.
Frank, John 3 above, 5 under.
Frank, Frederick 2 above, 4 under.
Getman, Frederick, Jr., above 2, under 1.
Herter, Henry, 5 above, 16, 6 under.
Helmer, Frederick, Jr., 2 above, 3 under.
Helmer, George, 2 above, 4 under.
Hills, George, Jr., 5 above, 2 under.
Hills, George, Sr., 4 above.
Helmer, Philip, 3 above, 7 under.
Herter, Nicholas, 6 above.
Herter, Lawrence, Sr., 3 above, 1 under.
Herter, Frederick, 5 above, 4 under.

Helmer, Adam 2 above, 1 under.
Helmer, Elizabeth, 1 above, 8 under.
Hess, Augustinus 2 above, 2 under.
Ittig, Marks, 6 above, 5 under.
Ittig, Christian 4 above 6 under.
Iray, the widow, above 1, under 6.
Myer, Michael, 4 above, 3 under.
Myer, Mary, 4 above, 2 under.
Myer, Frederick, 2 above, 5 under.
Myer, Jacob 4 above, 6 under.
Myer, Joseph 2 above, 5 under.
Miller, Henry, above 5.
Oxner, Mary above 1, under 4.
Pesausie (Passage), Margaret, 1 above 4 under.
Pesausie (Passage), John 2 above, 2 under.
Pypher, Jacob, 5 above, 4 under.
Fetry, Catherine, above 1, under 4.
Petry, Barbara above 1, under 4.
Petry, William, 2 above, 5 under.
Rigel, Christian, 2 above, 4 under.
Rigel, Frederick, 2 above, 5 under.
Raspell, Mark above 3, under 5.
Rankin, Elizabeth above 1, under 2.
Steale, Rudolph above 2, under 2.
Sharer, Margaret above 1, under 2.
Schuyler, Ann above 1, under 4.
Shoot, William above 2, under 3.
Steinwax, the widow, above 1, under 4
Smith, Nochals, 2 above, 3 under.
Smith, George, 6 above, 2 under.
Smith, Adam, 3 above, 4 under.
Smith, John, 2 above, 1 under.
Starring, Adam, Jr., 3 above, 1 under.
Spoon, Nicholas above 5, under 2.
Volmer, Thomas, 3 above, 5 under
Weber, Jacob, Jr., 3 above, 1 under.
Weber, Peter, 4 above, 3 under.
Weber, Jacob G., 2 above, 2 under.
Weber, George J. N., 2 above.
Weber, Frederick, 2 above.
Weber, George above 2, under 1.

Half Allowance

Such as have lost houses and barns but have some grain left and are put on half allowance:

Bellinger, Peter, above 4, under 4.
Crim, Jacob, above 3, under 5.
Fox, John, above 2, under 5.
Folts, Jacob, above 4, under 5.
Folts, Conrad and Peter, above 5, under 5.
Getman, Frederick, Sr., above 5, under 3.
Ittick, Michael, above 4, under 4.
Osterhout, John, above 2, under 5.
Basehaur, Jacob, above 5, under 3.
Steale, Fiedrick, above 6, under 5.
Starring, Adam, Sr., above 2, under 4.
Weber, Nicholas H., above 2, under 7.
Wents, George, above 4, under 3.

Outlying Districts

Such as lived distant from Fort Dayton and were obliged to leave their habitations all the summer and

have lost part of their effects and are on half allowance.
Broadhack, Jacob, above 2, under 1.
Bellinger, John, above 3, under 6.
Davie, John, above 2, under 6.
Demuth, Mark, above 5, under 6.
Fulmer, Conrod, above 3, under 3.
Flock, Peter, above 2, under 2.
Frank, Timothy, above 2, under 5.
Kast, Frederick, above 5, under 4.
Kast, Gertrude, above 1.
Lighthall, Nicholas, Sr., above 2, under 1.
Lighthall, Nicholas, Jr., above 2, under 1.
Myer, John, above 2, under 6.
Strobell, Christopher, above 3.
Weber, George, above 5, under 1.
Weber, Nicholas, above 2, under 4.

Absent Owners

Such as are absent at present but have lost houses, barns and most of their effects:
Clapsattle, Andrew, above 2, under 2.
Deygart, William, above 7, under 6.
Herter, Lawrence, Jr. above 2, under 3
Hills, Nicholas, above 3, under 7.
Nellis, George, above 5, under 1.

Signed of the Petition

Signed by the principal officers and inhabitants of the German Flatts:
Bellinger, Colonel Peter
Bellinger, Lieut. Col. Frederick
Frank, Frederick.
Getman, Capt. Frederick
Herder, Capt. Henry
Helmer, Lieut. Adam
Petri, Justice William

Prisoners of War from Clinton Papers
Vol. 2, Page 596, Dec., 1777

Tallma, Harmanus
Lawrence, Daniel
Lawrence, Nathaniel
Betts, Daniel
Hayes, John
Phillips, David
Kennedy, Thomas
Terjay, John
Verbryck, Bernardus
Verbryck, Samuel Garritson

Vol. 6, Page 723, March 27, 1781

Townsend, Samuel

Vol. 6, Page 724, August 2, 1780

Shoemaker, Elizabeth
Sharer, Anna
Sharer, Margaret
Staring, Anna
Clyne, Elizabeth
Clyne, Margaret

Clyne, Maria

List of Prisoners of War, Albany and Tryon

Vol. 6, Page 731, Year 1781

Boon, William
Wright, Zadock, Major
Werthoff, George
Boetger, Andries
Rahia, Ernest
Hartman, Paulus
Muller, Johannis
Gleyseman, Frederick
Walters, Andreas
Albeas, Conraedt
Schinneman, Hendrick
Bruineman, Henrick
Bruns, Christian
Brunner, Ludwig
Gelt, Ludwig
Bar, Christian
Bonse, John Henry Zacherias
Kempsy, Johannes
Coolman, Gebhard
Eggers, Julius
Meynecke, John Otto
Kogh, Andries
Peatzhold, George
Israel, Godfred
Smith, Christian
Neese, Frederick
Keeping, Frederick
Eylers, Johan
Hoffman, Christopher   Papist Hendrick
Kreykenbom, Hendrick
Beeler, Cunrad
Sieringer, Jacob
Norff, Michael
Aple, George
Plugh, Johannuis
Burghdoff, Hendrick
Just, Christian
Kogh, Hendrick
Weegenar, Carle
Henecke, Hendrick
Weather, John
Westfahlen, Frederick
Myer, Carle
Leedeke, John
Bruns, Adolph
Keenholtz, Christopher
Lawenstien, Jacob
Rysnard, Johan Henry
Heleman, Andries
Streder, Frederick
Lauwas, Frederick
Miller, Henrick
Cartner, Christopher
Hoofman, Jury
Cogh, Henrick
Parks, James
Arse, Isaac
Hoofer, Adam

State Prisoners Belonging to N. Y. State Confined in Provost Gaol

Vol. 2, Page 723, Year 1777

Miller, William, West. Co., Mar. 23, 1777.

Tolman, Horamaunos, Orange, Apr. 28.
Champenois, Thos. Westchester, Oct. 2
Vantasle, Peter, Westchester, Nov. 18
Winter, Joseph, Dutchess, March 24.
Van Tassle, Cornelius, Westchester, Nov. 18.
Marshal, Nah'l., Westchester, May 24
Brudige, James, Westchester, April 12
Philips, David, New York, April 20
Hunt, John, Westchester, April 21
Norris, Oliver, Suffolk, Aug. 7.
Griffing, Nath, Suffolk, July 2.
Thomas, Richard, Suffolk, May 17.
Dimon, Jonath, Suffolk, Dec. 28.
Hopper, John, New York, March 5.
Rider, Stephen, Queens, April 28.
Conkling, David, Suffolk, Aug. 8.

Tories Detained for Refusing to Take Oath of Allegiance

Ellis, James
White, Alexander
Dole, James
Cumming, John
Cuyler, Henry
McKenzie, William
Overfaigh, Zach
Sparding, John
Marsh, Daniel
Booker, Benjamin
Graves, John
Bell, Richard
    Last two mentioned as having escaped.
Wing, Abraham, Jr. released on bonds

Taken Nov. 18, 1780 at Veals Ford Vol. 6, Page 722

Townsend, Samuel
Brush, Major

Exchange of Prisoners Vol. 4, Page 50, Sept. 19, 1778

Lush, Stephen
Van Tassel, Corn's.
Dole, James

Troops Captured at Fort Montgomery Ask for Arms, Wages, Rations Due Them

Vol. 4, Page 205, Oct., 1778

Darcos, John, Serjt.
Slote, Cornelius, Serjt.
Humphrey, William
Humphrey, George
Humphrey, James
Stinson, William
Henry, Robert
Carmichael, John Blakeny
Contine, Moses
Wilson, Andrew
Seers, Eliphant
Vanorsdall, John
Cooper, Robert
Wool, Robert
Wood, James
Miller, James

McMullen, John
Scoat, William

Vol. 4, Page 206, Oct., 1778
Schaack, H. V., takes message for leniency to be shown prisoners to G. Clinton.

Vol. 4, Page 795, May, 1779
Crane, Joseph, taken near Tapan. Officers appeal for his exchange.

Vol. 5, Page 951, July, 1780
Punderson, Dr. Cyrus

Vol. 6, Page 494, Dec., 1780
Hamman, Col. James suggested his exchange for Col. Floyed
Van Tassel, Lt. Jacob
Reynals, Lt.
Keyler, Lt.

Vol. 6, Page 514 Exchange of Prisoners Dec., 1780
Van Schaack, Henry for Samuel Townsend
Van Schaack, David and Mathew Goes for Philips and Smith.
Mathews, Fletcher for Jesse Brush

Prisoners Captured and Confined in Canada
Williams, Isaac and Peter
Townsly, Henry
Williams, Elias
Vincent, Cornelius
Gould, Samuel
Bethuel, Daniel
Vincent, Benjamin
Vreland, Michael
Loitle, John
Durham, James

Taken at Fort Vreland, July 28, 1779
Vol. 6, Page 605
Neily, John
Martin,............
Tyrgit, Thomas
Watts, John
Miles, William
Armitage, Bailey &
Doyg, John
Furney, John

Prisoners in Canada
Vol. 6, Page 708, March 19, 1781
Smith, George for Capt. John Wood, if dead, exchanged for Joshua Drake
Smith, Patrick
Shepard, William

Vol. 6, Page 762, April 11, 1781
Bloore, Joshua, for Parson Stuart
Former at Albany Goal, bondsman for Stuart.

Vol. 7, Page 274
Stuart, Rev. John for either Messrs. Gordon, Harper, Snyder or Fonda
Vol. 7, Page 290, Sept, 1781
Simmons, Lieut.

American Officers. Prisoners in L. I. Petition for Relief After Nearly Three Years of Captivity

Vol. 5, Page 750-752, May, 1780
Allison, Wm., Colo.
Bruyn, Lt. Colo.
Livingston, Will, Lt. Colo.
McClaghry, James, Lt. Colo.
Hamman, James, Lt. Col.
Logan, Saml., Major
Godwin, Henry, Capt.
Teller, James, Capt.
Carpenter, Neh., Qr. Master
Gilchrist, Adam, A. C. G. F.
Brewster, Henry, Lieut.
McClaughry, John, Ensign
Hunter, John, Lieut.
Humphrey, James, Capt.
Jackson, Patten, Lieut.

Vol. 5, Page 721, March 21, 1779
Woodworth, William, taken March 21, 1779 at Skeensborough
Pendleton, Solomon, Lieut.
Fenno, Ephran, Capt.
Gilliland, James, Art.
Hallsted, Benjamin, Lieut.
Pawling, Henry, Lieut.
Swartwout, Henry, Ensign
Furman, John, Lieut.
Kronkhite, James, Capt.
McArthur, Alex'r., Lieut.
Mott, Ebenezer, Lieut.
Keeler, Isaac, Lieut.
Swartwout, Corn's., Capt. Lt. Artillery
Van Tassel, Jacob, Lieut.
Reynolds, Nathaniel, Lieut.
Crane, Isaac, Adjt.
Dodge, Samuel, Jr., Lieut.
Lush, Stephen, Maj.
DuBois, Zacharius, Capt.
Laggert, Abraham, Ensign
Glean, Oliver, Q. M. Gen.
Magor, Hamnil

Vol. 7, Page 283, Sept., 1781
McKenny, Mrs. Margaret

Vol. 7, Page 158, Aug., 1781

Exchange of Prisoners
Covenhoven, Mr.
Hake, Mr.
Taller, Mr.

To Be Exchanged for British Prisoners Held by the Continentals 1780
Vol. 6, Page 451
Abail, David
Shart, Peter
Harris, Capt.
Abell, Anthoney
Miller, Peter
Snyder, Jeremiah
Snyder, Elias
Sammons, Frederick
Newkirk, Jacob
Newkirk, William
Abell, David
Short, Peter

Vol. 4, Page 292, Nov., 1778
Stacey, Lt. Col., taken prisoner at Cherry Valley

Colonial Census of 1710

List of Palatines Remaining in New York; Census of West Camp; The Orphan Apprentice List.

From Vol. III Documentary History of New York

LIST OF THE PALATINES RE-
MAINING AT NEW YORK, 1710

———

Figures denote age.

Almerodrin, Anna, wid., 67

Ableman, Peter, 42
Ableman, Anna Margareta, 32

Badner, Johan Paul, 19

Bronck, Matheis, works in ye Govr.
  Gard, 50
Bronck, Anna Christina, his daugh-
  ter, 22
Bronck, John Hendrick his son, 16

Baumin, Magdalena wid., 29
Baumin, Johan Niclaus, 15

Bornwaserin, Maria Cath, wid., 26

Baschin, Frances, wid., 40
Baschin, Margaretha, 20

Beijerin, Susannah wid., 30
Beijerin, Susannah Maria, 1

Batzin, Anna Cath, 38
Batzin, John Ludwig, 7

Bruiere, Jeane, 18
Bruiere, Jacque, 15
Bruiere, Susannah, 6

Buers, Ludwig, 32
Buers, Maria Cath, 28
Buers, Catharine, 3

Benderin, Anna Maria, wid., 44
Benderin, Eva Catharina, 12
Benderin, John Matheus, 8

Brilmannin, Helena, orph. x, 17

Bressler, Valtin, 41
Bressler, Christina, 36
Bressler, Anna Eliz, 14
Bressler, Anna Gertrude, 12
Bressler, Andreas, 9
Bressler, Anthony, 5
Bressler, Maria Agnes, ½

Baer, Johannes, 40
Baer, Anna, 27
Baer, John Fred, 10
Baer, John Jacob, 4

Cramerin, Anna Maria, wid., 38
Cramerin, her eldest sone x, 18
Cramerin, Maria Eliz, 12
Cramerin, John Hendrich, 7
Cramerin, Anna Catharina, 5
Cramerin, Juliana Maria, 1½

Castleman, Christian, 36
Castleman, Anna Judeth, 27
Castleman, Eva Maria Cath, 12.

Dietrich, Anna Eliz. orph., 20
Deitrich, Anna Gertrude, 12

Daunermarker, Christopher, 28
Daunermarker, Christina, 28
Daunermarker, Cath. Eliz, 8
Danemark, Anna Hargt., wid., 58

Dausweber, Melchoir, 55
Dausweber, Maria Christina, 20
Dausweber, Anna Maria, 17

Deible, Johannes, 38
Deible, Anna Catharina, 7

Dorner, Johannes, 36
Dorner, Anna Margaretta, dead, 40

Erbin, Anna Catharina wid., 44
Erbin, Eliz Catha, 9

Elich, Andreas, 37
Elich, Anna Rosina, 23
Elich, John George, 3

Engelle, Johannes, 31
Engelle, Anna Christina, 12
Engelle, Anna Maria, 8
Engelle, Anna Eliz, 4

Erkel, Bernhard, 53
Erkel, Anna Maria, 43

Falck, Arnold, 36
Falck, Anna Eliz, 35
Falck, Johannes, 6

ffucks, John Peter, 31
ffucks, Anna Margt, 24

Fucks frau, Johanna Eliz, 22

ffelton, John Wm., x, 30
ffelton, Christina, 28
ffelton, Anthoni, 11
ffelton, Anna Clara, 17

Frederich, Conrad, 52
Frederich, Anna Maria, 45
Frederich, John Peter, 14
Frederich, John Conrad, 13

Feversback, Deitrich, 21A

Garlack, Peter, 37
Garlack, Magdalena, 39
Garlack, Margaretta, 12

Greisler, Johan Phillip, 40
Greisler, Catharine, 40
Greisler, John George, 11
Greisler, Johannes, 7

Gossinger, Johan Henrich, 31
Gossinger, Anna Eliz, 27
Gossinger, Anna Margt, 2

Gablin, Anna Maria, 34
Gablin, Anna Maria, 7

Galete, Maria, wid., 38
Galete, Sarah Margaret, 7
Galete, Jacob, 4

Grauin, Anna Cath., 40
Grauin, Anna Eliz, 18
Grauin, Anna Sophia, 10
Grauin, Johannes, 11

Grauberger, Philip Peter, 29
Grauberger, Anna Barbara, 33

Hoffman, Hermanus x, 30
Hoffman, Maria Gertrude x, 30
    These two remains at Hackensack
at John Lotz's.
Heidin, Anna Maria, wid., 50

Hauch, Lucas, dead, 44
Hauch, Anna Magda, 45
Hauch, Maria Cathar, 16
Hauch, Maria Margt, 18

Hauch, John Jacob, 13
Hauch, John George x, 12
Hauch, Maria Eliz x, 11
Hauch, Johannes, 4

Hebmannin, Maria Cath, wid., 40
Hebmannin, Anna Engel, 21A
Hebmannin, Gertrude, 14
Hebmannin, Anna Magdalena, 11

Hartwig, Caspar, 39
Hartwig, Anna Eliz, 39
Hartwig, Johan Bernhard, 8
Hartwig, Johan Lorentz, 6
Hartwig, Magdalena, 10

Henneschid, Michael, 36
Henneschid, Anna Catharina, 30
Henneschid, Casper, 11
Henneschid, John Peter, 1
Henneschid, Maria Sophia, 6

Hellich, Conrad, 30
Hellich, Anna Marie, 26
Hellich, Johannes, dead, 1

Heisterbach, Niclaus, 53
Heisterbach, Johan Jacob, 4
Heisterbach, Christina Cath, 10

Jung, Johannes, 32
Jung, Anna, 35

Jungens, Niclaus, works in ye Govr
    gard, 38
Jungens, Anna Magdalena, 25

Klein, Hironimus, 38
Klein, Maria, 38
Klein, Amalia, 12
Klein, Anna Eva, 14
Klein, Anna Eliz., 6

Kornman, Peter Jacob, dead, 51
Kornman, Anna Conigunda, dead, 52
Kornman, Anna Conig, 24
Kornman, John Christopher, 12A

Kuatz, Johannes, 40

Keiser, John Matheus, 23

Kuhner, Benedictus, 36
Kuhner, Anna Felice, 40
Kuhner, Jacob A., 4
Kuhner, Eva Barbara, 9
Korning, Ludolf, 50
Korning, Otillia, 50
Korning, Catharina, 16
Korning, Anna Dorothea, 15
Korning, Conrad, 7

Lucas, Frantz at New Rochelle at Mr.
    Chadden, 38
Lucas, Maria Eliz. his daughter, 20
Lucas, Frantz, 13
Lucas, Anna Maria, 9
Lucas, Anne, 7
Lucas, Anna Catharina, 4
Leicht, George Ludwig, 66

Leicht, Anna Margatta, 58
Leicht, Johan Henrich, 24
Leicht, Anna Eliz, 20

Lein, Conrad, 56
Lein, Maria Marga, 46
Lein, Juliana, 18
Lein, Margareta, 14
Lein, Anna Maria, 12
Lein, Abraham, 10
Lein, Conrad, 7

Lickard, Bernhard, 25
Lickard, Justina, 32

Lohrentz, Johannes, 43
Lohrentz, Anna Margaretta, 39
Lohrentz, Anna Eliz, 15
Lohrentz, Magdalena, 13
Lohrentz, Anna Barbara, 11
Lohrentz, Alexander, ½

Lintzin, Apollonia, wid., 40
Lintzin, Anna Catha, 16
Lintzin, Anna Margt, 13
Lintzin, Anna Eva, 6

Laukin, Anna Elizabeth, 42

Lenhard, Johan, 5
Lenhard, Eva Catharina, 12

Lampertin, Eliz., wid., 47
Lampertin, Erhard A., 13
Lampertin, Frantz Adam A., 11

Melchlin, Sittonia, wid., 41
Melchlin, Anna Maria, 11
Melchlin, Anna Eliz, 8

Mengelsin, Anna Maria wid., 27
Mengelsin, John Carolus, 3
Mengelsin, Anna Maria, 5
Mengelsin, Juliana, 1½

Meyin, Maria, wid., 45
Meyin, Anna Eliz., 9

Monen, Maria, 23
Monen, John Phillips, 2

Maulin, Anna Eliz, wid., 42
Maulin, Anna Catharina, 13
Maulin, Anna Ursula, 16
Maulin, Catharina, 12
Maulin, Anna Maria, 5

Maul, Frederick, 31
Maul, Anna Ursula, 31
Maul, John Jacob, 4
Maul, Anna Catharina, 5
Maul, John Paul, orph., 12

Morellin, Anna Eva, wid., 48
Morellin, Anna Apolonia, 18
Morellin, Anna Barbara, 11

Mullerin, Elizabeth, wid., 42
Mullerin, Jacob, 15
Mullerin, Melchoir, 13

Mullerin, Niclaus, 6
Mullerin, Anna Engell, 3

Mullerin, Catharina, wid., 36
Mullerin, Hans George, ½

Meserin, Margaret, wid., 50
Meserin, Johannes, 15
Meserin, Susan Cath, 10

Neff, Fred'ch, dead, 34
Neff, Johan, dead, 8

Newkirk, Johan Henrich, 36
Newkirk, Anna Maria, 33
Newkirk, Johannes, 11
Newkirk, John Henrich, dead, 8

Offin, Magdalena, wid., 32
Offin, Johan Jacob, 8
Offin, Anna Barbara, 6

Planck, Johannes, 43
Planck, Maria Margt, 32
Planck, Johanna Eliz, 14
Planck, Ludwig Henrich, 6

Nollin, Elizabeth, wid. x, 66

Niesin, Maria, wid., 38
Niesin, Maria Magdalena, 15

Onin, Maria Barbara, 36

Pseffer, Michael, 32
Pseffer, Anna Maria, 28

Reichin, Anna Maria, orph., 17
Reichin, Anna Margt, dead, 8
Reichin, Hans Thomas A, 12

Romer, George x, 30
Romer, Eliz x, 26

Roschman, Johannes, 33
Roschman, Anna Eliz, 30
Roschman, Maria Cath, 9

Rosin, Umbert, 45

Rusin, Anna Conegunda, wid., 44
Rusin, Anna Catharina, 14
Rusin, Anna Margaretta, 10
Rusin, Maria Catharina, 8

Rorbaalin, Anna Eliz, Wid., 34
Rorbaalin, Anna Morga, 11

Richter, Andreas, 47
Richter, Anna Maria, 45
Richter, Andreas, 16
Richter, Anna Barbara, 9

Schmidt, Henrich, 54
Schmidt, Anna Eliz, 54
Schmidt, Clements, 24
Schmidt, Wilhelm, 20
Schmidt, Hans George, 13
Schmidt, John Niclaus, 9

Schmiut, Anna Maria, 18

Schumacher, Daniel. 30
Schumacher, Anna Maria, 36
Schumacher, Hans Niclaus, 8

Scherin, Maria Margt wid., 23

Schutzin, Maria Cath, wid., 40
Schutzin, Hans Valentine, 17
Schutzin, Maria Catherina, 12
Schutzin, John Henrich, 3

Stuckrath, Hans Wm., 37
Stuckrath, Anna Margaretta, 28.
Stuckrath, Anna Clara, 10
Stuckrath, Catharine, 4
Stuckrath, John Marcus, ½

Schullzin, Anna Eliz., wid., 22

Strud, Christina, 40
Strud, Maria Ursula, 28
Strud, Catharine, 13
Strud, Anna Maria, 11
Strud, John Jacob, 9
Strud, Maria Catharine, 13

Simendinger, Ulrich, 38
Simendinger, Anna Margaretta, 36
Scahtz, John Deitrich, 38
Scahtz, Magdalena, 42
Sachtz, Hans Peter, 14

Starenburger, Johan Jacob, 45
Starenburger, Catharina, 33
Starenburger, Johan Langsert, 14
Starenburger, Anna Cathar, 12
Starenburger, John Jacob, 11
Starenburger, John Adam, 5

Schmidtin, Margaretta, wid., 27
Schmidtin, Johan Daniel A, 4

Salbachin, Elizab., 15

Sieknerin, Anna Apolonia wid., 44
Sieknerin, Johannes dead, 9
Sieknerin, Johan Jacob, 7

Storr, Michael, 38
Storr, Anna Marg, 48
Storr, Eliz. Catharine. 12

Sacksin, Anna Maria, wid., 30

Schneider, Johan Wm. x, 28

Schoneborin, 25

Teffa, Daniel, 30
Teffa, Marianna, 11
Teffa, Abraham, 7

Trilhauser, Johannes, x, 23

Vogdt, Simon, 30
Vogdt, Christina, 26

Werner, Christopher, 35

Werner, Maria Magdalena, 23
Werner, John Matheus, 3

Wickhaus, Peter, 32
Wickhaus, Eliz Catharina, 31
Wickhaus, Maria Catha, 15

Wannermacher, Johan Deitrick, 28

Weisin, Susannah, 36

Wenerick, Baltzar, 40
Wenerick, Elizabeth, 30
Wenerick, Hans George, 9
Wenerick, Johan Maltheis, 6
Wenerick, Maria Eliz., 17

Wenerich, Benedictus, 32
Wenerich, Christina, 33
Wenerich, Frantz, 5
Wenerich, Johannes, ½

Weidnecht, Andreas, 40
Weidnecht, Margaret, 40
Weidnecht, George Fred, 13
Weidnecht, John George, 11
Weidnecht, Anna Eliz, 9

Wormserin, Anna, widdow, 36

Zwickin, Veronica, wid., 39
Zwickin, Marcus, 31
Zwickin, John Martin, 6
Zwickin, Anna Margaretta, 14

Zangerin, Johanna, wid., 33
Zangerin, Peter, 13
Zangerin, Johannes, 7
Zangerin, Anna Catharina, 10

Zolner, Hans Adam, 52
Zolner, Maria, before Baumersin, 40

WEST CAMP

Statement of Heads of Palaten Families and Number of Persons in Both Towns of ye West Side Hudsons River. Winter 1710

LEGEND

Col. 1—Men.
Col. 2—Lads from 9 to 15.
Col. 3—Boys 8 and under .
Col. 4—Women.|
Col. 5—Maids 9 to 15.
Col. 6—Girls 8 and under.
Col. 7—Total of persons.

	1	2	3	4	5	6	7
Arnold, ——	1	0	0	2	0	0	3
ahl, ——	1	0	0	1	1	0	3
Bendor, Valinten	1	0	0	1	0	0	2
Brandau,	1	1	0	1	0	0	3
Becker, Jno.	1	1	0	0	0	0	2
Becker, Peter	1	0	0	1	0	0	2
Bayherin, Elisab.	0	0	1	1	0	0	2

Caselman, Jno. ffrid 1 1 0 2 0 0 4
Conterman, Jno. ffred ...1 3 0 1 0 0 5

Draberin, Ana Maria 0 2 0 1 0 0 3
Diebel, Peter 1 0 0 1 1 0 3
Dimouth, Jacob 1 1 0 1 2 0 5
Dietrich, —— 1 1 2 1 0 0 5

Ehman, Thomas 1 0 0 0 0 1 2
Eberhard, John 1 0 0 0 0 0 1
Eikertin, Gartrud 0 1 0 1 0 1 3
Egner, Peter 1 0 0 1 0 0 2
Emrich, Jho Michel 1 0 0 1 0 0 2
Emrichin, Ana Mar. 0 0 0 1 1 0 2

Fidler, Godfrey 1 0 0 1 0 0 2
Friedrich, Jno. Adam 1 0 0 1 0 0 2
Frolich, Stephan 1 0 0 1 2 1 5
Franck, Jno. 1 0 0 0 0 1 2

ffauldkinberg, Valin 1 0 1 1 0 0 3
Gerlach, Jno. Christ Ctp. 1 2 0 1 0 1 5

Helen, Georg 2 0 0 1 1 0 4
Hofman, —— 1 0 0 1 0 0 2
Hastman, Herman 1 2 0 1 3 1 8
Highrin, Maria 0 0 0 1 0 0 2
Hardel, Adam 1 0 1 1 1 0 4

Jungin, Elisab. 1 1 0 1 0 1 4

Keller, Frank 1 0 1 1 0 0 3
Kremer, Anthony 1 0 0 1 0 0 2
Kerner, Nicolaus 1 1 1 1 1 0 5
Keiseler, Peter 1 0 1 2 0 0 4
Kuntz, Anna Maria 0 0 0 1 0 0 1
Keifer, Jno. Wm. 1 1 0 2 2 0 6
Kiel, George Wm. 1 0 0 1 0 1 3
Kocherthaies, Mr. 1 0 0 0 0 0 1
Kelmer, Philip 2 2 1 1 2 0 8
Krantz, Jno. Hen. 1 0 1 1 1 0 4

Leher, Jno. 1 1 0 1 1 1 5
Lapin, Agnus 0 0 0 2 0 0 2

Mauer, Peter 1 0 0 2 0 0 3
Muller, Philip 3 1 0 1 1 1 7
Mirckle, Fred 1 2 0 1 3 0 7
Man, Henrich 1 0 0 1 0 0 2
Marsterstork, Alb. ffrid 1 0 0 1 0 0 2

Mand, Jacob 1 0 0 2 2 0 5
Muller, Wilheim 1 0 0 1 0 0 2
Meyer, Christian 1 0 0 1 0 0 2
Merdin, Conrad 2 1 0 1 0 0 4
Moor, Henrich 1 0 0 1 0 0 2
Mullerin, —— 0 0 0 1 1 0 2

Overbach, Peter 1 0 0 1 0 0 2

Ross, Andreas 1 0 0 0 0 0 1
Richart, Joseph 1 0 0 0 0 0 1
Rigel, Godfrey 1 0 0 1 0 0 2
Ritzbacus, Jho. 1 1 0 1 0 1 4

Spanhimer, Jno. Georg .1 0 0 1 2 1 5
Schaffer, Georg 1 0 0 1 0 0 2
Scheffer, —— 1 1 0 1 0 0 3
Scherman, Henrich 1 1 0 2 0 0 4
Straub, Jno. 1 0 0 1 0 0 2
Streiten, Magde 0 2 0 1 0 1 4
Schlimer, Matheus 1 0 0 2 0 0 3
Schram, Jno Henrich ...1 2 0 1 2 0 6
Sweden, Elizab. 0 0 0 1 1 0 2
Stubenrau, Georg Hen. .1 0 0 1 0 0 2
Schutzin, Catha. 0 0 0 1 0 0 1
Schib, Hyron 1 0 0 1 0 0 2

Tousweber, Melch. 1 0 0 2 0 0 3

Voschell, Peter 1 0 0 1 0 0 2
Voschell, Augustin 2 2 0 1 0 0 5

Welhelmin, —— 0 0 0 1 0 0 1
Wolleben, Valentin 1 0 0 1 0 0 2
Wolleben, Philip 1 0 0 0 0 0 1
Wagner, Peter 1 0 0 1 0 0 2
Wohleben, Peter 1 1 1 1 1 0 5
Weiden, —— 0 1 0 1 1 1 4
Weller, Hyronimus 1 0 1 1 0 0 3
——————————.............3 0 0 1 0 0 4

TOTALS

Men, 77.
Lads 9 to 15, 36.
Boys 8 and under, 13.
Women, 84.
Maids 9 to 15, 33.
Girls 8 and under, 14.
Total of persons 257.

Volunteers for Canadian Expedition 1711

List of Palatines Who Volunteered for the Expedition Against Canada in 1711.

Palatine Volunteers for the Expedition Against Canada; 1711

QUEENSBURY

Bergman, Andreas
Bellenger, Fred
Breigel, Geo.

Dopff, Jno Peter
Dilleback, Martin
Dachstader, George

Eckard, Nicklaus

Feeg, Johannis
Finck, Frantz
Feller, Niclaus

George, Wm., Lieut.

Haber, Christian
Hagedorn, Cristo
Hoffman, Hen.
Hagedorn, Peter

Jung, Henrich

Kuhn, Jacob
Kuntz, Mattheus
Kisler, Johannis

Leyer, Johan

Muller, Geo.
Mathias, Geo.
Munsinger, Jno. Jac.
Mathous, Henr.

Nelles, William
Nehr, Carl

Reinbolt, Mattheus
Reisch, Jno Jacob
Reichert, Werner

Schurtz, Andreas
Schaid, Antho.
Schaffer, Fred
Sein, Jno. Pet.
Schnell, Jacob
Schaffer, John

Wiser, Johan Cond, Capt.
Widerwachs, Hen.
Weber, Niclaus
Webber, Jacob

Zaysdorf, Johannes
356 men, women & children in this Town.
A True Coppy from the Original.
HENRY MAYER.

HAYSBURY

Palatine Volunteers for the Expedition Against Canada

Dales, John Wm

Bauch, Christian

Cup, Jacob

Dientzer, Paulus

Foltz, Melch.
ffucks, John Christopher. See photostat. Was he "Capt."

Gottel, Niclaus

Hayd, Peter
Hammer, Henr.
Hambuch, Jno. Wm.

Ittich, Mich

Kyser, Johan

Laux, Phillip
Langen, Abraham
Laux, Niclaus

Reitchoff, Paulus

Schaff, John Wm
Segendorf, John
Schultz, Jno Jacob

243 men women & child,

FROM HUNTERSTOWN; 16 JULY
1711

Anspach, Baltz

Bell, Frederick
Bender, George

Goldman, Cond.

Hills, Christ.
Huppert, David

Koch, Geo. Lud.
Kerchmer, Gro.
Keller, Conrad
Kobell, Jacob
Kneskern, Jno Peter, Capt.

Musig, Veil

Roschman, Johannes

Schawerman, Conrad
Sex, Henrick
Schulteis, Johannes
Schaffer, Reinhard
Schmidt, Jno Geo.
Schumacher, Tho.
Schmidt, Peter
Schwall, Johan
Stahl, Rudol.

Uhl, Carl
Uhl, Jno. Hen.

Warno, Jacob

336 men women and child.

ANNSBERG

Bruckhart, Ulrich
Busch, Danl
Bitzer, Herman
Blass, Johannes
Bonroth, Johannes
Bernhard, Johannes
Bast, Jacob
Bellinger, Hen.
Bellenger, Marcus

Orendorff, Jno. Hen.
Conradt, Jno. Hen.

Dings, Jacob
Dill, Jno Wm

Ess, Jacob
Fischer, Sebastian
Fehling, Hendrick

Hayd, Niclaus

Kuhn, Samuel
Kuhn, Conrad
Kradt, Johan
Kammer, Johan Wm.
Klein, Henrick
Kuhn, Valtin

Linck, Jno. Wm

Mentegen, Ferdo
Maisinger, Cond

Netzbach, Jno. Mart.

Petry, Joh Jost

Rieffenberg, Jno Geo.
Rauch, Casper
Ruffener, Thos
Ruhl, Niclaus

Schaffer, Gerhard
Spies, Peter
Schue, Johannes
Schneider, John Wm
Stuper, Hen. Balt.
Schneider, Johan
Schaffer, Phill
Schmit, Ludw.

Sittenich, Christ
Schmidt, Jno. Hen.
Schmidt, Adam Mic

Theis, Jno Phill

Winedecker, Hartman, Capt.
Winter, Henrich
Weis, Johannes
Walbourn, Jno. Adn

Zeller, Hans Hen.
Zeller, Johannes
Zerbe, Jno Phill
Zerbe, Martin

250 men, women & children.

A True Coppy   from the Original.
HEN. MAYER.

The foregoing was taken from Documentary History of New York. Vol. III by E. B. O'Callaghan, published by the state printer, Weed, Parsons & Co. of Albany in 1850. The list as originally published was not classified alphabetically, as arranged below, but otherwise appears here exactly as found in the volume above mentioned. No change has been made in the spelling and many names will be found which have undergone changes in the years since 1710. The suffix "in" denoting feminine gender appears to have been used indiscriminately thereby confusing the uninitiate as to the real name. Possibly this was due to the ignorance of the custom on the part of English clerks who recorded the name. Wherever the "in" appears it should be construed as meaning feminine gender as for instance Meyer (male), Meyerin (female). The lists are classified and will be in four sections, viz: The New York list, the West Camp list, the list of volunteers of 1711 and the apprenticed children or orphan list. These names are all that appear pertaining to the Palatine settlers published in Vol. III of Documentary History.

NAMES OF THE PALATINE CHILDREN APPRENTICED BY GOV. HUNTER. 1710-1714.

Date	Names of children	age	Parents	Bound to	of
1710 Aug. 31	John Philip Lepper	12	Orphan	John Hallock	Brookhaven
Sept. 14	Justina Mona	13	Orphan	H. Vanderhull	New York
14	George ffrederick	13	Conrad Weiser	S. Smith	Smithtown
21	Daniel Artopee	12	Orphan	Jno. Johnston	New York
21	Phillips Daniel	13	Orphan	Jno. Johnston	New York
22	Anna Margt Lamberton	13	Elizth Lamberton	Jno Deane	New York
22	Jno. Paul Denbig	7	Orphan	S. Phillips	New York
22	Hans Jerick Coons	6	Orphan	Saml Mulford	East Hampton
22	Hans ffellacoons	15	Orphan	Caleb Heathcote	Scarsdale
25	Anna Barber	9	Orphan	Rem Jorissen	Near the Ferry, Kings
25	Adam Creiner	13	Anna Maria Creiner	Jos. Hunt Jr.	Westchester
26	Hans Jerick Paer	8	Johans Paer	Richd Smith	Smithtown
26	Anna Cathrina	11	Magdalen Drum	Paul Droilhet	New York
26	Johannes Lodowick Trorit	9	Orphan	Laur Van Hook	New York
26	Susan Maria Harmin	7	Orphan	Jasper Hood	New York
26	Anna Maria Harmin	14	Orphan	Laurce Van Hook	New York
27	Hanna Catrina Laparing	16	Orphan	Andw Mead	New York
28	Hendrik Porter	14	Orphan	Garret van Horne	New York
28	Mary Trum	15	Trum	Richd Willet	New York
Oct. 14	Anna Margt Wolfe	13	Orphan	John Garreau	New York
16	Hans Bastian Gatian	12	Sara Catrin Bastian	Geo. Elsworth	New York
17	Jno Barnard Ruropaw	10	Orphan	Jno Sebringh	at the Ferry Kings
17	Anna Sibella Shefering	10	Ann. Maria S.	Dr. John Nerbury	ferry, L. I.
18	John Conearhart	9	Margt Otteene	Robt. Walter	New York
18	ffrederick Pather	7	Margt Otteene	Harman Rutghert	New York
18	Anna Catrina Haver	10	Margt Otteene	Jacob Goelet	New York
18	Maria Elizth Negilzin	11	Margt Otteene	Joseph Latham	New York
19	Han Jerick Livisten	12	ffrawnick Swieter	Derk Philps Conine	New York
19	Peter Pyfrin	6	Orphan	John van Horne	New York
19	Willm Pyfrin	10	Orphan	John van Horne	New York
23	John Conrad Petre	12	Orphan	Robt Livingston	Livingston Manr
23	Jerit Castnor	13	Orphan	Michl Hawdon	New York
23	Garrit Lamberton	12	Widw Lamberton	Michl Hawdon	New York
24	Magdalena Lizard	13	Widow Lizard	Wellm VandeWater	New York

Date	Name	Age	Parent / Status	Bound to	Residence
Oct. 24	Catrina Lizard	15	Widow Lizard	Isaac Stoutenburgh	New York
Oct. 24	Lizard, Elizabeth	13	Widow Lizard	James Leigh	New York
Oct. 24	Hans Gerit Lizard	10	Widow Lizard	John Symons	New York
Oct. 26	John Peter Zenger	13	Widw. Hanah Zenger	Wm. Bradford, Printer	New York
Oct. 30	Thoms Reich	12	Orphan	Saml Palmer	Momereneck
Nov. 1	ffrances Lamberton	10	Wdw Lamberton	John Hicks	Flushing
Nov. 6	Jacob Berliman	1	John Berliman	Henry Wileman	New York
Nov. 15	Jno Paul Schmidt	6	Orphan	Nathl Kay	Rhode Island
Nov. 20	Magdalen Brilman	12	Orphan	Lancaster Symes	New York
Nov. 21	Jerit Taylor	15	Taylor	Thos Noxon	Kingston
Nov. 23	Johns Coenrt Matheis Horner	15	Orphan	Enoch ifreland	New York
1711 Jan. 12	Jacob Oysterberk	3	Orphan	John Williams	Fairfield, Con.
Jan. 12	Margaret Oysterberk	7	Orphan	Hugh Nesbitt	Stratford, Con.
Jan. 15	Hans Hendrk Schilts	8	Orphan	R. Livingston	Livingston Mass
Jan. 15	Wyart Webber	8	Orphan	R. Livingston	Livingston Mass
Jan. 15	Jonah Smith	10	Henry Smith	R. Livingston	Livingston Mass
Jan. 15	Anna Catha Rear Pachin	12	Orphan	R. Livingston	Livingston Mass
Jan. 15	Anna Christian Patchin	4	Orphan	R. Livingston	Livingston Mass
Jan. 15	Johannes Schilts	10	Orphan	R. Livingston	Livingston Mass
Jan. 16	Mary Catharina Hendrick	15	Orphan	Daniel Ebbetts	New York
Jan. 19	Christian Angle	8	Orphan	James Elmes	New York
Jan. 19	Anna Maria Angle	2	Orphan	Mary Robinson	New York
Feb. 6	Arnout Sweet	13	Orphan	Laur. VanGhulen	Communapong, N. J.
Mar. 21	James Bruere	14	Orphan	Rip Van Dam	New York
Mar. 21	Peter Lonie	9	Orphan	Abm Lackerman	Richmond
Mar. 23	Mary Catha Schutsen	12	Mary Kathe Schutsen	Thos Bayeux	New York
Apr. 9	Nichs Tedry	14	Jacob Tedry	Thos Wiggins	Jamaica L. I.
Apr. 11	Katha Rose	9	Anna Rose	Thos ffell	New York
Apr. 11	Anna Margt Rosse	10	Anna Rose	Alexr Moore	New York
Apr. 12	Elizth Woolfe	8	Orphan	Wm. Commons	New York
Apr. 17	Johannah Elizth Weizer	7	Orphan	Albert Terhena	Flatlands
Apr. 17	Peter De Mott	13	Orphan	Cornelis Wyckoff	Flatlands
Apr. 19	Jacob Berliman	11	John Berliman	Nathl Kay	R. Island
Apr. 27	Elizabeth Rapell	13	Orphan	Arthur Knight	New York
June 2	Jno Willm Smith	14	Orphan	Jacob Rutsen	Ulster
June 2	Simon Helm	8	Peter Helm	John Rutsen	Kingston
1712 May 2	Maria Mangley	2	Anna Maria M.	Kathe Provost	New York
May 2	Charles Mangley	6	Anna Maria M.	ffredk Seabringh	Kings
1714 May 22	Anna Elizth Angle	5	Orphan	ffrancis Salisbury	Kattskill
May 5	Mary Angell	11	Orphan	Geo Willocks	Elizabethtown

HISTORIC SHRINES OF THE MOHAWK VALLEY

ORISKANY BATTLEFIELD
MONUMENT

GENERAL HERKIMER HOME

MONUMENT TO UNKNOWN SOLDIERS
OF ORISKANY

Roster of Oriskany Heroes

The list of names following comprise the combined lists of 1884 and 1921. There are duplicate names which may indicate two individuals and again it may be that two of the same name were engaged. Heretofore the 1884 list and the 1921 list have been published separately. In the following list they have been combined and classified for the sake of clarity

The list also includes a number of names procured by Nelson Greene and others and which appeared in Greene's splendid work in four volumes entitled "The Mohawk Valley, Gateway to the West," published by the Clark Publishing Company, 1925. Other name have been added by individuals who have furnished satisfactory proof, many from the pension papers of the participants. To date this is the most comprehensive list assembled. That it is incomplete is accepted and acknowledged. That other names will be yielded through further research, is to be expected. This most important battle will always remain somewhat obscure because of the fact that so many were killed or disabled, that no accurate record was obtained. Inasmuch as the direction of the battle was under the Committee of Safety, and this was soon afterwards absorbed by the new state government and active written returns were either lost or were never committed to writing, the roster which follows has been built up name by name, and under most difficult circumstances. The desire for a complete roster of participants at Oriskany still remains as a task for future historians.

Key to References

1 Killed.
2 Died in action
3 Prisoner of war
4 Missing
5
6 Wounded

Brigadier General

Hercheimer, Nicolaus 1

Colonels

Bellinger, Peter
Cox, Ebenezer 1
Klock, Jacob
Visscher, Frederick 6

Lieutenant Colonels

Bellinger, Frederick 3
Campbell, Samuel
Flock, John
Veeder, Volkert
Wagner, Peter
Walrath, Heinrich

Brigade Majors

Frey, John 3-6

Majors

Bleven, John 1
DeGraff, Isaac
Eisenlord, John 1
Klapsattel, Enos 1
Newkirk, John
Sieber, Wilhelm 1
Shoemaker, Han Yost
Van Slyck, Hermanus 1
Van Vechten, Anthony

Second Major

Clyde, Samuel

Surgeons

Petry, Dr. Wilhelm 6
Younglove, Dr. Moses 3

Captains

Bauman, Jacob 1

Bell, George H. 6
Brodbeck, Johann (Bigbread) 6
Copeman, Adam
Copeman, Adam
Davis, John James 1
De Graff, Immanuel
Deifendorf, Heinrich 1
Deichert, Wilhelm
Demuth, Johann
Deygart, John 1
Diefendorf, Jacob
Dillenbach, Andreas 1
Eckler, Henry
Fox, Chrstof W. 6
Fox, Christoph 1
Frank, Frederick
Gardinier, Jacob 6
Getman, Frederick
Hans, Christian
Helmer, Frederick 1
Herchheimer, George
Hoover, John
Ittig, Michael
Keyser, John
Klock, Jacob G.
Pettingale, Samuel 1
Rector, Nicholaus 6
Seeber, Jacob 1
Seiber, Jacob
Small, Jacob 1
Snook, William
Tuthill, Stephen
Van Evers, Rymier
Visscher, John
Wemple, Johannes
Yates, Robert

Lieutenants

Bailey, Joseph
Bailey, Joseph
Campbell, Robert 1
Dunlap, John
Fox, Frederick
Gardinier, Samuel 6
Grant, Petrus 1
Gray, Samuel
Grinnell, James 1
Groot, Peter 6
Hans, Yost
Heath, Nathaniel 1
Helmer, George 6
Helmer, George 6
Hiller, Jacob 1
Horning, Dederick
Loucks, Peter
McMaster, Daniel

Petrie, Wilhelm
Petrie, Dietrich M. 1
Petrie, Hans Yost 1
Putman, Victor
Putman, Richard

Quackenbush, Abram D.

Swart, Jeremiah
Scholl, Johann Yost
Timmermadrr, Heinrich 6 (?)
Van Alstyne, Martin
Van Horne, Thomas
Voltz, Jacob
Wagner, Peter, Jr.

Sergeants

Brandt, Christian 1
Comb, Uriel 1
Diefendorf, John Jacob
Garlock, Charles 1
Petrie, Nicholas 1
Piper, Andrew
Ritter, John 1
Steinway, Arnold 1

Corporals

Finck, Christian 1
Iser, Frederick 1
Keyser, Michael
Mereness, William 1
Tuthill, Stephen 1

Privates

Alter, Jacob
Aradt, Abram
Bauder, Melchert 1
Baluwadt, Major 3 (suppposed murdered)
Baumann, Jacob
Baun, John
Becker, Hendrich
Bell, George Henry
Bell, Joseph 1
Bell, Nicholas
Bellinger, Adam
Bellinger, Wilhelm P.
Bellinger, Peter F.
Bellinger, John P.
Bellinger, John
Bellinger, Adam
Bellinger, Johann
Bellinger, Wilhelm P.
Bettinger, Martin
Berge, Peter
Biddleman, Adam
Billington, James 1
Billington, Samuel 1
Boyer, Johann
Bowman, Frederick
Brooks, Naome
Brooks, Naome
Bush, George
Casselman, John
Chawgo, Jacob 1
Christian, Frederick
Clemons, Jacob
Clemens, Jacob
Clock, John I.

Collier, Jacob
Cone, Samuel
Cone, Samuel
Cook, John 6
Countryman, John
Covenhoven, Peter 6
Covenhoven, Isaac
Covenhoven, Abraham
Covenhoven, Cornelius
Covenhoven, Jacob
Cox, William
Cunningham, Andrew 1
Crouse, George
Crim, Jacob
Dachstadter, Johnn
Davis, Daniel
Davis, Benjamin 1
Davis, Martinus 1
Deichert, George
Deichert, Johann 1
Deichert, Peter S.
Dickson, James
Diefendorf, Johann
Diefendorf, Johan
De Graf, Eamanuel
Dorn, Peter
Dunckel, Garret
Dunckel, Nicholaus
Dunckel, Peter
Dunlap, John
Dunlap, William
Dunlap, ...
(3 brothers)
Dygert, Peter
Edic, Jacob, Sr.
Ehle, Peter 3
Ehle, William
Elwood, Isaac 1
Empie, Jacob 1
Everson, Adam
Eyer, Frederick (Oyer)
Eyer, Friedrich
Eyster, Johann
Fehling, Jacob 1
Fehling, Heinrich 1
Fehling, Heinrich N.
Finster, John
Flint, Adam
Flint, Alexander
Flint, Cornelius
Flint, John
Flint, Robert
Flock, John
Foltz, Conrad 6
Foltz, Peter 1
Folts, Peter
Fonda, Adam
Fox, Philip
Fox, Karl
Fox, Christoph
Fox, Friedrich
Fox, Peter
Fox, Wilhelm
Franks, Andrew 6
Frank, Adam
Frank, John 1
Froelich, Valentin
Gago (Chawgo), George 1
Gardinier, Samuel

Garlock, Eleas 6
Garter, John
Garter, John, Jr.
Goertner, Peter
Goertner, Georg
Gray, Silas
Gray, Nicholaus 1
Gray, Silas
Graves,
Gremps, John (15 years)
Gross, Lorenz
Hahn, Conrad 1
Hall, William
Hall, William
Halter, Johann A.
Hand, Marcus
Hand, Marcus
Hann, Conrad 1
Hanson, Henry
Harter, John A.
Hawn, Conrad
Helmer, Johann Adam
Henner, Peter 1
Herkimer, George
Herkimer, Joseph
Herkimer, Hendrick
Herkimer, Philip
Hess, Augustine
Hess, Frederick
Hess, Conrad
Hess, Augustine, Jr.
Hess, George
Hess, Johannes 6
Hiller 1
Hoover, Jacob
Horning, Adam
Horning, George
Horning, John
Horning, Lanert
House, Conrad 1
House, John
Hoyer, George Frederick
Hufnagel, Christian 1
Hunt, Abel 1
Hunt, Timothy
Hunt, Peter 1
Huyck, John
Jackson, Joseph 1
Jones, Judas
Jones, Judah
Kaufman,
Keesler, Adam
Keesler, Jacob
Keller, Andreas
Keller, Jacob
Keller, Solomon 1
Keller, John 6
Keller, Henry
Keller, Jacob A.
Keller, Jacob
Kessler, Adam
Kessler, Jacob
Kessler, Johann
Keyser, John
Keyser, Henry
Keyser, Bernard
Kilts, Conrad
Kilts, Conrad
Kilts, Peter

Klapsattel, Jacob (Clapsattel)
Klock, Jacob I.
Klock, Adam 1
Klock, John J.
Kopernall, Richard (Coppernoll)
Kraus, Georg
Kraus, Robert (Crouse) 1
Lampman, Henry 1
Lapper, Jacob 1
Leonardson, John
Lentz, Jacob
Levy, Michael 1
Lighthall,
Lighth'all, Nicholas
Lighthall, Francis 3
Lighthall, George
Lindner (Linter), George
Lohnus, Heinrich
Longshore. Solomon
Lonas, John
Loucks, William 6
Markell, William
Markell, Jacob
Martin, Philip 6
Mauer,
Mauer,
Mauer, Conrad
Mathias, Hendrick 1
McMaster, Hugh 6
Merkel, Jacob 1
Newkirk, Garret
Merkel, Wilhelm 1 (Markell)
Merckly, William 1
Meyer, Jacob
Meyer, Jost
Miller, Jelles
Mowers, Conrad
Mowers (brothers)
Mowers (brothers)
Moyer, Jacob 1
Moyer, Ludwick
Muller, Heinrich
Muller, Jelles
Muller, Johann P.
Murray, David
Nellis, Christian
Nellis, Joseph
Nellis, Johann P.
Nellis, Philip 6
Nestel, Peter
Neuman, Joseph
Nelson, Paul
Paris, Esaak 1 (Isaac)
Paris, Peter 1
Peeler, Jacob
Petrie. Johann 1
Philips, James 1
Philips, Cornelius 1
Pickert, Bartholomew
Pickard. Adolph 6
Pickard, John 6
Pickard, Nicholaus
Price, Adam 6
Putman, Ludowick
Putman, Martinus 1

Radnor, Jacob 6
Ratenhower, Godfrey 1
Rasbell, Frederick 6

Rasbach, Friedrich
Rasbach, Marx
Rasbell, Frederick
Raspnor, Georg
Ravsnor, George 1
Reibson, Mathias 1
Ritter, Jacob
Ritter, Henry
Ritter 1
Ritter, Jacob 1
Rose, Willard
Rose, Willard
Roth, Johann
Ruff, Johannes
Saltsman, John 6
Sammons, Thomas
Sammons, Jacob
Sammons, Samson
Saunders, Henry
Scholts, George
Schaefer, Wilhelm 6
Scherer, Christian 1
Scherer, Pedagogus
Schimmel,
Scholl, Heinrich
Schultz, Georg
Schultz, Johann
Schnell, Christian
Schnell, Johann
Schnell, Friedrich 1
Schnell, George 1
Schnell, Jacob 1
Schnell, Johan 1
Schnell, Joseph 1
Schnell, Peter
Schnell, Sophromus 1
Schumacher, Thomas
Schuyler, Philip 1
Schuyler, William
Seeber, Henry 6
Seitz, Heinrich
Seitz, Peter
Serviss, Christian
Serviss, George
Shaull, George
Shults, Johan
Sieber, Adolph
Sieber, Adolph, Jr.
Siebert, Rudolph
Siller,
Silberbach, Johann G.
Sitts, Henry
Smith, Henry
Smith, George
Snell, Suffrenus
Sparks, Pearl 6
Sponable, John 3
Spore, John
Stevens, Frederick 1
Steele, Dietrich
Stevens, Amasa
Staring, Heinrich
Stevens, Frederick
Stowitz, Philip G. 1
Suits, John I.
Sulbach, Garret 6

Terwilliger, James
Thumb, Adam
Thornton, James

Thompson, Henry
Timerman, Conrad
Timerman, William
Van Alstyne, Philip
Van Alstyne, Martin G.
Van Antwerp, John 1
Van Deusen, George
Van Driesen, Peter
Van Epps, Jan
Van Epps, Charles
Van Evera, Reemer
Van Horn, Henry
Van Horn, Henry
Van Horn, Cornelius
Van Horn, Cornelius
Van Horn, Abram
Van Slyke,
Van Slyck, Jacobus
Van Slyke, Nicholas 1
Van Vechten, Derrick
Vatterly, Henry 1
Veeder, Johannes
Veeder, Volkert
Veeder, Abram
Veeder, Hendrick
Vedder, Henry
Visscher, Harmon
Visger, John
Vrooman, Hendrick
Wagner, George 6
Wagner, Jacob
Wagner, Johann
Wagner, Johann
Walrath, Garret 3
Walrath, Jacob
Walrath, Nicholas 6
Walter, George 6
Weaver, George J.
Weaver, George M.
Weber, Jacob
Weber, Peter J.
Westerman, Peter 1
Wildrich, Michael
Windecker, Frederick
Windecker, Nicholas
Wormuth,
Wohleben, Nicholas
Wohloofer, Adam (Wohleben)
Worloofer (Wohleben), Johann 1
Wohloofer (Wohleben), Richard
Worloofer (Wohleben), Peter
Wrenkle, Lorenz
Wright, Jacob 6

Yates, Robert
Yerdon, Nicholaus 6
Yerdon, John
Yonker (Youker), Jacob 3
Young, Peter
Young, Richard
Young, Godfrey 6
Zimmerman, Heinrich, Pen. Papers.
Zimmerman, Jacob
Zimmerman, Conrad
Zoller, Jacob 1
Zoller, Andrew 3

Spencer, Thomas (Indian) 1
Atyataronghta, Lt. Col. Louis, Indian

officer.
Tewahangaraghkan, Capt. Han, Indian officer.

Names of Soldiers who Fought at Oriskany, whose Names are not on the Oriskany Roster

Han Adam Helmer, killed at the Battle of Oriskany.
John G. Helmer.
Also a brother of John G. Helmer (name unknown) killed at Oriskany.
Captain Peter Bowman (husband of Catharine Helmer) killed at Oriskany.
Smith, Nicholas, Sr., killed at Oriskany

Additional Names in Greene's Gateway to West

Ayer, Frederick 1
Basehorn, Jacob Lt.
Bell, Jacob 1
Bellinger, Frederick Private
Bellinger, John, Lt. 1
Bellinger, John Frederick 1
Billington
Casler, John
Casler, Jacob
Casler, Adam
Covenhoven, John
Davy, Thomas, Capt. 1
Demuth, Hans Marks
De Graf, Nicholas
Dunckel, Francis
Fonda, Adam, Lt. Col.
Fonda, Jelles
Folts, Jacob, Lt.
Fox, Christopher P., Capt.
Fox, Charles
Frank, John, Sgt.
Graves, Capt. 1
Gross, Lorenz, Capt.
Hartman, Adam
Harter, Henry, Capt.
Hess, David
Helmer, Philip
Hill, Nicholas
House, Henry 1
House, John Joseph, Lt.
House, Christian, Capt.
Klock, John
Lepper, Wyant (Pen. Papers)
Marlett, John
McMaster, David, Lt.
Miller, Adam
Nellis, John D.
Newkirk, John
Petrie, John Marks
Petry, Richard, Lt. 1
Petry, Joseph 6
Pettingale, John 1

Putnam, Victor C., Lt.
Putnam, Victor
Renckel, Lawrence 1
Schumacher, Rudolph
Schell, Christian
Schnell, Jacob F. 1
Schnell, John, Jr. (probably refers to 2nd Johan in Oriskany roster) 1
Schnell, Jacob 1
Seeber, Suffrunes 1
Seeber, James 1
Seeber, Lt. John
Sommer, Peter
Spencer, Henry (Oneida Indian interpreter) 1

Steel, Rudolph
Van Epps, Everett 6
Van Evera, John
Walrath, Henry, Lt. 3
Walrath, Henry 3
Wohleben
Wohlelver, Abram
Woolheber, Dederick 1

———

Names Furnished by Mrs. C. W. Crim

Huyck, Henry
Herkimer, George (14 years old aide to Gen. Herkimer)
Pruyne, Peter
Walrath, William

Tryon County Militia, 1st. Regiment.
COL. SAMUEL CAMPBELL.

The first of the four Tryon County Militia regiments is usually known as Campbell's Regiment or as Clyde's Regiment. The territory from which this regiment was drawn was known as the Canajoharie country or precinct and was all the land from the "Noses" to the east, to Little Falls to the west, lying altogether on the south side of the river. Concerning the regiment S. L. Frey in his treatise "The Minute Book of the Committee of Safety" says on pp. 122: "There were two colonels in the first regiment Tryon County Militia, according to 'New York in the Revolution'—Campbell and Ebenezer Cox. The regiment was at Oriskany and Cox being killed, Colonel Campbell was in command and brought off the regiment or what was left of it. He was also colonel of a battalion of Minute Men, presumably a local organization for the protection of Cherry Valley. The family was Scotch-Irish and came to Cherry Valley with several others in 1741, from New Hampshire. In the massacre of Cherry Valley Mrs. Campbell and her four children were among the prisoners and were not exchanged until 1780. Col. Campbell died in 1824, aged 86 years. Judge William W. Campbell, author of the 'Annals of Tryon County' was his grandson. Samuel Clyde was Lt. Colonel but afterwards raised to Colonel. He was a very efficient officer and rendered valuable aid to the cause throughout the war. He was in command at Fort Plain in 1783, when Washington visited the valley. In the massacre at Cherry Valley Col. Clyde escaped by hiding in the woods. He was in the assembly in 1777-8 and sheriff 1785 to 1789.

Key to References

1 Killed at Oriskany.
2 Died in action.
3 Prisoner of war
4 Missing.
5 Engaged at Oriskany.
6 Wounded.

TRYON COUNTY MILITIA
Colonels

Campbell, Samuel 5
Cox, Ebenezer 1

Majors
Deygert, Peter S.
Copeman, Abraham 5

Adjutant
Seeber, Jacob 1
Quarter Master
Pickard, John
Surgeon
Frank, Adam
Younglove, David

Captains
Bowman, John 1

Brown, Matthew
Copeman, Adam 5
Davey, Thomas 1
Devendorf, Henry 1
Deygert, Jost
Diffendorff, Jacob 5
House, Joseph
Leyp, Adam
Roof (Russ), John
Van Everen, Ryner 5
Weyser, Nicholas
Wilson, Japes

Lieutenants
Adamy, Peter
Arnt, Abraham
Barth, Nicholas
Brate, Henry
Braun, Conrad
Campbell, Robert 1
Conderman, George
Deygert, Nicholas
Dunlap, John 5
Grinnall, James 1
Heath, Nathaniel 1
House, John Joseph 5
Horning, Dedrick 5
Matthews, Jacob

Powell, Charles
Schneyder, Jacob
Seeber, John
Seeber, William
Shrumling, Henry
Van Alstine, Martin C. 5
Van Everen, John 5
Windecker, Hanes

Ensigns
Bellinger, John L.
Cunderman, John
Ellwood, Richard
Flind, Adam
Hanes, Jacob
Myer, Henry 3
Van Every, Cornelius
Walrath, Henry

Corporals
Martinus (Metneus), Wm. 1

Sergeants
Garlock, Charles 1
Petry, Nich'l. 1

**Additional Names on State Treasur-
er's Pay Books**
Wagoner, Englehardt, Lieut.
Pickert, John, Ensign
Young, Jeremiah, Ensign

Enlisted Men
Adamy, Peter
Ale, Peter.
Ale, Christian
Apel, Henry
Arnat, Abram 5
Alter, Jacob 5

Batenauer, Jacob
Batenauer, George
Barndt, Christian, Sgt. 1
Bearmour, Henry
Becker, Henry
Becker, Peter
Beellinger, Adam
Bell, Fredrick
Belleanger, Frederick
Beliner, Heinrick
Bellinger, Adam 5
Bellinger, Philip
Bellinger, William
Bendeman, Peter
Besner, Jacob
Bettinger, Martin
Benteman, Simmon
Bickerd, Henry
Bickerd, Isaac
Biling, William
Billinger, William
Bitelman, Peter
Blats, George
Bleats, George
Bohall, Adam
Bolier, Frederick
Bolt, Fillip
Boom, Fredrick K.
Boss, Christian

Bost, Christian 3
Bost, Joh's 2
Botman, Adam
Brate, James
Brisenbecker, Balser
Broukman, Godfret
Bruckeman, John
Bruckman, Godfrid
Brunner, Christian
Bush, George
Butcluter, John
Euterfield, James

Cannan, Matthey 3
Castler, Thomas
Christman, John
Clapsattle, William
Clapsedel, George
Clebsater, William
Clock, Joseph
Cockton, Thomas
Cohat, Adam
Cohert, Adam
Conterman, John
Contryman, John 5
Contryman, John M.
Coon, John
Crais, George
Cramer, Godfred
Cramer. Joast
Casler, Peter 2
Coppernoll, Richard 5
Cox, Williamm 5
Crouse. Rob't. 1
Crouse, Geo. 5
Creamer, John
Creamer, Joseph
Crimm, Jacob
Crisman, John
Crosmen, Frederick
Crouse, Friederick
Crows, George
Crum, Adam
Crum, Jacob
Cuff (colored)
Cunderman, Cunrath
Cunderman, Frederick 2
Cunderman, John J.
Cunderman, Marius
Cuntrman, Adam
Cuntryman, Cunrad
Curtner, Peter
Cypher. John

Damuth. Richard
Darwind, Bindier
Dasler, John
Deck, Henry
Defendorf, Jacob H. R.
Demult, Richard
Demuth, Dederick
Devery, Arent
Devy, Adam
Deygert, Nichlas
Didenbeck, Baltus
Diefendorff. H. Jacob
Diefendorff. Johannes
Diefendorff. John J. 5
Diefendurff, John 5
Diefendurff, John, Jun.
Dietrich, Dewald
Dilenbeck, Baltus

Dilenbeck, Martin
Dinstman, Antony
Dinstman, Denis
Docksteader, John
Dreisselmann, Christian
Dunckey, Frank 5
Dunckey, Nicholas 5
Dunckel, Peter 5
Dunckell, Garrett 5
Dunkle, George
Dunlap, John
Dunlap, William
Dus Ler, Jacob
Dusler, John
Dusler, Marx
Dychert, Thabolt
Dygart, Sevrinus 3
Dygert, Henry
Dykert, Henery
Dickson, James 5
Dunlap, 3 brothers 5

Eatkens, William
Eckler, Christ Sogel
Eckler, Christstofel
Eckler, Ernest
Eckler, Hanos
Eckler, Henry
Eckler, Henry, Jun.
Eckler, Johannes
Eckler, Lenet
Eckler, Pitter
Ehl, Christian
Ehl, Peter
Ehle, Anthony
Ehle, Harmanus
Ehle, John
Ehts, Adam
Ehts, Christopher
Ehts, John Christ.
Ehts, William
Elfendorf, Debois
Ell, John
Ellwood, Benjamin
Ellwood, Isaac 6
Elvendorf, Tobias
Elwood, Peter
Embody, Henry
Estter, John C.

Failing, Henry N. 5
Farbus, Nichlas
Faubele, Johnas
Feeble, John
Fehling, Andreas
Fehling, Henry 6
Felling, Jacob 1
Felling, Nicholas
Felling, Peter
Fetterly, John
Fetterly, John T.
Fouston, John
Flack, Peter
Flind, Alexander
Flint, Alexander 5
Flint, Cornelius 5
Flint, John 5
Flint, Robert 5
Folkert, John
Folyg, Peter
Forbush, Johnes
Fork, Isaac

Forre, Adam (see Furry)
Fosse, Adam 3
Foster, John
Foster, Moses
Fox, Peter
Fox, William
Frantz, Stoffel
Fretcher, Conraed
Flint, Adam 5
Fuks, Peter
Fun, Adam
Furro, Rudolph (see Furry) 3

Gago, Geo. 1
Galger, Isaac
Garlock, Adam
Garlock, George P.
Garlock, Jacob
Garlock, Philip
Gelly, Thadeus
Gerlack, Gorge
Gerlack, Han Christian
Gerlack, Henry
Gerlock, George W.
Givit, Fridrick
Givet, John J.
Goertner, Peter 5
Goertner, George 5
Grim, Jacob
Gros, Capt. Lawrence 5

Hahn, Conrad 1
Haber, Jacob
Haberman, Jacob
Hack, Fredrick
Haffer, Jacob
Hake, Frederick
Hako, Fradrick
Harning, Lienert
Haus Adam
Haus, Henrick
Haus, Peter
Heerway, Charles
Helmer, John
Helmer, John G.
Helmer, Joseph
Helmer, Jost
Henry, Andrew
Hess, George
Hess, Henry
Heuth, Joshua
Heyntz, William
Hicky, George
Hicky, Michal
Himer, William
Hines, Andrew
Hootmaker, Adam
Hoover, Jacob
Horning, Adam 5
Horning, Dederick
Horning, George 5
Horning, John 5
Horning, Lanert 5
Hous, Harman
House, George 3
House, Conrad 1
House, Jacob 3
House, John
House, Joseph
House, Jost C.
House, Nicholas 3
House, Peter 3

Jackson, Joseph 1
Jacob, Henry
Johns, William
Jordan, Adam
Jordan, Casper
Jordan, Casper L.
Jordan, Casper
Jordan, George
Jordan, John
Jordan, John Peter
Jordan, Nicholas
Jorden, John P.
Jorden, Peter
Jung, Jacob
Jung, Thommes
Jungijo, Jacob

Kellar, Jacob
Keller, Andras
Keller, Andres, Jun.
Keller, Felix
Keller, Gasper
Keller, Jacob R.
Kelly, Thomas
Kelmer, John
Kerlach, Henry
Kesles, Thomas
Kessler, Peter
Killy, Thomas
Kling, Ludwig
Knausz, Johanens
Knautz, John
Knieskern, Pitter
Knouts, George
Koemer, Johannes
Korning, Adam
Kretsinger, Jacob

Lambert, George
Lambert, Peter
Lambert, Peter, Jun.
Lambert Peter, Sen.
Lampert, Peter
Lape, John
Lappius, Daniel
Lentner, George 5
Leeve, Philip
Leipe, John L.
Lepert, Fredrick
Levey, Michael 1
Leyli, Simon
Lint, Georg
Lints, Gorg
Lipe, John
Lipe, John, Jun.
Loucks, Peter
Loux, Jost
Low, Lawrence Gras
Lure Philip,
Longshore, Solomon 5
Louns, Henry 5
Lurzdemann, Simon (

Mai, Henrich
Marten, Robert
Mayby, David
Mayby, Joseph
Mayer, H. Henry
Mayer, Jacob
Mayer, Jacob S.
Meier, Matthew
Meyer, Henrick
Meyer, Henrick S.

Mathias, Henry 1
Meyer, Jacob
Meyer, Jacob R.
Meyer, Johan Henrick
Meyer, Solomon
Mier, John
Miler, John C.
Miller, Conraed
Miller Dionysius
Miller, Garret
Miller, John
Monk, John, Jun.
Monke, John
Moone, James
Moos, Pitner Rufus
Morfey Henry
Moyer, David
Moyer, John
Murphy, Henry
Murphy, Thomas
Myer, Matthias
Myers, Dewel
Myers, John
Myre, Henry
Myre, John
McCartey, Dunkon
McCartey, John
McFie, Alexander
McKillip, John
McLonis, Jurry
McVagulhen Peeter

Neles, Cris John
Neles, Rowerd
Neles, Willem
Nelles, Christian
Nelles, George
Nelles, Gerry
Nelles, Henrick
Nelles, Henry
Nelles, Henry N.
Nelles John
Nelles, Wiliam
Nellies Gerry
Nelis, Henry
Nellis, Jacob 2
Neteherly, John
Netherly John H.
Netherly, John I.
Nolgert, John

Ohn, Jacob
Outerman, Jacob
Ovendurff, Conrad

Paba, Ernst
Parsheall, James
Pauly, Jacob
Phenes Michael
Price, Adam 6
Pickard, John 6
Pritchard, Nich'l. 5
Pier, House, Joh's. 2
Pickard, Cunrad
Pickerd, Adolph 6
Pickerd, Nicholas 5
Pickert, Conradt
Pickert, George
Pigner, Tise
Plets, George
Plough, Nichlas
Plunes, John
Price, George

Qollinger, Henry
Quackenbos, Honter Soct
Quackenboss, Isaac
Quackenbush, David
Quackenbush, Jeremiah
Quakenbush, Peter
Quollenger, Gosper
Quollinger, Andrew

Radenaer, Jacob 6
Radimour, Jacob
Ransier, George 1
Ratnower, George
Ratnower, Jacob
Ratnower, Godfrey 1
Reasnor, James
Reinhartd, Willem
Remer, Jacob
Remer, John
Remer, Martin
Revershon, John Peter 3
Ribsorner, William
Rice, John
Riebsomer, Matteys 1
Riverson, John Peter
Rodgers, Samuel
Roneons, Jonathan
Ronnin, John, Jun.
Roof, John
Roseel, John
Roth, John 5
Ruff, John
Runnins, John, Jun.
Runnins, John, Sen.

Sacknar, John
Sander, Henrick 5
Scheat, Andony
Schefer, Adam 3
Schiely, Martin
Schimmel, Francis
Schneck, George
Schneider, Michael
Schreiber, Steffan
Schuyler, David 3
Schuyler, Jacob 3
Schuyler, John Jost
Schuyler, Nicolas 3
Schuyler, Peter P.
Schyler, David, Jun.
Scoulen, Essias.
Scoulen, Tosseos.
Seaber, John W.
Seeber, Jacob
Seeber, John 5
Seyber, John
Shall, Henry
Sheafer, Adam 3
Sheafer, Henry
Shelly, John
Shimel, Dietrich
Shairmar, Geo., Corpl., 3
Shoemacher, Rudolph 5
Seeber, Suffrenus 1
Seeber, Adolph 5
Seeber, Adolph 1
Seeber, James 1
Seeber, Henry 6
Shireman, George 3
Shmit, Hendrick
Shnyder, Gottlib
Simmerman, Conratee

Simmeman, Henery
Sits, Headrick 5
Sits, John 5
Sits, Nichlos
Sitts, Peter
Sitz, Baldes
Smidt, Philip
Smith, Johannes
Smith, John 3
Smith, Philip
Snake, George
Snyder, John
Sober, Jacobus
Spalsbeck, John
Sparback, Martinus
Sparks, Pearl 6
Stansell, Nicolas
Steinmetz, Philip
Stensell, George
Stensell, Nicoles
Stensell, William
Stephen, John
Strawbeck, Adam
Stroback, Fradrick
Strobeck, Jacob
Sulenger, Gosper
Suller, Andrew
Suller, Gosper

Tailor, Nathan
Tetterly, John H.
Thompson, Aaron
Thompson, John
Thompson, Thomas
Thompson, William
Tillenback, Martin
Tom (colored)
Tucks, Peter
Tulling, Henry
Tygert, Henry

Ullendorf, Daniel
Ulsever, Stephen
Ulzhaven, Bastian
Uthermark, John B.
Uttermark, John J.

Van, Johannes
Van Allstine, Abraham
Vanallstine, Abraham C.
Van Allstine, Peter
Van Alsten, Cornelius C.
Van Alstin, Harmans
Vanalstine, Cornelius
Vanalstine Cornelius J.
Vanalstine, John
Vanalstine, John G.
Vanalstine, John M.
Vanalstine, Martin
Vanalstine, Martin A.
Vanalstine, Martin G. 5
Vanalstine, Philip 5
Vanalstyn, Peter
Van Camp, Isaac
Van Campen, Cornelius
Van Dusen, Geo. 5
Vatterly, Henry 1
Van Derwarken, Harmanus
Vanderwarker, Joshua
Van Derwartin, Joshua
Van Eaverak, John
Van Everen, John
Van Slike, George

Van Slyke, Garret 3
Van Slyke, John

Wagener, Engelhard
Waggoner, Isaac
Waggoner, Jacob
Wagner. George
Wagner, Jacob 5
Wagoner, Gorge
Wagner, John 5
Walrath, Garret 3
Wallart, Hannes
Wallrad, Georae
Wallrate, Adolph
Wallrate, Frederick
Wallrate, Jacob
Walse, Conraed
Walse, Conraed, Jun.
Walse, Jacob
Walrad, Jacob
Walrate, Henrick
Walrath, George
Walrath, Henry
Walrath Jacob
Walrath, William
Wals, Cunrath
Wals, Cunrath, Jun.
Wals, Cunrath, Sen.
Warmood, Pete
Warmorte, Petter
Warmuth, John
Wath, Jacob
Westerman, Peter 1
Wiele, Henry
Wiele, Joss Henry
Wilson, James

Windecker, Fredrick
Windker, Nicolas
Winn, John
Wohlgemuth, John
Wohlgemuth, Wiliam
Woldorf, Johannes
Wolkemood, John
Wollever, John 3
Woolerod, Nich's. 2
Wollever, Nicholas
Woolf, Jacob
Wormut, John
Wright, Jacob 6

Yates, Chris P.
Young, Adam
Young, Andreas
Young, Andrew
Young, Christian
Young, Christian A.
Young, Crist, Jun.
Young, Frietrick
Young, Godfred 6
Young, Henry
Young, Henry P.
Young, John
Young Joseph
Young, Jost
Young Lodwick
Young, Peter
Young, Robert
Young, Thomas
Yerdon, John 5
Yerdon, Nich'l. 6
Young, Richard 5

Zoller, Andrew 3

FORT PLAIN BLOCK-HOUSE.[1]

Col. Jacob Klock's Regiment

Second Tryon County Militia·in the Revolution.

In presenting the names of the men in Col. Jacob Klock's Regiment a word of explanation seems necessary in order to avoid confusion and outline the exact scope of the work. It should be borne in mind that this work is confined to but one of the five regiments in Tryon County. In collecting the names the editor has frequently received names which belong to other regiments and these are of course so classified and will be treated at a future time.

In 1772 Sir William Johnson divided Tryon County into five districts after the county was set off from the county of Albany. The districts were as follows: Mohawk, the eastern portions east of "The Noses"; the Palatine district, that portion on the north side of the river from "The Noses" to Little Falls and extending north to the Canadian line; the Canajoharie district on the south side and occupying the same breadth as the Palatine, extending south to the Pennsylvania line; the Kingsland district, that portion on the north side of the river west of the Palatine district and the German Flatts distric: which was on the south side of the river extending from Little Falls to Fort Stanwix and south to the Pennsylvania line.

The Tryon county committee apparently followed this general division at first but after the death of General Herkimer who was in the Canajoharie district the Kingsland and German Flatts regiments were consolidated and a fifth regiment created embracing Cherry Valley and the section adjacent under Col. Harper. Roberts New York in the Revolution gives the division as follows:

First Regiment—Col. Samuel Campbell, Col. Ebenezer Cox, Lt. Col. Samuel Clyde.

Second Regiment—Col. Jacob Klock, Lt. Col. Peter Wagner.

Third Regiment—Col. Frederick Fisher, Col. Frederick Visscher, Lt. Col. Volkert Veeder.

Fourth Regiment—Col. Peter Bellinger.

Fifth Regiment—Col. John Harper, Major Joseph Harper.

There were also separate divisions as Battalion of Minute Men un der Col. Samuel Clyde; Asosciated Exempts, Capt. Jelles Fonda and tour organizations of rangers under Capts. John Wynn, Christian Getman, John Kassellmann and Capt. John Breadbake (Bigbread).

Klock's Regiment is taken largely from New York in the Revolution, a state publication which was issued in 1904. The list of names is from state pay rolls sent in by Col. Jacob Klock and is undoubtedly correct as to those in the regiment subsequent to 1780 when the state government first began to function. Prior to that and especially at the battle of Oriskany when the entire man power of the valley wa; under arms there were no returns made for the reason that the battle was fought before there was a state government. The only records of those engaged in that battle are those gleaned from pension papers, private papers and family tradition. This has been a work of years and has been engaged in by historians for many years back. The present work is the first attempt to treat the subject by regiments and is far from complete. Recourse has been had to the Oriskany roster of names, as well as Greene's "Gateway to the West" which contains the best roster yet published. We are also indebted to many family historians who have collaborated liberally in preparing this list. We know that we have fallen way short and that many of those not marked were in the battle of Oriskany. We can only hope that in the fulness of time additional evidence may come to light whereby these men may receive the honor they deserve. In recording the names as prepared from state pay rolls undoubtedly many repetitions occur. The nature of the service called for many short time services and consequent duplicate pay rolls. The carelessness of army clerks in recording names coupled with the apparent indifference of the men themselves in the matter of spelling often led to duplication of one individual. But on the other hand there were so many of the same name that it is impossible to attempt correction, for fear of robbing some individual of the honor to which he was entitled. The difficulty will be appreciated when we point out that there were during the war three Major Foxes, all bearing nearly the same christian name, two of them being named Christopher and one Christian. Three distinct and separate George Nellises were engaged and there seems to have been at least five Jacob Klocks, all separate individuals. As for Timmerman and Zimmerman, Crouse and Krouse, Failing and Phelan, Dillenbeck and Tillebagh and others there is seemingly a hopeless maze. And yet each of these is capable of separation and in the course of time it is reasonable to expect that many of the heroes will receive just recognition.

In giving the roster of Klock's Regiment the editor is indebted to so many sourecs that proper acknowledgment by individual name is avoided for fear of omission, but the editor wishes to convey his appreciation to all who have assisted and without such aid frankly admits the task would not even be attempted. The work should not rest here and it is to be hoped that any additional information will be forwarded in order that corrections and additions may be added for a future edition.

Key to References

1 Killed at Oriskany.
2 Died in action.
3 Prisoner of war.
4 Missing.
5 Engaged at Oriskany.
6 Wounded.

OFFICERS

Colonel
COL. JACOB KLOCK, 5

Lieutenant Colonel
Lieut. Col. Petter Wagoner 5
*Lt. Col. Ebenezer Cox 1-5

Major
Maj. Anthony Van Vechten 5
Maj. Tannes Van Slyke 1-5
Maj. Christian William Fox 5
Maj. Christopher Fox 5
Maj. John P. Frey 3-5-6
Maj. John Eisenlord 1-5
Maj. Hermanes Van Slyke 1-5
Major Henry Merchell
Maj. John Decker

Captains
Capt. Frederick Gettman 5
Capt. Andreas Dillenbeck 1-5
Capt. John Brodbeck 5-6
Capt. Severines Cook   z
Capt. John Dygert 1
Capt. Peter S. Dygart 5
Capt. John Cassellman 5
Capt. Christian House 5

Capt. Philip Helmer 5
Capt. John Hess 5
Capt. —— Hoover
Capt. Johanes Kayser 3-5
Capt. Severinus Kloch
Capt. Christopher W. Fox Maj. (Sept 29, 1780) 5-6
Capt. Chris P. Fox 1-5
Capt. Nicholas Righter 6
Capt. Johannes Russ
Capt. John Zilly 3
Capt. Henry Miller 5-6
Capt. Rudolph Kock
Capt. Abram Cuddiback
Capt. Jacob R. Dewitt
Capt. Levinus Klock
Capt. Rudolph Koch, Jr.

Adjutant
Adj. Samuel Gray 5
Adj. Andrew Irvin

Quartermaster
Quartermaster Jacob Aaker
Surgeon
Surgeon Johann George Vach (Fox)

Lieutenants
Lieut. John Bellinger 1
Lieut. John Adams
Lieut. Adam Bellinger 5
Lieut. Harman Brewer
Lieut. Richard Coppernoll 5
Lieut. Lodowick Nellis
Lieut. John Schall
Lieut. John Sutz
Lieut. Hendrick Timmerman 5-6
Lieut. John Timmerman 2
Lieut. John P. Sutz
Lieut. Samuel Vanetta

Lieut. John Van Slyck 2
Lieut. Nicholas Coppernoll
Lieut. Jhon Koch 5
Lieut. Isaac Paris 1-5 (murdered)
Lieut. Christian House 5
Lieut. Peter Loucks 5
Lieut. Peter Wagner 5
Lieut. Mathew Woermuth 2
Lieut. Jacob Conrad Klock 3

Corporal

Corporal Peter Lampman 6
Corporal John Bayard
Corporal Valentine Bayard
Corporal ——— Casselman
Corporal Jacob Christman
Corporal Philip Dehoist

---

* Fernow places Col. Lieut. Ebenezer Cox under Col. Nicholas Herkimer of the 1st Battalion (Canajoharie district) but at one time he was in charge of the Kingsland, later in the fourth Battalion in the list of casualties given by Fernow Cox is placed in Col. Klock's regiment.

Ensigns

Ensign George Fey
Ensign Peter Grems
Ensign Peter Sitz 3
Ensign Conrath Timmerman 5
Ensign Nicholas Van Slyck
Ensign Christian Gerlock (1763)
Ensign Frederick Timmerman

Sergents

Sargent Bayard Cayser
Sargent Peter H. Dygert
Sargent Andrew Grey
Sargent John Grems 5
Sargent Beads Kern

Additional Names on State Treasurer's Pay Roll

Lieut. John Eigenbroot.
Lieut. John Finck
Lieut. William Fox
Lieut. Honyost School 5
Ensign George Ecker
Ensign George Wagoner 3
Ensign Nicholas Walrath
Ensign Frederick Zimmerman

Privates

Acker, John
Adamy, Peter
Acker, Adrahan
Apply, Jacob 2
Arkson, John
Baun, John Geo. 1
Bacchus, John
Bader, Melgert 5
Bagley, Andrew
Bailer, Joseph 5 (Bailey)
Baker, Joseph
Bader, Michael
Baldsperger, Johannes
Balsby, Peter

Baum, John George 1-5
Balsle, Andrew
Barder, Nicholas
Bates, Michael
Baul, Simeon
Baul, Samuel
Baum, Frederick
Baum, Philip
Bayer, John
Beacker, Henry
Bealer, John
Buyie, John B.
Bealor, Joseph
Beaum, Philip
Becker, Henry 5
Becker, Philip
Bellinger, Adam 5
Bellinger, Wm. P. 5
Bellinger, Fredich 1-2-5
Billington, Samuel 1
Bellington, James 1
Becker, Peter
Bealor, Joseph
Beeler, Jacob
Beely, Jacob
Bellinger, Henrich
Bellinger, Jost
Bellinger, Peter 5
Billington 5
Bicker, Corse
Bishelt, Charles
Bishet, Charles
Blessen, Lorance
Blessus, Lorents
Bishop, Charles
Bost, Andres
Boush, George 5
Braun, Christien 5
Bratt, Henry
Bratt, Jacobus
Brewer, John
Brewer, William
Brower, William
Brunner, Jacob
Bush, George 5
Bush, Julius
Backer, Thomas 3
Backter, John
Backter, Michael
Bader, Mebzer
Badman David
Barsh, Adam
Barsh, Ludolph
Bellinger, John 1-5
Bowen, Frederick
Brower, Helmer
Brown, John
Buyer, John P. 5
Buyer, Valentine 3
Bedheg, John
Beekman, Theophs

Calutia, Thomas
Candon, John
Casselman, John 5
Casselman, Peter 3
Clock, John I. 5
Chawgo, George 5-6
Cook, John 5-6
Comb, Uriel (Serg.) 1
Christman, John
Clapper, Christian

Clapsattle, Andrew
Clapsattle, William
Claus, George
Clements, Jacob 5
Coleman, Henry
Conningham, Henry
Comb, Uriel 1
Conningham, William
Conterman, John 5
Coppernoll, John
Coppernoll, William
Crama, Jacob 5
Cramer, Andreas
Cranse, Jacob
Crim, Hendrick
Crounhart, George
Cworhart, Georg
Cruysler, George
Culman, Henry
Cunningham, Johannis
Cunningham, William
Consolly, Benjamin
Casselman, Barth'w.
Casselman, Barthe
Casselman, John
Cayser, John
Chambers, Jacob
Clake, Joseph
Coch, Casper
Cole, Wilhelmus
Cook, Casper
Cratzer, Leonard
Crause, Leonard
Crisler, George
Crouse, John
Crouse, Joseph
Cuddeback, Peter
Curdendolph, Solomon
Cuykindolph, Peter

Dackson, John
David, Adam
Davis, Joseph
Deacke, John
Deacker, Hendrick B.
Deavies, Jacob
DeHarsh, Philip
Dellenbag, Hendrick
Dellenbag, John
Deygert, Peter S. 5
Deygert, J. Petrus 5
Dygert, Rutderph
Deygert Salbiegenus P.
Deygert, Severines H. 5
Deygert, Soeferinus
Dillenbagh, Martin
Depuy, Benjamin
Dillenbach, Henry
Dillenbach, John
Dockstader. Nicholas
Dorn, Peter 5
Dum (Thum), Nicholas
Dum (Thum), Melchoir
Dum (Thum), Conradt
Dygert, John 5-1
Dygert, William H.
Dygert, Peter 5
Duslar, Jacob
Dure, John
Dusler, William
Dygert, George 5
Dygert, Seffreanes

Dygert, Servinis P.
Dygert, William
Depuy, Samuel
Deezlaer, William
Dummer, Nicholas
Durm, Adam
Dygert, Peter D., Jr.
Dykeman, Joseph
Dygert, Henery
Dygert, Nicholas
Dygert, Peter W.
Dygert, Sefferinus, Jr.
Dygert, Sepinus P.
Dygert, Sepinus H.
Dygert, Sestheanes
Dygert, Sovrinus
Dygert, Sovrinus H.
Dygert, William. Jr.

Eading, Conrad
Eadle, George 3
Eadle, Hendrick
Eaker, George, Jr.
Eaply, Philip
Ecker, Abraham
Ecker, Johannes
Eckler, Henrich 5
Egenbrode, John 5
Egenbrode, Peter
Eher, Nicholass
Ehle, Peter 5-6
Ehle, Wm. 5
Ehll, Michel
Eigenbrade, George
Ekar, George
Ecker, Nicholas
Ellwood, Isaac 5-6
Embie, Philip 3
Emge, Johnnes
Emge, Johannes, Jr.
Emge, Philip
Emphe, John
Empie, Adam
Empie, Andrew
Empie, Jacob 1-5
Empie, Frederick
Empie, John
Empie, John F.
Empie, John, Jr.
Empie, Philip
Engus, John
Erichman, Gottfried
Erksen, John
Eigenbrod, Peter I.
Eigenbrod, Peter I.. Jr.

Faling, Jacob 1-3-5
Faling, Philip
Feanes, Michael
Feather, William
Fehling, Jacob 5
Fehling, John 5
Fert, Jacob
Fey, George, Jr.
Filling, John
Finch, Christian 1-5
Finch, Hanyost
Finck, Andrew
Finck, Christian 5-1
Finck, Hanyost
Finck, John
Fitcher, Coenrad
Flander, Henry

Flander, Jacob
Flander John
Flander Tenus
Fon, Stoffil
Foneyea, John
Forbush, Bartholomew 3
Fykes, George
Ekly, Michael
Fort, Andres
Fox, Daniel
Fox, Philip W. 5
Fox, Peter 5
Fox, Charles 5
Fox, Christopher 5
Fox, Frederick 5
Fox, Joseph
Fos, Peter 5
Fox, William 5
Foy, George
Frealing, Jacob 5
Frebach, George
Freihtad, Johann
Frelich, Felte
Frelich, Francis
Frelich, Jachiob
Frelich, Valentine 5
Freytery, J. G.
Fritcher, Henry
Frolich, Jacob
Fry, Jacob 5
Furneay, John
Fykes, Philip
Forbush, Nich. 3
Farbush, John 3
Felling, George
Fevinegea, John
Finch, John
Finch, William
Finck, William, Jr.
Fink, William
Fishback, Henry
Flander, Daniel
Foltz, Hanjost
Foltz, Melchoir
Fox, Consider
Frest, Jacob
Frimmer, Christian
Fritcher, Conrad
Feeling, John D. 3
Feeling, John J. 3
Fox, Peter P.
Fox, Philip
Fox, Stoffel
Fridagh, George

Gorofe, Henray
Graen, John
Graff, Christian
Gram, John 5
Grant, John
Gray, Adam
Gray, Nicholas 5-1
Grany, Andrew
Gray, John
Gray, Robert
Gray, Samuel 5
Greay, Adam
Greay, Andreas
Greay, Robert
Greh, Robert
Grembs, Hendrick
Grems, Peter, Jr.

Gross, Lawrence, Capt. 5
Guywitz, Frederick
Gaaff, Christ
Garter, John 5
Garter, John, Jr. 5
Gamon, Elias
Gamaur, Ezekiel
Garnaur, Jacob
Gearne, Charles
Getman, John, Jr.
Gramer, Andrew
Gramer, Godfrey
Grause, Leonard
Gring, John
Gross, Henry
Guloch, Christian
Guywick, Fred'k.
Garlock, Adom 3
Garrison, John
Gerder, Henrich
Gerlack, George
Gerlock, Adam
Gerlock, Philip
Gerlag, Adam
Gerlag, Philip
Gerlock, William G.
Getman, Christian
Getman, George
Getman, Johannis
Getman, Peter
Getman, Thomas
Ginder, Henry
Glantz, John
Grant, Petrus, Lt. 1

Haberman, Jacob
Habner, Andrew
Haeman, Peter
Hainer, Hendrick
Hallenbolt, Andrew
Hanson, Henry, iLeut. 2
Hanner, Peter 1
Harkimer, Abraham
Hart, Conradt
Hart, Henry 2
Hart, Daniel
Hart, John
Hause, Adam
Hauss, George 6
Hawerman, Jacob
Hayney, Henry
Heaber, John
Headeach, Daniel
Heds, Hen'd. ((authority I. A. Frye)
Heer, Casper
Hees, Johannes
Heiney, George
Heintz, Andreas
Hallebolt, Andrew
Hellebolt, Dennis
Hellebould, Tunis
Hellegas, Conrad
Helegas, Peter 3
Helmer, Henrich
Helmer, John 3
Helmer, Philip, Jr.
Helmer, Adam
Helmer, Lenerd
Helmer, Lenerd L.
Helmor, John
Helwig, John

FORT KEYSER, FROM AN OLD DRAWING

This old stone residence was located near the Battle Field of Stone Arabia (October 19, 1780) and was occupied by members of Klock's Regiment. Here the dead and wounded were taken after the battle. No trace of the Fort remains.

GRAVE OF PIONEER

Still standing. The stone marks the grave of Hendrick Klock, pioneer born 1760 and died at the advanced age of 97. He was the first of the Klocks. His son Col. Jacob Klock is buried in the same cemetery but no marker indicates the exact spot where this defender of the frontiers lies buried. The place is known as Klock's cemetery and is about a half mile east of the village of St. Johnsville, N. Y.

OLD PALATINE CHURCH

The above edifice slightly remodeled still stands. It was the first place of worship of many of Klock's Regiment. Here too was the military training grounds of the militia for many years after the Revolution. It is located on the Mohawk Valley Turnpike, three miles east of St. Johnsville.

Heoman, Peter
Herkimer, Abraham
Herkimer, Gerg 5
Herkmere, Jost
Herkimer, Nichol
Herring, Henry
Hertiss, Andreas
Hess, Christian
Hennes, Peter 1-5
Hess, Daniel
Hess, Henry
Hess, John Frederick
Hess, David
Heyney, Frederick
Hillts, John
Hoeman, Peter
Hodge, Israel
Honsaied, George
House, Adam
House, Harman
House, George
House, Elias
House, Frederick
House, Peter, Sergt. 2
Hordig, Andrew
Hiltz, Peter
Huffnagel, Christian 1-5
Hutmacher, Adam
Hyney, George
Huyck, John 5
Huger, Jacob 5
Huber, John 5

Janea, Christian
Johnston, William
Jordan, Casper
Jacker, George
Jordan, George
Juger, Jacob
Juger, John
Jung, Jacob, Jr.
Jung, Lutwig
Jacker, George

Kaufman 5
Kalley, George
Kaseman, Bertel
Kasselman, Johannes
Keaber, John
Kern, John
Keasselman, John, Jr.
Keasselman, Peardle
Kees, Henrich
Keiltz, Peter
Keller, Solomon 5
Keller, Jacob 5
Keller, Andreas 5
Keller, Felix
Keller, Kasher
Keller, Piter
Keller, Jacob A. 5
Keller, John 6
Kelley, Thomas
Kelley, George
Kern, Beads
Kern, John
Kerm, Michael
Kessler, Conrath
Kessler, Joseph
Kessler, Mergertt
Keyser, Hanjost 5
Keyser, Barnard 5

Keyser, Henry 5
Keyser, Michael 5
Kiles, Conrath
Kiley, Henrich
Killes, Peter 5
Kilts, Conrath 5
Kilts, Peter 5
Kilts, Adam
Kilts, Conrath 5
Kilts, Nichelas
Kilts, Peter 5
Kilts, Peter N.
Kilts, Phililils
Kilts, Philip
Kinm, George
King, John
Klock, Adam 1
Klock, George G.
Klock, Hendrick
Klock, Hendrick J.
Klock, Hendrick
Klock, Henry, Sr.
Klock, Jacob H. I. 5
Klock, John 5
Klock, Joseph
Klock, John I. 5
Klock, Jost
Knap, William
Koch, Beadus
Koch, Kasparrus, Jr.
Kooch, Rudolph
Kramer, John
Krause, Leonard
Krays, Johannes
Kreams, Hendrick
Krembs, Henry
Kremer, Gotfrey
Krems, John
Kretser, Leonard
Kring, Johannes
Kring, John Louck
Krouse, Jost
Kroust, Jost
Kuhl, Philip
Kurn, Carl
Kurne, Charley
Kyser, Hanyost
Kyser, Hendrick
Kyser, Michel
Klock, Hendrick I.
Keller, Andrew, Jr.
Kack, Casper
Kallenvolt, Andreas
Keadman, John
Kellen, Raspur
Kelmer, Hend'k.
Kelmer, Leonard
Kern, Earl
Kess, Christian
Keyser, Barent
Keyser, John 5
Keyser, Joost
Killer, Andrew
Killey, Andrew
Klock, Coenrad 3
Klock, George H.
Kortright, Moses
Krien, John
Krien, Peter
Krembs, Peter, Jr.
Kring, Ludwig

Kring, John
Labdon, Daniel
Lambert, Peter
Lamoman, Peter
Lampford, Peter
Lampman, Henry 1-5
Lanks, Henry A.
Lanks, Henry A., Jr.
Lasher, Garrit
Lasher, Gavoet
Lasher, John
Laucks, Adam 5
Laucks, Adam A.
Laucks, George 3
Laucks, Henry W.
Laucks, Jacob
Laucks, John
Laucks, Piter 5
Laucks, William 5-6
Laux, Conrad
Laux, Jacob
Laux, Dietrick
Laux, Hendrick
Laux, Peter 5-3
Laver, Conrad
Lawyer, Conrad
Leaning, Jacob
Leasher, Garnet
Leather, Christian L.
Leather, John
Ledder, Christian
Ledder, John
Lelly, Toyn
Lerhri, Johann Caspar 2
Lentz, Jacob 5
Lephard (Lepper), John
Lepper, Frederick
Lepper, Jacob 1-5
Loucks, William 5
Lepper, Wyant 5
Loucks, Wiliam 5
Loux, Adam
Loux, Jacob
Loux, William
Lobdell, Daniel 3
Lobdell, Isaac 3
Lutz, George
Lapius, Daniel
Lilly, John
Lenter, Jacob
Lessinger, Nichs.
Lighthall, Francis 3
Lighthall, Nicholas 5
Little, Francis
Lighthall, George 5
Lighthall — — 5
Leschr, Gerred
Lesher, John
Long, Hendrick
Loucks, Henry
Loux, Derick
Lowen, Coenread
Lonas, John 5
Lower, Conradt 3
Lygert, William H.
Lower, John 3
Lyke, John, Sr.

McArder, John

Macknoo, James
McArder, Duncan

March, Stephen
Marinus, Abraham
Martin, Alexander 5-6
Martin, Philip 5-6
Merckel, Peter
Mayer, Gewalt
Merckel, Gewalt
Merckel, Wm. 1-5
Merkill, Jacob 1
Merkill, Richard
Merckley, Wm. 1
Meyer, Deobald
Meyer, Deowald
Meyer, Johannes
Meyer, John
Meyer, Theobald
Miller, Conrad
Miller, Garret
Miller, John 5
Miller, Samuel
Miller, Henry 5
Murray, Thomas
Myer, Jacob 5
Markle, Dirk
Myer, Jacob 2 (Lieut).

Nelles, Andreas
Nelles, Gorg 3
Nelles, Henry
Nelles, George
Nelles, Joseph 5
Nelles, John 5
Nelles, Lodowick,
Nelles, Peter
Nelles, Philibs 5-6
Nellis, Christian 5
Nelles, William
Nellis, Joseph
Nells, George
Nestel, Andrew
Nestel, George
Nestel, Gottlib
Nestel, Peter 5
Nestel, Gottlib
Nestel, Henry
Nestel, Martin
Nestel, Mearty, Jr.
Newman, Joseph 3-5
Nalley, John
Neer, Casper
Nellice, Robert
Nellis, Deobolt
Nellis, Hend'k.
Nellis, John H.
Nellis, Lips
Nellis. Peter H.
Nellis, Peter W.
Neoman, Peter
Nelson, Paul 5
Nichols, Simon
Nisbet, Charles
Nyney, George
Nellice, Peter, Jr.

Osterroth, Frederick
Omehie, John
Palsberger, John
Peaker, Adolt
Peaker. Philip
Paris. Peter 1-5
Pellinger, Joseph
Peters, Joseph

Phenis, Michel
Phillips, James 1
Pickard, Conrad
Pickard, Jacobus
Pickerd, John 3-5
Pickert, Adolph 5-6
Pitry, Hancost 5
Plant, Johannis
Plapper, Christian
Potman, Arent
Price, John
Putnam, David
Putnam,, Richard, Ensign 5
Putnam, Martinus 1
Paris, Isaac 1
Patry, John
Peatrie, Joseph
Pellinger, Adam
Pellinger, Adam P.
Petrie, Joseph
Petry, Will 1
Pier, Ernest
Pickerd, Barth'w. 3
Post, Nicholas
Perfer, John 3

Raisner, Jacobus
Rapspel, Frederick 5-6
Rattenaur, Jacob 5
Read, John
Reeder, Hendrick
Remesnyder, John
Richard, Jacob 5
Richter, Nicholas
Rickerd, Bartholomew
Rickert, Lodowick
Rickert, Ludwick
Rikert, John
Ritter, John 1-5
Ritszman, Johannes
Rob, John
Roller, Andrew
Root, Christian
Ropp, George
Rosencrantz, George
Rosekrans, Nicholas
Ruff, Michael
Rust, George
Ratmonz, Jacob
Realer, John
Retz, Conradt
Rickerd, Conrath
Rodman, David
Rouse, Elias
Ruff, John
Rumsnider, Henry 3

Salbag, Hangrist
Saltsman, John 5-6
Saltsman, George
Saltsman, Henry
Schultheis, Johannes
Schaffer, Henrich
Schaffer, John
Schall, Georg 5
Schebber, Johannes
Scheffer, Jacob
Scheit, Peter
Schnel, Adam
Schnel, Adam
Shultis, John 5
Sholl, John Jost 5
Shults, Johannes, Jr. 5

Silback, John 5
Schulds, Johannes 3
Schulds, Wm., Sergt. 3
Schuldye, John, Jr.
Schuldys, John 5
Sutt, Peter
Sutz, Peter 3
Schuls, Hemrich
Schuls, Jacob
Schultagiss, Georg
Shuls, Hemrich 3
Schultz, Jacob
Schultz, John 5-3
Schultz, John
Schupp, Nichlaus
Seaker, Philip
Seart, Jacob
Seeber, Conrad
Seeber, John 5
Seelbach, Johannis
Serd, Jacob
Shaffer, John
Shaffer, Nicholas
Shait, Peter
Shall, Johan Yost
Shaver, Bartholomew
Sheffer, Jacob
Shiely, Mantus
Shill, Jacob
Shite, Peter Shittser
Shittser, Hendrick
Should, George 5
Shouldis, Hendrick
Schouldis, John
Schultis, Jacob 5
Shults, Henru
Shults, George 5
Shults, William 5-3
Shutthers, George
Sietz, George
Sits, George
Sits, Hendrick 5
Slutz, Jhames
Smeath, James
Smith, Paltes
Smith, Baltus
Smith, Baltus S.
Smith, Bolzar
Smith, George 5
Smith, Henry 5
Smith, James
Smith, Matthias
Smith, Nicholas, Sr. 1
Smith, Nicholas, Jr.
Smith, William
Sneek, George
Snell, Adam
Snell, George 1-5
Snell, Jacob 1-5
Snell, John 1-5
Snell, John F. 1
Snell, John J.
Snell, John P.
Snell, Nicholas
Snell, Peter 5-6
Snell, John 1
Snell, Jacob 1
Snell, Sefrinus 1-5
Spalsperder, John
Spank Nebel, John 3-5
Spracher, Conrath

Snell, Frederick, Jr. 1-5
Snell, Joseph 1-5
Snell, Jacob F. 1-5
Snell, Johan, Jr. 1-5
Snell, Johan 1-5
Snell, George 5
Soner, Henry 2
Sponable, John 3-5
Spracher, George, Jr.
Spracher, John
Spreacher, Conrad
Spreecher, George, Jr.
Spreacher, John
Spucher, George
Spucher, George, Jr.
Spucher, John
Stahll, Rudolph
Stam, Jacob
Stamn, George
Stamm, Lawrence 2
Staring, Adam
Staring, Jacob 3
Steak, George
Steanole, Nicholas

Stenbey, Jeremiah
Stencil, Nicholas
Stencil, William
Stenfell, George
Streader, Nicholas
Straher, John
Straub, William
Streeber, Nicholas
Streter, Christian
Strubel, Christopher
Sults, Peter
Sulbach, Garret, 3-5
Suts, Derick
Suts, John 5
Suts, Peter 5
Suts, Peter P.
Sutz, Richard
Syphert, Godfrey
Sulback, Christian
Sutts, John, Jr.
Swartwout, James
Syfert, John
Shultis, John
Smith, George
School, Henyost
Schulds, Will
Sebein, John
Selback, Christian
Shafer, Barth'w.
Shaffer, Henry
Shaffer, Jacob
Shall, George
Shaver, Henry
Sheely, Martin
Shiffer, Nicholas
Shell, Adam, Jr.
Shell, John
Sholl, Hanyost
Sholl, John
Sholl, John Jost
Sholl, Joseph
Shults, Johannes, Jr.
Shults, William
Shutter, Henry
Shyle, Peter
Silback, John
Silleback, Christian

Silleback, John
Slycke, Wm. S.
Smith, Philip
Sneck, George
Snell, Adam, Jr.
Snell, Epinus
Snell, Han Joost
Snell, John I.
Snell, John Job
Snell, John S.
Snell, Joost
Stansill, George
Stansill, Nicholas
Steecher, John
Steedr, Nicholas
Steenbergh, Jeremiah
Stephens, Amasa 2
Stensell, George
Saltsman, Henry, Jr.
Subar, John
Suber, Coenradt
Teed, Samuel
Temerman, Jacob J.
Temerman, Jacob
Thumb, Adam 5
Thousler, William
Thum, Conrad
Thum, Nicholas
Tillenbech, Hendrick
Tilm, Nicholas
Timberman, John
Timmerman, Adam
Timmerman, Jacob L. 5
Timmerman, Jacob, Sergt. 2
Timmerman, Jacob T. 5
Timmerman, Christian
Timmerman, Conrath L. 5
Timmerman, Hendrick L. 5
Timmerman, Jacob L.
Timmerman, John
Timmerman, John G.
Timmerman, William 5
Temerman, Jacob 3
Tread, Samuel
Tucker, George
Tucker, Jacob
Tucker, Johannis
Tygert, Peter S.
Tyger, George
Timmerman, John I.
Tonyea, John
Ullendorff, Daniel
Utt, Francis

Van Alstine, Nicholas 5
Van Alstine, Marten C. 5
Vanderwerke, John
Vander Werke, Thomas
Vander Werke, William
Van Etten, Jacobus
Van Lichel, Samuel
Van Loon, John
Van Slick, Adam
Van Slick, Copes
Van Slick, Nicholas
Van Slick, Samuel
Van Driesen, Peter 5
Van Slick, William
Van Slyck, John
Van Slyck, Nicholas 1-5
Van Slyck, Adam

Van Slyck, Jacobus 5-3
Van Slyck, Samuel
Van Slyck, William
Vedder, Arnout
Voss, Nicholas
Vach, John George
Valter, Christian
Van Aken, Daniel
Van Derwerken, John
Van Derwerken, Jochim
Van Derwerkin, Th's
Van Etten, Samuel
Van Etter, Levi
Vaninwegen, Cornelius
Vaninwegen, Harmanus
Van Slyck, Nicholas G.
Van Vetta, Samuel
Van Slyke, Herman 1
Visger, John 5

Wabel Hendrick
Wafel, George
Wafel, Henry
Wafel, John
Wafel, William
Waggoner, George 5-6
Waggoner, Joseph
Waggoner, John 5
Waggoner, Jost
Wagoner, Engelhard
Walder, Adam
Waldter, George 5
Wallrath, Adam
Walter, George 5-6
Wallrath, Hannes
Walrath, Heinrich
Walrath, Isaac
Walrath, Nicholas 5-6
Wallratt, Jacob 5
Walrad, Adolph
Walrad, Jacob 5
Walrad, Gerhart 3-5
Walrad, Jacob
Walrad, John 3
Walrad, Peter
Wallrath, Isaac
Wallrath, Nicholas 5-6
Walrath, Adolf 3
Walrath, Friterick
Walrath, Henrich 5
Walrath, Henry 5
Walrath, John A. 3
Walrath, Jacob H. 5
Walt, Christian
Walter, Adam
Werner, Christian
Werner, Charles A.
Walter, George 5-6
Walter, Christian
Waltz, Conrad
Waltz, George
Walvel, Johann Gerg
Warmooth, Christian
Warmouth, Nathaniel
Warmooth, Peter
Warmouth, William
Warmouth, Peter J.
Warmouth, William
Warmud, John, Jr.
Warmut, Christean
Warmwood, Mathias, Lieut. 2

Warmwood, Peter
Wasel, Adam
Wasel, George
Wasel, Henry
Wasel, John
Wasel, William
Wassell, Henry
Wassell, George
Water, William
Weack, Sefrnus
Weak, John
Weaver, Jacob 5
Weaver, Nichalas
Weber, Nicoltss
Weimer, Andrew
Werner, Andrew
Werner, Elexander
Wessel, George
Wessel, George W.
Wesser, Nicholas
Wick, John
Wick, Michael
Williams, Eliser
Williamson, Eliser
Winckel, John
Windecker, Nicholas 5
Windecker, Jacob
Windeker, Frederick 5
Winn, John
Woleben, Nicholas 3-5
Wolever, Peter 5
Wormud, Mattis
Wormwood, John
Wormwood, William
Wyles, George
Wyner, George
Wyner, John
Wafel, Adam
Walrath, Peter I.
Walrat, Adam A.
Walrath, Henry A. 6
Warner, Andrew
Wavil, George
Westfall, Abraham
Wavill, Henry
Westfal, Simon
Wormwood, Peter
Wormwood, Peter T.
Walder, Christian

Yanney, Christian
Yoran, Jacob
Yorna, Jacob
Young, Adam
Yound, Andree
Young, Christian
Young, Gottfried 3-5-6
Young, Jacob
Young, Jacob, Jr.
Young, Lodowick
Younglove, Moses 3-5
Young, Ludwick
Young, Nicholas
Young, Richard 5
Yucher, George
Yuker, George
Yung, Ludwick
Yuger, Jacob 3
Yuran, Jacob
Yuger, Jacob

Zessinger, Nicholas

Zimman, Jacob L.
Zimmerman, Christian
Zimmerman, Conrad 5
Zimmerman, Jacob 3-5
Zimmerman, Henry 5
Zeaming, Jacob

Zeeckley, John
Zeely, John, Lieut. 3
Zimmerman, Deobolt
Zimmerman, George
Zimmerman, John

COL. MARINUS WILLETT

A regular army officer who succeeded in command of the Mohawk Valley militia towards the close of the war. He was stationed at Oriskany during the siege and later was stationed at Fort Dayton and Fort Plain. He led the militia in the Battle of Johnstown, October 25, 1781, known as "the last Battle of the Revolution." In his narrative he speaks very highly of the valor of the Mohawk Valley Militia and indeed he could not do otherwise. Wherever he led the men of the valley were willing to follow. Something of the ravages of war may be learned from Col. Willett's letter to Washington on taking command of the militia. He wrote from German Flatts (Herkimer), July 6, 1781 as follows: "Out of 2,500 men at the beginning of the war not 1200 remain liable for military duty and those fit will hardly exceed 800."

Tryon County Militia, 3rd Regiment
Col. Frederick Fisher

The Third Regiment, usually known as Col. Fisher's or Vischer's, was composed of militia from the present east end of the county, or the Mohawk district. This included both sides of the river eastward of the Noses nad ran to the county line east of Amsterdam. The men were drawn largely from the Fonda settlement, then Caughnawaga, this being the principal settlement. Owing to the proximity of the Johnsons, this regiment was handicapped by their influence during the early stages of the war. Col. Frederick Fisher stood alone in defiance of the Johnsons at one time. He was born February 22, 1741 and died June 9, 1809. He was Colonel of the Militia during the war. After Johnson deserted Johnstown he was in charge of the fort there. When Sir John Johnson invaded the valley early in 1780 by way of Johnstown his Indians fell on the Fishers and killed and scalped the Colonel and his two brothers, Captain John and Harman. His sisters escaped but the aged mother was struck down by a tomahawk. Both the mother and Col. Fisher recovered. He was afterwards first Judge of Montgomery county common pleas. He was a member of the Committee of Safety for the Mohawk District prior to the outbreak of the war. Lt. Col. Volkert Veeder was a prominent officer. He was Lt. Col. of the 5th Albany Militia and then of the Third Tryan County Militia. His name appears to be spelled both Veeder and Vedder. There were seventy-five men in the service by the name Veeder and Vedder.

Key to References

1 Killed at Oriskany.
2 Died in action.
3 Prisoner of war.
4 Missing.
5 Engaged at Oriskany.
6 Wounded.

COLONEL FREDERICK FISHER6
(Scalped by the Indians and left for dead at Caughnawaga, October 25, 1781).
Lieutenant Colonel Volkert Veeder 5
Lt. Colonel Adam Fonda 5
Major John Nukerk
Major John Bluen (Bliven) 3-6
Adjutant John G. Lansingh, Jr.
Adjutant Gideon Marlatt (Ensign)
Adj. Peter Conyn
Quarter Master Theodorus F. Romine
Quarter Master Abraham Van Horn
Quarter Master Simon Veeder
Surgeon John George Folke
Surgeon William Petry
Major John Blauvelt 1
Major Isaac DeGraff 5

Captains

Degrauf, Amaunniel 5
Fisher, John 5

Fonda, Jelles 5
Gaerdenyer, Jacob 6
Hogoboom, Dirik
Littel, John
Mabie, Harmanus
Marselis, Isaac
McMaster, David
Putnam, Gerrit
Rees, Samuel
Snook, William 5
Veeder, Abraham
Wemple, Andrew
Wemple, John 5
Yates, Robert 5
Yeomans, Joseph
Davis, John James 1

Lieutenants

Bennet, Amos
Deline, Benjamin
Dockstetter, Nicklis
Ernest, Christ
Gardinere, Samuel 6
Hall, William
Lard, William
Newkirk, Gerritt
Oline, Benjamin
Printup, Josop
Pruy, Francis F.
Quacenbosh, Abrahand 5
Quackeubush, Mc W.

Quackeubush, Vincent
Schuler, Lorentz
Snook, John
Swart, Isaias J.
Van Bracklen, Garett S.
Van Horn, Thomas
Van Olynde, Peter
Van Veghten, Derick
Vroman, Henry H.
Yates, Peter
Yong, Peter
Groot, Petrus 6
Hunt, Abel 1
McMaster, Daninel 5
McMaster, David 5

Sergeants and Corporals

Corporal Steven Tuthill 1
Sgt. Evert Van Epps 6

Ensigns

Lewis, Henry
Potman, Rechrt
Putman, Francis
Stone, Conrad
Stone, Gorg
Van Bracklen Garrett G.
Vroman, Peter
Harrison, Thomas
Pierce, Ephraim
Van Vaughn, Teunis

Brigade Major

Fry, John 3

Additional Names on State Treasurer's Pay Books

Lieutenants

Beverly, David
Dinghardt, Jacob
Hubbs, Charles
McMaster, James
Prentiss, Joseph
Putnam, Victor
Quackenbush, Myndert W.
Reynuer, Francis
Swart, Jeremiah 5
Swart, William
Woodworth, Solomon

Enlisted Men

Acker, John
Aker, Gorge
Albrant, Hendrick
Albrant, Henry
Algire, John
Allen, William
Anderson, William
Antus, Coenrad
Antus, John
Any, Jacob
Archer, Ananias
Baker, Adam
Barbat, John
Barcly, Isaas
Barnhart, Charls
Barnhart, John
Barhydt, Thunis
Barkill, Lowis
Barnes, Jacob

Barnes, John
Barns, Aron
Bayer, John, Jun.
Billings, James
Beakemen, Eshemeal
Beddle, Benijah
Bell, John
Bell, Matthew
Bellinger, Christian 3
Bellinger, Philip 3
Berkley, Isaes
Berlett, John
Berrey, Nicholas
Berry, William
Beverly, David
Beverly, Thomas
Bodin, John
Bogards, Henry
Bogert, Henry
Booldman, John
Boshart, John
Bove, Nicholas
Bowman, John 2
Breem, John
Brewster, John
Brothers, John
Bunn, Jacob
Bun, John
Burch, Jeremiah
Butler, Thomas

Cachey, Andrew
Cady, Nathalen
Cagal, John
Caimon, Andrew
Caine, John
Caine, Peter
Caine, Thomas
Calyar, Isaac
Campbell, John
Campbell, Nathaniel
Campel, Samul
Cane, Samuel
Cannan, Andrew
Canner, John
Carrall, John
Cas, Peter
Catman, William
Carey, William
Chrasse, Francis
Chrisse, Simon
Clark, William
Clemant, John
Clement, Lambert
Cline, Adam
Cloes, Reuben
Cobon, William
Cochran, Andrew
Cock, Petter
Cogmen, Jacob
Cohenut, Jacob
Colun, William
Colyar, Jacob 5
Colyer, John
Colyer, Willim
Comrie, James
Connelly, Hugh
Conner, James
Conradt, Joseph
Conyne, John
Corsaart, David

Cossaart, Tracis
Cossote, James
Coughvennhover, Isaac
Coughenhover, John 5
Counrad, Nicholes
Cocenhove, Abraham 5
Covenhoven, Isaac 5
Covenhoven, Peter 6
Covenhioven, Jacob 5
Covenhoven, Carnelles 5
Cunningham, Andrew 1
Crackenberch, Adam
Crackenberch, George
Crannell, Thomas
Crans, Henry
Croll, John
Cromert, Aaron
Cronkhite, Abraham
Crook, Christopher Forn
Crossett, Benjmin
Crossett, John
Crowley, Jeremiah 3
Crummel, Herman

Dachsteter, John F.
Dachstetter, Frederick F
Dachstetter, Markus
Davis, Benjamin 1
DeGraff, Nich'l. 5
Daline, Benjamin
Dallimthis, James
Dann, John
Dannel, John M.
Darrow, Jiohn
Dasinham, John
Daukstetor, Frederick H.
Davis, Isaac
Davis, Martinus 1
Davis, James, Jr.
Davis, John
Davis, Thomas
De Eifix, Max
Deline, Benjamin
Deline, Isick
Deline, Ryer
Diefendorff, Jacob
Diline, Willim
Dingman, Gerrit
Dingman, Jacob
Dingman, Peter
Dingman, Samuel
Divis, Abraham
Dockstader, George A.
Dockstader, John H.
Dockstader, Henry H.
Dockstader, George
Docksteder, Adam
Docksteder, Haniskel
Dockstader, Nicholas H.
Docksteter, Leonhart
Dockstetter, Henrich
Dockstetter, Nicolas
Dopber, Robert
Doranberagh, John
Doren, Alicksander
Dorn, David
Dorn, John
Doron, Jacob
Dorp, Mattias
Doucksteter, John
Doughstedar, Jacob

Doyle, Stephen
Dum, Richard
Dunham, Ebenezer
Dunham, John
Dunn, James

Eargesengar, John
Earnest, Jacob
Eaten. Elezar
Eaton, Ephraim
Eel, Nichel
Eighter, John , Corporal 2
Eliot, Jacob
Eliot, Andrew
Elliot, Joseph
Ellis, John
Eman, Jacob
Ener, Peter
Eney, John
England, Benjamin
Eny, George
Eny, Godfret
Ernest, Jacob
Eten, Efrim
Eten, Elezer
Eten, James
Eten, Tomes
Eversay, Adam 5
Eversen, John, Jun.

Farguson, Willim
Fars, Christian
Ferrel, Charles
Fishar, Harmanis 5
Fisher, John
Fie, George, Jun.
Fine, Andrew
Fine, Frances
Files, Jiohn
Fishback, Henry
Fithpatrick, Peter
Fonda, Adam 5
Fonda, John
Forgason, Daniel
Forrest, Matthew
Fowler, James
Frakk, Henry
Frank, Adam 5
Frank, Albart
Frank, Andrew 6
Frank, John 1
Frank, Jacob 2
Frank, Henry
Fredreck, Jacob
Frederick, Peter
Frederick, Francis
Fredrick, Phillip
French, Ebenezer
French, Josuf
Frenk, Henry
Fuller, Abraham
Fuller, Isaac
Fuller, Michel

Gallenger, Henry
Gardenar, William
Gardener, Martin
Gardinier, Martyn J.
Gardinier, Matthew
Gardinier, Nicholas
Gardinier, Nicholas T.
Gardenir, Abraham

Garsling, Peter
Gerdanell, John
Gibson, William
Giles, John
Goihnet, John
Grace, Owan M.
Graft, Jacob
Grass, Phillith
Gray, Silas 5

Hagal, John
Hagal, Magal
Hains, John
Hall, Jacob
Hall, John
Hall, Peter
Hall, William 5
Han, Jacob
Hann, Peter
Hanna, James
Hanna, William
Hansen, Ficktor
Hansen, Nicholas
Hanson, John
Hanson, Richard
Hanson, Henry 5
Hand, Marcus 5
Hare, James
Harpper, Archiball
Harrison, Harmanis
Harrison, Peter
Harrison, Tomis
Havinser, Torc
Helmer, John
Henn, Marks
Herring, John, Sen.
Hird, Leonard
Hoch, Georg
Hodges, Abraham
Hoff, Richard
Hoff, Richard, Jun.
Hogoboom, John
Hogoboom, Peter
Hogoboom, Christian
Holdenbergh, Abraham
Horn, Jams
Horn, Mattis
House, Jacob
Hubbs, Alexander
Hubbs, Charles
Hulsbarker, Addem
Hunt, Timothy 5
Hutchson, Edward

Inxale, Joseph

Jones, James
Jones, Harmanus
Jones, Richard
Johnson, Andrew
Johnson, John
Johnson, Robert
Johnson, Ruliph
Johnston, Witter
Juman, David
Jurry, John

Kartright, Hanry
Keech, James
Keech, Jorge
Keelman, Jacob
Keith, Jacob
Kell, Nicolas

Keller, Jacob
Kelly, Peter
Kennedy, James
Kenneday, Robert
Ketcham, Ephraim
Kiley, Henry
Kitts, John
Kitts, John, Jun.
Kline, John
Kline, Martin

Lacess, Samul
Lane, Daniel
Lane, Jacob
Lannen, Rechert
Lapper, John
Lawis, David
Leets, David
Lenardson, James
Lenardson, John 5
Lenardson, Timothy
Lennes, William
Lever, John
Lewis, Adam
Lewis, David, Junr.
Lewis, Frederick
Lewis, John
Lewis, William
Leyd, Richard
Leypert, Jacob
Liddel, John
Lincompetter, Mighael
Link, John
Linox, John
Loyde, Daniel

Mabee, Peter
Mambt, Willem
Mannes, Hugh M.
Marlat, Michael
Marlatt, Abraham
Marlatt, Gideon
Mason, John
Mave, John
Mayer, Jacob
Mayer, Jacob, Junr
Marlatt, John 5
Marlatt, Thomas
Martin, John W.
Martin, Peter M.
Martin, Philip 6
Mashel, John
Mason, Jacob
McArthur, Daniel
McArthur, Donald
McArthur, Duncan
McCallum, John
McCollam, Findlay
McClumpha, Thomas
McCredy, William
McDonald, James
McDonald, Nicholas
McGraw, Christopher
McGGraw, Danel
McGraw, Dennis
McGraw, John
McGraw, Dainnel
McGraw, Wm.
McKenney, Daniel
McMaster, Hugh 6
McMaster, James
McMaster, Robert

McMaster Thomas
McNaugnten, Petar
McRadey, William
McTaggert, James
Mears, Thomas
Melone, John
Mets, Henry
Meurinus, William
Miller, Fredrick
Miller, Adam 5
Miller, Gorge
Miller, James
Miller, Jillis 5
Miller, Johan
Millroy, Aexander
Mower, ——— 5
Mower, ——— 5
Mower, Conrad 5
Moyen, Jacob 3
Montgomry, Peter
Montek, William
Moon, Jacob
More, Conrad
More, John
Mount, Joseph
Mount, Samuel
Mower, Barrant
Mower, George
Mower, Henry
Murdorph, Gorge
Murray, David 5
Musner, John
Myers, George
Myers, Peter

Nelley, John
Newkirk, Abraham
Newkkerk, Garret 5
Newkerk, Garrit C.
Newkirk, John 5
Nukerck, Jacob

Ogden, Daniel, Sen.
Ogden, David
Panter, Ulrich
Pater, Francis
Patteson, Adam
Percy, Ephraim
Peters, Joseph
Peters, Joseph, Jun.
Pettingell, Henry
Pettingell, Jacob
Pettengell, John 1
Pettingell, Joseph
Pettingell, Samuel 5
Pettingell ,William
Phileps, Abraham
Philes, Henry
Philips, Henry
Philips, Corn'ls 1
Philips, Phillip
Philipse, James 1
Philipse, Volkert
Phillips, Jacob
Phillips, John
Phillips, Lewis
Phillips, William
Phillipsa, Harmanis
Phillipsa, John
Pickes, John
Plank, Adam

Plank, John
Polmanter, Thomas
Polmateer, John
Polmateer, Willem
Potman, Aaren
Potman, Adam
Potman, George
Potman, Hendrik
Prentes, Daniel
Prett, John
Prime, David
Prime, Henry
Prime, Petter 5
Prine, Luis
Printup, William
Pruime, John
Pruyn, John
Pruyne, Henry
Putman, Cornelys, Jun.
Pntman, David
Putman, Factor
Putman, Fredrick
Putman, Hanry
Putman, Jacobus
Putman, John
Putman, Lewis
Putman, Lodiwick 5
Putman, Victor 5
Putman, William
Pyrune, Daniel

Quack, John
Quack, Petar
Quack, Willem
Quackinboss, Nicholas
Quackenbush, Abraham, Jun.
Quackenbush, David
Quackenbush, Isaac
Quackenbuss, John G.

Redy, Charles
Reed, Conrad
Renins, Samul
Rankin, James 3
Richardson, Jonathan
Riker, Henry
Rinyens, Samuel
Roberson, Robert
Robeson, George
Robison, Joseph
Roelofson, Abraham
Rogers, John
Rogers, Samuel
Roges, Samuel
Rombough, Ausmus
Romeyn, Theodorus F.
Romien, Nicholas
Romien, Abraham
Runyans, John
Runyens, Henry
Rury, Henry
Rury, Henry
Rury, William
Ruse, Jacob

Salsbury, John
Sammons, Frederick 3
Sammons, Sampson 5
Sammons, Jacob 5
Sammons, Thomas 5
Sammore, Frederick
Saron, Philip

Sarvis, Frederick
Sarvis, Richart
Scarbury, William
Schaffer, John
Schoonmaker, Thomas
Schot, Joseph
Schramling, Henry
Schrambling, Dewald
Schuler, Lorentz
Schuts, Joseph
Scoot, Joseph
Scott, James
Scott, Joseph
Semple, Hugh
Semple, Samuel
Serves, Christian 5
Servies, Philip
Serviss, George 5
Servos, Christian
Servos, John
Shaddack, Tomis
Shaffer, James
Shaddock, Jams
Shasha, Abraham
Sharpenstine, Jacob
Shasha, William
Shasha, Abarham
Sheham, Butler
Shelp, Fredrick
Shew, Godfrey
Shew, Henry
Shew, Jacob
Seber, Henry 6
Schuyler, Wm. 5
Shew, John
Shew, Stephen
Shilp, Frederick
Shilip, Christian
Shinner, Tomes
Ship, George F.
Shoemaker, Thomas
Shoemaker, Tomis
Shoemaker, Rudolph
Sillebach, Christayane
Sillibogh, Hincrist
Sillibig, John
Simpson Nicholas
Simpson, Henry
Sixbary, Adam
Sixbary, Cornelus
Sixberry, Bangnen
Sixberry, Cornelius, Jun.
Skinner, John
Slack Martinis
Smith, Harmanus
Snook, Henry
Snyder, Adam
Southwoth, Willam
Spencer, Jonathan
Spencer, Aaron
Spencer, Nathan
Spoor, Nicolas
Spore, John 5
Stabits, Michael
Stale, Gorg
Staley, Henry
Stall, Joseph
Stalye, Roulof
Starn, Adam
Starn, Philp

Starin, Frederick
Starin, John
Staring, Joseph
Stephens, Amasa 5
Sterman, Christiana
Stern, Neckliss
Sternberg, Christian
Sternbergh, Jacob
Sternbergh, Joseph
Stine, William
Storme, Jacob
Strail, John
Stuart, William
Stung, Peter
Swart, Benjamin
Swart, John
Swart, Walter
Swart, Tunis
Sylmur, Marsster

Thompson, Henry 5
Thornton, James 5
Tanner, Jacob
Terwilliger, Hermanus 3
Terwilliger, James 5
Thelm, John
Thompson, James
Timmerman, Christian
Tims, Michael
Tontill, Joseph
Tyms, Michael

Ulman, Burnt
Ulman, Johanes
Ulman, Leonard

Vadder, Isaak
Vaghte, John
Van Allen, Jacob
Van Antwerpen, John Jun.
Van antwerper, John, Sen.
Van alstene, Jacob
Van Alstin, Gilbert
Van Alstine, Abraham
Van Alstine, Cornelius
Vanalstine, Isaac
Vanalstine, John
Vanbrakel, Malkert
Van Bralan, Gisbert
Van Bracklen, Alexander
Van Bracklin, Garret G
Vandelinder, Benjamin
Vandeusen, Abraham
Van Deusen, Harpert
Van Darwark, Willim
Van Dewarck, Thomis
Vanderwerken, Albert
Van Derwerkin, Gasper
Van Dewerkin, John,
Van Duzen, Mathu
Van Duzen, Gilbert
Van Eps, John 5
Van Geyseling, Peter
Van Horn, Cornelius 5
Van Horn, Henry
Vanhorn, John
Van Husen, Albert
Vanolinde, Benjamin
Van Olinden, Benjamin
Vanolynde, Jacob
Van Sice, Cornelius
Vansickler, Ryneer,

Vanslick, Nechless
Van Vorst, Jelles
Van Wurst, Jelles
Vedder, Albert
Veeder Abraham 5
Van Epps, Charles 5
Van Horn, Abram 5
Young, Peter Warren 5
Veeder, Volkert 5
Veeder, Hendrick 5
Veeder, John J.
Veeder, Cornelius
Veeder, John 5
Ven Husen, Albert
Venolinde, Benjam
Vinter, William
Vroman, Henry H. 5
Vroman, Simon
Vrooman, Henry B.
Vrooman, Isaac
Vrooman, John J.
Vrooman, Peter
Walrath, Adolphus
Wampal, Cornelius
Wampel, Handrick
Wample, John
Wample, William
Wart, Andrew
Wart, Matise
Weart, John
Weaver, Nicholas
Weener, Peter

Weks, Sammul
Wemple, Barent
Wemple, John T.
Wemple, Myndert
Weser, Nicholas
Wile, Christian
Wiley, Nicholas
Williams, Daniel
Willson, Aliner
Willson, John
Wilson, Abner
Wilson, Andrew
Wilson, Samuel
Wiser, John
Witbeker, Leonard
Wheeler, Isaac
Whiler, Henry
White, Edward
Wood, William
Woodcock, Abraham
Woodcock, John
Woodcock, Peter
Woodworth
Woodworth, Selah
Wright, David
Yanney, Christian
Yanney, Henry
Yoran, Jacob
Yost, Peter
Young, George
Young, Lodowick
Young, William

DEDICATING THE MEMORIAL GATEWAY AT ORISKANY BATTLEFIELD, AUGUST 6, 1929

Mayor Harry V. Bush of Canajoharie, President of the Mohawk Valley Historical Society, Delivering the Dedicatory Address. Inset, the late Col. John W. Vrooman of Herkimer, Founder of the Society and Known as "The Grand Old Man of the Mohawk Valley."

Tryon County Militia, 4th Regiment
COL. PETER BELLINGER

Reviewed and edited by L. F. Bellinger, Lt. Com. U. S. N., Retired, of Atlanta, Ga. Mr. Bellinger is the author of the Bellinger Family series and has spent many years in research pertaining to the Revolutionary period in the Mohawk Valley.

—

The Fourth Regiment known as Bellinger's was recruited from the man power of the German Flatts settlement and included the former Kingsland or Fairfield district. It was composed of many seasoned veterans of the French wars of 1757 and all of the older people remembered vividly the destruction of their village in November of that year. Samuel L. Frey in his notes in the back of his work, "Minute Book of the Committee of Safety," says: "Peter Bellinger, Colonel of the Fourth Regiment, Tryon County Militia, was born 1726. He married Delia Herkimer. He was a most efficient officer and an ardent patriot. He led his regiment at Oriskany. Lt. Colonel Frederick Bellinger, of the same regiment was taken prisoner. There were thirty Bellingers in the service. At a meeting of the Committee of Safety August 26, 1775 he appears as a Lt. Colonel for the German Flatts and Kingsland Regiment. The Colonel selected was Honyoost Herkimer who died. This advanced Peter Bellinger to the rank of colonel. At the same meeting Col. Nicholas Herkimer was chosen as delegate from the four districts as Chief Colonel and Commander."

Col. Peter Bellinger HELD the frontier!

Fort Stanwix was an outpost, burned at midday two years before the end of the war by its own garrison no doubt.

With houses, barns, farm buildings and crops burned; with cattle, food, animals and horses driven off, there was no material object for the inhabitants of German Flatts to remain in that vicinity. They started to leave! Had they left German Flatts, Canajoharie would have become the frontier town. Col. Peter held the people in German Flatts by threatening to take their few remaining effects from them. With crops destroyed and with nothing to eat, how could any of them be held? In a cataclysm in San Francisco followed by fire, it required presidential authority backed by promises of congressional leaders of both parties to enact special legislation, before the army fed the destitute. Col. Peter could not await orders. The initiative was his, and his only. He ordered rations to be issued the sufferers from the supplies at Fort Herkimer, and reported his action through proper channels to the governor, who disclaimed in writing any responsibility for, and the consequences of, this act. The governor's brother, Gen. James Clinton criticised that use of rations, stating that some were not destitute enough to feed on government rations

Nevertheless, both men and women mounted guard twice daily, walked post in Fort Herkimer and Fort Dayton and held the frontier through the perilous years of 1779 to 1783. What could the politicians do to Col. Peter in consequence of his prompt action? Evidently Col. Peter agreed in the thought accompanying that query. The next move was up to the politicians and they forgot all about it so far as following up the breach of regulations was concerned.

ORISKANY

Col. Peter's action at Oriskany is alone sufficient to commend him to us forever! Quoted from Max Reid's "Mohawk Valley" is the following:

General Herkimer "ordered Col. Bellinger and the soldiers who had not yet crossed the causeway to retake the hill. Dashing through the hail of lead on both flanks the stalwart Palatine Germans stormed the hillside firing to kill as they went and then meeting their antagonists with the swinging blows of clubbed muskets. Regaining the hilltop, they formed themselves into circular squads, leaving the bottom of the fatal ravine to the dead and dying" * * * After three-quarters of an hour the enemy began to concentrate upon the Americans from all points. * * * "Noticing this movement the Americans on the plateau formed themselves into circles and their resistance from that moment became more effective." * * * Col. Peter's rush at the enemy had caused them to forsake their American prisoners temporarily and as Adam Miller relates, the Palatines who were prisoners from the rear guard, immediately joined Col. Peter's men and re-entered the fight. * * * * The General withdrew the troops under Col. Bellinger and Capt. Jacob Gardinier from the east side of the ravine. "Formed into a circle, each man protected by a tree or log, they were ordered to adopt a new mode of bush fighting * * * two men to take each tree." Capt. Gardinier's men after being rescued by Col. Peter as related, fought the major part of the battle under Col. Peter.

Oriskany cannot compare with modern battles in numbers engaged, though "many important battles" of the War of 1812 had less than 1000, and some less than 500 engaged. In per cent of casualties, (Committee of Safety reported 150 returned safely) and in the important consequences resultant from the battle, it ranks high in historical works entitled "Decisive Battles of America." Some New Englanders may not call Oriskany a "Battle", but it certainly was a FIGHT!

What won that fight?

In any surprise and ambush confusion reigns. Ordinary military tactics were useless in the swamp and woods. So far as known, only two tactical orders were given, viz.:

"Put two men behind each tree."

"Form the men in circles." (They were surrounded).

St. Leger's success meant supplies and reinforcements for Burgoyne, with no necessity for the Battle of Bennington, fought ten days after Oriskany. The fight at Oriskany insured the surrender of Burgoyne. Burgoyne's surrender insured the French alliance. The French fleet insured the surrender of Yorktown. Oriskany made possible the birth of the new nation. Oriskany was made possible by the directive actions of two men, General Herkimer and his brother-in-law Col. Peter Bellinger, each giving one of the two orders mentioned above.

Their action is memorialized in the picture of Oriskany by Chaplin, described by the late Col. John W. Vrooman, as quoted:

"It has General Herkimer at the left talking with Colonel Bellinger. Both men are pointing. Mr. Petrie is bandaging General Herkimer's wounded leg."

This picture was rediscovered by Harry V. Bush of Canajoharie. From the Battle of Oriskany, August, 1777 to the Battle of German Flatts, Col. Peter Bellinger carried on as The Frontiersman of New York!

References—Max Reid's, "The Mohawk Valley," pp. 423, 424.
U. S. Pensions of Revolutionary war, numbered S23644 and R17772.
Clinton's "Public Papers," Vol. IV, page 49.
Greene's "Old Fort Plain," page 363.
New York Historical Association, "New York History," January, 1928, page 102; April, 1932, page 129.

Explanatory References

1 Killed at Oriskany.
2 Died in action.
3 Prisoner of war.
4 Missing.
5 Engaged at Oriskany.
6 Wounded.

Col. Peter Bellinger 5

Adjutant George Demuth

Quarter Master Peter Bellinger, Jr.

Lt. Col. Fred'k. Bellinger 3-5

Tinus Clappsaddle 1

Captains

Helmer, Frederick 1
Dygert, Wm. 5
Demuth, Hans Mark 3-6-5
Frank, Frederick 5
Gettman, Frederick 3
Herder, Henrig 5
Huber, Henry
Ittig, Michael
Small, Jacob 2
Starring, Henrich

Lieutenants

Campbell, Patrick
Demuth, Hannes
Folts, Jacob 5
Petry, Detrick Marcus 1
Frank Timothy
Helmer, George 6
Myer, Jacob
Smith, John
Weber, George A.
Weber, Peter
Walrath ,Henry 3

Ensigns

Bellinger, Hannes (A)
Mayer, John
Petry, Jacob
Starring, Adam A.
Bellinger, Johannes F. 2 (B)
Hiller, Jacob 1

Corporals

Iser, Frederick 1

Additional Officers

Additional officers taken from original pay rolls before the Capitol in Albany was burned, and taken from the original U. S. pension application papers.

Lieutenants

Basehorn, Jacob. He resigned the year after Oriskany. See U. S. pension S23644.

Fox, Frederick, member of committee of safety, assemblyman during Rev. War, numerous descendants

around Mohawk, Groton, Olean, Wellsville. First supervisor German Flatts.

Roof, John, mentioned in U. S. pension S23644.

Sergeants

Bellinger, Frederick called Hoffrich. Descendants numerous around Mohawk, Ilion, Michigan, Georgia.

Folts, Melchoir, of Frankfort. Said to have commanded Henry Herter's Company after the captain moved to Columbia county. See pension W25951.

Frank, John. Orderly sergeant under Capt. Michael Ittig who was Mem. of Assembly 1777 and under his brother Frederick Frank who superseded Ittig after Oriskany. First Judge in Herkimer Co. Was in the "Last Battle of Rev. War 1783", U. S. pension S23644.

Meyer, Michael afterward became Major General of Militia. Married a daughter of Capt. Henry Herter.

Stale, George, now spelled Steele.

Smith, George, an expert penman who inscribed records in many family Bibles. From North Herkimer.

Corporals

Belinger, John, possibly the same as Major John of Utica, died 1815.

Dockstader, John, son-in-law of Lt. Col. Frederick P. Bellinger. Descendants in Phelps, N. Y.

Herter, Lorens, grandson of Patentee. Too many of this name for identification.

Shoemaker, Domas, son-in-law of Patentee, Lorentz Herter. Descendants numerous in Mohawk and vicinity. Son of Patentee Thomas who was a Lieut. in 1733.

Drummers

Wohleber, Pitter. See notes under Pvt. Pitter Wohleber, later died 1829.

Weaver, John ⸺

Hilts, John. He was also a footracer. Carried message Fort Dayton to Fort Stanwix and return same day.

Fifer

Weaver, George M. He played at the gallows for Hon Yost Schuyler who was released at the last moment for special service. Utica descendants.

Enlisted Men

Ahrendorf, Frieterich
Ahrendorff, Piter
Ahrentarff, Peter
Ahrentorff, Gorg
Armstrong, Archibald
Armstrong, John
Ayer, Frederick 1
Badcock, John
Balthaser, Breih (C)
Bany, Ichabod
Bauman, Adam (D)
Bauman, Frederick (D)

Bauman, Georg A.
Bauman, Jacob
Bauman, Johannes
Bauman, Nicolas (D)
Bauman, Stophel
Becker, Henrich 5
Betrer, Jacob (1)
Bell, G. Henry 6
Bell, Jacob 1
Bell, Nicolaus 5-2 (E)
Bell, Thomas
Bellinger, John Frederick 1
Bellinger, John 3 (F)
Bellinger, Peter 2 (G)
Bellinger, Peter B.
Bellinger, Peter P.
Bellinger, Stoffel
Bendel, Catren
Bender, Jacob
Benrich, Frans
Bercki, Jacob (H)
Berckie, Peter (H)
Berdrick, Frantz
Bersh, Lutwig (I)
Bell, Frederick 2 (J)
Bell, Joseph 1 (E)
Bellinger, Wilhelm P. 5
Bellinger, John 5 (F)
Biddeman, Adam 5
Bargy, Peter 5 (H)
Bersh, Rudolph (I)
Beshar, Jacob (K)
Betrer, Jacob
Bonny, Ichabod (L)
Bouman, Adam (D)
Bouman, Frederick (D)
Bouman, Nicholas (D)
Breidenbucher, Balthass (C)
Breidenbue, Baldes (C)
Brothack, Jacob
Brothak, Bartholomay
Brothock, John
Burcky, Peter, Senr. (H)
Burti, Jacob
Byrky, Jacob (H)
Byrky, Peter (H)

Campbell, John
Campbell, Ludwig
Camples, Patrick
Casler, Conrad
Casler, Jacob H. 5
Casler, Jacob J.
Casler, Jacob, Junr.
Casler, John 5
Casler, John T.
Casler, Adam 5
Casler, Nicholas (M)
Casler, Peter
Casler, Malger (N)
Chitter, John
Chokin, Thomas
Christman, Frederick 3-5 (O)
Christman, Fritrich
Christman, Jacob (P)
Christman, John
Christman, Nicolaus
Clapsattel Andrew
Clapsattle, William
Clements, Jacob 5

Clements, Philip
Clenicum, John (Q)
Cline, William
Cochen Thomas
Coken, Dome
Colsh, John, Senr.
Colsh, John, Junr.
Connghem, Willem (Q)
Corroll, George
Cox, Fauet
Cox, Fesser
Cram Jacob
Crantz, Hanry (S)
Cremm, Jacob
Cristman, Jacob (P)
Cunicum, Willem (Q)
Cunningham, John (Q)

Davis, Daniel 5
Dabush, Jacob (T)
Dachsteter, Georg 3
Dachsteter, John 5 (U)
Dachsteter, Piter
Davis
Davis, George
Davis, John
Davis, Peter
Dawie, John
Daygert, William A.
Deisellman, Chrisdian
Demote, Marx (V)
Demuth, Diterich
Demuth, John
Demuth, Marx (V)
Deavy, John 2
Dinges, Hannes
Dinus, Jacob 3
Dom, Meger
Dunuss, Jacob

Edie, Frederick
Eeisemann, Stephen 3 (W)
Etig, Gorge
Eyseman, Johannes
Eeiseman, Stephen 3 (W)
Eckler, Leonard 3

Feelis, Jacob
Finster, John 5
Flack, Pitter (X)
Flock, Peter (X)
Follick, Thomas
Folmer, Christian
Folmer, Conrad
Folmer ,Thomas
Folmer, William
Fols, Conrath C.
Fols, Georg
Fols, Jacob
Fols, Melger (Y)
Fols Peter 5
Folts, Conrad 5-6
Folts, Jost
Foltz, John Jost * 5
Fox, Friederich
Fox, John (Z)
Frank, Henry
Frank, John 5
French, Henrich
Fux, Hannes (Z)
Gettman, Frederick, Junr.

Gettman, Petter
Gortner, Peter
Getman, Conrad
Getman, Frederick 3

Hiller, 1
Hawn, Conrad 1
Helmer, John Adam 5 *
Harter, Henry 5
Harter, John A. 5
Hunt Peter 1
Harlam, Adam (a)
Hartch, Adam (b)
Hartman, Adam 5-6 (a)
Hatz, Peter
Hayer, Georg
Hebrissen, Martin
Heller, John 3
Helmer, Frederick
Helmer, Frederick A.
Helmer, Philip 5
Hendert, John
Herchmer, Jost
Herckmer, Abraham
Herkemer, John
Herkimer, George 5
Herkimer, Nicholas
Herkimer, Joseph 5
Herkimer, Henrich 5
Herder, John (b)
Herder, Lorens 3
Herder, Niklas
Herter, Frederick, Junr (b)
Herter, Lawrence
Herter, Lorens
Herter ,Lorens F.
Herter, Lorens N.
Herter, Lorens P. 3
Herter, Nicolas
Herter, Nicolas F.
Herter, Philip
Herter, Philip F.
Hes, Conrat (c)
Hesler, Morten
Hess, Augustinus 2
Hess, Christian
Hess, Conrad (c)
Hess, Fridrik
Hess, George
Hess, John 6
Heyer, George (e)
Hever, George Frederick (e)
Heyer, Peter (e)
Hils, Georg (d)
Hils, Hannes
Hilt, George N.
Hilts, John
Hiltz, Georg (d)
Hiltz, George G.
Hiltz, George, Junr.
Hiltz, George N.
Hiltz, Gotfrid
Hiltz, Hannes
Hiltz, Laurence
Hiltz, Nicolas
Hochstrasser, Christian
Hoffstader, Christian
Hoyer, George (e)
Hoyer, Gorg Friederich (e)
Hoyer, Peter (e)

Huber, John
Hyser, Martin

Ittig, George (f)

Itig, Marck 2
Ittig, Christian 3
Ittig, Conrath
Ittig, Frieterich
Ittig, Jacob 5
Ittig, Jacob J.
Karle, George
Kast, Frederick
Keller, Nicolaus
Kessler, Adam 5
Keller, George Nicholas 3
Kelsch, John, Junr. (R)
Kelsch, John, Senr.
Kesler, Hannes
Keller, George 3
Kesler, Nicholas (M)
Kesslar, Conrat
Kessler, Jacob John
Kesslar, John 5
Kessler, Jacob 5
Kessler, Jacob J.
Kessler, John P.
Kessler, Johney
Kessler, Joseph
Kessler, Melger (N)
Kiltz, Georg
Kiltz, Laurants (d)
Koch, Jost
Klapsaddle, Jacob 5
Krans, Michel (S)
Krantz, Heinrich (S)
Kreim, Jacob
Kuran, Michael (g)
Kyler, Nichlas (N)
Lantz
Leithal, Abraham (i)
Lentz, Jacob
Lentz, John 2
Lentz, John, Junr.
Lentz, Peter
Lighthall, George
Lighthall, Nicholas 5
Lithall, Abraham (i)
Moyer, Jacob 1
Myer Jacob 5
Moyer, Ludwig 5
Macnod, Jeams
Manderback, John
Mauyer, Nicklas
Mayel, Matthias
Mayer, Frederick
Mayer, Henry
Mayer, John
Mayer, Joseph
Mayer, Mates (j)
Mayer, Michel (j)
Mayer, Nicolas
Mayer, Piter
Moyer, John 2
Meller, John
Miller, Henrich
Miller, Johannis
Miller, John, Junr.
Miller, John, Senr.
Miller, Nicolaus

Miller, Fette
Miller, Valentine
Millor, Hanry
Molter, Jacob
Molter, Peter
Moyer, Frederick
Moyer, Hanry
Moyer, Joseph
Moyer, Margeris (j)
Moyer, Peter
Muller, John
Multer, Jacob
Multer, Piter
Munterba, Hannes
Myer, Josaph 5
Myer, Michel (j)
Myndnbach, Johanne
McNutt, James
Nash, James, (k)
Nesch Schims
Newkerk, Benjamin

Oxner, Nicholas 2
Ogt, Georg
Ohrendorph, Frederick, Junr.
Ohrendorph, Frederick, Senr.
Ohrendorph, George
Ohrendorph, Peter
Osterhout, John
Osteroth, Johannes
Osterttout, John

Petrie, Hanjost, Sgt. 6 d. Aug. 30, 1777
Pedery, Marx (l)
Petry, Diterich
Peifer, Jacob (m)
Pesausie, John (k)
Petrey John Marx 5
Petri, Daniel 2
Petri, Jacob 3
Petri, Johannes
Petri, Joseph 6
Petry, Marx
Petry, iDterich
Petry, John 1
Petry, John M.
Petry, Jost
Phyfer, Andrew 5-3
Phyfer, Jacob 3 (m)
Piper, Antoore
Piper, Jost

Rabold, Georg
Rasbach, John
Regel, Godfray (pp)
Remah, George (n)
Rickel, Christian (pp)
Riema, Georg (n)
Riema, John (n)
Riema, John Senr.
Rigel, Frederick 3
Rima, Johannis, Junr. (n)
Rima, John, Senr.
Rimer, Hannes (n)
Rosekrantz, Nicolaus (o)
Ryan, John
Rasback, Frederick 5
Rasbach, Mark 5
Renckel, Lawrence 1 (p)
Ritter, Jacob 1
Ritter, 1

Ritter, Henry 5
Roof, Johannes 5
Roof, John 5
Sharriar, Christian 1 (q)
Sharriar 1
Shaull, Henry 5
Shimel 5
Schuyler, Philip 1
Skinner, Isaac 2 (t)
Shiffen, George 2
Shall, Fredrick
Shell, John
Shoemaker, Christopher 3 (r)
Shoemaker, Frederick
Shoemaker, Hanjost (r)
Shoemaker, John 3
Shoemaker, Jost
Shoemaker, Thomas 3-5 (r)
Shute, Frederick
Shute, William (s)
Simer, Gesom (t)
Smith, John (u)
Smith, Nicholas 2
Smith, William
Sneck, George
Spon, Nicklas
Spoon, Werner
Stahring, Attam, Senr.
Stahring, George
Stale, Gorge (v)
Staring, Adam 3
Staring, Adam J.
Staring, Conrat
Staring, Henrich 3-5
Staring, Margred (w)
Staring, Nicklas
Staring, Peter
Starring Nicholas, Senr.
Starring, Nicholas
State, George (v)
Steal, Ditrick
Steale, Adam
Stehl, Ditetrich
Stering, Adam
Stearing, Valentine 2 (w)
Schell, Christian 2-5
Schell, Johannes
Schenck, Georg
Schieff, Georg
Schmid, Friedrich
Schmit, Adam
Schmit, Frederick
Schmit, John (u)
Schmit, Jost
Schmit, Peter
Schumacher John
Schumacher, Stiffel (r)
Schut, Wiliem (ş)
Seimer, Isack (t)
Stinway, Arnold Sgt. 1
Stowitts, Philip G. P. 5
Stevens, Fred 1
Straubel, Stoffel (x)
Strobel, Christoph (x)
Tinis, Jacob
Tinis, John
Usner, Peter Gorg
Van Slyck, Jacobus 5
Weaver, George

Weaver, Nicholas H.
Weaver, Nicholas, Junr.
Web, Nicolas G.
Weber, Frederick
Weber, Frederick G (y)
Weber, Frederick, Junr.
Weber, George
Weber, George F.
Weber, George, Junr.
Weber, George M. 5 (y)
Weber, Jacob 2
Weber, Jacob G.
Weber, Jacob J. 5
Weber, Jacob N.
Weber, Jacob, Senr.
Weber, Johannes
Weber, Michel
Weber, Nicolas
Weber, Nicolas G.
Weber, Nicolas H.
Weber, Peter
Wederstine, Henry
Wents, George
Widerstein, Henry
Widrig, Jacob 3
Widrig, Michael 5
Witerig, Georg
Witrig, Conrat
Witterstein, Henrich
Wohleben, Abraham (z)
Wohleber, Abraham 5-6
Wohleber, Jacob
Wohleber, Pitter 5   (z)
Woleben, Jacob
Wolff, Johannes
Wolleben, Peter
Wollerver, Abraham (z)
Wolleben, Niclas 5 (z)
Wohleber, John 1
Wohleber, Richard 1 (z)
Weaver, Peter James 5

Weaver, Jacob 5
Walrath, Henry 3
* John Adam F. Helmer, Hans Marcus Demuth and Johan Jost Folts, were the three scouts selected by Gen. Herkimer to penetrate the enemy lines and carry a message to Gen. Gannesvoort of the beleagured Fort Stanwix. The identity of the 3rd scout Johan Jost Folts was not discovered until 1930 when Lt. L. F. Bellinger-rescued the information from pension papers of John Adam F. Helmer, later published in full in the Helmer Family book by Pascoe Williams and issued from the Enterprise press of St. Johnsville. John Adam F. Helmer appears as a private in Bellinger's regiment but he was a lieutenant in the Rangers (Scouts) under Captain John Bigbread. The exploit of these three scouts in reaching Fort Stanwix is classed among the outstanding examples of personal bravery in the Revolutionary war.

Capt. Hans Marcus Demuth was related to the other two scouts but just how is not known. Johan Jost Folts married a Bellinger girl and Helmer also. Capt. Peter Bellinger was father-in-law to the following patriots: Lt. Adam F. Helmer the scout; Lt. Timothy Frank, Sergt. George Smith, the expert penman; Christian Scherer, prisoner of war; Abraham Lighthall, pensioner; Abraham Wohleber, pensioner who was scalped and his feet frozen.

Bellinger, Hannes A

REFERENCES FROM LIST, 4TH REGIMENT

A—Hannes Bellinger, may be the Major John of Utica, born 1760, died 1815, no living descendants; or he may be more probably John P. Bellinger of Jacksonburg, born 1743, died 1820, married second a daughter of Col. Peter, and with numerous descendants around Mohawk, Ogdensburg and elsewhere.

B—Johannes F. Bellinger, son of Lt. Col. Frederick, born about 1755, killed 1780, married Ernestine Herter, the "It" girl of the Rev. War., has descendants in Greenwood, Neb.

C—Breitenbucher, Baltus, is the way Dominie Rosenkrantz spells it. Three spellings for the one man.

D—Bauman, Bouman, are now Bowman. The names of Adam, Frederick and Nicholas are possibly repeated on the lists, though they may be in separate families.

E—Bell, Nicolaus, was son of George H. Bell, Member of Assembly 1778, and nephew of General Herkimer, father of Col. Jost Bell of the War of 1812; killed 1781. His widow Christina........ was the first wife of Col. Peter Bellinger's oldest son, Peter, Jr. who had in a joke promised to marry Christina, if Nicolas was hurt. Descendants of Christina now live in Little Falls, Oneida, Jefferson county and California, but none are named Bell so far as I know.

F—Bellinger, John Frederick. Killed at Oriskany in all the records. Not identified among the families printed in the Enterprise. He may belong with the Philip Bellinger family from Andrustown, which family moved to Minden after Oriskany. Wilhelm P. further down the list is of this family and is also given in Campbell's "Minute Men." Peter B. Bellinger may be of this family. Peter P. Bellinger, is thought to be son of Col. Peter, afterward was promoted from Pvt. to Q. M., married Christina .... as given above and has numerous descendants. Stoffel Bellinger is Christopher F., son of Lt. Col. Frederick P. Descendants are numerous in Mohawk, Ilion, New York city and Schenectady. John Bellinger may belong to the Philip and Adam Bellinger tribes.

G—Bellinger, Peter killed 29 June, 1778. He left a son, Daniel of Warren, who had a daughter Elizabeth, married Henry S. Devendorf and may be had other descendants. So far, no descendants of this hero have been proven.

H—Bercki, Byrky, Bargy (modern spelling) Jacob and Peter are no doubt the same men. Peter, Senr., is a third man and Jacob Burti may be the effect of writing seven names for three men, of the Bargy family of Frankfort.

I—Bersh, Ludwig and Rudolph. Modern spelling is Barse. Descendants live in Ilion.

J—Bell, Frederick, killed in Andrustown, details given in Mrs. Hatch's stories of that place. Descendants live near there.

K—Beshar, Jacob is probably the same man as the Lieut. Pesausie, John— has a spelling nearer that of Bassache (pronounced about the same). All descendants have made of their names either Basehorn or Passage. They married into Cristman and Shoemaker families and descendants now live south of Mohawk.

L—Bonny and Bany are pronounced the same and Ichabod is the one man who belongs to both names, of course.

M—Casler, Nicolas, son of Jacob, married Gertrude, daughter of Col. Peter Bellinger. Descendants are still in Little Falls. The other name Kesler, Nicholas, may or may not be the same man. Families prided themselves on their retention of family names in those days.

N—Casler, Malger and Kessler, Melger are of course the same individual Casler, Melchoir—Matthew.

O—Christman, Frederick, may be the same man as Fritrich. Descendants are in Columbia, Mohawk and Herkimer. Senator F. W. Cristman of Herkimer can furnish details.

P—Cristman, Jacob is the same as Jacob Christman and is doubtless the first settler of Utica who married Ernestina Bellinger, probably the sister of Major John who died 1815.

Q—Cunningham, Clenicum, John are probably the same man, likewise are Connghem, Willem and Cunicum, William. Descendants live in Mohawk.

R—Colsh, John, Sr., spelled Kolsch in the church records and Kelsch, John, Jr. (same two men). It may be an alteration of Kilts and Hilts.

S—Crantz, Krantz, Henry is the same man. His second wife was also the second wife of Frederick Hess, Sr. Descendants are in South Columbia and Cattaraugus county.

T—Dabush, Jacob, the name may be Davis.

U—Dachsteter, John, son-in-law of Lt. Col. Frederick P. Bellinger, a U. S. Rev. War pensioner, with descendants in Phelps, N. Y.

V—Demote, Demuth, Marx. One man possibly, but if they are two men they are nephews of Capt. Marx. The only known descendants of this family come from the Adjutant George. They live in Perth Amboy, N. J.

W—Eiseman, Stephen and Eysamen, Steffe are the same man whose name as a prisoner is spelled Easeman. His wife and baby were killed by Indians. His sons married into Col. Peter Bellinger's family. Descendants live in Herkimer, Little Falls, Rome, Syracuse, Black Lake.

X—Flack, Pitter and Flock, Peter are the same man. Flagg who married Sophia Wohleben, daughter of Nicolas the Patentee. He was a pensioner, brother-in-law of "Hoffrich" Bellinger. Lived in Columbia.

Y—Fols, Melger—Melchoir Folts same man as Sergt. Folts of Frankfort. Descendants of this family are distributed from Ilion to Arizona.

Z—Fox, John and Fux, Hannes are the same man, brother of Frederick Fox, who was a Lt., Mem. of Com. of Safety, Assemblyman and Supervisor Both are sons of Christopher the Patentee and neither with boys old enough to be soldiers. Getmans and Harters are numerous all over Herkimer county.

a—Harlam, Adam and Hartman, Adam, thought to be the same man. His descendants married into the family of John Shoemaker. Only a few are left, south of Mohawk.

b—Hartch, Adam, thought to be a misspelling of Herter, Herder, Hurder (in the 1790 census) Herrther in the Bible records, now spelled Harter. Descendants are all over Herkimer county, St. Lawrence county and in Oklahoma and Savannah, Ga. All come from Lorentz Herrther Patentee, first owner of the Herrther Bible (see the Enterprise).

c—Hes, Conrat and Hess, Conrad are the same man. He appears in various pension records. All the Hess's mentioned here are from Augustinus and his father Johannes, the Patentees. Descendants are in Glens Falls, Mohawk, Columbia, Rochester, Otsego county, Texas.

d—Hils, George; Hiltz, George; Kiltz, George are all the same man. Hiltz, Laurence and Kiltz, Laurants are one man. From this family come two books of military tactics 1743 and 1750. They married Starings and Harters and lived south of Mohawk.

e—Heyer, Hever and Hoyer are merely three men, not six.

f—Ittig, George and also Etig, George seem to be the only duplication in this family. Descendants numerous from South Ilion to Paterson, N. J. Now spelled Edick.

g—Kuran, Michael, as a Mohawk Dutch name it looks more like Michael Curran.

h—Kyler, Nichlas, sounds more like Nicholas Schuyler if one pronounce it at normal speed.

i—Leithal, Abraham and Lithall, Abraham are one. He, George and Nicholas, brothers, come from a Schenectady family. Abraham's wife Catharine Bellinger, signed her pension application at age of 106. She died at 110. Descendants are in Mohawk and in Michigan.

j—Moyer, Myer, Mayel, Mayer, Mauyer are spellings of the same name at different times. Matthias Mates and Margeris are thought to be all one man, named Matthew Myers. Michel Mayer and Michel Myer are believed to be the same as the Sergeant Michael Myers, later Major General of Militia. There were several families of Meyers; one family were Jews, another came from Perth Amboy, N. J. Descendants run from Georgia, New Jersey, Toledo to Ilion, Mohawk, Ontario county, Schenectady and New York city.

k—Nash, James. Same man as Nesch, Schims, ie. James—Schims.

l—Pedery, Petrey, Petrie, Petry and Betrer are all from the couple of original Palatine families. Descendants are from Port Ewen, N. Y. to Hibbing, Minn., all over Herkimer, Jefferson and St. Lawrence county.

m—Peifer, Phyfer, Jacob, same man, descendants in Mohawk, Herkimer, Ilion, Frankfort, Buffalo. Phyfer and Piper, Andrew and Antoore, same man, descendants came through Col. Peter's descendants, Shoemaker and others, are scattered from Columbia to Syracuse.

n—Remah, George and Riema, George, same man. Riema and Rima, John Jr. and Sr., same men. Rimer, Hannes, one man and all possibly come from the Riemenschneider family, from the Bush settlement of that name, north of Little Falls.

o—Rosekrantz, Nicolaus. Descendants named Rosegrants now live near Ogdensburg. Others must live around Little Falls but cannot yet be located.

p—Renckel, Lawrence, the name was spelled Rincken by Dominie Spinner and is now Rankin. Married into Col. Peter Bellinger's family. Descendants in Danube and Little Falls.

pp—Regel, Godfray; Rickel, Christian. These two men are of the same family. Riegl was the spelling by some of the Dominies. The Patentee was Godfrey Reele. The modern spelling is Reall or Reals. They moved to Deerfield, thence to Manlius. No descendants known, unless some are in Little Falls and in Manlius.

q—Sharriar, Christian, married a Bellinger girl, daughter of old Capt. Peter. Two daughters captured by Indians when Lucinda Bellinger, daughter of John P. was shot out of the butternut tree in ravine on lot 35 near Fort Herkimer. One girl married George Edick, the other Peter Fox. Descendants in Mohawk and Columbia.

r—Shoemaker, Schuhmacher, all from Thomas the Patentee, Lt. in 1733. Hanjost, son of Rudolph the neutral, had descendants in Cincinnati and Toledo. Thomas put up a pitiful wail to Gov. Clinton for his captive wife to come home and care for his five small children. Read it in Gov. Clinton's papers. Descendants all over southern part of Herkimer county. Thomas was father-in-law of Frederick Bellinger, Jr of War of 1812.

s—Schute, William and Schut, Willem, same man. Of this family probably Appolonia Schuttin, born 1702 married Lorentz Herrther; the Bible record still exists. No descendants of Schut are known. One was a son-in-law of Nicholas Wohleben.

t—Simer, Gesom—Gershom Skinner, miller at Littls Falls when mill was burned. He was a partner (in the mill) of Frederick Fox. The Fox and Skinner families intermarried. Descendants are in Mohawk and Columbia. Seimer, Isack, Skinner, Isaac same man.

u—Smith, John; Schmid, John. Probably no duplications in this Smith family of North Herkimer and of Utica.

v—Stale, State, George are same individual. Steal, Steale and Stehl, now are all spelled Steele. Descendants are in Ilion, Herkimer and Columbia.

w—Staring, Margred may be Malger, Melger, Melchoir, Matthew. Stahring, Stearing, Stering all are really Staring, though even modern spelling makes Stauring and Sterling of it. Descendants are in Ilion, Frankfort, Albany. I doubt any duplications in this family even with two Adams and two Nicholas. Intermarriages with Hess, Fox and Bellinger families were numerous.

x—Strobel, Christoph and Straubel, Stoffel, same man. Descendants in Herkimer.

y—Weaver, Web, Weber are all from the three Patentees. Frederick G. married into Lt. Col. Frederick P. Bellinger's family so did the daughters of Jacob G. "King" Weaver, the fur king partner of J. J. Astor. George M. of Utica married into Col. Peter Bellinger's family. Descendants live in New York city, Herkimer, Ilion, Utica and Jefferson county. There appear to be no duplications in this family except for the Fifer at the gallows of Hon Jost Schuyler.

z—Wohleben, Wohleber, Wollerver, Abraham. All three are believed to be the same man. With feet frozen, the flesh coming off and with his head scalped, his pension describes his being laid up for about two years, and that he and Nicolas his nephew both served in the Battle of German Flatts, August, 1783. Abraham was scalped Oct. 15, 1781. Sergt. and Judge John Frank in his pension papers gives the same battle, same year, three affidavits. Wohleben's papers give two affidavits to that effect U. S. pension R17772. Peter Wolleben's death notice by Dominie Spinner, recites that Peter escaped from the battlefield of Oriskany "with his father." Although Benton has Nicholas, the father dying two years before the war. This death notice means an additional bar for all descendants of this family. Won, Niclas is thought to be Wolleben, later moved to Fort Plain. Descendants in Shoemaker, Flagg, Bellinger, Schute and Woolaver (modern spelling) are in North Ilion, Manheim, Mohawk, Columbia, Jefferson county and Georgia.

NOTE—S. L. Frey in the back of his book says that the Tory, Honyoost Herkimer was born 1751 and became Colonel of the Fourth Regiment. This duty is inconsistent with the age of twenty-four years. In the Militia records in 1733 there was a Lt. Johan Jost Herkemer. In 1768 among "Lieutenants wanted" is Han Jost Herkemer, Jr. and August 26, 1775, 6th Co. of 4th Regt. is Capt. Hanyoost Herkemer, and in the 8th Co. is Capt. George Herkimer, leaving Johan Jost Herkemer, Sr. for the Colonel who died the same month "about 80 years old," which is too old for service, and too soon for Hon Jost Herkimer, Jr. to have become a Tory. I suggest omitting the debatable question. Benton's History of Herkimer County page 71 and page 85 gives all the officers of the 4th Regt. but no Lt. Col. Henry Walrath. (Green's Gateway to the West," Vol. 1, page 849.—Ed.)

Likewise Tinus Clapsaddle as a major*. This name is short for Augustinus Clapsaddle. He was a pension applicant though, so was George H. Bell, Capt. so called. 5th Co., Capt. Peter Bellinger. In 1762 he was reported "too old and unfit for service" and Conrad Frank was made captain in his place. Conrad died 1773 and it looks as if Capt. Peter, about the same age as Col. Hon Jost Herkimer, was reinstated. Capt. Peter was naturalized 1715, 60 years before the 5th Co. was formed.

NOTE—On John Bellinger, many of him—take your choice! The original pay rolls show 1779 (June-November inclusive) in the Co. of Capt. Henrig Herder, Ensign Hannes Bellinger, the son of the late Lt. Col. Frederick P. and among the privates, all living around Fort Dayton, Hannes Bellinger who served a day or two in each month less than Hannes Bellinger, Jr., who because of those few days difference in service is regarded as son of Hannes. For a hint to searchers it is suggested the elder Hannes may be a brother of Philip, married 1849 and to Adam, born 1840, all, of the Andrustown family which moved to Minden after Oriskany. Note in the Stone Arabia church records, births to Johannis Bellinger and Elizabeth Barbara (possibly Folts or Devendorf) Aug., 1760, May 27, 1763, March 20, 1765.

In the same Co., 1780 appears John belinger Corp. All the above, lived north of the river. Just to make it harder in Capt. Frank's company around Fort Herkimer, south of the river, was a private who was on the pay rolls 18 days in 1779 and 22 days in 1780 and 19 days in 1778 all in June and July.

Going back to the 5th Co. the Capt. was Peter Bellinger, the Ensign was John P. Bellinger which in this case no doubt shows that "P" means son of Peter, not son of Philip. Father and son both went "out" as officers when the 5th Co. and the 9th Co. were consolidated under Michael Ittig and later under Frederick Frank. The list of officers of the 5th Co. appears to show that Ensign John P. was son of Capt. Peter Bellinger. And yet many researchers think Col. Peter is the son of Capt. Peter. Peter because of a deed for lot 23 of 1765, between them. In that case John P. was a brother of Col. Peter and in 1794 married as second wife his brother's daughter as her second husband. Capt. Peter in 1782 deeded lot 34 to his son Hoffrich and in 1784 a lot in one of the newer Patents to his daughter Dorothea, wife of Abraham Wohleben (Wolleaber-Woolaver). Also in 1790 is living on lot 34 John Bellinger and his brother (?) Hoffrich (2 John Frederick).

Here's hoping some descendants straighten out all these Johns and find out which John was prisoner of war. If John is found to have had a wife named Catharine, help may be extended through the Enterprise as follows: From 1785-1800 appear three Johns, each of whom had a wife named Catharine. Their three families have been carefully segregated by the writer after working twenty years on the segregation.

*   "Green's Gateway, pp. 845.

Chokin, Thomas, Cochen, Thomas, Coken, Dome, same man.

Carroll, George, Karle, George same man Carroll.

Nacnod, Jeams, same man as McNutt, James or possibly now McNought.

Molter, Jacob, Molter, Peter are same men as Multer, Jacob and Multer, Piter.

Rapold, George. Name was spelled Rappoll and Rappool in St. Johnsville Church records. It is probably same as Rappelye or Rapelje.

Usner, Peter George was very likely named Ochsner or Onner in the church records.

Dawie, John, same man as Deavy, John, now perhaps Davy.

Cram, Jacob, Cremm, Jacob, Kreim, Jacob are all three the same man, Crim.

Tryon County Rangers and Exempts

Exempts were men too old for active duty, but who were called out in emergencies to repel invasion In the battle of Oriskany all were called and it was not uncommon for father and son to fight side by side. In several cases three generations were represented Rangers were the scouts of that day. They were selected from the militia. John Frank, a pensioner, says: "the local militia were classed into classes of eight or ten and sometimes fifteen men and each group was required to furnish one man, either on order of the governor or Committee of Safety." They enlisted for nine months and virtually "lay out" along the frontiers to detect Indian movements. They were the "eyes of the army." They went on foot, subsisted as best they could, and carried the responsibility of protecting the settlements against surprise.

Battalion of Minute Men

Col. Samuel Campbell
Capt. Francis Utt
Lieut. Adam Lipe
Lieut. Jacob Matthias
Ensign William Suber

Enlisted Men

Ayle, Christian
Ayle, Peter
Ayles, William
Bellinger, William
Bohall, Adam
Bydaman, Simon
Countreyman, Counradt
Countryman, John
Cramer, John
Crows, George
Dedrick, David
Duncle, Nicholas
Duncle, Peter
Dunkle, Gerrit
Endler, Michal
Felling, Henry John
Felling, Henry Nicholas
Felling, Peter
Fock, John 5
Harld, Henrey
Hickey, George
Jones, William
Jordan, Adam
Jordan, Casper
Jordan, George
Jordan, John

Keller, Andrew
Kerlack, Adam
Kerlack, George
Kesler, Thomas
Kessler, John
Korey, Benjamn
Lapp, Daniel
Lipe, John
Miller, Deonyceons
Netherly, John
Netherly, John, Junr.
Othermark, John B.
Plats, George
Schall, Hendrick
Schall, Matthyas
Schall, John
Scrembling, Henry
Scremling, David
Seeber, Jacob
Stansel, Nicholas
Steffan, John
Truax, John
Ulshaver, Bastian
Wahadt, George
Walradt, William
Westerman, Peter
While, Henry
While, Youst Henry
Woulkermouth, John
Wourmouth, John
Wourmouth, Peter
Young, Jacob
Young, John
Young, Peter

ASSOCIATED EXEMPTS

Capt. Jelles Fonda
Lieut. Zepheniah Batcheller
Lieut. Abraham Garrason
Ensign Samson Sammon
Ensign .... Lawrence

Enlisted Men

Algyre, Jonn
Allin, Thomas
Alt, Johannis
Anderson, Duncan
Ansley, Samuel
Antes, Jacob
Barmore, William
Barry, Guilbert R.
Bashan, Jacob
Benson, Jonathan
Bickle, John
Boshart, Jacob
Boss, Heinrich
Bridelburgh, Baltus
Brook, Robert
Cameron, Angus
Cochnet, Jacob
Collins, Richard
Conner, Edward
Cratchenberger, Conrate
Creesy, John
Cromel, Jacobes
Cromnel, James
Crossett, Benjamin
Crossett, James
Crotchinbrge, Conrad
Crowley, Jenemiah
Dachstetter, Marx
Dachstetter, Nicolaus
Dochstader, Frederick
Dockstader, John H.
Dop, David
Dunn, Richard
Ecker, John
Ensign, Lawrance
Everas, Adam (see Everson)
Everson, Adam (see Eversas)
Everson, John
Fey, Jacob
Finck, Mattgred
Fonda, Adam
Fonda, John
Frederick, Barent
Frichert, Henry
Froman, Henry
Fyes, George
Fyles, George
Graft, Jacob
Hall, John
Hall, William
Hanson, Barent
Hanson, Richard
Harde, Johannes
Herring, John
Hover, Johannes
Hower, Nicholas
Johnson, Androw
Kelder, Henry
Kelder, John
Kilts, Johannes
Kinkead, Crownidge
Kitts, Jacob

Krose, Moses
Ladde, Johannes
Lenardson, Timothy
Marlatt, Mark
Marseles, John
Mason, Jeremiah
Michard, Henry
Mickle, John
Miller, Philip
Momtrute, Steven
Morgan, John
Morger, John
Myers, Michael
McCollum, John
McDonad, John
McDonnel, John
McGlashen, Robert
McGrigor, Duncan
McIntire, John
McKenny, John
McKinney, John
McKerque, Duncan
McManus, Hugh
McMarlinger, Duncan
McMarten, Duncan
McVain, Daniel
Nanes, Joseph
Nest, Johannes
Perine, Daniel
Perine, David
Phile, George
Philips, Abraham
Philips, William
Plants, John
Platto, James
Poter, France
Putman, Cornelius
Quackenbush, David
Remise, John
Reyer, John
Rickle, John
Rightmyer, Johannes
Roase, James
Robertson, John
Ruport, Adam
Ruport, D.
Rykert, Hendrick
Ryer, Henry
Sammons, Jacob
Schwob, Michel
Seeber, Henry
Schieb, George Friderick (see Sheep)
Shanck, George
Shaver, Nicholas
Shew, George
Shew, Steven
Shewmaker, Hanjost
Shoeman, William
Sixberry, Corneliu
Smith, Arent
Smith, Conradt
Smith, Cornelius
Smith, Daniel
Smith, John
Snell, Robert
Staring, John
Staly, Jacob
Stealy, Jacob
Stoner, Nicholas
Terwillegen, Harmanis

Vactor, John
Vorhis, John
Van Alstine, Cornelius A.
Van Alstyne, C. V.
Van Antwerp, John
Van Bracklen, Gysbert
Van Bracklen, Nicholas
Vanderwerke, Johannis
Vanderwerkin, Albert
Vandesen, Melgert
Van Deusen, Jacobus
Van Deusen, Matthew
Van Dewarkin, Class
Van Dewerken, Jacob
Van Dewerker, Henry
Van Eps, Charles
Van Eps, Evert
Wallace, William
Wallrad, Johannes
Walters, John
Well, John
Wemple, Barent
Wemple, Hendrick
Whitekar, Thomas
Wilson, John

RANGERS

Cap. John Winn
Lieut. Lawrence Gross
Lieut. Peter Schremling

ENLISTED MEN

Adamy, Peter
Andrews, Lewis
Anthony, John
Atkins, William
Bellinger, Adam
Bush, George
Bush, Wiliam
Bratt, James
Christman, Nicholas
Cogdon, John
Countryman, Johannes
Embody, Henry
Dingman, John
Franck, Adam
Freeman, Joseph
Fritsher, Conradt
Gueenall, James
Hamilton, James
Hayes, Thomas
Heath, Josiah
Hellegass, Peter
Helmer, Godfried
Hornung, Burent
House, Elias
House, George
House, Johanjost
House, John
Jackson, Joseph
Johnston, Richard
Kaach, John
Kennedy, Samuel
Kesslaer, Johannes
Kook, William
Kremer, Johanjost
Kronckhite, Abraham
Lampford, Peter, Jr.

Lampford, Peter, Sr.
Leathers, Ezekiel
Lepper, Fredrick
Liewry, Jacob
Llump, Thomas
Mackly, Felix
Maybee, John
McCollum, John
McDonad, John
Nellis, Christian
Nellis, Wiliam
Ogden, Daniel
Pickerd, John
Price, Adam
Reebsamen, Francis
Reebsumen, Johannes
Roader, Jacob
Roorey, William
Scotten, Josiah
Seger, Fredrick
Shilip, Christian
Snyder, Gonlieb
Snyder, Johannes
Stensell, Nicholas
Stensell, William
Stevens, Samuel
Styne, Conradt
Timmerman, Jacob
Van Der Warke, Gershom
Vander Warke, James
Van Slyck, George
Weaver, Jacob
Young, Richard

RANGERS

Capt. Christian Getman
Lieut. James Billington
Lieut. Jacob Sammans

ENLISTED MEN

Agin, Joshua
Biller, Miche
Box, John
Brame, John
Canton, John
Coplin, Samuel
Coppernol, Adam
Coppernol, Richard
Cratzer, Leonhart
Crum, John
Dop, John
Earl, William
Empie, Jacob
Fishbock, Jacob
Flander, Hendrick
Flune, John
Fralick, Felter
Freman, Richard
Fry, Jacob
Fuller, Isaac
Fuller, Michel
Getman, Thomas
Hails, John
Hart, Conrad
Hart, Daniel
Hawk, George
Hodges, Abraham
Hoyney, Fredrick

Hoyney, George
Hulser, John
Jenne, Christian
Karin, William
Kind, William
Kring, Ludwick
Kufe, Johanes
Leather, Christian
Leather, Johanes
Loux, George
Miller, Johanes
Mills, Cornelius
Phillips, Philp
Rickard, Jacob
Saltsman, George
Saltsman, George, Jr.
Shafer, Hendrick
Shuell, John
Shuell, Peter
Smith, Bolzer
Smith, John
Spankrable, Johanes
Storing, Jacob
Strader, Nicholas
Sutes, Johanes
Tusler, Jacob
Vrooman, Hendrick
Vrooman, Minehart
Vananwarp, John
Vanderworkin, Hendrick
Vanderworkin, John
Vanderworkin, Martin
Walliser, Christian
Williams, Nehemiah
Wormwood, Christian
Wormwood, Johanes

RANGERS

Capt. John Kasselman
Lieut. John Empie
Ensign George Gittman

ENLISTED MEN

Backer, John
Bickerd, Rdolph
Dusler, Jacob
Empie, John
Ettigh, Coenrad
Fry, Jacob
Gittman, Peter
Harth, Daniel
Haynes, George
Hortigh, Andrew
House, Peter
Kasselman, John

Kretzer, Leonard
Kulman, Henry
Shuell, John
Smith, Henry
Smith, William
Strater, Nicholas
Tillenbach, Christian
Vander Werke, John
Walter, Adam
Walter, Christian

ADDITIONAL NAMES

The following names are found in the Oriskany roster, Vol. 1 of Green's Gateway to the West, but do not appear among the Tryon County Regiments found in New York in the Revolution. The Battle of Oriskany was fought under the direction of the committee of safety and before the state government was functioning. Those who were killed or wounded or disabled from further action might easily have been overlooked by those who prepared the roster of soldiers, depending on the state papers. The list of soldiers follows:

Cone, Samuel
Eyer, Fredich
Eysler, John, Remansnyderbush
Garlock, Elias
Graves, Capt.
Hans, Marcus
Hill, Nicholas
Jones, Juda
Lewis, Atyataronghta, Oneida Indian officer.
Peeler, Jacob
Putnam, Lt. Victor C.
Piper, Sgt. Andrew
Rose, Willard
Seibert, Rudolph
Shaeffer, William
Spencer, Thomas, Oneida Indian
Stephens, Frederick
Spencer, Henry, an Oneida
Shoemacker, Maj. Han Yost
Van Vechten, Derrick
Vedder, Henry
Zoller, Jacob

Tewahangarghkan, Capt. Han Yerry, Indian officer.

These names while they do not appear among the Tryon County Militia Regiment will be found in the Oriskany Roster.

Johnson's Ledger

NAMES OF RETAINERS OF THE GREAT SIR WILLIAM

Many Scotch Names Found. Presumably Many Were Retainers Who Joined Sir John Johnson's Grens.

The following names appear in the ledger in Sir William Johnson Hall at Johnstown, N. Y. and were copied from the Morning Herald of Gloversville and compied by John T. Morrison, of Johnstown, N. Y. Said list was rearranged by Frank Bogaskie, Deputy County Clerk of Fulton County.

Achey's Son, Tenant.
Auguson, Tenant.
Anderson, John
Allen, Thomas
Archer, Annanias
Augustus, Fort

Bennett, James
Brader, John
Belladoe, Tenant, 3 times.

Cameron, Alexander
Cameron, Angus
Cameron, Donald
Cameron, Hugh
Cameron, John, 2 times
Cameron, John McOsee
Cameron, William
Cameron, Owen
Christholm, Alexander
Christholm, William
Crosset, James
Cotter, James
Campbell, David
Chew, Esq., Joseph
Clemants, Matthias, Tenant, Royal Grant.

Duldrigen, Tenant.

Faix, Hendrick
Ferguson, Peter
Ferguson, Alex.
Friel, John

Faix, Jr., Peter, Tenant.
Gulache, Tenant, 2 times.
Glenri, Tenant, 2 times.
Glennorison, Tenant.
Grant, Archibald
Grant, Alexander
Grant, Angus
Grant, Duncan
Grant, Donald
Grant, Finlay
Grant, John
Grant, Peter
Grant, Philip
Hagart, John
Haynes, John

Jeacocks, John
Jeacocks, David

Kennedy, Alexander
Kessener, William
Keer, William
Koghnot, Jacob
Keller, Nicholas, Tenant, Royal Grant

Lundee, Tenant.

Moyer, Jacob, Tenant, Royal Grant.
McArthur, Duncan
McCleman, John
McCune, David
McDonald, Donald
McDonald, Archibald
McDonald, Duncan
McDonell, Allen, 2 times
McDonell, Duncan
McDonell, Alex
McDonell, John, 7 times
McDonnell, Kenneth
McDonnell, Ronald
McDonell, Roderick
McDonnell, John, 2 times
McDonnell, John Ray
McDowell, Alexander
McGilles, Donald
McGilles, Jr., Donald, Tenant.
McGraier, Donald
McIntosh, John
McKay, Angus
McKenzie, Hugh
McLean, Donald
McPherson, Alexander

McPherson, Lochlin
McPherson, Murdock
McPherson, William
McLeod, Donald
McLeod, Malcolm
McLeod, Murdock, 2 times
McLeod, Normand
McLeod, William
Monroe, Hugh
Murchinson, Duncan
Murchinson, John
Murchinson, John, Jr., Tenant.
Murphy, Timothy

Ogh, Han Ury, Tenant, Royal Grant.
Rein, Nicholas, Tenant, Royal Grant.
Picken, Robert
Quin, Michael

Ross, Donald
Ross, Finley
Ross, Philo
Ross, Thomas
Ross, Thomas
Russell, Daniel
Robinson, Richard
Sneck, Jr., George, Tenant, Royal Grant.
Sneck, Han Ury, Tenant, Royal Grant.
Swouple, Michael
Taylor, Tenant.
Urchard, William
Waltz, Conradt, Tenant.
Yinney, Peter

Nicknames and Equivalents

Various Corruptions of Christian Names in Use Among Early German Families.

A proper understanding of the various nicknames and equivalents commonly used by the early settlers is necesasry in order to avoid multiplication of individuals. It is this penchant which has burdened the records. Because we have in history and early documents George, Gerg, Yerry, Jerry Klock it is assumed by the uninitiate that they were separate individuals. Aside from the fact that there was a George Junior, no other individual of the time existed The list appended will be helpful to students of the book of names. It is contributed by Lt. L. F. Bellinger.

JOHAN JOST—John Joseph, Han Jost or Honyost.
GEORG—(George), Jorg, Jurgh, Yury, Urie, Jurie.
JOHN JORG—John George, Hon Yurrie or Han Yerry.
JOHAN NICHOLAS—Han Nichol, Honikol, Honicle.
JOHAN FRIEDRICH—Han Fried, Honfrie, Hoffrich, Fritz.
PHILIP—Lips.
CHRISTIAN—Chris-John.
JOHAN CHRISTIAN—Hon Kriss.
CHRITOPHER—Stophel, Stuffle.

MATTHIAS—Tice.
VALENTINE—Tine.
DEOBALD—Dewalt, David.
DIETRICH—Dietterich, Richard.
CONRAD—Coonrad.
MELCHOIR—Meljor, Melchert, Matthew.
RUDOLPH—Dolph, Rudy
LUDOLPH—Luiof, Dolph.
WILHELM--Veelie (Juvenile).
ADAM—Ad.
AUGUSTINUS--Tenys, Denus, Deen, Dean.
CATHARINE—Caty, Katie, Catherina.
MARGRETHA—Greta, Marcate, Marget Peggy.
ROSINA—Sina, Seenie.
MARY MAGDALENA—Lena, Lany, Maria Lena.
MARY—Polly, Bolly, Bally, Batty.
ELIZABETH—Elesebeth, Lisbeth, Liz. Lieszbet, Betsey, Bess, Beth, Lizzie.
APPOLONIA or APOLONE—Abalona Abigail, Nabby.
ANNA—Nancy, Agnes.
GERTRUDE—Gertie, Charity.
ON LIESZ—Anna Elizabeth.
CHIM—Jim.
ERNESTINA, Ernstien, Errenstien, Teena.
LUCINDA—Cindy .

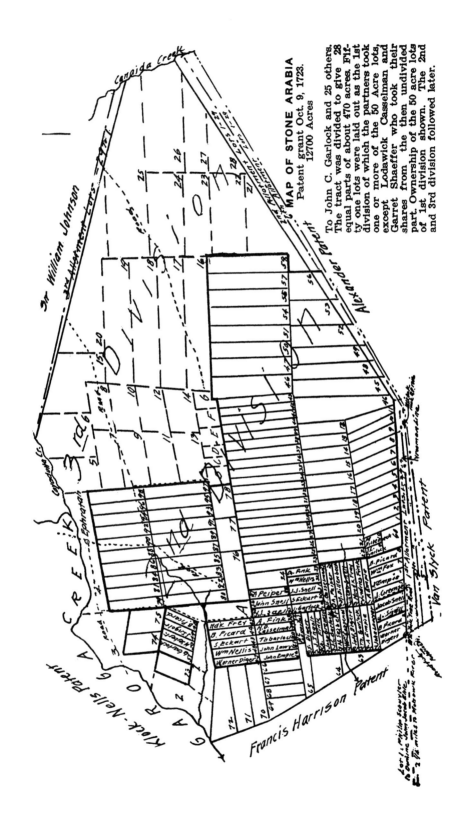

MAP OF STONE ARABIA
Patent grant Oct. 9, 1723.
12700 Acres

To John C. Garlock and 25 others. The tract was divided to give 28 equal parts of about 470 acres. Fifty one lots were laid out as the 1st division of which the partners took one or more of the 50 Acre lots, except Lodawick Casselman and Garret Shaeffer who took their shares from the then undivided part. Ownership of the 50 acre lots of 1st division shown. The 2nd and 3rd division followed later.

Committee of Correspondence and Safety

Tryon County

In producing the names of the Committeemen who composed the various Correspondence Committees later to be known as the Committee of Safety some explanation may be of interest. These were the men who held the reins of government during the formative period of the present government. They were the very first to foresee the coming of a new era. They began cautiously as a Committee of Correspondence, hoping against hope that their letters of remonstrance would bring a headstrong King and Parliament to see the light of reason. To one who cares to follow the minutes of the committee it is easy to trace the gradual hardening in tone which leads from remonstrance to defiance. At this stage, with the burden of government transferred from the King and Parliament to the sturdy shoulders of the Committeemen the change is noted in the title. It became the Committee of Safety. And as such they levied the militia, administered justice, punished the guilty, confiscated public property and carried on in every way as a governing body. It should be recalled the Battle of Oriskany was fought under the direction of this governing body, and that the burden of decision, affecting the destinies of the entire people of the valley rested on the committee. The names presented herewith are taken from the book known as the Minute Book of the Committee of Safety, with introduction by J. Howard Hanson and notes by Samuel Ludlow Frey. The latter had the original minutes, which are still extant, before him. His work is probably the best authority that can be consulted. The Committeemen are given here in order that all names connected with the Revolution in the Mohawk valley may be incorporated in one volume. Many of these names are duplicated elsewhere in the military records. Many lost their lives during the war and all suffered financial loss. Perhaps among them were some who were too old for military duty but their services as committeemen will not be forgotten. They carried on at a time when only self reliance would suffice. They were the living building stones on which the republic was reared.

Palatine District

Clock, Jacob
Clock, John, Jr.
Ecker, George, Jr.
Finck, Andrew, Jr.
Fox, Christopher W.
Fox, William, Jr.
Frey, John
Marlatt, John
McDougal, Daniel
Nellis, Christian
Paris, Isaac
Reber, Andrew
Van Slyck, Harmanus
Van Vechten, Anthony
Wagner, Peter
Yates, Christopher P. (Chairman)
Zimmerman, Lawrence

Canajoharie

Campbell, Samuel
Cox, Ebenezer (Clerk)
Cox, David
Clyde, Samuel
Eisenlord, John
Henry, Thomas
Herchimer, Nicholas
Heints (Heintz), Henry
Moore, John
Pickert, John
Pickert, Conrad
Seeber, William
Seeber, Jacob
Tygert (Dygert), Warner

Mohawk

Bliven, John
Fonda, Adam
Lane, Daniel
Merlatt, John
McMaster, James
Sammons, Sampson
Schuyler, William
Van Horn, Abraham
Visscher, Frederick
Vedder, Volkert
Yates, Abraham

German Flatts and Kingsland

Ahrendorf, Frederick
Demoth, John
Fox, Frederick
Franck, John
Harter, Henry
Herkimer, George
Hess, Augustinus
Helmer, Frederick
Ittig, Michael
McDougal, Duncan
Petry, John
Petry, Marcus
Petry, William
Wall, Edward
Weaver, Jacob N.
Wentz, George

Albany County

NAMES OF THE MEMBERS OF THE ALBANY COMMITTEE OF CORRESPONDENCE

The following names of the Albany Committee and adjoining precincts is taken from the volume of minutes published by the State of New York in 1925. This volume gives the minutes in detail under date of each separate meeting. From this we have gathered all the names as they appear in the book. While this takes us out of the Mohawk Valley and down the Hudson we deem it proper to incorporate them into the present work because of their intimate relations with the Committeemen of the Mohawk Valley. It was in the upper Mohawk that the far flung battle line was drawn across the wide frontier threatened by Canada at the north and the Iroquois from the west. As the supplies and munitions came up the Hudson and thence to the front and as communications from the front passed through Albany there naturally grew up relations which compelled their treatment as an entire group. In some instances men will be found who belonged to two or more of these committees. Their names have therefore been duplicated in order that their full activities may be of record. Following the Albany names those of the outlying districts north and south are added under their separate divisions. The Oath of Secrecy appears in the Albany book and as it breathes the spirit of the times we reproduce it in full. A careful reading ought to present a picture of the state of the times which could produce an instrument of that character.

The Oath of Secrecy

We the subscribers do swear on the Holy Evangelists of Almighty God that we will not devulge or make known to any Person or Persons whomsoever (except to a Member or Members of this Board) the name of any Member of this Committee giving his vote upon any controverted matter which may be debated or determined in Committee, or the arguments used by such Person or Persons upon such Controverted Subject, and all other such matters as shall be given hereafter in charge by the chairman of this Committee to the Members to be kept secret under the sanction of this Oath, until discharged therefrom by this Committee or a majority of the subscribers or the Survivors of them, or unless when called upon as a Witness in a Court of Justice.

NAMES OF THE ALBANY COMMITTEEMEN

Albany Committee of Correspondence

Abeel, David
Abbott, John
Acker, Thos.
Adgate, Matthew
Albert, Bernard
Allen, Ebenezer
Ashman, Justus

Ball, Johanats
Ball, John
Baldwin, Heze
Bancker, Flores
Barber, Joseph
Barclay, John
Barret, Thomas
Bay, John
Beardsley, Jehiel
Becker, Peiter
Becker, Johannes, Jr.
Beebe, John
Beetis, Joseph
Becker, Abraham
Benidict, Elisha
Brown, Wm.
Beeckman, John H.
Beeckman, John M.
Beeckman, John Jac.
Beringer, Friderich
Bleecker, John, Js.
Bleecker, Henry
Bleecker, John N.
Bleecker, Jacob
Bleecker, Jacob, Jr.
Bleecker, Rr.
Bogart, Henry I.
Bogert, Isaac
Bomel, G. V.
Borst, Jost
Bostwick, Elijah
Bratt, John A.
Bratt, Anthony E.
Brat, Peter
Bries, Henry
Bronck, John L.
Bronck, Peter
Bronck, Philip
Bronck, Reitgert
Brown, Thomas

Clark, Joseph
Clarke, Jeremiah
Clauw, Wm.
Cluet, Gadus
Cook, Michael (Vander Cooke?)
Collins, Tymans
Connyne, Philip
Conner, Lancaster
Covell, Simeon
Cuyler, Abraham
Cuyler, Corn P.
Cuyler, Jacob

Dean, Stewart
De Freest, Isaac
De Lancey, Stephen
De Ridder, Wouter

Dennis, John
Denison, James
Dick, Nicolas
Doty, Cornelius
Douglass, Asa
Douw, Andries
Douw, Peter W.
Douw, Volkert P.
Dumond, John B.
Dunning, Michael
Dyne, Baret

Edger, David
Eights, Abraham
Esselstyn, Gabriel
Esselstyn, Richard

Fiero, Hendrick
Fisher, Bastiaen
Fitch, Mr. Nehemiah
Flint, Asa
Fonda, Abraham D.
Fonda, Isaac, Ds.
Fonda, Isaac
Fonda, John A.
Fonda, John D.
Fonda, Laurance
Fonda, Peter A.
Fort, Harmen
Fort, John
Ford, Nathanael
Frisbe, John
Frisbee, Philip
Fryer, Isaac

Gansevoort, Leon'd
Gansevoort, Peter
Gardner, Othniel
Gardineer, Dirck
Gilbert, Elisha
Gorden, James
Goes, Isaac
Grant, Eleazer
Graves, Stephen
Groot, Corneles
Groesbeeck, Geirit
Groesbeck, Wouter N.
Guernsey, Peter

Harris, Nicholas
Hanson, John P.
Herrick, Capt.
Hodges, Isaac
Hogan, Henry
Hogeboom, Lawrence
Hoogkerk, John
Hubbell, Jabez
Hull, Daniel
Humphrey, Cornelius
Hun, William
Huntington, Amos

Jewett, Edward

Knickerbocker, John, Jr

Lake, Abraham
Lansing, Henry R.

Lansing, Jacob, Jr.
Lansingh, Rutger
Lansing, Jacob F.
Lansing, Isaac
Lansing, Gerrit, Jr.
Lawyer, Johannis
Leake, Henry L.
Lincoln, Hosea
Linking, Joseph
Livingston, Walter
Losee, Joshua
Lush, Stephen

Maybe, Albert
Mackbride, Samuel
McCarty, David
McCrea, John
McCrea, Samuel
McClallen, Robert
McClung, John
McFarlin, Andrew
Magee, James
Marden, Friederick
Marselis, Gisbert
Marselis, Henry
Marselis, Nicholas
Marvin, Stephen
Midelbrook, Heskiah
Migow, Robert
Millard, Jehoida
Miller, Peter
Moore, Charles
Mosher, Jabez
Muller, Corn's
Mynderse, Barent

Oathout, Abraham
Oberacker, Michal
Ouderkirk, Jacob

Perse, John
Palmer, George
Parrot, James
Patrick, William
Powell, Wm.
Pratt, David
Preston, Levy
Price, John
Pulver, Hendrick

Quackenboss, Henry

Rockefeller, Philip
Rose, Johannis P.
Rose, Peter
Roseboom, John
Roseboom, Jacob, Jr.
Roseboom, Myndt
Rogers, Philip
Row, Joseph
Rowland, Col. Sam'l.
Ryckman, Peter

Sayles, Ezekiel
Scharp, Peter
Schaver, Jacob F.
Schermerhorn, Jacob C.
Schuyler, Phi. P.
Schuyler, Stephen J.
Sexton, James

Silvestor, Peter
Skinner, Calvin
Smith, Philip
Snyder, Zacharias
Spalden, Isaac
Spencer, James
Spencer, Israel
Staats, Henry
Sternberger, David
Stringer, Sam'l.
Swart, Jacobus
Sweeper, Thomas
Sweetman, Thos.

Tayler, Ezekiel
Taylor, John
Tayler, John
Ten Broeck, Abraham
Ten Broeck, Dirck
Ten Broeck, General
Ten Broeck, John
Ten Broeck, John J.
Ten Broeck, Leonard
Ten Broeck, Samuel
Ten Broeck, Wessel
Ten Eyck, Abraham
Ten Eyck, John H.
Ten Eyck, Jacob C.
Ten Eyck, Meynat S.
Thorn, William
Thorn, Jonathan
Tillman, John
Toll, Charles H.
Turner, Ichabod

Van Aalstyne, Reymier
Van Aelen, John A.
Van Aernam, Isaac
Van Allen, Barent
Van Allen, Jacobus
V. Antwerp, Lewis
Van Antwerp, Wm.
Van Bergen, Anthony
Van Bommell, Gerrit
Vanbergen, William
Vanderepoll, Barent
Van Den Bergh, Nich's
Van Der Bergh, Corn. J.
Van der cook, Michel
Van Der Volgen, Corns
Van Der Volgen, Nicholas
Van Driessen, Henry
Van Detten, Arent N.
Van Dyck, Cornelius
Van Ernum, Isaac
Van Ingen, Dirck
Van Loon, Albartus
Van Loon, John
Van Nesst, Ferdinandus
Van Ness, John
Van Ness, William
Van Orden, John
Van Orden, Hezekiah
Van Ornam, Isaac
Van Rensselaer, David
Van Rensselaer, Henry J.
Van Rensselaer, Philip
Van Rensselaer, Ph.
Van Santvoordt, Corn
Van Schaick, Anthony

Van Schaick, Stephen
Van Schaick, Gosen A.
Van Slyck, Corns A.
Van Veghten, Henry
Van Veghten, Henry
Van Vechten, Sam'l.
Van Vechten, Tenis Ts.
V. Vechten, Philip
V. Rensselaer, Jer
V. Rensselaer, K.
V. Rensselaer, R.
Veder, Necoles
Veeder, Volkert
Veeder, Class
Venor, James
Vere, Hendrick
Vischer, Bastejaen T.
Visscher, Mat.
Vroman, Adam
Vrooman, Barent
Vrooman, Isaac
Vrooman, Isaac
Vroman, Jonas

Wayt, Wm.
Wells, Edmund, Jr.
Wells, Edmund, Sr.
Wenne, Jasber
Wemple, Abraham
Wemple, Abraham
Wemple, Myndt. M.
Wendell, Har's P.
Wendell Henry
Werner, George
White, George
Whiting, W. B.
Wilson, James
Williams, John
Williamson, Jacobus
Winnie, Daniel
Winne, Peter L.
Winne, Matthew
Wincope, Nicholas
Wire, John
Witbeck, Andries
Wood, Joseph
Woodworth, Gershom
Wright, Job

Yates, Azraham J.
Yates, Abraham, Jr.
Yates, Peter W.
Yates, Robert
Young, Benjamin
Younglove, John
Young, Jo.

Schoharie and Duanesburgh

Ackerson, Thomas
Ball, Johannis
Budd, Daniel, Dr.
Becker, Abraham
Becker, Joseph
Becker, Johs., Jr.
Becker, Peter
Burst, Jost
Dietz, Wm.
Lawyer, Johannis

Laraway, Derrick
Rechter, Hendrick
Schoolcraft, Laurence
Sternberger, David
Sternberg, Nicholas
Swart, Peter
Vrooman, Adam
Vrooman Col. Peter
Vrooman, Samuel
Vrooman, Jonas
Vrooman, Isaac
Warner, George
Zielie, Lt. Col. Peter
Zielen, Peter W.
Zimmerman, Jacob
Zimmer, William

Johannes Ball, a thorough going whig was chairman of the committee from its organization to the end of the war. It consisted generally of six members, and underwent some changes to meet the exigencies of the times. The above persons were believed to be members in the course of the war.

Saraghtoga

Ashman, Justus
Bradshaw, Wm.
Bryant, Alexander
Bacon, Samuel
Dickinson, Dan'l.
Dunning, Michael
Fish, John
Hart, Richard
Jones, Jonathan
Lansingh, Peter
Marvin, Ebenezer
Marvin, Stephen
McCrea, John
Miller, Jehoida
Palmer, George
Rodgers, Philip
Rogers, John
Row, Joseph
Sales, Ezekiel
Schuyler, Collo.
Swart, Dirck
Schuyler, Hars.
Swart, Jacobus
Taylor, John
Van Den Bergh, Corn's
Van Woert, Petrus
Van Veghten, Corn's
Vrooman, Adam
Wright, Job

Corporation of Cambridge

Allen, Ebenezer
Ashton, James
Blair, John
Brown, Wm.
Becker, David
Coville, Samuel
Clarke, Jeremiah
Curtis, Comfort
Doty Cornelius

Hodges, Samuel
Morrison, Thos.
Millenton, John
McKellup, John
McKellus, John
Preston, David
Powell, William
Rigg, Edward
Robinson, Archibald
Smith, Henry
Smith, Nathan
Van Woert, Lewis
Wells, Joseph
Whiteside, Phineas
Wells, Edmund, Sr.
Wells, Edmund, Jr.
Wire, John
Woodsworth, Gersham
Younglove, John
Younglove, Joseph

Grote Imboght

Dedrick, Zacharias
Mendersea, Henry
Mire, Christian
Marten, Frederick
Sax, Johannis
Ten Broeck, John
Van Orden, John
Van Schaick, Gosen
Van Orden, Hezekiah

Kinderhook

Burgart. Lambert
Clauw, Wm.
Goes, Lucas J.
Goes, Matthew, Jr.
Gardineer, Dirck
Humphrey, Corns
Van Ness, John
Van Allen, Jacobus
Van Alstyn, Peter S.
Van Schaack, Henry
Van Schaack, Peter
Van Vleck, Abrm. J.
Van Schaack, Corn., Jr.
Van Der Pool, Barent
Vosburgh, Peter
Witbeeck, Andries

Schonectady

Cuyler, John, Jr.
Cuyler, Corns.
Fonda, Abraham
Glen Henry
Lansing, Gerrit G.
Mabee, Albart
McFarlen, Andrew
Mitchell, Hugh
Mynderse, Rynier
Oothout, Abrm
Peek, John
Roseboom, John
Schermerhorn, William
Teller, Jacobus

Ten Eyck, Myndert
Van Ingen, Dirck
Van Driesan, Henry
Van der Wolgen, Cornelius
Van Patten, Aaron
Van Slyck, Cornelius P.
Vedder, Alexander
Veeder, Nicholas P.
Vrooman, John B.
Vrooman, Isaac
Wemple, Abraham
Wendell, Hermanus H.
Wendle, Ahasueras
White, William
Wendell, Hars
Wilson, James
Yates, Chris
Young, Benjamin

Cocksakie and Katskill

Bronck, John L.
Bronck, Richard
Bronck, Peter
Bronck, Philip
Barker, James
Conine, Philip
Oathout, Henry
Van Bergen, Hendk.
Van Lone, Mathias
Van Bergen, Wm.
Van Veghten, Samuel
Van Loon, Albartus
Van Loon, John
Van Bergen, Anthony
Van Loon, Hubartus
Von Loon, Albartus

Ballston

Brown, Thomas
Benedict, Elisha
Chiles, Increase
Collins, Tyranus
Culver, Nathaniel
Gorden, James
Gilbert, Elisha
Grant, Eleazer
Hubble,. Jabez
Kellog, Aaron
Lothrop, Mellitiah
Mitchell, Andrew
Middlebrooks, Hezekiah
Miller, Elisha
Mudge, Abraham
McCrea, William
McCrea, Samuel
Sweetman, Thomas
Tayler, John
White, Jonas
Wadsworth, John
Wheeler, Edward
White, Stephen

Manor of Livingston

Fonda, John A.
Jansen, Dirck

Livingston, Walter
Livingston, Peter R.
Livingston, Henry Beekman
Lepaier, Jacob F.
Pulver, Hendrick
Schaver, Jacob F.
Smith, Philip
Ten Broeck, Samuel
Wynkoop, Petrus
Ten Broeck, Leon'd.

Claverack

Cantine, Peter
Esselstyn, Richard
Fonda, Peter
Fonda, Lawrance
Ford, Jacob
Gernryck, Zechariah
Graves, Stephen
Hutchinson, Solomon
Hogeboom, Stephen
Hogeboom, Lourance
Hogeboom, Johannis, Jr.
Hopsapple, Johannis
Jackson, Wm.
Kinney, Stephen
Kinney, Roger
Van Ness, Peter
Meaker, Robert
Muller, Corns. S.
McKinstry, Thos.
McKinster, John
Pratt, David
Rey, Christiaen
Spaulding, Isaac
Ten Broeck, John
Ten Broeck, Jeremiah
Van Rensselaer, Robt.
Van Deusen, Johannis
Yates, Robert

Schagtekoeke Dis.

Bratt, John
Bleecker, John Js.
Cook, Michael
De Wandelaer, John
Eastwood, Benjamin
Ford, Nathaniel
Groesbeeck, Wouter N.
Groesbeck, John W.
Howard, Matthew
Hanson, John P.
Holstead, Thos.
Hicks, Benjamin
Knickerbocker, John
Kipp, Ignas
Ketchum, Samuel
Lansing, Jacob
Oakley, Elisha
Overacker, Michael
Quackenbush, Harme
Rowland, Samuel
Toll, Carol H.
Thorn, Wm.
Vielen, Lewis H.
Van Antwerp, Lewis

Van Nest, Ferdinand
Van Der Cooke, Michael
Van Bummel, Gerrit
Van Veghten, Dirck
Wilsey, Cornelius
Winne, Garret
Yates, Peter

Nistegaone and Half Moon

Brevoort, Henry
Cluet, Gerardus
Fonda, Isaac
Fordt, John
Fordt, Harmen
Groot, Cornelius
Groet, Abraham
Hegeman, Adrian
Lansingh, Rutger
Tayler, Ezekiel
Losee, Joshua
Tymese, Corns.
Van Der Karr, Dirck
Van Antwerp, Wilhelms.
Van Schoonhoven, Guert
Van Vranken, Peter

Sinkaick and Hosick District

Abbot, John
Bratt, Daniel B
Breese, Henry
Bries, Henry
Berrisly, Jehiel
Brown, Thomas
Bosley, Jos.
Fonda, John
Gifferd, Joseph
Hadlock, James
Hodges, Isaac
Jewett, Edward
Johnson, John
Lake, Henry
Lansingh, Isaac
Lampman, Michel
Ouderkerk, Jacob
Palmer, Fenner
Smith, David
Shepard, Benjn.
Tallmage, Josiah
Van Rensselaer, John
Van Rensselaer, David
Vrooman, Adam
Wood, John
Wayt, Wm.
Walder, John
Walice, John

Bennington District

Brush, Nathan
Clark, Nathan
Dewy, Elijah
Hatheway, Simon
Robinson, Moses
Robinson, Samuel
Wemple, Benjamin
Wood, Ebenezer

Manor of Rensselaerwyck

Anderson, Joseph
Bratt, Peter
Banker, Florus
Berger, Frederick
Beeckman, John H.
Deniston, James
Fonda, Ab. D.
Fonda, Abraham
Hoakesly, Robert
Hull, Daniel
Lansing, Abrm. J.
Lansing, Jacob F.
Lansing, Jacob Ja.
Mindertse, Barent
McCarty, David
McGee, James
Nicoll, Franci
Oathoudt, Henry
Quackenbush, Henry
Staats, Jochim
Schuyler, Stephen J.
Slengerlandt, Teunis
Schermerhorn, Jacob C.
Schuyler, Peter
Schuyler, Philip P.
Ten Eyck, Coenraedt
Tillman, John
Tillman, Christopher
Turner, Ichabod
Van Rensselaer, John
Van Rensselaer, Killiaen
Van Bergen, Gerrit C.
Van Veghten, Lucas
Van Vechten, Philip
Van Aelstyn, Rynier

Van Den Mergh, Corn. G.
Van Den Bergh, Ab.
Van Schaick, Anthony
Veeder, Volkert
Visscher, Bastiaen T.
White, George
Winnie, Daniel P.
Winne, Levynus

Kings District

Buck, Daniel
Culver, Nathaniel
Douglas, Asa
Dyer, Barret
Edgate, Matthew
Frisbe, Philip
Fitch, Nehemiah
Gray, John
Guernsy, Peter
Herrick, Daniel
Mostwick, Elijah
Muney, John
Pratt, Elisha
Waterman, Asa
Wood, Joseph

German Camp

Kortz, John, Jr.
Lincoln, Hosea
Rockefeller, Philip
Rose, Peter
Ten Broeck, Wessel
Scharpe, Peter

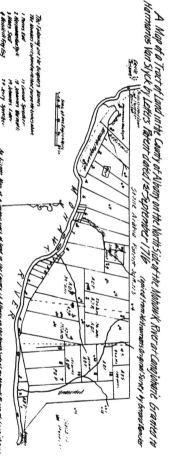

MAP
BURNETSFIELD PATENT
April 30 1725

The original purchase from the Indians was for "24 English miles along the river and as far back on each side as they wished but the colonial Governor allowed each patentee only 100 acres. This was given in 30 acres as the town site and 70 acres wood lot. The names are as copied. Petition for patent Jan. 17, 1723. Purchase was dated July 9, 1722. Thirty or more families from Schoharie settled on the land in 1723 and were given land certificates. The patent was issued April 30, 1725. The petitioners were John Jost Petrie and Conrad Rickert in behalf of themselves and other patentees. There were 46 lots of 100 acres each side of the river. Some split as noted. The village of Herkimer now occupies part of the above patent. Copied for the Enterprise and News, by Boyd Ehle, C. E.

THE FRANCIS HARRISON PATENT, EXTENDING FROM EAST CREEK TO NELLISTON ON NORTH SIDE OF RIVER PURCHASED FROM INDIANS IN 1722

The Indian treaty held at East Creek in 1722 resulted in the above purchase for 700 beaver skins. It was purchased in behalf of King George of England. In 1723 the property was sold by the crown to the Albany company consisting of John Haskell, John Schuyler, Harmanus Wendell, Governor Barnet and others who divided it as shown in the map. The site of St. Johnsville Lot 14 and 15 was apportioned to John Haskell (15) and Capt. Philip Schuyler (14). The original holder immediately resold to the Palatine early settlers. In fact there is reason to believe there were settlers already on the land awaiting the completion of the Indian purchase in order to get clear title.

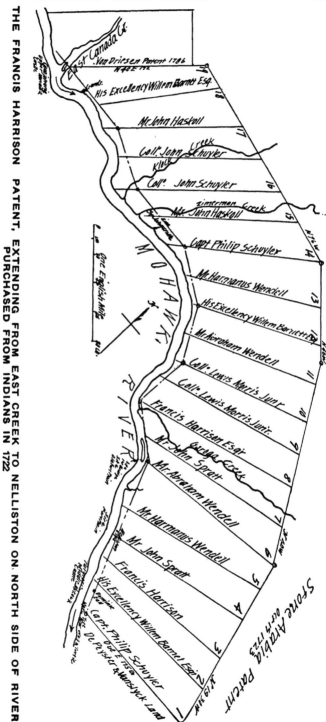

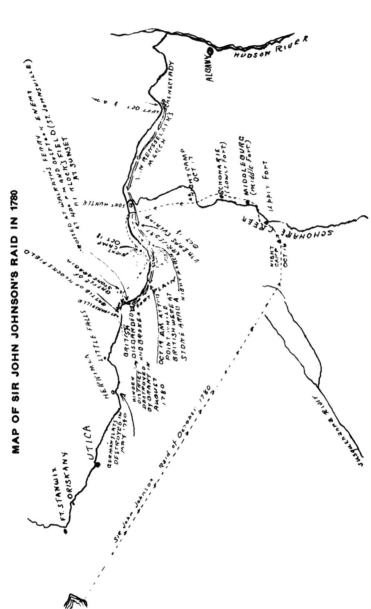

MAP OF SIR JOHN JOHNSON'S RAID IN 1780

Showing how he swept down the Schoharie Valley and swung up the Mohawk leaving death and destruction in his wake. At St. Johnsville his force was shattered. Dotted line shows course taken by enemy. Parallel lines show march of General Van Rensselaer in pursuit.

INDEX

TO THE KOCHERTHAL CHURCH RECORDS

(Pages 15 to 50 inclusive)

Key to Alphabetical References

The numeral following each name refers to the page number. The letter refers to the status of the individual. As follows:

c   Child
d   Died
m   Married
p   'Parent
s   Sponsor
r   Received in Holy Communion

Example—Flegler, Zacharias, p24, p26, s25, m41, m43. From this we learn he was a parent on page 24 and 26, acted as a sponsor at a baptism on page 25 and was married to a second wife on page 41 and to his third on page 43.

Aigler. Christian, p18, s18, s19
    Andreas, c18
    Maria Eva, p18
Aigner, Peter, p26, p47
    Anna Margretha, p26, p32, p37
    Johann Peter, p32
    Johann Fridrich, c32
    Johann Balthasar, d47
    Susanna Margretha, c26
Aignor, Peter, p37
    Johann Balthasar, c37
Asmer, Philipp, 44
    Anna Barbara, m44
Anspach, Maria Barbara, c37
    Anna Maria, p37
    Balthasar, p37
Arsen, Wilhelm, 16
    Elizabeth 16
Arnold, Christina, r40
Albertson, Johann, s23
Amstach, Johann Peter, c28
    Anna Maria, p28
    Balthasar, p28
Artopoeus, Johann Adolph. s17

Bakus, Johann Reichart, p35
    Maria Barbara, c35
Backus, Maria Elisabeth, s23
    Elisabeth, p24
    Johann Peter, c24
    Agnes, m41
    Sebastian, 41
    Reichart and his wife Elizabetha Catharina, s30
    Elisabeth Catharina, s23, p35
    Anna Margretha, s38, r40
    Johann Reitz, s21, p24, s38, r39
    Johann Reitz, child of, d47
Baender, Johann Henrich, c35
    Johann Valentin, s16
    Veltin, p35
    Jerg, s34
    Johan Georg and his wife, s23, s31
    Anna Margretha, s16, p35
    Anna Maria, s31, s32
Baggs, Andreas, s22
Ball, Johann, 43
    Maria Ottila, m43

Bardorf, Martin, s35
Bardorst (orf), Catharina Elisabetha,
   r39
Barthel, Elisabetha, s28, m46
   Andreas, r39
   Henrich, p46
   Johan Andreas, s28
   Maria Margretha, s28
   Philip Balthasar, r39
Bast, Johann Henrich, p21
   Anna Dorothea, p21
   Anna Maria c21
Bason, Niclaus, s24
Batz, Anna Catharina, m43
   Fridrich, 43
Bauch, Christian, p17
   Anna Dorothea, p17
   Anna Margretha, c17
   Christian and his wife, p31
Baumann, Maria Catharina, p35
   Adam, m43
   Anna Maria, m42
   Anna Margretha, s23
   Johann Adam, p35
   Henrich, 42
   Margreth, s35
Baunert, Johann Georg, r40
Beck, Johanna Maria, r40
Becker, Elisabetha, m42
   Anna Juliana, c33
   Anna Catharina, m42
   Anna Elisabetha, p22, p25, s28, s29,
      p33
   Conrad, m46
   Catharina, s49
   Hermann, s49
   Johann Michael, 42
   Johann Henrich, 42
   Johann Peter, p25
   Johann Jacob, m45
   Johann Christian, c25
   Johannes, p22, c22
   Johann, s22, 42, p45
   Peter, s32, p33
   Sebastian, p46
Beer, Johann, m43
Bernhard, Anna Elisazetha, c29
   Anna, p29
   Jost, s24
   Johann, s19
   Johannes, p29
   Johann Ulrich, s20
Berenhard, Elisabetha, s17, c17,
   Anna Maria, p17
   Johann, p17
Barnard, Johannes, p48
   Maria Margaret, c48
   Anna Eulalia, p48
Bertram, Martha, s20
Behr, Hermanus, s49
Bellinger, Marcus, s27
   Johann Henrich, s20
   Peter, s31
Bell, Johann Jacob, c23, p23
   Anna Maria, p23, s34
   Johann Fridrich, p23
Bellross, Christoph, m43
Behringer, Johann Henrich, c27

Conrad, s26, p27
Beringer, Anna Elisabeth, p21, p27
   Conrad, p21
   Maria Elisabetha, c21
Berg, Johann Christian, r40
   Johann, r39
Berman, Jacob, s21
Bertold, Anna Margretha, 48
   Adam, 48
Bertsch, Jan, s36
Berurer, Johann s30
Best, Christina, p49
   Jacob, s25
   Johann Hermann, c49
   Johann, p49
Bestuh, Daniel, s28
Bitzer, Peter, s30
   Maria Catharina, s28
Bitzwig, Anna Maria, s28
Blanick, Maria Catharina, s17
Blast, Anna Maria, m43
   Adam, 43
Blettel, Johann Jacob, p15
Boeshaar, Anna Catharina, p34
   Johann, c34
   Jacob, p34
Boemer, Johann Adam, c21
   Elisabetha, p21
   Hans Jorg, p21
Bohnenstihl, Nichlaus, p28
   Anna Margretha, p28
   Susanna Margretha, c28
Bohl, Lastar, 42
   Anna Sophia, m42
Bois, Wilhelmina, p20
   Henrich, p20
   Pieter, c20
Bond, Rachel, s22
   Jannike, p22
   Johan, p22
   Mattheus, c22
Border, Maria, s26
Borner, Johann Georg, m41
Brack, Michel, p29
   Anna Maria, p29
   Johann Michel, m46
   Maria Catharina, c29
Brandau, Anna Christina Elisabeth,
      c36
   Elisabeth Catharina, p36
   Elisabeth Catharina, s36
   Elisabetha, p28
   Hannes, s50
   Johann Fridrich, c28
   Johann Wilhelm, p22, s26, p28, p36
   Johannes, c22
   Liesbeth, c50, p50
   Maria Elisabetha Catharina, p22
   Nicklas, p50
   Wilhelm, s38
Bransan, Johann Wilhelm, s50
Brauchler, Anna Magdalena, c27
   Johann Jacob, c27
   Johann Henrich, p27
   Magdalena, p27
Braun, Johann Philip, r39
Bredfort, H., 48
Brein, Maria, c18

Elisabetha, p18
Johann, p18
Brendel, Anna Agatha, p16
  Anna Margretha, c16
  Caspar, p16
Bretsch, Catharina, p24
  Anna Maria, c18
  Catharina, p18
  Johann Ludwig, c24
  Ludwig, p18, s21, p24
Brehjis, Margretha, m44
  Christoph, 44
Brick, Anna Maria, c26
  Johann, p26
  Maria Barbara, p26
Brigel, Johann George, s29
Brinck, Matteus, m42
Brucker, Margretha, r39
Bruckhard, Ulrich, r40
Bruen, Margretha, 16
  Christian, 16
  Johan, 16
Brunck, Niclaus, c24
  Anna, p24, m46
  Christina, s38
  Mattheus, p24, d47
Bruschi, Elsgen, p35
  Margreth, c35
  Weinsan, p35
Buck, Maria Gerdaut, s26
Burckhard, Anna Elisabeth, c49
  Amalia, p36, p49
  Anna Maria, s25
  Anna Margreth, s29, m45
  Elisabetha, d47, m44
  Johanens, c49
  Johann Martin, s33, r40
  Johann, 44, p45, p46
  Johann Conrad, c36
  Johann Peter, s29, m46, p49
  Peter, s33, s36, p36
Burgard, Peter, p50
  Maria, c50
  Mattie p50
Busch, Anna Maria, s17
Butt, Anna Catharina, s21
Buvnat, Paul, s20

Cast, Johann (see Kast), s34
Castlemann, Anna (see Kasselman,
  Kessel, Kissel), p19
  Anna Maria Judith, p17, p25, p36
  Anna Elizabeth, s16, m44
  Anna Maria, p29
  Christian, p25, p17, p36, p29
  Dietrich, s21
  Eva Catharina, c17
  Johann Ludwig, r40
  Johann Dietrich, p19, 44
  Johann Peter, c29
  Maria Justina, c25
  Sophia Magdalena, c36
  Wilhelm, c19
Caputz, Dorothea, s28
Caputzgi, Margretha, s34
Caputzgin, Anna Margretha, s27
Castin, Anna, s22
Caujun, Fransa 46

Belicka m46
Chisem, Anna, p18
  Annike, p25
  Christina, c25
  Henrich, p18, s21, p25, 46
  Jan s25
  Margretha, s21
  Robert, c18
Chamborary Johann, s17
  Barbara Elisabetha s17
Christian, Andreas Christian, c35
  Elisabeth, p35
  Pieter, p35, m44
Christman, Johann, s30
  Gertraut, s34
Clerk, William, s18
Clotter Paul, 41
  Susanna, m41
Coblentzer, Elizabeth Margretha, m41
  Johann Peter, 41
Congreve, Carolus, 15
Connrath, Johann, r39
Conrad, Anna Catharina, s34
  Johann Henrich, s23, s34, m46
Conterman, Anna Eva, c26
  Andreas Frantz, p33, m45
  Elisabetha, c33
  Johann Fridrich, p26, p33, p45, d47
  Jacob, c33
  Maria Barbara, p26, p33
  Sibylla, p33
Corhof, Maria Catharina, r39
Crump, Johann, m42
Cun, Anna Catharina, c31, p31
  Veltin, p31
Cuntz, Maria Catharina, p21, s24
  Anna Margretha, p19
  Johann Jacob, m45
  Johan David, c19
  Johann, p21, s24
  Ludwig, c21
  Matheus, p19, s20, p45, p46
  Philip, s29
  Philipp Henrich, m46
Curring, Johann Ludolph, s23
  Anna Catharina, m43
  Catharina, s19
  Ludolst, 43
  Ottilia, s34
  Rudolph, s22

Dachsetter, Anna Elizabeth, s21, p34
Dachstetter, Georg, p34
  Johann Fridrich, c34
Dausweber, Anna Magdalena, p22
  Johann Melchoir, p22, 41, m42
  Maria Barbara, m41
  Maria Regina, c22
DeBois, Abraham, c18
  Pannicke, p18
  Pieter, p18
Decker, Arianicke, s24
  Gabriel, c50
  Georg Johann, p24
  Geritt, p50
  Gertrud, p50
  Johanna, c24
  Joris, s24

Jurg Jan, p49
Margaret, c49, p49
Maria, p24
Demuth, Alexander, 44
Anna, s30
Anna Maria, s26, s33, s36, r39
Anna Maria Dorothea, s21
Dietrich, r39
Georg, s29
Gerg, s27, m44
Johann Fridrich, r40
Destuh, Daniel and his wife Barbara, s33
Deteutscher Janike, p27
Rudolph, c27, p27
Diehl, Hananias, s17
Diestenbach Anna Barbara, p27
Johann Conrad p27
Dietrich Agnes, s28, s33
Anna Catharina, c50
Anna Margareta, p21, c48, s48
Anna Maria, c37, p37
Catharina, c50
Christian, s28, p45, p50
Eva, p48, p50
Friderich, p50 (2), p48
Hans Wilhelm, s48, s49
Johann Christian, s25, s35, p37
Johann Wilhelm, c21
Jorg Wilhelm, p21
Margareta, m45, p50
Margrete, s49
Maria, c50
Maria Cathrina, s50
Dihl, Ananias, p26, p36
Elisabetha, p26, p36
Johann Henrich, c36
Johann Peter, c26
Dillenbach, Anna Margretha, c23
George Martin, widower, m44
Jorg Martin, p23, m44
Sara Catharina, p23
Dings, Jacob, s18
Dippel, Anna Barbara, s17, m42
Anna Catharina, p21, p26, c26, s34
Anna Eva, c21
Anna Maria, r40
Johann Peter, p21, p26
Peter, s27
Philipp, 42
Diestenbach, Dorothea, c27
Dobus, Abraham, p37
Jann, c37
Doerner, Anna Margretha, r39
Dolest, Anna Margretha, s33
Dopf Anna Maria, s27
Johann, p36
Margretha, m44
Peter, 44
Dopp, Johann Peter, s34, c36
Dorn, Anna Margreth, p29, p36
Latzarus, p29, p36
Maria Barbara c29
Michael, c36
Drechsler, Anna Catharina, c27
Catharina, p27
Peter, p27

Driesen, P. V., 35
Drum, Maria Catharina, s29
Duntzbach, Anna Elizabeth, s26
Elisabeth, s35

Eberhard, Anna Sibylla, p22, s49
Johannes, p22, s49
Johann Georg, c22
Johann, m43
Ebert, Anna Catharina. r40
Eckhard, Adam, p22, p27, p34
Anna, p27, p34
Anna Elisabetha, c27
Anna Catharina, c22
Johann, Georg, r39
Johann Peter, c34
Elisabetha Catharina, p22
Maria Barbara, r39
Magdalena, s24, s34
Ehmann, Thomas, m43
Eimer, Johannes Peter, r39
Eigner, Peter, s37
Eichler, Andreas, s50
Elsaesser, Paul, 42
Gertrauda, m42
Elswa, Faemige, p18
Benjamin, p18
William, c18
Elig, Hans Jurge, s50
Andreas, s18, p18
Anna Rosina, p18
Christian, c18
Ellich, Andreas and his wife Anna
Andreas, s35, s36, s29, p35, m45.
Anna Sophia, p35
Johann Wilhelm, c35
Sophia, s32
Souphia, d47, s35, s36
Emerich, Margreth, p38
Anna, c33
Anna Catharina, c24
Anna Elisabetha, s23
Anna Margretha, p19
Anna Margretha, s24, s24, p26, p23, s37
Catharina, s49
Elisabetha, p24, c26
Hannes, s50
Johann Michael, p24, m43
Johann, s24
Johannes and wife, p26, p33, p38, c38, s38
Johanna Catharina, c19
Johann Peter, 43
Johann, s24, s25
Johannes, p19
Maria Martha, m43
Endters, Johann Wilhelm, c34
Bertram, p34
Maria Christina, p34
Engel, Johannes, r39
Erhard, Maria Catharina, c20
Anna Margretha, p20
Simeon, p20
Eschenreuter, Anna Margreth, s30, r39

Esswein, Thomas, 42
 Anna Elisabetha, m42
 Elisabetha, s17
 Jacob, p27, p38
 Johann Wendell, s27
 Margretha, p27
 Veronica, c37

Falck, Anna Elisabeth, p25, p28
 Arnold, p25, p28, s32 (2), d47
 Gertraut, c28
 Johann Peter, c25
Falckenburg, Agnes, c28
 Anna Gertraut, c19
 Elisabetha Maria, p19, p28
 Gertrud, s49.
 Hans Veltin, s21
 Johann Hieronymus, c28
 Johann Valentin, p19, p28, s25
 Veltin, s26
Falckner, Justus, Rev., 15, 16
Feegen, Elisabetha Barbara, m44
Feegan, Johann, 44
Feg, Catharina, r39
Feeg, Anna Margaretha, c31
 Anna Maria, s17, s31, p31
 Johann, p45
 Johann Peter, p31
 Johannes, p17
 Leonard, m45
 Maria Margretha, p17, c17
Fees, Christina, s49
 Henrich, s49
Fehling, Henrich, p31
 Maria Kunigunda, p31
 Niclaus, c31
Fehlinger, Anna Kunigunda, p25
 Johann Jacob, c25, p25
Feller, Catharina Elisabeth, p35
 Johann Niclaus, c35
 Johann Philipp, p35, m46
 Maria Elisabetha, c23, p23
 Niclaus, p23, p46
Fidler Elisabeth, s34
 Johann Gottfrid and wife, s34
Finck, Andreas, p23, s30
 Frantz, m44
 Jacob, c23
 Johann Adam, 44
 Maria, p23
Finckel, Anna Catharina, p23
 Johann Philipp, c23, p23
Fischer, Andreas, c51
 Johann, m40, s22
 Johannes, 15, p16, s18, p51
 Margretha, c16
 Maria, p16, s22
Fisher, Maria, p16, s22, r39
Fischerin, Maria Barbara, p51
Flegler, Anna Magdalena Elizabetha,
 c24
 Eve Anna Elizabetha, p24, s25, p26
 Elisabetha, s21
 Simon, c26
 Zacharias, p24, p26, s25, m41, m43
Forster, Margretha, r40
 Susanna Margretha, s32
Fowles, William, s16

Franck, Johannes, s22, m43
Francke, Johann, s19
Frey, Catharina, s34
 Henrich and wife, s31
Freymeyer, Anna Eva, c20
 Anna Elisabetha, p20
 Johann Michael, p20
Friedrich, the wife of Conrad, s18
Fridrich, Johann Adam and wife Re-
 gina, 29
 Johann Adam, s21
 Johann Conrad, r39
Fritz, Maria Elizabetha, s24
Frehd, Maria Margretha, s28
Fridrich, Maria Regina, s22
Friderich, Regina, s21
Froehlich, Anna Catharina, c24
 Anna Elisabetha, p24
 Appollonia, s19, p24, s27, p33
 Bernhard, c33
 Johannes, c24
 Johann Valentin, p24, s33
 Stephan, p24
 Veltin, s30, p33
Fuchs, Christoph, p23
 Anna Maria, r39
 Johanna Elisabetha, p23
 Johann Philipp, s23, c23
Fuehrer, Johann, s21, s27, m44, d47
 Anna Maria, c49
 Catharina, p49, p50
 Henrich, c50
 Johannes, s28
 Valntin, p49, s32
Fuhrer, Valentin p50
Fulz, Catharina, s19
Fux, Christina, s30

Gans, Anna Catharina, c19
 Gertrud, p19
 Johann, p19, m41
German, Anna Cahtarina s27
 Anna Catharina, s26
 Jacob ,s27,
Gerlach, Anna Margretha, s22
 Conrad's widow, s18
 Johann Peter, s23
Gerystler, Catharina, s25
Gesteler, Anna Louisa, s21
Giesser, Sibylla, m43
 Johann, 43
Giller, Barbara, p19
 Franz, p19
 Joseph, c19
Gisler, Anna Lucia, p23
 Johann Hermann, c23
 Peter, p23, p33, s36
Gistler, Anna Lucia, p33
 Johan Georg, c33
Glock (see Clock, Klock), Henrich, p20
 Johannes, c20
 Maria Margretha, p20
Glopp, Anna Magdalena, p31
 Johann Peter, m43, s20
 Peter, s24, p31
 Susanna c31
Gockel, Anna Christina, r39
Goebel, Anna Margretha, s16

Goettel, Daniel, r39
Gormann, Jacob, s33
Gratt, Gabriel, s50 (2)
   Gabriel, s50
   Greetje, s50
Grad, Anna Elisabetha, c26
   Johann, p26, s26
   Wlaburga, p26
Graad, Maria Margareta, s50
Gransche, Elisabetha, s22
   Omyla, s22
Grauberger, Anna Barbara, s23, p21
   Johann Fridrich, c21
   Philip Peter, s19, p21, s22
Greisler, Anna Catharine, p27, c27
   Catharina, p24
   Johann Hieronymus, c24
Greissler, Johann Philip, p24, p27
Grems, Anna Apolonia, p16
   Johannes, p16
   William, c16
Greysler, Johannes, r40
Groster, Anna Catharina, s31
Gulch, Ana Catharine, p52
   Melchoir, p52
Guchin, Heinrich, c52
   Magdalena, c52
Guntermann (See Countryman, Kon-
   derman, Andreas, r40
   Anna Barbara, s22
Guss, Mattheus, s22

Haas, Anna Barbara, c18
   Anna Catharina, r39
   Anna Elisabeth, c17
   Anna Sabina, c26
   Catharina, p22
   Jannike, c22
   Johann Niclaus, s27
   John, p22
   Maria Sabina, p26
   Niclaus, p17, p26
   Rosina, p18, p25
   Sabina, p17
   Simon, p18, p25, s26
   Zacharia, c25
Haber, Christian, m44
Haeger, Johann Fridrich, s22, s24, s38
   Johann Fridrich, Rev., m46
Hagedorn, Johann Peter, s17
Hagendorn, Johan Peter, s26
   Maria Gartraut, r39
   Peter s32
Ham, Catharina, p49
   Johannes Peter, c49
   Peter, p49
Hambuch, Johann Wilhelm, 30, m46
Hambuck, Johann Wilhelm, s27
Hamm, Anna Catharina, c27
   Anna aCtharina Sibylla, p27
   Peter, p27
Hammer, Hans Henrich, s20
Hanor, Johann, m41
Hanti, (or Meautl). Conrad, s36
Hartman, Anna, s28
   Anna Maria, m41
   Conrad, 41
   Johann Hermann, s30
Hassmann, Elisabeth, r40

Hastmann, Elisabetha s29
Hauck, Anna Elisabeth, p34
   Anna Margretha, c34
   Georg, p34
Haug, Lucas, 43
   Magdalena, m43
Haupt, Anna Catharina, r39
   Cathrina, c28
   Gertraut, p28
   Philipp, p28
Hauss, Christian, m42
Hayner, Johannes, s20
Heckman, Maria Gertraut, r40
Heidorn, Henrich, m43
Heil, Anna Catharina, s29
Heller, Johann Philipp, s27
Helm, Johann Peter, s20
Helmer, Anna Catharina, m42
   Antonius, 42
Hemer, Elisabeth, s35
Hemler, Elisabetha, p31
   Johann Gottfrid, c31
   Leonard, p31
Henrich, Frantz, c30
   Johann Lorentz, s36
   Lorentz, p30
   Regina, p30
Hendrickson, Abraham, c18
   Isaac, p18
   Judith, p18
Herchemer, Jerg, s31
Herdel, Anna Margretha, p23, s26
   Anna Margretha, s19, s26
   Elisabeth, s32, s38
Herder, Johann Michael, s23
Hertel, Adam, s19, p23, s25, p28, m46
   Adam, child of d47
   Adam, wife of, d47
   Eva Maria, c28
   Margretha, p28
Hertel, Maria Elisabeth, c23
Hess, Anna Catharina, p29, c34, p34
   Anna Maria, c29
   Catharina, s26
   Johann, s19, p29, s26, p34, m43
   Niclaus, s18
Hettich, Anna Maria, p17
   Conrad, p 17
   Johannes, c 17
Hettman, Gartraut, s34, (2)
Heu, Litcken, 16
Heydorn, Henrich, s28
   Maria Barbara, s29
Heyl, Catharina, m45
   Johann Wilhelm, p45
Heypert, Anna Elisabetha, r39
Hill, Carolus 40
   Maria, m40
Hochdihl, Jacob, 46
Hoener, Johann and his wife Cathar-
   ina, s34
Hoerner, Margretha, m42
Hoenig, Anna Elisabeth, c35
   Magdalena, p35
   Michael, p35
Hof, Adam, p35
   Anna Catharina, p35
   Johann Phillipp, c35

Hofmann, Anna Elalia, p17
  Anna Mara, s17, c17
  Dietrich, p17
  Esther, p25
  Herman, s23
  Jannike, c25
  Jacob, p20
  Maria Elisabetha, p20
  Mattheus, c20
  Zacharias, p25
Hoffman, Ester, 29
  Rennalt, c29
  Zacharias, p29
Hofmann, Gabriel, p19
  Joseph, c19
  Susanna, p19
Horning, Gerhard, s27
  Sophia, s29
Hornung, Anna Sophia, m45
  Gerhard, d47
  Sophia, s2r
Hostmann, Anna Catharina, p24
  r39
  Conrad, p20
  Eva Margretha, p20
  Gabriel, m43
  Gabri el, m43
  Johann Peter, c20
  Sebastian, c24
Huen, Anna Gertrauda, m41
  Dietrich, 41
Huenschick, Michael, s24
Humbel, Elisabetha, m43
  Jerg, 43
Humel, Anna Margretha, p38
  Hermann, p38
  Peter, c38
Hummel, Hermann, p33
  Johann Georg, c33
  Margretha, p33
Hupfer, Anna Catharina, p27
  David, p27
  Jacobina Maria, r39
  Sophia, c27

Ifland, Anna Maria, s31
  Johann David, s19
Ittich, Johann s31

Jan, a negro, p32
Jaeger, Christina Elisabetha, s20, p30
  Johann, c30
  Wendell, p30
Janson, Maria, p22, 16
  Peter, 16, p22, c22
Jorg, Johann Niclaus, c18
  Maria, p18
  Wilhelm, s18, p18
Jung (Young), Anna Elisabeth, s35
  Anna Margretha, p20, p32
  Anna Veronica, p30, p36, p50, p49
  Catharina Elisabetha, c30
  Elisabetha, s30, s21 (2)
  Eva Maria, c36
  Gertrudt, c49
  Henrich, p20, p32, s35
  Johann Henrich, Anna Margreth,
    twins, c32

Jacob, widow of, p22
Jan Matthias, p50
Jerg Hans, 44
Johann Adam, c34
Johann Eberhard, s24
Johann Mattheus, s20, s26, s29, p30, p36, m44, p49
Johann Quirinius, d47
Johannes, c50
Magdalena, s19
Magdalena, wife of Niclaus, s24
Maria Catharina, c20, p34
Niclaus, s24, d47
Theobald, p34

Kaehl, Jorg Wilhelm, s26
Kanikli, Peter Samuel, 16
  Emicke, 16
  Johannes, 16
  Samuel, 16
Kaputzgi, Jacob, s33
  Anna Magdalena, s33
  Anna Margretha, p40 m46
  and wife, s29
  Anna Dorothea, r40
  Johann Jacob, p46
Kehl, Anna Sibylla Catharina, s21
  Gerdraut, s26, s36
  Georg Wilhelm, s29, s33
  Jorg Wilhelm, s21
  Jerg Wilhelm, s36
  Sibylla Catharina, s38
Keller, Frantz, p29, s30
  Barbara, p29, s30
  Johann Wilhelm, c29
Kernick, James, s38
Kestler, Anna Margretha, p31, p34
  Anna Catharina, c31
  Johann, p31, c34, p34
Keyser, Anna Margretha, c35, p35
  Johann, p35, m42
Kiever, Christina, p49
  Balthasar, p49
  Catharina, c49
  Henrich, c49
Kilmer, Eva Margretha, p49
  Georg, p49
  Johann Wilhelm, c49
Kistler, Eleonora Catharina, s20
  David, s20, s32
Klein, Adam, p31
  Amelia, s25, s33
  Anna Maria, s27, m46
  Anna Maria Clara, c31
  Anna Catharina, p31
  Elisabeth, s49
  Johann, s26, s38
  Hieronymus, s22 s24, s28, p46, s48
  Maria, s28, s32, s50
  Maria Margretha, s25, s26
Klug, Johann Georg, p17
  Johannes, c17
  Susanna p17
Klumm, Anna Margretha, c33
  Johann Georg, c19
  Philipp, p19, p33
  Veronica, p19, p33

Kniestberg, Anna Maria, c32
   Elisabetha Barbara, p34
   Elisabetha, p32
   Johann Godtfrid, c34
   Johann Peter, p32, p34
Kobel, Jacob, p23, s23
   Anna Maria, p23
   Johann Henrich, c23
Koch, Anna Maria, s19
   Jorg Ludwig, s19
Kocherthal, Christian Joshua,   Rev.,
      c52
   Benigna Sibylla, s29, s30, s35,   s36,
      c52
   Joshua, p16, s25, s30, p52
   Louisa Abigail, c16
   Susanna Sibylla c52
   Sibylla Charlotta, p16, d47, p52
Koerner, Anna Magdalena, p19, p26
   Catharina Elisabetha, c26
   Johann Adam, c19
   Johann Niclaus, p26
   Niclaus, p19
Kohl, Georg Wilhelm, s50
   Gertruda, s19, s50
   Jurge Willem, s50
Kopp, Johann Adam, s34
   Anna Sophia, s17
Kornmann, Anna Kunigunda, m42
Korb, Gebje, p50
   Hendrick, p50
   Jannetje, c50
Kraemer, Antoni, p29, r42
   Anthon, r39
   Gertaut, p29, s33
   Johannes, c29, s34
Krantz, Johann Henrich, p22,   p24,
   Anna Catharina, p22, s24, p24, p29,
      p36
      p29, p36
   Conrad, 43
   Elisabetha, s28, s36, m43
   Henrich and his wife, s32
   Johann, m41
   Johannes, c24
   Johann Wilhelm, c36
   Maria Elisabetha, c29
Kraus, Jacob, d41
   Anna Maria, m41
Kreystler, Johann Georg, r40
Kreiser, Catharina, p17
   Johann Philipp, p17
   Johann Henrich Valentin, c17
Kuester, Anna Maria, s20, s32, m46
   Johann Wilhelm, s28, p46
   Johann Balthasar, s21, s35, s37, r39
   Wilhelm, s24
Kuster, Catharina Susanna, r40
Kuestler, Susanna, s26
Kugel, Anna Margretha, m43
   Johann, 43
Kuhlman, Catharina, s38
   Johann, s30
Kuhn, Veltin, p20
   Anna Catharina, p20
   Johanna Elisabeth Margretha, c20
Kun, Elisabetha, s37
Kunz, Johann Wilhelm, s49
Kuntz, Margretha, s17

Kurtz, Lorentz Henrich, s17
   Maria Margretha, s17
   Margretha, s35
La Gransche, Entike, s25
   Johann, s25
Lambert, Anna Elisabetha, s27
Lamed, Anna Elisabeth, s17
   Johannes, s17
Lamert, Johann, s26
   Wife of Johann, s38
Land, Anna Margaretha, s31
Landgrast, Jerg and his daughter An-
      na Elisabetha, s32
Landmann, Peter, p47, m47, r39
Lang, Abraham and wife, s37
Langry, Maria Catharina,   wife of
      Abraham, s20
Last, Anna, p31
   Anna Dorothea, c31
   Johann Georg, p31
   Johann Just, s31
Lastner, Johann Peter, p21
   Juliana Elisabetha, c21
   Magdalena, p21
Lauck, Abraham, p20, p30
   Anna Christina, c30
   Catharina, p20, p30
   Elisabetha, m43
   Jacob, 43
   Maria Catharina, c20
Launert, Anna Catharina, c30
   Anna Margretha, p30
   Jerg, s30
   Johann Georg, s34, m45
   Philipp, s28, s29, p30, p45
Laur, Arnold, 42
   Maria Agnes, m42
Lauer, Johann Mettheus, r40
Laux, Anna Elisabetha, s28, s30, p30
   Dietrich and wife, s32
   Johann Adam, c31
   Johann Dietrich, p31
   Johann Just, s34, p45
   Johann Peter, r40
   Johann Wilhelm, c30
   Maria Elisabetha, m45
   Maria Margretha, r39
   Niclaus, p30
Leer, Anna Margretha, c22
   Johann, p34
   Johannes, p22
   Ottilia Helena, c34
   Sibylla Catharina, p22, p34
Lehmann, Anna Elisabeth, c36
   Anna Margretha, c30
   Clemens, p27, p30, p36, m44, d47,
      p50
   Johann Wilhelm, c27, s27, s35
Lehman, Wilhelm and wife Maria, s32
Leich, Elisabeth, p19
   Georg Ludwig, m43
   Johann Eberhard, c24
   Johann Henrich p19
   Ludwig, p24
   Maria Martha p24
   Philip, c19

Leick, Anna Catharina, c34
  Johann p34
  Maria Barbara, p34
Lein, Conrad, p23
  Johann Peter, c23
  Margretha, p23
  Margaretha, r39
Leitz, Johannes, s48
  Maria Barbara, s48
Leman, Anna Maria, c50
  Gertrud, p27, p30, p36, p50
  Maria Eva, s50
  Willem, s38, s50
Lerck, Wilhelm, s26
  Henrich, s38
Lesch, Johann Adam, s17

Lescher, Bastian, s37
Liboscha, Maria Johann, 51
  Susanna, 51
Linck, Anna Eva, p26
  Anna Gerdraut, c26
  Wilhelm, p26
Lisemus, Anna Maria, s23
Lispenaer, Abigail, s16
Listenus, Anna Barbara, r40
Listenius, Anna Maria, p19, m44
  Bernhard, p19
  Christianus, c19
Loehn, Anna Margretha, p34
  Johann, c34, p34
Loeshaar, Jacob, s23
  Maria Elisabetha, p16, c16
  Sebastian, p16
Loiner, Abigail p48
  Robert, c48
  William, p48
Loockstad, Elisabetha, p18
  Georg, p18, m41
  Georgius, c18
Lorentz, Alexander, c17
  Anna Margretha, p17
  Henrich and his wife s23
  Johannes p17
  Henrich, s18
Losch, Elisabetha, r39

Loscher, Conrad, r40
  Johann Bastian, s48
  Johann Georg, r39
Losting, Andreas, c22
  Cornelia, p22
  Peter, p22
Louck, Abraham, m42

Lucka, Maria Elisabetha, s17
Luckhard, Bernhard, child of, d47
Ludwig, Susanna Catharina, s37
Lueckhard, Bernhard, p24, p28,   s33,
  p33
  Johann Bernhard, p18
  Johann Daniel, c28
  Johann Peter, c33
  Johann Wilhelm, c18
  Johannes, c24
  Justina, p18, s22, p24, s25, p28, p33
Lued, Johan Leonard, s16

Luetken, Daniel, s16
  Daniel ,M. D., 15

Lun, Elisabetha, p27
  Marcus, c27
  Samuel, p27
Lutt, Anna Catharina, s33, m46
  Barthas, r39
  Johann Balthas, s35
Lutz, Anna Magdalena, m43
  Johann Christoph, 43

Maemig, Ferdinand, p46
  Maria Elisabetha, m46
Maerten, Johann Conrad, p24, p28
  Johann Fridrich, c24
  Johann Henrich, c28
  Maria, p24
  Maria Elisabeth, p28
Manck, Anna Veronica, s26
  Eva Catharina, s21, s30
  Jacob, child of, d47
Mancken, Anna Veronica, m44
  Jacob, 44
Manges, Johann. s26

Mann, Henrich, s23
  Johann Henrich, p19
  Johann Peter, c19
  Maria Elisabetha, p19
Mannich, Maria Elisabetha, r39

Martenstock, Albrecht, p33
  Albrecht Dietrich, p21, c21, p28
    p38, m41, 48
  Daniel, c33
  Elisabetha, p21, p28, p33, s37, p38,
    48
  Johanna Maria Sophia, c28
  Maria Christina, c38
Martin, Conrad, s26
  Maria, s26
Matthes, Anna Maria, s27, m45
  Maria Apollonia, m41
  Peter, 41, p45
Matteus, Henrich, p46
  Sabina, m46
Mattheus, Conrad, c34
  Georg, p34
  Jerg, s20, p31
  Johan Jacob, c31
  Maria Catharina, p31, p34
  Maria Sibylla, s21
Mauck, Jacob, s19

Mauer, Anna Catharine, p23
  Anna Margreth, c23
  Johann Georg, r39
  Peter, p23
Maul, Anna Catharina, s36
  Anna Elisabetha, c37
  Anna Julian, s21
  Anna Margareta, s49
  Anna Maria, c23
  Anna Ursula, p23, p32, p37
  Christoph, s23, s30
  Fridrich, s21, s24, s25, s27, s28, p37
    s50
  Johann Fridrich, p32
  Johann Jacob, s49
  Johannes, c32
  J. Fridrich, p23
  Ursula, s36

Maurer, Anna Catharina, 30, p30
Dorothea, s27
Johannes, c30
Johann Peter, s19
Jorg, s27
Peter, s24, p30, s37
Mayer, Anna Gertraut, p38
Catharina, c38
Christian p38
Mehs, Henrich, s17
Meinhard, Burckhard and wife, s18
Mendes, Maria Christina, s31
Menges, Anna Eva, s21, p29, s33, p36
Anna Elisabetha, c29
Gerdraut, c36
Johannes, p29
Mengis, Johann ,s17, s33, s35, p36
Merckel, Anna Barbara, p21, p24, p33
Eva, c33
Elisabetha, c38
Fridrich, p21, p24, p33
Johann Adam, c21
Johann Fridrich, p38
Johann Jacob, s31
Maria Elisabetha, c24
Mertin, Margaretha, s22
Mertz, Anna Catharina, m41
Elisabetha, r40
Johann, 41
Sophia Elisabeth Margaretha, r39
Meyer, Anna Christina c35
Anna Maria, c21, m45
Christian, p19, p26, s25, p30, p35
Gerdraut, s36
Johann and wife Barbara, s32
Johann Fridrich, p45
Johann Peter, c30
Maria Barbara, s35
Meyrer, Anna Gertraut, p19, p26, p30, p35
Anna Kunigunda, p21, p31
Henrich, p21, p31
Johann Henrich, c31
Johan Wilhelm, c26
Maria Elisabetha, c19
Meyser, Johann Michel, s34
Moessig, Johann Heinrich, c28
Maria Catharina, p28, s37, p38
Susanna, c38
Veit, p28, p38
Mohr, Anna Catharina, c21
Anna Margretha, p21
Heinrich, p21, s27
Johann, r39
Philipp, s21, s33, s37
Moor, Anna Margreth, p30
Catharina Elisabeth, c30
Christina, p28
Elizabeth, p31
Henrich, s28, p30
Johann, p31
Johann Georg, c31
Philipp, r40
Philipp Henrich, c28
Philipp Wilhelm, p28, s30, s35
Motsch, Juliana, s21
Michael, Georg Andreas, c28
Maria Barbara, p28

Niclaus, p28
Michel, Anna Barbara, p32
Elisabetha Margretha, c32
Henrich, p45
Johann Henrich, r40
Johann Niclaus, p32
Susanna, m45
Susanna Gerdraut, r39
Minckler, Johann, m42
Minkler, Anna Margretha, p23
Jacob, c23
Kilian, p23
Migrigri, Letischa, 16
Peter, 16
Mueller, Anna, s27
Anna Catharina, s27
Anna Eva, s36
Anna Elisabeth, s20
Anna Elisabetha, m44
Anna Margretha, s23
Anna Maria, s21, m41
Catharina, p32
Christian, m45
Eva, s33
Elisazetha, s16, s17, c37, m43
Georg, 43
Johann, s16, s22, s34, 44
Johannes, s21, (2), c32, c49
Johann Christian, p37
Johann Georg, 41, p45
Johann Philipp, c17
Margretha, p37
Maria Catharina, m43
Maria Elisabeth, s36
Philip, p17, s19, s20, s30, p32, 43
Samuel, s27
Muller, Anna Sibilla, s48
Bartel, r39
Christiana Clara, r40
David, s36, p49
Margrete, p49
Muenckler, Anna Margretha, c27, p27
Anna Maria, c27
Kilian, p27
Mustirr, Catharina, m41
Johann Jacob, 41

Naeher, Carl, s28, p32, m41, m45
Naehrung, Johann Henrich, 16
Neher, Anna Constantia, p32
Johann Fridrich, c32
Netzbacher, Anna Margaretha, c30
Barbara Elisabetha, p23
Johann Henrich, c23
Johann Martin, p23
Martin, p25, p30
Netzbaecher, Anna Barbara, p25
Anna Maria, c25
Neukirch, Anna Benigma c,30
Anna Maria, p25
Maria Catharina, c25
Johann, s32
Johann Henrich, p25, p30
Neus, Abraham, p17
Anna Elisabeth, c17
Neurich, Anna Maria, s23, p30

Noecher, Anna Constinia, p35
   Anna Maria, c35
   Carl, p35
Noll, Bernard, s28, s33
Nuess, Johann Heinrich, r39

Oberbach, Anna Maria, c25, s50
   Christina, s27
   Elisabetha, s19, p25, s33, p33
   Elisabetha Magdalena, s33
   Jerg, s30, 47
   Johann Christian, c25
   Johann Georg, s19, c30
   Johann Peter, c20, p20, s20, p25,
      s25, p30
   Maria Christina, s19, p20, p25, p30,
      c33, s36
   Peter, s20, p25, p33, s36
Oemich, Anna Catnarina, p38, r39
   Jerg Adam, s32
   Johann Adam, r39
   Lorentz, c38
   Niclaus, p38
Ohmich, Anna Catharina, p29
   Anna Maria, c29
   Niclaus and his wife, s28, p29
Ohrendorf, Henrich, p35
   Anna Margretha, p35
   Maria Elisabetha, c35
Onderling, Anna, m44
Ormen, Richard, s33

Peeter, Anna Maria, s19
Persch, Anna, s22
Petri, Anna Gertraut, c31, s31
   Anna Margretha, s19
   Cordula, p31
   Philipp, s19, m44
   Johann Just, p31
Pfeister, Andreas, r39
Pfester, Anna Maria, p18, s32
   Johannes, c18
   Michael, p18, s18
Pfuhl, Anna Catharina, c25
   Anna Sophia, p25
   Peter, p25, m42
Philipp, Anna Catharina, s37
   Magdalena, s26, s49
Philip, Catharina, s49
   Johann Peter, s49
   Peter, s49
Planck, Christina, c30
   Johann, s18, p18, s24, c25, p25, p30,
      d47 (2), p47
   Johann Elisabetha, r39, m47
   Johann Michael, c18
   Killian, p22
   Maria Margretha, p18, c22, p25, p30
Plass, Elisabetha, p26
   Johann, p26, s28
   Johann Wilhelm, c26
Pletel. Jacob, p51
Plettel, Elizabeth, 15
   Johannes, 15
Pletelin, Ana Elisabetha, p51
   Anna Sara, c51

Catharine, c51
   Margretha, c51
Plettol, Elisabetha, m41
   Jacob, 41
Pliest, Johann Emerich, s29
Plirs, Johann Emmerich, s22
Poehler, Johann Henrich, r39, m41
Porster, Maria, wife of Jacob, s20
Practer, Helena, 16
   Joseph, 16
Presier, Valentin, s17
Propeet, Maria Barbara, r39
Propert, Anna Maria, s37
Propper, Anna Elisabeth, s49
   Johann Jost, s49
Prusie, Gertraut, s25
   Gabriel, s25
Prusti, Gabriel, s27
   Gertraut, s27
Pulfer, Anna Catharina, s19
Pulver, Johann Wendel, s27

Rau, Catharina, c48, p48
   Catharina Elisabetna, s26, s27
   Fridrich, r40
   Friderich, p48
   Gerdraut, s28
   Johann Georg, r39
   Johann Niclaus, s35
   Michael, s48
   Niclaus, s28
Rauersee, Gertraud, p20
   Hermann, p20
   Meinhard, c20
Rauh, Catharina Elisabetha, m46
   Niclaus, p46
Rausch, Anna Christina, r39
Rauscher, Martin, r39
Rautenbusch, Anna Barbara, m42
   Johann, 42
Rauw, Anna Maria, p50
   Catharina, c50
   Michael, p50
Reckfel, Anna, r39
Rees, Andreas, s35
   Benjamin, p35
   Cathariana, s35
   Gertraud, p35
   Henrich, c35
Reichard, Hans, 43
   Johann Bernhard, c22
Reichart, Anna Constantia, m45
   Anna Maria, s19, p22, p26, s35,
      m43, 48
   Elisabetha Catharina Backus, p29
   Joseph, s19, p22, p26, s28, s34, s35,
      m42, p45
   Johann Mattheus, c29
   Johann David, c26
   Johann, p29
Reisdorst, Anna Margretha, s33
Reiter, Henrich and his wife, s23
Reitschaft, Johann Paul, m41
Rennau, Henry, s16, p51
   Heinrich, c51
   Johanna, s16, p51
   Lorenz, c51

Reuter, Anna Juliana, p19, p27, p36,
      48, s49
   Eva Catharina, c36
   Henrich, p19, p27, s28, p36, s36, 48
   Johanna Elisabetha, c19
   Johann Herman, s49
   Johann Fridrich, c27
   Juliana, s24, s32
   Liesabeth, s50
Richter, Andreas, p27, 44
   Anna Barbara, r40
   Anna Maria, m44
   Anna Maria, s24
   Elisabetha, s24, p27
   Johannes, c27
Risch, Johann Jacob, s17
Risom, Anna, s18
   Hensic, s18
Ritscher, Anna, p36
   Johann Conrad, p35
   Maria, c36
Rohrbach, Anna Catharina, 29,   s30,
      m46
Rohrbauch, Anna Catharina, s27
Roos, Catharina, s22
   Ephraim, m44
   Wilhelm, s22, 44
Roschmann, Anna Elisabetha, c26, p26,
      s27, r39
   Johann, p26, s29
   Johannes s27
   Maria Catharina, r40
Rose, Andreas, s18
   Peter, 16
Rosenquest, Alexander, s17
Roth, Johann, 15
Ruebenich, Elisabetha, m41
   Mattaeus, 41
Rued, Johann Georg, s31
   Johann Michael, r39
   Johann Peter, r39
Rueger, Anna Margretha, p21, p24
Reuger, Johann Philipp, p21
   Johannes, c21
Ruehl, Anna Catharina, c24, 35
   Anna Dorothea Margretha, p33
   Gottfrid, s21
   Gottfried, p24
   Gottfrid and wife, s31
   Niclaus, p33
   Niclaus, s31
Rusch, Anna Magdalena, r39
Rusmann, Elisabeth, p49
   Johann, p49
   Johannes, c49

Saalbach, Johann Smith, s48
   Maria Margretha, s48
Saderland, William and wife, s16
Saltmann, Anna Margretha, p38, c38
   Georg, p38
Saltzmann, Amalia, r40
Salzmann, Georg, m46
Savoy, Anna Elisabeth, c34, p34
   Joseph, p34
Schaarmann, Anna Catharina, m41
   Conrad, p29

   Henrich, 40, m42, p45
   Johann Henrich, s22, 29
Schauermann Johan Emerich, c29
   Maria Salomo, p29
   Sibylla, m45
Schaefer Elisabetha, 16
   Maria Margretha, p16
   Maria Catharina, s20
Schaeffer, Johann, s31
Scheffer, Johannes, s50
Schaeffer, Justis Henrich, 16, p16
Schaib, Anna Catharina, p38
   Catharina, s28
   Fridrich, c38
   Hieronymus, p38
Schaester, Agnes, p21, p25, p29, s35, p38
   Anna Elisabetha, s20
   Anna Margretha, s20, s31, r39
   Anna Maria, p17, p29, s35
   Dorothea, p32, p37, d47
   Elisabeth Catharina, c37
   Elisabetha, c37
   Fridrich, s34
   Georg, m45
   Gerhard, p17, r40
   Henrich, s29, s37
   Jacob, p45
   Jerg, s27, p29
   Jerg Philip, c29
   Johann Adam, c29
   Johann Henrich, c21, s35, r39
   Johan Niclaus, s20
   Johann Philipp, c25
   Johann Werner, s30
   Johannes, c38
   Jost Henrich, p21, p25
   Just Henrich, p38, m41, 48
   Justus Henrich, 29
   Maria Catharina, s20
   Maria Sophia, c17
   Valtin, r40
Schaster, Anna Sibylla, r40
   Margretha Elisabeth, r39
   Maria Margretha, s22, m45, 48
Schester, Johann, s21, p35, c35
   Johann Veltin, s35
Schall, Maria Elisabetha, s23
Schauser, Michael, 42
Schister, Philipp, p45
Schampnor, Daniel, p20
   Johanna, p20
   Paul, c20
Schauer, Johann Michael, r40
   Magdalena, m42
Schedp, Jacob, s23
Schef, Anna Maria, s50
Scheff, Anna Margreta, p50
   Lisabeth, c50
Scheib, Anna Catharina, p26
   Anna Catharina, p32, s33
   Anna Maria, c26
   Hieronymus, p26, p32, s33
   Maria Elisabeth, c32
Scherp, Anna Barbara, p48
   Anna Maria, s48
   Jacob, s48
   Johan Jacob, c48
   Jurgen Henrich, p48

Scherer, Theobald, wife of, Justina, s27
Scheset, Johann Wilhelm, s34
Schleicher, Anna Catharina, m41
 Anna Margretha, p17
 Catharina Elisabeth, s25
 Johann Adam, c17
 Johann, Georg, p17, 41
Schlemer, Anna Eva, c21
 Mattheus, p21
Schlemmer, Anna Elisabetha, c33
 Anna Veronica, p21, s23, p26,, p33
 Maria Catharina, c26
 Maria Gerdraut, c26
 Mattheus, p21, s26, p26, s29, p33, s33
Schley, Anna Maria, m46
 Johann Michel, p46
Schlitzler, Maria Elisabetha, s21
Schmid, Adam, s25
 Adam Michael, s17
 Anna Catharina, s25, p25
 Anna Elisabetha, p19, c25, s32, r40, p50
 Anna Maria, m44
 Bernhard, s28
 Christina, p49
 Conrad, s29
 Elisabeth, p37
 Elisabetha Margretha, p23, p29
 Eva, p37
 Georg, s25
 Georg Adam, s19
 Henrich, s25, 44
 Johann Adam, r40
 Johann Georg, p19, c23, r39
 Johann Henrich, p25, c37, m41, 44
 Johann Peter, p23, s28, s29, p37
 Johannes, Peter, c49
 Johannes, c29
 Jorg Ludwig, c19
 Justus Adam, p49
 Ludwig, m42
 Margaretje, c50
 Maria Barbara, r39
 Maria Catharina, r40
 Nicklas, s27, s36, p37, 40, r40, p50
 Peter, p29, m41, m46
 Susanna, Catharina, c37
 Wilhelm, s49, p50
 Wilhelmus, c50
Schmidt, Gertrauda, m41
 Maria Elisabeth, s50, p50
Smid, Paul, s49
Schnell, Johann Just, s31
Schneider, Agnes, c35
 Anna, p27
 Anna Barbara, p30
 Anna Catharina, m45
 Anna Gerdraut, p28
 Anna Margretha, s37
 Anna Maria, s23, c28, s38
 Antoni, p33
 Anthonious, m45
 Dietrich, p45
 Elsie, s48
 Henrich, p27
 Jacob, p30

Johann Dietrich, p45
Johann Georg, 30, s33, m47
Johann Henrich, c30
Johann Samuel, c27
Johann Wilhelm, s26, p28, s30, p47
Johannes, s38
Margreth, s34, p35
Susanna Margretha, s28
Schnitt, Johann Jacob, p17
 Johanna Elisabetha, c17
 Maria Elisabeth, p17
Schott, Helena, s18, p21
 Hargreth, c21, s25
 Wilhelm, s18, p21
Schraemmle, Johann Henrich, s23
Schramm, Anna Maria, p35, p37, s49
 Catharina, s35
 Friderich, s32, p35, p37, s38, m46, p48, s49
 Henrich, s23, s28, s33, p46, s50
 Johann William, c35
 Johann Henrich, c37
Schram, Margretha, s26, s50
 Maria, c48, p48
Schreib, Catharina, s28
 Hieronymus, s25
Schreiber, Albrecht, p20
 Anna Margretha, c20
 Eva, p20
Schuch, Gerdraut, s26
Schuertz, Andreas, p37
 Anna Catharina, s26, c37, m45.
 Jerg, s37
Schuett, Anna Maria, p29
 Henricus, c18
 Peter, c29
 Salomon, p18, p29
Schuetz, Benjamin, c25
 Johan Michael, 15, p25
Schuetze, Jannicke, 15, p18
 Maria, 15, p25
Schumacher, Anna Barbara, 18, s19
 Anna Maria, p24
 Barbara, r39
 Daniel, p24
 Dorothea, s30
 Jacob, s34
 Johann Jost, c24
Schuemann, W. Harmannus, 15
Schut, Catharina, s50
Schultz, Anna Elisabetha, m43
Schutz, Conrad, s32, s34, p45
 Susanna, s31
 Georg, 43
Schuertz, Catharina Appolonia, p37
Schurtz, Eva, s20
 David, r40
Schuh, Eva, s38
Schuenemann, Herman, m43
Schultheis, Elsabetha, s31
 Johann, m42
Schultheiss, Johann George, s19
Schwisser, Anna Catharina, p51
 Johanns, c51
 Lorens, p51
Schweitzer, Laurenz, p16
 Catharina, p16
 Johann Heinrich, c16

Seegendorf, Adam, p46
    Anna Gertraud, m46
Segendorf, Hermann, p34
    Johann Georg, c34
    Maria Catharina, s27
Segendorst, Hermann, s20
    Maria Catharina, s37
Sehn, Anna Gertraud, wife of Peter,
    s25
Seibert, Jerg Adam, c32
    Anna Maria, p32
    Johann Martin, p32
Sexer, Anna Magdalena, r39
Seybold, Georg, s34
Simon, Anna Elisabetha, c32
    Anna Maria, p20, p32
    Johann Michael, m41
    Johann Wilhelm, p32
    Johann Ulrich, c20
    Wilhelm, p20
Sittig, Christian, s20
Sixt, Anna Elisabeth, s34
    Christina, p30, p34
    Christina Elsabeth, c30
    Elsabeth, s30
    Gertraut, c34
    Henrch, p30, s30, p34
Soller, Adam, d47
Soeller, Johann Adam s21, m42, m44
Speickermann, Anna Catharina, s26
    Catharina, s28
    Anna Elisabetha, p20, p28
    Anna Maria Catharina, c28
    Johann Hermann, s26, m41
    Philip Peter, c20
    Sebastian, p20, p28, s30
Spohn, Anna Catharina, p31
    Anna Margretha, c25, s25
    Anna Maria, p25, p36
    Adam, s23, p25, s32, p36, m44
    Henrich, p31
    Johann Henrich, c23, m43
    Johann Niclaus, c31, 44
    Johann Peter, p23
    Maria Catharina, p23
    Maria Elisabeth, c36
    Werner, 44
Sponheimer, Anna Margaretha, c16
    Anna Maria, p16, s22
    Johann Georg, p16, s22
Spoon, Adam, s28, p32, s50
    Anna Maria, p32, s50
    Maria Eva, c32
Spoor, Annika, p30
    Isaac, p30
    Johann, c30
Springstein,   Catharine, 16, p18, p37,
    c37
    David, s18
    Georg, 16, p18, p37
    Gertrauda, 16, c18
    Maria, 16
    Melchoir, 16
    Samuel, 16
Stahl, Anna Agatha, s26
    Anna Elisazetha, s21
    Anna Maria, c20
    Anna Ursula, p20, p28

Johann p20, s25, s35
    Johannes, s27, p28, s32
    Johann Henrich, c28
Stehl, Maria Dorothea, s34
Staring, Anna Margretha, c19
    Niclaus, p19
Starring, Adam and wife, s31
    Anna Maria, p32
    Johann Adam, p32, m44
    Maria Catharina, p19, c32
Steiger, Catharina, s26
    Johann Niclaus, r40
Stein, Anna Maria, c21, p21
    Maria, s19
    Martin, p21, m43
Steis, Elisabetha Magdalena, r39
Sternberger, Jacob, p22, r39
    Johann Lampert, r39
    Philippus Hieronymus, c22
Steuber, Balthas, s26
Storr, Anna Kunigunda, c19
    Elisabeth, p19
    Elisabetha Ottilia, s22
    Michael, s17, p19
Straub, Johann, s22
    Johannes, s24
    Maria Elisabetha, s22, s24
Straup, Johann Jacob, c34
    Johann Wilhelm, c26
    Johannes, p26, 29, p34, p38
    Maria Elisabetha, p26, c34, c38, p38
Streid, Anna Catharina, p49
    Friderich, s28, s38, p49
Sertie, Anna Christina, s36
    Anna Maria, r39, c49
    Catharina, r39
    Ludwig, 43
    Magdalena, m43
    Ursula, r39
Stubenrauch, Anna Catharina, p23, s24
    Georg Henrich, c23
    Henrich, s24
    Jorg Henrich, p23
Stuber, Anna Elisabeth, r40
Stueber, Maria Catharina, r39, m41
Stueckenrad, Johann Wilhelm, s18
Stump, Johann George, s20, s34
Stupp, Anna Elisabetha, c31
    Catharina, p31
    Martin, p31
Sutz, Amilia, c33
    Andreas, c24
    Dietrich, p24, s37
    Johan Dietrich, p45
    Johan Peter, s25, m45
    Magdalena, s36, p24
    Anna Margreth, p33
    Peter, p33

Taeter, Anna Maria, p33
    Jerg, p33
    Maria Magdalena, c33
Tales, Anna Margretha, p27
    Johann Wilhelm, c27, p27
Taus, Anna Albertina, r39
Tesch (or Yesch), Johann   Henrich,
    s29

Testu, Maria Barbara, s28
Thaeter, Anna Maria, p36
   Georg, s28, p36
   Gerg and his _wife Anna Maria,
     s29, m[45] *⸱⸱
   Johann, p45
   Johannes, c36
   Lorentz, s38
Thais, Johan Philipp, r39
Theis, Christina, s25
Thibaux, Elias, c17
   Job, c17
   Maria, p17, c17
   William, p17
Thomas, Anna, p31
   Anna Eva, s23
   Jerg, p31
   Johann Henrich, c31
   Johan Peter, s31
Thonius, Anna Catharina, m47
   Anna Demuth, s20
   Anna Maria, s25
   Stephan, p47
Thonus, Christina, s25
Thonusen, Margretha, s30
   Peter, s30
Tobich, Johann Peter, r39
Tonese, Peter, s35
Tonius, Christina, s35
Tonnius, Anna Christina, s33
Trambauper, Magdalena, s21
Traut, Elisabetha, s32
Treber, Anna Maria, m42
   Johann, 42
   Sebastian, s24, s39
Thombauer, Anna Christina, c22
   Anna Elisabetha, c32
   Johan Niclaus, p32
   Magdalena, p22
Trombour, Dietrich, c37
   Johannes, c38
   Magdalena, p32, p37, p38
   Niclaus, p22, p27, p38,
Turck, Isaac, 52

Uhl, Christina, s36

Van Orde, Temperans, s49
   Willem, s49
Voess, Christina, s37, s38
   Henrich, s37
Volck, Andreas and wife, s18, p18, 15,
     p22, p51
   Anna Catharina, 15, p18, s18, p51
   Anna Maria, c18
   Carloss, 15
   Catharina, p22
   Georg Hieronymus, c51
   Johannes, c22
Volckin, Anna Gertrauda, c51
   Maria Barbara, c51
Vollbart, Anna Gartraud. r39
Voltz, Anna Eva, s20
   Melchoir, s20
Von De Bogard, Jacobus, s20
Von Husum, Anna, p22
   Jannicke, c22

Maria, s22
Rennier, p22
Volkart, s22
Von Kleck, Pieter, s20
Von Loon, Albert, p23
   Alberth, s25
   John, c23
   Maria, p23, s23
   Marion, s25
Von Nordstrandt, Jan, m46
Von Schaak, Arend, p25, p36
   Jannike, c25
   Maria, p25, p36
   Margreth, c36
Von Thesen, Abraham, s18
   Jacobina, s18
Vorst, Jacob, p18, c18
   Maria, p18
Vorstung, Abraham, p25
   Clara, p25
   Isaac, c25
Vosburg, Cornelia, p32
   Gertraud, s32
   Jacob, c32
   Jan, p32
   Peter, s32
Voshel, Anna Catharina, c19
   Peter, p19
   Maria, p19

Waegelin, Anna Maria, p29
   Johann Georg, c29
   Johann Michael, p29, s36, m41
Wagner, Maria Margretha, s22
   Peter, s19
Waid, Gertraud, m46
Waidnecht, Johann Michael, s17
Walbuer, Maria Elisabetha, r39
Waldron, Maria Elizabeth, s35
Wallrath, Anna Maria, p20
   Christina Elisabetha, c20
   Gerhard, p20
   Johann Adam, s34
Wambach, Catharina, s50
   Wilhelm, s50
Wanner, Agnes Barbara, p31
   Anna Barbara, p34
   Johann Ludwig, p31
   Johann Michael, c31
   Ludwig, p34
   Maria Dorothea, c34
Wanemacher, Anna wife of Dietrich,
     s19
   Anna Margretha, p17
   Johann Dietrich, p17, p22
   Johann Michael, c17
Wannenmacher, Anna Kunigunda, s18,
     p22
   Elsabetha Ottilia, c22
   John, m42
Warmer, Aliken. p33
   Cornelius, p33
   Jan and wife, s33
   Johannes, c33
Warno, Sibylla, r39
Weberin, Eva Elisabetha, c51
   Eva Maria, p51

Weber, Anna Elisabetha, 15, p16, p51
    Jacob, 15, p16, s23, s31, s32, p51
    Johann Herman, 15
    Johannes, c16
    Ottilia, s32
Weerich, Maria Elisabeth, r39
Weid, Anna Catharina, s30
    Gertraut, s25
Weidnecht, Andreas, s21
    Margretha, s21
Weidmann, Anna Margretha, c29
    Anna Ursula, p29
    Martin, p29
Weigand, Anna Catharina, s16, p51
    Anna Maria, 15, 16, r38
    Georg, s18, c51
    Michael, s16, p51
    Tobias, c51
Weigandin, Ana Maria, c51
Weight, Goodith, p18
    Isaac, c18
    William, p18
Weishard, Margretha, s18
Weisser, Conrad, s34
Weller, Anna Juiana, p22, p25, p29,
        p33, s33
    Hieronymus, p22, c25, p25, s28,,
        p29, p33, s38, d47
    Johann Friderich, c22
    Johann Heinrich, c33
    Johann Hieronymmus, s23
    Johann Wilhelm, c29
Wenerich, Benedict p17
    Christina, p17
    Johannes, c17
Wennerich, Johann Georg, r40
Wenn, Anna, p24, p32
    Anna Elsabetha, c24
    Duerck, p24, m44
    Rebecca, c32
    Richard, p32
Wenne, Jannetje, s50
Weniger, wife of Ulrich, s30
Werner, Anna Gertraud, m44
    Appolonia, c19
    Christoph, p19
    Johanna Elisabeth, s19
    Magdalena, p19
    Maria Magdalena, r39
    Michael, s36, 44
Whoerner, Ludwig Ernst, 42
Wickhaus, Elisabetha Maria, p19
    Maria Magdalena, c19
    Peter, p19, s21
Widerwachs, Andreas, r40, p48
    Anna Barbara, p48
    Anna Cecelia, p20
    Johann Georg, c20
    Johann Henrich, p20
    Henrich, s23, s28
    Maria Catharina, s25
Wiederwachs, Johann Bastian, c48
Wihler, Edwart, p45
    Robert, m45
Wihs, Johann, s17
Windecker, Barbara Elizabetha, p20,
        p31
    Hartmann, p20, p31

Johann Henrich, c20
    Johann Georg, c31
Winter, Anna Kunigunda, s36
    Anna Margretha, s26
    Anna Maria, s26
    Johann Georg, r39
    Johannes, r39
    Kunigunda, r40
    Lydia, 16
    Maria Catharina, r39
Wis, Anna Elisabetha, s20
Wolf, Anna Gartraud, m44
    Anna Margareta, p50
    Bertram, 44
    Johann, p50
    Johann Adam, c50
Wollbach, Engelbertus, m42
Wolleben, Anna Margretha, p27, c27,
        c34
    Anna Maria Dorothea, c28
    Johann Niclaus, s20, s31, r39
    Johann Philipp, s25, p27
    Susanna, p28, p34
    Veltin, p34
    Valentin, p28
    Wallrath, 43
Wolst, Anna Margretha, s36
Wooden, Anna wife of Johann, s19
Wormster, Anna, m42
    Sebastian, 42
Worms, Catharina, p49
    Johann Daniel, r39
    Margreta, c49
    Daniel, p49
Wuest, Maria Appollonia, s17
Wulfen, Anna Elisabetha, c32
    Anna Margretha, p32
    John, p32
Wulsten, Anna Margreth, p35
    Gottfrid, Sr., and his wife, s28
    Gottfrid Sebastian, c35, s35
    Jan, p35
Wust, Anna Catharina, r39
    Anna Gerdraut, r40
Wynscop, Ernst, 50
    Johannes, 50

Zech, Anna Magdalena, p17
    Johann, s17
    Johann Adam, c17
    Johannes, p17
Zeh, Georg Johann, r39
Zerb, Anna Elisabetha, s38
    Anna Kunigund, c36
    Elisabeth, p28
    Johan Jacob, p36, r39
    Johann Philipp, s23, m41
    Maria Catharina, p36
    Maria Margretha, c28
    Martin, p28
    Wife of Martin, s25, r40
    Philipp, s17
Zerber, Catharna, p48
    Jacob, p48
    Maria Barbara, c48
Zeller, Anna Maria, c31, p31
    Henrich, p31

Zimmerman, Anna Margretha, s32
    Jacob, s20
Zipperlin, Anna Maria, s18, s22, s27
    Johann Bernhard, s22
    Johann Bernhard, s22, s26,   r39,
        m43
    Johann Fridrich, s38
Zoeller, Johann and his wife, c35
Zoller, Maria Catharina, p32

Zufeld, Anna Catharina, p23, p27, p33
    Anna Margretha, c33
    Anna Maria, c27
    Anna Regina, c23
    Anna Sibylla, c23
    Jerg, p27, p33
    Johann Georg, s20
    Jorg, p23
    Jurg Adam, r40

General Herkimer's Home, Town of Danube. Herkimer County

CPSIA information can be obtained at www.ICGtesting.com
Printed in the USA
LVOW10s2216111016

508365LV00013B/135/P

9 780806 302317